The Cambridge Companion to *West Side Story*

Over sixty years after its opening night, *West Side Story* is perhaps the most famous and beloved of twentieth-century musicals and stands as a colossus of musical and dramatic achievement. It not only helped define a generation of musical theatre lovers but is among the handful of shows that have contributed to our understanding of American musical identity at mid century. Bringing together contemporary scholars in music, theatre, dance, literature, and performance, this *Companion* takes a multi-disciplinary deep dive into every aspect of *West Side Story* and offers fresh perspectives on this well-loved musical that also provide a springboard for broader discussion of the genre. Organised thematically, chapters range from Broadway's history and precursors to *West Side Story*; the early careers of its creators; the show's score with emphasis on writing, production, and orchestrations; issues of class, colourism, and racism; New York's gang culture; and how the show's legacy can be found in popular culture throughout the world.

PAUL R. LAIRD is Professor Emeritus of Musicology at the University of Kansas. As a scholar of musical theatre, he specializes in the careers of Leonard Bernstein and Stephen Schwartz. With William A. Everett, he co-edited three editions of *The Cambridge Companion to the Musical*.

ELIZABETH A. WELLS is Professor of Musicology at Mount Allison University in Sackville, New Brunswick, Canada. Her first book on *West Side Story* was published in 2011 and won the American Musicological Society's Music in American Culture award.

Cambridge Companions to Music

Topics

The Cambridge Companion to Ballet
Edited by Marion Kant

The Cambridge Companion to Blues and Gospel Music
Edited by Allan Moore

The Cambridge Companion to Caribbean Music
Edited by Nanette de Jong

The Cambridge Companion to Choral Music
Edited by André de Quadros

The Cambridge Companion to Composition
Edited by Toby Young

The Cambridge Companion to the Concerto
Edited by Simon P. Keefe

The Cambridge Companion to Conducting
Edited by José Antonio Bowen

The Cambridge Companion to Eighteenth-Century Opera
Edited by Anthony R. DelDonna and Pierpaolo Polzonetti

The Cambridge Companion to Electronic Music, second edition
Edited by Nick Collins and Julio D'Escriván

The Cambridge Companion to the 'Eroica' Symphony
Edited by Nancy November

The Cambridge Companion to Film Music
Edited by Mervyn Cooke and Fiona Ford

The Cambridge Companion to French Music
Edited by Simon Trezise

The Cambridge Companion to Grand Opera
Edited by David Charlton

The Cambridge Companion to Hip-Hop
Edited by Justin A. Williams

The Cambridge Companion to Jazz
Edited by Mervyn Cooke and David Horn

The Cambridge Companion to Jewish Music
Edited by Joshua S. Walden

The Cambridge Companion to K-Pop
Edited by Suk-Young Kim

The Cambridge Companion to Krautrock
Edited by Uwe Schütte

The Cambridge Companion to the Lied
Edited by James Parsons

The Cambridge Companion to *The Magic Flute*
Edited by Jessica Waldoff

Instruments

The Cambridge Companion to *West Side Story*

edited by

PAUL R. LAIRD
University of Kansas

ELIZABETH A. WELLS
Mount Allison University, Canada

CAMBRIDGE
UNIVERSITY PRESS

CAMBRIDGE
UNIVERSITY PRESS

Shaftesbury Road, Cambridge CB2 8EA, United Kingdom

One Liberty Plaza, 20th Floor, New York, NY 10006, USA

477 Williamstown Road, Port Melbourne, VIC 3207, Australia

314–321, 3rd Floor, Plot 3, Splendor Forum, Jasola District Centre,
New Delhi – 110025, India

103 Penang Road, #05–06/07, Visioncrest Commercial, Singapore 238467

Cambridge University Press is part of Cambridge University Press & Assessment,
a department of the University of Cambridge.

We share the University's mission to contribute to society through the pursuit of
education, learning and research at the highest international levels of excellence.

www.cambridge.org
Information on this title: www.cambridge.org/9781108489959

DOI: 10.1017/9781108784849

First published 2024

A catalogue record for this publication is available from the British Library.

Library of Congress Cataloging-in-Publication Data
Names: Laird, Paul R., editor. | Wells, Elizabeth Anne, 1964– editor.
Title: The Cambridge companion to West Side story / edited by Paul R. Laird, Elizabeth A. Wells.
Description: [1]. | Cambridge, United Kingdom ; New York, NY : Cambridge University
Press, 2024. | Series: Cambridge companions to music | Includes bibliographical references
and index.
Identifiers: LCCN 2024019524 | ISBN 9781108489959 (hardback) | ISBN 9781108747752
(paperback) | ISBN 9781108784849 (ebook)
Subjects: LCSH: Bernstein, Leonard, 1918–1990. West Side story. | Bernstein, Leonard,
1918–1990 – Performances. | Musicals – History and criticism. | Race in musical theater. |
Puerto Ricans in musicals. | Robbins, Jerome. | Laurents, Arthur.
Classification: LCC ML410.B566 C34 2024 | DDC 782.1/4092–dc23/eng/20240430
LC record available at https://lccn.loc.gov/2024019524

ISBN 978-1-108-48995-9 Hardback
ISBN 978-1-108-74775-2 Paperback

Contents

ix

Figures

Music Examples

Contributors

ERNESTO ACEVEDO-MUÑOZ is Professor of Cinema Studies and Chair of the Department of Cinema Studies & Moving Image Arts at the University of Colorado-Boulder.

EMILY ABRAMS ANSARI is Assistant Dean of Research and Associate Professor of Music History at Western University, Canada.

ERICA K. ARGYROPOULOS is an independent scholar and musicologist based in Tulsa, OK.

KATHERINE BABER is Associate Professor and College of Arts and Sciences Associate Dean at the University of Redlands, CA.

JANE BARNETTE is Associate Professor in the Department of Theatre and Dance at the University of Kansas.

JOHN M. CLUM is Professor Emeritus of Theater Studies and English at Duke University, NC.

WILLIAM A. EVERETT is Curators' Distinguished Professor Emeritus at the University of Missouri–Kansas City Conservatory.

GONZALO FERNÁNDEZ MONTE is a Spanish musicologist and pianist who works as a musical theatre performer and teacher in Madrid.

AINO KUKKONEN is Visiting Researcher at the University of the Arts Helsinki.

PAUL R. LAIRD is Professor Emeritus of Musicology at the University of Kansas.

LAURA MACDONALD is Assistant Professor in the Residential College in the Arts and Humanities at Michigan State University.

DUSTYN MARTINCICH is Professor of Theatre and Dance at Bucknell University, PA.

MARTIN NEDBAL is Associate Professor of Musicology at the University of Kansas.

PHOEBE RUMSEY is Senior Lecturer in Musical Theatre at the University of Portsmouth in the UK.

ANNE SEARCY is Assistant Professor of Music History at the University of Washington.

HELEN SMITH is an independent musicologist and conductor in the UK.

SYLVIA STONER-HAWKINS is Senior Artist-in-Residence in Voice at Skidmore College, NY.

STEVE SWAYNE is the Director of the Montgomery Fellows Program and the Jacob H. Strauss 1922 Professor of Music at Dartmouth College, NH.

ELIZABETH A. WELLS is Professor of Musicology at Mount Allison University in Sackville, New Brunswick, Canada.

Preface

PAUL R. LAIRD AND ELIZABETH A. WELLS

West Side Story premiered at New York's Winter Garden Theater on 26 September 1957, well over six decades before the publication of this book. It was a remarkable moment in the history of the American musical theatre when four bold artists – Jerome Robbins, Leonard Bernstein, Arthur Laurents, and Stephen Sondheim – joined to create a profoundly serious work that strongly influenced the future of musical theatre. The show's staying power in American culture – and internationally – has been remarkable. Numerous shows from the period have persisted in the repertory, but few have remained as famous as *West Side Story*. What made it so much a part of the national conversation was the 1961 film, directed by Robert Wise. It starred Natalie Wood – one of Hollywood's most enduring stars – won ten Academy Awards and gathered a huge worldwide audience. The film and numerous recordings helped provide the show's score with staying power. With music by Bernstein and lyrics by Sondheim, the songs 'Somewhere', 'Tonight', 'Maria', and others remain significant in the American national songbook. Choreography by Robbins was also a major part of the film, making his dances ubiquitous. An important part of *West Side Story*'s continuing appeal derives from it being an adaptation of *Romeo and Juliet*, one of Shakespeare's most famous plays.

Steven Spielberg became a major fan of *West Side Story* when as a boy he heard the Broadway original cast album. In late 2021 he realized a dream when his film appeared. Although on first release it did not prove very popular, the film offers a fresh interpretation of the show and addresses controversial aspects of the original film, such as eschewing use of brownface makeup for actors playing Puerto Ricans and casting many Hispanic actors. Spielberg largely hired Puerto Ricans to play the Sharks and their girlfriends, including actors with both light and dark complexions, as one might observe from the island's population. The 2021 film appeared when a new variant of the COVID-19 virus threatened in the USA, likely limiting the number of older fans going to theatres. The film failed to prove popular with the youth market, but its very appearance demonstrated that *West Side Story* remains an important title in the American musical theatre. The editors of this volume certainly knew about Spielberg's film, but that was not the sole reason why this essay collection seemed like a good idea. The show is controversial by its very nature for several reasons. It occurs in the context of juvenile gang violence, a problem when the show opened and one still unsolved in the USA. Although Puerto Ricans are American citizens and free to move anywhere in the country, many Americans consider them immigrants because English is not their first language and, regrettably, racism endures in the United States. *West Side Story*, therefore, remains topical in the 2020s. Combine these perspectives with the work's exceptional qualities – a wonderfully distinctive score, a terse book that is an imaginative adaptation of *Romeo and Juliet*, and the fascinating use of choreography – and one perceives a show that will long continue to be significant in the Broadway legacy.

Changing cultural standards affect our perception of the show, and there are commentators who deride four white males creating a story that involves Puerto Ricans, or who criticize the show's representation of minorities and women. A wide palette of analyses and opinions about various aspects of the show appears herein, providing a rich internal conversation concerning the careers of its creators before they wrote the show, various aspects of *West Side Story*, and its complicated legacy. Most of the volume concerns the Broadway original but various chapters also consider the films, revivals, and productions elsewhere in the world. Our volume benefits from perspectives of different disciplines: musicology, theatre, dance, and film, and those who work from a variety of theoretical approaches. At a time when scholars rigorously critique the American past concerning issues of race, gender, and class, it is important for us to do the same with Broadway musicals, recognizing a property like *West Side Story* for the ground-breaking show that it was but also noting that our perceptions have changed and will continue to do so.

Part I involves shows in Broadway history that served as precursors for *West Side Story*; the early careers of Jerome Robbins, Leonard Bernstein, Arthur Laurents, and Stephen Sondheim; and the show's original producers. William A. Everett reviews the genre's history, describing shows that concerned immigrant experiences, race, politics, knife violence, and the allure of Latin music and cultures. He demonstrates that *West Side Story* was hardly the first show to address such issues. Helen Smith approaches Bernstein's musical theatre career before 1957, including the ballet *Fancy Free* and the Broadway show that it inspired, *On* the Town; the opera *Trouble in Tahiti*, which played briefly on Broadway; *Wonderful Town*; and *Candide*. In the process, Smith illustrates the variety that Bernstein and his collaborators brought to these scores and that his previous works foreshadowed his great success in *West Side Story*. Phoebe Rumsey follows Robbins's career from a young upstart in a modern dance school, through his years of apprenticeship, to his early shows with Leonard Bernstein. John M. Clum provides a background on Arthur Laurents, who had many successful properties and film scripts before writing *West Side Story*. Steve Swayne details Sondheim's brief career before coming on as the junior member of the team after meeting Arthur Laurents at a post-show party. *West Side Story* faced an uncertain path when Cheryl Crawford pulled out as lead producer a few months before rehearsals began. Roger Stevens stayed on as a silent partner with Harold Prince and Robert Griffith saving the project when they signed on, an important aspect of the show's history covered by Laura MacDonald in her chapter.

Part II concerns the show itself and its context at the time of its initial Broadway run. Paul R. Laird considers the show's score with emphasis on the writing process, orchestrations, Bernstein's compositional efforts at dramatic unification, and commentary on salient features of each major number. Katherine Baber considers aspects of race and gender, and their intersection with both 'white' and 'Puerto Rican' characters within the story, and the 'other' character of 'Anybodys'. Jane Barnette offers an essay on *West Side Story*'s relationship with its Shakespearean model, concentrating on their similarities and contrasts in spirit, the palimpsests between the works where *West Side Story* shows resonances of *Romeo and Juliet*, how geographical concerns affect the adaptation, and whether either work conforms to the technical definition of a tragedy. Ernesto R. Acevedo-Muñoz dives deeply into the Latinx elements of the work, where the authors may have misunderstood or downplayed the value of some of the Puerto Rican characters, but arguing that the musical remains valuable for the cultural work that it does. Erica K. Argyropoulos investigates *West Side Story* in the context of class and such related lenses as race, concentrating on Bernstein and demonstrating the relative lack of consciousness that he showed concerning the advantages he enjoyed over most minorities. Argyropoulos ties this to the show by noting the limited understanding its creators showed of Puerto Ricans and in Bernstein's cultural appropriation of Latinx musical tropes in the score. Elizabeth A. Wells revisits the gang culture of the 1950s in America, and how popular representations of gangs and violence in New York streets inform the authors' response to this aspect of the work.

Part III includes four essays in which the authors explore aspects of the show's legacy. Sylvia Stoner-Hawkins provides a detailed description of Bernstein's vocal writing and of the types of voice that perform each part. She also comments on the singing heard on the most famous recordings of *West Side Story*. Dustyn Martincich assesses the choreographic legacy left by Robbins through the work and how he revolutionized musical theatre dance. Martin Nedbal paints a fascinating picture of *West Side Story* abroad, particularly its incarnation in a German-language version where the translation resulted in the subtle rewriting of some of the work's literary themes. The final essay, written by several specialists, concerns the show's early presence in the Soviet Union, Finland, and Great Britain, and includes a survey of touring and professional productions in Spain. These are merely several examples of the show's international imprint, which now also involves two films released sixty years apart. Our reaction to this musical and our interpretation of it will continue to develop, but it would seem that *West Side Story* will long be 'somewhere' in popular culture throughout the world.

Acknowledgements

The completion of a volume like this is not possible without the participation and assistance of many people. First we must thank our contributors, who willingly shared their expertise and time, first writing these wonderful chapters and then working with us while we edited them. Our writers included scholars with whom one or both of us have collaborated and others with whom we have not worked before, and to all of them we express our deep gratitude for their enthusiasm for the project and their patience while we completed it. Obviously, we have all fought through the complications brought on by the pandemic while working on this project, especially the challenges it caused in our teaching lives, which lengthened the editing process and slightly delayed the volume's submission. Discussions recently and over the years with a number of our writers, and others in our field, have assisted our knowledge and perspectives on *West Side Story*, Bernstein and his collaborators, and their place in the history of the musical theatre and its repertory. We thank these many people for their contributions to our work and understanding.

We express our deep appreciation to our editor Kate Brett of Cambridge University Press and her assistant Abi Sears, who patiently answered numerous questions and were both instrumental in bringing this collection to print. We feel honoured to be part of *The Cambridge Companion* series, which has become such an important part of publishing for general and scholarly readers in both music and theatre. We both thank our institution and their libraries and staffs for their assistance in making our research for this volume possible. Thanks to Marie Carter (now retired) and Hannah Webster of the Bernstein Office for their assistance in securing necessary permissions for the book and to Georgia Stratton of Concord Music Publishing for her help. We also appreciate Steve Swayne's help in securing permissions from Stephen Sondheim's office to publish the lyrics that appear in his chapter on the young Sondheim. We thank the New York Public Library, SOM Produce, and Photofest for their assistance in securing photographs for the book. Sara McClure, a PhD student in musicology at the University of Kansas, prepared the volume's index. We thank Sara for her meticulous and timely efforts. We also appreciate Adrian Hartsough for producing a musical example.

Paul Laird dedicates this volume to his wife Joy Laird, who has patiently listened to him enthuse about Bernstein and especially *West Side Story* for more than forty years. Elizabeth A. Wells dedicates this volume to Branden Olsen, her partner in crime and musicology, without whom she could not have completed this volume.

Permissions

PART I

Before *West Side Story*

1 | Performing Social Relevance in the American Musical before *West Side Story*

WILLIAM A. EVERETT

A boy from one immigrant group and a girl from another are in love, much to the ire of their respective families. Two rival ethnic groups go to a dance at a local hall, and tensions are high. While these scenarios sound as if they belong to *West Side Story*, they are actually plot points from *The Mulligan Guard Ball*, a musical comedy from 1879. The similarity between the scenarios leads to the idea of palimpsests, where echoes of earlier works appear in later ones. According to the Chicago School of Media Theory at the University of Chicago, a palimpsest is

> a parchment or other writing surface on which the original text has been effaced or partially erased, and then overwritten by another; manuscript in which later writing has been superimposed on earlier (effaced) writing. In other words, a palimpsest is a 'multi-layered record.'[1]

This notion helps us understand how various themes continue to appear and reappear in the American musical. The musical theatre is a gigantic palimpsest of multiple historical and stylistic layers, various folds where things get hidden, and typographical features such as venues, creators, and performers. Some subjects seem to permeate musicals for a time, then disappear, only to return decades later, while others seem to have a fairly solid presence. Among those that maintain a continual presence is the broad notion of social relevance. Following Bruce Kirle's now commonplace thesis, musicals are products of the time and place of their creation.[2] Therefore a significant part of any musical's identity rests within its contemporary social–cultural relevance. This chapter explores how a handful of socially relevant topics – immigrant experiences, race, knife violence, politics, and the allure of Latin America – were performed on Broadway musical stages before *West Side Story*'s appearance in 1957. Traces of these earlier shows in *West Side Story* reveal that the subject of this *Companion* resides in a continuum of musical theatre productions in which various palimpsests concerning social relevance can be discerned.

Immigrant Experiences

A vibrant musical theatre existed in and for various immigrant communities throughout the United States from the nineteenth century through World War II.[3] Performances in German, French, Spanish, Italian, Chinese, and Yiddish were common occurrences on ethnic stages across the country. Many of the shows that appeared on these stages concerned the immigrant experience – after all, the target audience for these productions consisted of immigrants.

One of the most significant figures in New York's German American theatrical scene was Adolf Philipp (1864–1936), an actor–singer–composer–playwright–impresario whose immigrant-themed works include *Der Corner Grocer aus der Avenue A* (1893), *Der Pawnbroker von der Eastside* (1894), and *Der Butcher aus der Erste Avenue* (1895). Philipp typically starred in his own productions. For example, in *Der Corner Grocer aus der Avenue A*, he played Hein Snut (translated as Henry (Big) Mouth), the title character who brings about the comeuppance of a former barber who lives beyond his means.[4] While most characters in the tale are German, the cast did include one Irishman, 'Herr' McGinty, who speaks Irish-affected German.[5] Philipp's music is direct in appeal and sentiment, with diatonic harmonies, regular periodic phrase structure, syllabic text setting (making the words easy to understand), and an abundance of waltz refrains. Such musical style befits the background of his central European immigrant characters and audiences.

German and Irish immigrants also feature in Edward Harrigan's *The Mulligan Guard Ball* (1879, revised 1883 and 1892, music by David Braham).[6] Harrigan created the character of the Irish immigrant Dan Mulligan in 1873, and played him in a series of 'Mulligan' musical comedies through the 1890s. In *The Mulligan Guard Ball*, Dan's son, Tommy, wants to marry Kitty,[7] the daughter of the German butcher Gustavus Lochmuller. Dan is very much against the idea and thinks his son should marry an Irish girl. To complicate matters, Kitty's mother, Bridget, is Irish and does not want her daughter to make the same mistake she did by marrying a German boy. Interethnic marriage is discouraged, as it is in *West Side Story*.

Central to the storyline of *The Mulligan Guard Ball* is the relationship between Irish immigrants and African Americans. From the 1850s, Irish immigrants and blacks were living in the same districts[8] and, though the Irish supported abolition, tensions arose as Irish immigrants began taking over the jobs of free blacks by offering to work at a lower wage.[9] The Irish, who had been what David R. Roediger terms one of the 'in-between peoples,'[10] since they were Northern Europeans but not Anglo-Saxon Protestants, were able to become white by aligning themselves with white groups, which they did. Drawing on the writings of James Baldwin, Roediger asserts, 'Joining in acts of racism against people of color made immigrants white over time.'[11] The Polish immigrants in *West Side Story*, Tony's community, would have also participated in this process of becoming white.

Since white immigrants took over jobs that paid wages, displaced blacks had to turn to self-employment and trades such as chimneysweeps and bootblacks.[12] These work-related tensions infuse *The Mulligan Guard Ball*. Dan Mulligan works at a gas factory, and Gustavus Lochmuller is a butcher. They both have stable incomes. By contrast, Simpson Primrose, one of the main black characters, is a self-employed barber. Significant in terms of performance, Primrose, along with the chaplain Palestine Puter, were played in blackface by 'Negro impersonators' Billy Gray and Johnny Wild.[13] The blacks resent the Irish in *The Mulligan Guard Ball*. Their 'Order of Full Moons,' which Puter calls a 'secret colored society to prevent de Irish from riding on horse cars,'[14] points back at groups who kept blacks from using public transportation.

The Irish Mulligan Guard and the black Skidmore Guard plan balls for the same evening. When the hall where the Skidmore Guards planned their ball is closed, they end up being moved to the Harp and Shamrock Hall, which had already been booked for the Mulligan Guard Ball. The Harp and Shamrock is a place, says Puter, where a Full Moon cannot go 'widout trouble.'[15] When the Skidmore Guard arrive, after fearing an ambush, they leave their muskets in the hat rack, but carry razors to protect themselves from the Irish, who Puter describes in strongly racist terms. The Mulligans and the Skidmores come to an agreement: the Skidmores will go upstairs and the Mulligans will take the ground floor. During the balls, the ceiling gives way, causing mayhem when the Skidmores fall through and land on top of the Mulligans. Racial tensions on both sides live at the surface of *The Mulligan Guard Ball*, as they do in *West Side Story*.

In 1947, almost seventy years after the first incarnation of *The Mulligan Guard Ball*, two musicals concerning immigrant experiences and relationships between races opened on successive evenings: *Street Scene* on 9 January (book by Elmer Rice, music by Kurt Weill, lyrics by Langston Hughes) and *Finian's Rainbow* on 10 January (book by E. Y. Harburg and Fred Saidy, music by Burton Lane, lyrics by Harburg). *Street Scene* includes immigrants from various European countries, while *Finian's Rainbow* features only an Irish father, daughter, and leprechaun.

Among *Street Scene*'s New York tenement dwellers are immigrants from Italy, Sweden, Ireland, and Germany. Playing into racist stereotypes, there's also a Jewish intellectual (Sam Kaplan, the romantic lead, a tenor) and a black janitor (Henry Davis, a baritone). The sundry cast of characters 'finds an analogue for its *ethnic* diversity in its *musical* diversity,' writes Stephen Hinton.[16] When it comes to musical depictions of immigrant groups, the 'Ice Cream Sextet' evokes the spirit of Neapolitan song not only through its fast-paced sections in 6/8 but also by being led by a quintessential Italian tenor, Lippo Florentino. Henry's 'I Got a Marble and a Star,' the second number in the show, likewise bears a strong blues influence, its style functioning as a racial signifier for African Americans.

Whiteness is performed through operatic-sounding music. The Maurrants – husband/father Frank, wife/mother Anna, and children Rose and Willie – are the generationally established white American family. Frank yearns for the 'safe and sound' world before the 'lousy foreigners' arrived. The Maurrants' music, as well as that of Rose's beloved, Sam, sets them – and their tragedies – apart from the other characters in the story. Musical style is not wholly segregated, for blues elements feature in the show's opening number, 'Ain't it awful, the heat?' and in Sam's aria, 'Lonely House.'

Finian's Rainbow, which its authors called 'a musical satire,' concerns Finian McLonergan and his daughter Sharon, who arrive in Rainbow Valley in the mythical state of Missitucky (a fusion of Mississippi and Kentucky) from Ireland with a pot of gold stolen from the leprechaun Og. Whereas *Street Scene* operates under the tenets of realism, *Finian's Rainbow* is a fable, rich in elements of fantasy. Unlike Senator Billboard Rawkins and his cronies, the sharecroppers who live in Rainbow Valley welcome Finian and Sharon. Rawkins remarks at one point, 'My whole family's been havin' trouble with immigrants ever since we *came* to this country [emphasis in original]!'[17] Rawkins's anti-immigrant, white supremacist attitude causes Sharon to wish, over the pot of gold, that he become black. Her wish comes true, and Rawkins experiences the racist slurs and treatment he so willfully lashed onto others. The Irish characters – Finian, Sharon, and Og – generally come across as the ones promoting antiracism, offering lessons to all the residents of Rainbow Valley. Likewise, it is their music, such as 'How are Things in Glocca Morra?,' 'Look to the Rainbow,' and 'Old Devil Moon,' that remain the most endearing songs from the show.

Race

Whiteness and racism run rampant throughout the history and legacy of the American musical. This is strongly evident in *West Side Story*, with Tony's immigrant Polish community having become white, something that is not possible for the Puerto Ricans, many of whom would have sub-Saharan ancestry as a result of the Spanish slave trade.

Minstrelsy, which consisted of performances by whites in blackface of imagined black experiences with overt racist language and mannerisms, flourished on American stages in the nineteenth century. Blacks also appeared in minstrelsy, donning the requisite blackface. In the African American musicals that began to appear with greater frequency around the turn of the twentieth century, John Graziano asserts that 'minstrelsy and racial pride coexist uncomfortably.'[18] A corollary exists in *West Side Story* with its juxtaposition of performed racial stereotypes amidst a quest for betterment among the Puerto Rican immigrants.

The team of Bert Williams (1876–1922) and George Walker (1872–1911) starred in a series of musical comedies about black experiences that included *In Dahomey* (1903, book by Jesse A. Shipp, lyrics by Paul Laurence Dunbar, music by Will Marion Cook) and *Abyssinia* (1906, book and lyrics by Shipp and Alexander Rogers; music by Cook and Bert Williams). In the former, a group of African Americans living in Florida journey to Dahomey as part of a colonization society, where they are imprisoned and sentenced to death before being rescued by the Williams and Walker characters.[19] *In Dahomey*, with its depiction of rule and order in Dahomey as being 'uncivilized,' endorses Ibram X. Kendi's remarks on the founding of the American Colonialization Society in 1817, 'Africans in America had received their knowledge of Africa and their racist ideas from White Americans.'[20] The African Americans in *In Dahomey* certainly saw themselves as superior to the 'savages' of Dahomey. They performed on stage what W. E. B. Du Bois proclaimed in 1900 at the First Pan-African Conference, 'To be sure, the darker races are today the least advanced in culture according to European standards.'[21] Du Bois, following assimilationist racist thought, advocated for gradual decolonization since in his estimation African nations were not yet advanced enough for independence. His words echoed those of his contemporaries who were saying the same thing about the colonies that the USA acquired after winning the Spanish-American War, places such as Cuba, Guam, the Philippines, and, relevant to *West Side Story*, Puerto Rico.[22]

The inappropriately heavy punishments for minor offenses from *In Dahomey* continued in *Abyssinia*. In the latter show, however, the

Abyssinians are viewed as culturally superior to their African American visitors by speaking a stilted parody of 'King's English,' while the speech of the African Americans evoked the demeaning sounds of minstrelsy.[23] The show opened in February 1906, three months before Franz Boaz gave his famous commencement address at Atlanta University. The noted anthropologist recalled the glories of precolonial West African kingdoms, telling the assembly: 'To those who stoutly maintain a material inferiority of the negro race, the past history of your race does not sustain [that] statement.'[24] *Abyssinia* played on a combination of these conflicting notions of racial pride and gradual decolonization, as would *West Side Story*.

Before Richard Rodgers (1902–1979) and Oscar Hammerstein II (1895–1960) became 'Rodgers and Hammerstein,' they each created works that dealt with race. Hammerstein's lyrics and libretti explored relationships between whites and various peoples of colour: indigenous nations in *Rose-Marie* (1924, music by Rudolf Friml and Herbert Stothart), Moroccans under French colonial rule in *The Desert Song* (1926, music by Sigmund Romberg), and African Americans in *Show Boat* (1927, music by Jerome Kern). In *Show Boat* Hammerstein and Kern offered a serious portrayal and interrogation of issues facing African Americans, especially during the miscegenation scene, when Julie's mixed-race heritage is revealed.[25] In Rodgers's case, the show was *Babes in Arms* (1937, book by Rodgers and Lorenz Hart, music by Rodgers, lyrics by Hart). To avoid being sent to a work farm as public charges after their parents go on the vaudeville circuit, Val and Marshall convince the sheriff that they can earn money by putting on a show. Among those who want to join the production are the African American siblings Irving and Ivory De Quincy. The wealthy white guy Lee Calhoun, who is underwriting the show and therefore is its producer, refuses to let the De Quincys perform on racist grounds. Val smacks him and sends the pair on stage for the show-within-a-show's dance-heavy finale, 'Johnny One-Note Ballet.' (Lee ends up pulling his financing, which drives Val and his friends to the work farm, but everything works out at the end. It is a musical comedy, after all.)

When it comes to Rodgers and Hammerstein as a team, race is central to three of their musicals: *South Pacific* (1949), *The King and I* (1951), and *Flower Drum Song* (1958), the latter appearing on the heels of *West Side Story*. While all three have been heavily criticized for their racist portrayals of Asian and Pacific cultures, they nonetheless perform ways in which different cultures interact, something that is central to *West Side Story*. White colonial attitudes dominate, even in *South Pacific*'s socially progressive dictate, 'You've Got to Be Carefully Taught.'

Opening the same year as *South Pacific*, *Lost in the Stars* (1949, book and lyrics by Maxwell Anderson, music by Weill) took place in apartheid South Africa and concerned a young black man, Absalom Kumalo, accused of killing a white man during a botched robbery. Called a 'musical tragedy,' the work reflects the experiences of the black community, embodied by the chorus that occupies the work's musical (and therefore dramatic) center, and Absalom's father, the preacher Stephen Kumalo.[26] Among the musical's most poignant moments is the choral anthem 'Cry, the Beloved Country' (its title taken from the Alan Paton novel on which the musical is based), sung immediately after the white judge sentences Absalom to death. The antiphonal effects of black and white choruses in 'Fear!' is a harrowing manifestation of the anxieties caused by white-against-black violence. Weill's idea of race-based choruses as characters is prescient of Bernstein's treatment of the Sharks and the Jets in *West Side Story*.

Two musicals by white creators that offered images of African American cultures became important touchstones for such representations: the Broadway opera *Porgy and Bess* (1935, libretto by DuBose Heyward, music by George Gershwin, lyrics by Heyward and Ira Gershwin) and Oscar Hammerstein II's adaptation of George Bizet's opera *Carmen*, *Carmen Jones* (1943, orchestrated by Robert Russell Bennett; film version 1954). Both feature entirely black casts (with the exception of small speaking parts for law enforcement characters in *Porgy and Bess*), and both have been interrogated for their staging of negative black stereotypes.[27] The rhapsodic score of the former and vibrant re-fashionings of Bizet's music in the latter have kept both works in the public consciousness. Similar remarks could be made about *West Side Story*, its racist depictions of Puerto Ricans, and its captivating music.

Knife Violence

The intense rage associated with knife violence, the close proximity of bodies, and the physical force required make this type of killing intensely personal and terrifyingly visceral.[28] When Tony stabs Bernardo in *West Side Story*, the scene becomes part of a stage legacy dating back to antiquity. In terms of the operatic stage, some of the most famous on-stage knifings include Don José's stabbing of the title character at the end of Bizet's *Carmen* (1875), Canio's double murder of Nedda and Silvio in Leoncavallo's *Pagliacci* (1892), Tosca's slaying of Scarpia in Puccini's *Tosca* (1899, first performed 1900), and the eponymous character's slaughtering of Marie under a blood red moon in Berg's *Wozzeck* (1914–1922, first performed 1925).[29]

Knifings also occur in the plots of Broadway musicals in the first half of the twentieth century, though not with the frequency they do in the second half. Two of the most famous (or infamous) occur in *Rose-Marie* (1924) and *Oklahoma!* (1943, book and lyrics by Hammerstein, music by Richard Rodgers). In *Rose-Marie*, Wanda stabs her husband, the aggressive drunkard Blackeagle. According to the libretto, the scene is played behind a stage gauze, something that removes its intense directness while also offering the possibility to literally magnify the crime – and its horror – through lighting and shadows. As in *Rose-Marie*, a character marked with violent tendencies dies by the knife in *Oklahoma!* Here it is Jud Fry, who falls on his own blade during a fight with Curly.

Other types of violence appear in Rodgers and Hammerstein musicals. For example, there's Billy's horrific spousal abuse of Julie in *Carousel* (1945) and in *The King and I*, the king's threatened beating of Tuptim and the brutal off-stage killing of her lover, Lun Tha. In the case of *The King and I*, the violence is linked to race in highly troubling ways, as it is in *West Side Story*.

Politics

A string of musicals from the 1930s employed satire as a way of addressing contemporary political and politicized issues. *West Side Story*'s 'Gee, Officer Krupke,' with its burlesque treatment of issues facing youth set to fast-paced razzmatazz music, has clear precedents in these shows.

The effervescence of musical comedy permeates a trio of works with songs by George and Ira Gershwin that played early in the decade: *Strike Up the Band* (1930, revised from 1927), *Of Thee I Sing* (1931), and its sequel, *Let 'Em Eat Cake* (1933). All three shows lampoon aspects of American political life at the time.

Morrie Ryskind's book for *Strike Up the Band* offers a satirical look at the motivations for war. In George S. Kaufman's scenario, the owner of a Connecticut-based cheese company underwrites a war between the USA and Switzerland in response to the Swiss protesting a US-imposed 50 percent tariff on imported cheese. As Howard Pollack asserts, the musical focused not on the absurdity of the war itself but rather on 'the intolerance, paranoia, hypocrisy, self-serving moralizing, and exaggerated patriotism on the home front.'[30] These qualities are clearly evident in the show's march-like title song.

Of Thee I Sing, with a book by Kaufman and Ryskind, includes the impeachment trial of a sitting US president, something considered remarkable at the time, since the only one to have taken place to date was of Andrew Johnson in 1868, and he was not convicted. In *Of Thee I Sing*, President John P. Wintergreen, who was elected on a platform of love, chose to marry a campaign worker, Mary Turner, who bakes delicious corn muffins, rather than Diana Devereaux, who won the beauty contest tied to his campaign. Diana vows revenge, causing bad publicity. Wintergreen's advisors suggest he resign to quell the public relations crisis, and when he refuses to do so, they impeach him. As the Senate is about to deliver its verdict, Mary enters and tells everyone that she is pregnant. The vice president, Alexander Throttlebottom, declares that there's no precedent for impeaching an 'expectant father,' and the case evaporates. Larry Starr succinctly describes the basic message of the show: 'American politics are haphazard, unburdened by principle, and readily swayed on the spur of the moment.'[31] Gershwin's music matches the dramatic need at any given point in the show, whether it's the campaign march 'Wintergreen for President,' the jaunty title song, the slightly syncopated love song 'Who Cares,' or the extended musical-dramatic sequences such as the Act 1 finale. Just as Bernstein will do in his indictment of social issues in *West Side Story*, music here serves specific dramatic purposes.

Let 'Em Eat Cake, as a sequel to *Of Thee I Sing*, features Wintergreen, Mary, and Throttlebottom, all played by the same actors who created the roles. Wintergreen has lost his bid for reelection to John P. Tweedledee, and when the Supreme Court denies the incumbent's request to overturn the landslide vote, he and his followers enter the garment industry and start a blue-shirt revolution, modeled on Hitler's brown shirts and Mussolini's black shirts. They stage a coup and Wintergreen becomes 'dictator of the proletariat' and turns the White House into the Blue House, after the colour of his revolution. When the League of Nations beats the US Supreme Court in a baseball game to settle war debts, Wintergreen and his cohort are sentenced to death by guillotine, only to be saved when Mary and the other wives enter wearing new fashions from Paris instead of the state-mandated blue blouses. Wintergreen ends up entering the dress-making business, Tweedledee becomes president of Cuba, and Throttlebottom becomes US president. The innate plot absurdities were perfect means to address the worsening economic depression, the ineptitude of government officials, and the rise of fascism in Europe. The show's only hit song was the counterpoint song 'Mine,' in which Wintergreen declares his steadfast commitment to Mary.[32] A much more famous counterpoint song, the 'Tonight' (Quintet), will feature prominently in *West Side Story*.

While the clothing industry was central to the satire in *Let 'Em Eat Cake* it was the lifeblood of *Pins and Needles* (1937), a revue featuring left-leaning sketches by Marc Blitzstein, among others, and music and lyrics by Harold Rome. Labor Stage, Inc. produced the show under the sponsorship of the International Ladies Garment Workers Union (ILGWU), with members of the union appearing on stage. According to Trudi Wright, a large part of the show's success came from its tempered political perspective.[33] Though still decidedly pro-worker and anti-fascist, it avoided overly radical sentiments, even with such progressively titled songs as 'Sing Us a Song with Social Significance,' 'Doin' the Reactionary,' and 'Four Little Angels of Peace Are We.'

The same night that the politically tempered *Pins and Needles* opened at the Labor Stage, 27 November, an overtly leftist work, this one entirely the creation of Marc Blitzstein, began playing at the Mercury Theatre. Audiences at *The Cradle Will Rock* experienced an 'oratorio version' of the work that featured Blitzstein at the piano and the principals, in street clothes, seated on a raised platform with the chorus on another platform behind them.[34] In Blitzstein's story, Larry Foreman, a mill foreman in Steeltown USA, organizes his fellow workers and gains the support of the town's underclass, including the prostitute Moll, against the capitalist Mister family (Mr. Mister, Mrs. Mister, Sister Mister, and Brother Mister) and Mr. Mister's anti-union Liberty Committee. Blitzstein's highly sophisticated score played at the banalities of much of the era's popular music, as in 'Honolulu,' while the show's leftist message came through in its polystylistic and austere-sounding numbers such as the title song, 'The Freedom of the Press,' 'Art for Art's Sake,' and 'The Nickel under Your Foot.' The show addressed numerous social issues of the time beyond unions and the intimidation of union organizers, including imperialist fantasy, student militia groups, hypermasculinity, and even the preciousness of classical artistes.[35] Blitzstein himself remarked that the show concerned the plight of the middle class and its need to look to the future, not the past.[36]

The tale of the work's first public performance on 16 June 1937 has become at least as famous as its content. With its genesis in the Works Progress Administration (WPA) Federal Theater Project, the show's unapologetic political content in terms of the New Deal and labor unions brought about an injunction against the performance, causing the theatre where it was scheduled to play (the Maxine Elliott) to be padlocked. A theatre broker for producer John Houseman and director Orson Welles found the Venice Theatre empty, booked it, and the troupe performed the decidedly pro-union show with Blitzstein alone on stage at a piano and the cast singing and speaking their lines from the audience, since their union prohibited them from performing on stage.[37]

Three weeks before *Pins and Needles* and *The Cradle Will Rock* began their Broadway runs, a show of a completely different ilk about New Deal policies opened. *I'd Rather Be Right* (1937, book by Kaufman and Moss Hart, music by Rodgers, lyrics by Lorenz Hart) concerns a young couple, Phil and Peggy, who want to marry. However, they do not think it prudent unless Phil gets a pay raise, something that won't happen until Roosevelt balances the federal budget. In a dream sequence, President Franklin Delano Roosevelt (played by George M. Cohan) tries all sorts of absurd ways to balance the budget, but, in the end, he is unable to do so and encourages the young couple to marry anyway, adding that he needs another term in office in order to balance the budget and restore the country's happiness. Most reviews deemed it a kindhearted attempt at political satire, with Roosevelt portrayed as, according to Garrett Eisler, 'a well-meaning grandfatherly figure surrounded by dubious advisors.'[38] The script sharply targeted various aspects of the New Deal – for example, the high taxes directed at the wealthy, Social Security, the Federal Theatre Project, and organized labor – to the point where numerous scholars, including Eisler, deem it essentially right wing.[39] The show includes Roosevelt's press conference number 'Off the Record,' performed in a style reminiscent of Gilbert and Sullivan as the creators jabbed at ineffective or unqualified government officials.

The New Deal also figures in the plot of *Knickerbocker Holiday* (1938, book by Anderson, lyrics by Anderson and Weill, music by Weill), which relates the story of Pieter Stuyvesant, the tyrannical governor of Manhattan in the seventeenth century.[40] Based on Washington Irving's satire, *The History of New York by Diedrich Knickerbocker* (1809), it takes a pre-existent text and infuses it with contemporary references, not completely unrelated to what Arthur Laurents did when transforming Shakespeare's *Romeo and Juliet* into *West Side Story*. Among the many politically charged songs in the show is 'How Can You Tell an American?', a duet for Washington Irving, who functions as the show's narrator and brings about a happy denouement, and Brom Broeck, the show's anti-Stuyvesant rabble rouser. Through sprightly music and clever list-song lyrics, the pair define an American as someone who cannot take orders (is defiant) and hates corruption (promotes justice). Other politically infused songs include the anthem-like 'One Touch of Alchemy,' in which Stuyvesant's democratic reform appears to be indistinguishable from tyranny, and the buoyant 'Ballad of the Robbers,' the Act 2 opening in which Irving observes that the real criminals run free while the good guys (Brom) are locked behind bars.

Bernstein, Blitzstein, and Weill

The socially conscious musicals from the 1930s certainly resonated with Bernstein. On 27 May 1939, while a senior at Harvard, he led the greater Boston premiere of *The Cradle Will Rock* at Harvard's Sanders Theatre with the support of the Harvard Student Union and several faculty sponsors.[41] Following Blitzstein's model, Bernstein played the piano on-stage (and from memory), announced the scenes, and played some bit parts. The production sparked controversy from a local politician, while the critics praised it.

On 14 June 1952, while on the faculty at Brandeis University in Waltham, Massachusetts, Bernstein conducted a concert performance of Kurt Weill and Bertolt Brecht's *The Threepenny Opera* as part of the university's Festival of the Creative Arts (which Bernstein founded). Blitzstein prepared the translation of the team's *Die Dreigroschenoper* (1928) and also served as the performance's narrator, echoing his role in the early performances of *The Cradle Will Rock*. This concert was the impetus for a 'Weill renaissance' in the 1950s that included a production of *The Threepenny Opera* at the Theater de Lys in Greenwich Village that ran 2,611 performances.[42]

The Allure of Latin America

In his 1933 inaugural address, President Franklin Delano Roosevelt dedicated himself and his administration to a 'Good Neighbor Policy' intended to improve relations between the USA and the nations of Central and South America. He emphasized cooperation and trade as the means to maintain this relationship, rather than military intervention. The plan kept Latin American nations aligned with the USA during World War II but began to unravel in the 1940s as the USA began to intervene in domestic affairs in Argentina, then elsewhere. Because of the Good Neighbor Policy, celebratory images of Latin America infused popular entertainment in the USA during the 1930s and 1940s, including Broadway musicals.

One instance was the football-themed campus musical comedy *Too Many Girls* (1939, book by George Marion, Jr., lyrics by Lorenz Hart, music by Rodgers). The story concerns a scandal-prone East Coast heiress, Consuelo Casey (despite her name, she's white), whose father sends her to his alma mater, Pottawatomie College in Stop Gap, New Mexico, to keep her out of trouble. He hires four bodyguards to watch over her, all of whom are college-age football players. Of course, she falls in love with one of them. In his breakout role, Cuban bandleader Desi Arnaz (1917–1986) played Manuelito, an Argentine star of prep-school American football (not soccer). Manuelito's love interest is Pepe, a student from Mexico. The Puerto Rican-born entertainer Diosa Costello (1913–2013) played Pepe, and in doing so, became known as the first Latina to appear on Broadway.[43] Manuelito and Pepe's race-based romantic segregation, along with the show's avoidance of interracial romance, leads to a racist idea of 'exotic but equal' when it comes to romantic couples in *Too Many Girls*. Individually and together, Pepe and Manuelito performed several cringe-worthy-titled songs that reflected a collective Latin American identity which erases cultural distinctions. After all, a Cuban actor is playing an Argentine character who performs the idea of Mexican music.

Feting South America was central to the revue *Sons o' Fun* (1943), which extolled the comic antics of the team Olsen and Johnson (vaudevillians Ole Olsen and Chic Johnson). Extravagant production numbers such as 'Thank You, South America' and 'Manuelo' featured dynamic performances by the Spanish-born flamenco team of Rosario and Antonio (also known as Los Chevalillos) and the future Hollywood icon, Brazilian Carmen Miranda.

References to Latin America continued to appear in musicals during the early 1950s. In *Guys and Dolls* (1950, music and lyrics by Frank Loesser, book by Jo Swerling and Abe Burrows), Sky Masterson takes Sarah Brown to Havana, where after drinking a 'Cuban milkshake,' which unbeknownst to her includes rum, she kisses Sky and sings 'If I Were a Bell.' The first act of Bernstein's *Wonderful Town* (1953, lyrics by Betty Comden and Adolph Green, book by Joseph A. Fields and Jerome Chodorov) ends with the high-energy 'Conga,' which begins with Ruth, a recent New York arrival, and a group of Brazilian naval cadets. Before the number ends, all of Christopher Street, where Ruth lives with her sister, have joined in the celebration.

* * *

West Side Story rests on a dynamic array of palimpsests, as this chapter demonstrates. The Broadway musical encompasses a rich heritage of shows concerning immigrant experiences, race, knife violence, politics, and the allure of Latin America. Building on performances of immigrant lives and race relations in *The Mulligan Guard Ball* through political satires in the 1930s to the nascent presence of Latinx actors and music in light of the Good Neighbor Policy, *West Side Story* forms an important part of the American musical theatre's ongoing legacy of social relevance.

Notes

1. The Chicago School of Media Theory, https://lucian.uchicago.edu/blogs/mediatheory/keywords/palimpsest/ (accessed 21 July 2020).
2. See Bruce Kirle, *Unfinished Show Business: Broadway Musicals as Works-in-Process* (Carbondale: Southern Illinois University Press, 2005).
3. For more on this phenomenon, see John Koegel, 'Non-English-language musical theatre in the United States,' in *The Cambridge Companion to the Musical*, 3rd ed., ed. William A. Everett and Paul R. Laird (Cambridge: Cambridge University Press, 2017), 51–78. For more on German-language musical theatre in New York, see Koegel, *Music in German Immigrant Theater: New York City, 1840–1940* (Rochester: University of Rochester Press, 2009).
4. For more on *Der Corner Grocer aus der Avenue A*, see Koegel, *Music in German Immigrant Theater*, 209–20.
5. Koegel, *Music in German Immigrant Theater*, 214.
6. The Mulligan Guard scenario grew from a song to a skit to a full-length show (*The Mulligan Guard Ball*) to a series (Katherine K. Preston, 'Introduction to this volume,' in *Irish American Theater: The Mulligan Guard Ball (1879) and Reilly and the 400 (1891), Nineteenth-Century American Musical Theatre*, ed. Deane Root, volume 10 ([New York: Garland, 1994], xvii). *The Mulligan Guard Ball* went through at least two expansions. The initial one-act version appeared in 1879 (the text of which is included in Richard Moody, ed., *Dramas from the American Theatre, 1762–1909* [Cleveland: World Publishing, 1966], 535–65), a two-act version in 1883, and a three-act version in 1892 (the basis for Preston's edition, published in *Irish American Theater*).
7. The daughter is Kitty in the 1892 version, the basis for this discussion. In the 1879 version, her name is Katy.
8. Noel Ignatiev, *How the Irish Became White* (London: Routledge, 1995), 47–50.
9. Ignatiev, *How the Irish Became White*, 128–29.
10. David R. Roediger, *Working toward Whiteness: How America's Immigrants Became White – The Strange Journey from Ellis Island to the Suburbs*, updated edition (New York: Basic Books, 2018), 13.
11. Roediger, *Working toward Whiteness*, 103.
12. Ignatiev, *How the Irish Became White*, 134.

13. Moody, *Dramas from the American Theatre*, 539.

14. Edward Harrigan, *The Mulligan Guard Ball*, in Preston, ed., *Irish American Theater*, 25.

15. Harrigan, *The Mulligan Guard Ball*, in Preston, ed., *Irish American Theater*, 26.

16. Stephen Hinton, *Weill's Musical Theater: Stages of Reform* (Berkeley and Los Angeles: University of California Press, 2012), 369.

17. E. Y. Harburg and Fred Saidy, *Finian's Rainbow* (New York: Random House, 1947), 50.

18. John Graziano, 'Images of African Americans: African American musical theatre, *Show Boat* and *Porgy and Bess*,' in *The Cambridge Companion to the Musical*, 3rd ed., 124.

19. For more on *In Dahomey*, see Marva Griffin Carter, *Swing Along: The Musical Life of Will Marion Cook* (Oxford: Oxford University Press, 2008), 56–67.

20. Ibram X. Kendi, *Stamped from the Beginning: The Definitive History of Racist Ideas in America* (New York: Bold Type, 2016), 147.

21. Quoted in Kendi, *Stamped from the Beginning*, 284.

22. Kendi, *Stamped from the Beginning*, 284.

23. Carter, *Swing Along*, 71.

24. Kendi, *Stamped from the Beginning*, 295–96.

25. For more on Hammerstein and race, see William A. Everett, 'Oscar Hammerstein II and the performativity of race and intersectional oppression in American musicals from *Show Boat* (1927) to *Carousel* (1945),' *Arti musices* 50, nos. 1–2 (2019), 355–75.

26. For more on the choral numbers in *Lost in the Stars*, see Foster Hirsch, *Kurt Weill: From Berlin to Broadway* (New York: Knopf, 2002), 302–09.

27. See, for example, Naomi André, *Black Opera: History, Power, Engagement* (Urbana: University of Illinois Press, 2018).

28. Eric Niiler, 'Knife vs. gun: what a weapon reveals,' www.seeker.com/knife-vs-gun-what-a-weapon-reveals-1768455243.html (accessed 21 July 2020).

29. Thank you to Isaac Brinberg for his work on pointing out connections between verismo opera and *West Side Story* and to Anthony Varner for his investigations into knife stabbings in operas.

30. Howard Pollack, *George Gershwin: His Life and Work* (Berkeley: University of California Press, 2006), 399.

31. Larry Starr, *George Gershwin*, Yale Broadway Masters (New Haven and London: Yale University Press, 2011), 92.

32. Pollack, *George Gershwin*, 551–53.

33. See Trudi Wright, '*Pins and Needles* (1937): everything in moderation,' *Studies in Musical Theatre* 7, no. 1 (2013), 61–73.

34. For more on this production, see Pollack, *Marc Blitzstein: His Life, His Work, His World* (Oxford: Oxford University Press, 2012), 180–82.

35. Pollack, *Marc Blitzstein*, 162.

36. Pollack, *Marc Blitzstein*, 163.

37. For more on this performance, see Pollack, *Marc Blitzstein*, 175–78.

38. Garrett Eisler, 'Kidding on the level: the reactionary project of *I'd Rather be Right*,' *Studies in Musical Theatre* 1, no. 1 (2007), 7.

39. See Eisler, 'Kidding on the level,' 7–24.

40. Foster Hirsch, *Kurt Weill on Stage: From Berlin to Broadway* (New York: Alfred A. Knopf, 2002), 164.

41. For more on the production and the professional and personal relationships between Blitzstein and Bernstein, see Pollack, *Marc Blitzstein*, 183–87.

42. bruce d. mcclung and Paul R. Laird, 'Musical sophistication on Broadway: Kurt Weill and Leonard Bernstein,' in *The Cambridge Companion to the Musical*, 3rd ed., 230.

43. '"Latin Bombshell" Diosa Costello donates costumes to Smithsonian,' Hispanic PR Blog, 15 September 2011, www.hispanicprblog.com/diosa-costello/ (accessed 24 July 2020).

2 | Bernstein on Broadway

HELEN SMITH

When the curtain rose in the Adelphi Theatre on 28 December 1944, and *On the Town* erupted onto the Broadway stage, it was the culmination of a journey for twenty-six-year-old Leonard Bernstein that had begun many years before, when a love of musical theatre had first been kindled in the young Lenny's heart. From an early age, Bernstein had absorbed every musical experience placed before him, and there was certainly an eclectic range on offer. In his piano lessons, started at the age of ten, he studied the standard repertoire of classical pieces, whilst at home he would play by ear popular melodies, ragtime and jazz music that he heard on the radio.[1] When attending the Temple Mishkan Tefila, Bernstein was captivated by the organ and choral music that was performed as part of the worship; from the age of thirteen he was taken by his father to concerts at Boston Symphony Hall.[2] One of Bernstein's first experiences of opera came when he played through four-hand piano arrangements with his younger sister, Shirley, and these explorations led to Lenny's initiation into the musical theatre on a very practical level: at the age of only sixteen, Bernstein began the tradition of mounting a musical production whilst the family were at their summer residence in Sharon, initially persuading other enthusiastic local young people to join in a rather satirical perform-ance of Bizet's *Carmen*.[3] Bernstein himself, unsurprisingly, took charge of various aspects of the show: 'Leonard was in charge of staging and chore-ography as well as the music. That he could cope without help from an experienced guiding hand, such as a drama teacher or music teacher, illustrates an early ability to organise and lead a large group of performers. His innate sense of theatre was already beginning to assert itself.'[4]

Bernstein's involvement with the theatre continued during his univer-sity days at Harvard, with two very significant events occurring barely a month apart in 1939: creating and conducting incidental music for the Classical Club's performance of Aristophanes' *The Birds*, and mounting a student production of Marc Blitzstein's headline-grabbing show *The Cradle Will Rock*. The first of these events marked Bernstein's conducting debut, while the second introduced him both to Blitzstein, who attended

19

the premiere, and also to the concept that perhaps composing in general, and for the theatre more specifically, could be a worthy vocation. However, Bernstein's head was turned as he began studying at the Curtis Institute in the autumn of 1939, and although he returned to Harvard to contribute more incidental music for *The Peace* in 1941, increasingly Bernstein's time was taken up with conducting and highbrow composing. It was only following a move to New York in 1942, and his famous debut conducting the New York Philharmonic on 14 November 1943, standing in for an indisposed Bruno Walter, that the theatre literally came knocking on Bernstein's door once again.

Fancy Free

Despite all the preceding events and experiences, it was to be through modern dance that Bernstein first reached the New York stage. The American choreographer Jerome Robbins was searching for a composer to collaborate with on his new American ballet, and the theatre designer Oliver Smith directed Robbins to Bernstein's studio in Carnegie Hall. Robbins described the meeting: 'We went up and saw him. I showed him my scenario, which was very well preceded [*sic*], it followed the story exactly as it is, and then he started composing.'[5] The resulting ballet, *Fancy Free*, opened at the Metropolitan Opera on 18 April 1944 and was an instant success: 'The music by Leonard Bernstein utilizes jazz in about the same proportion that Robbins's choreography does . . . It is a fine score, humorous, inventive and musically interesting. Indeed the whole ballet, performance included, is just exactly ten degrees north of terrific.'[6] *Fancy Free* follows three sailors on shore leave in New York City, hunting for female company for the twenty-four hours of freedom that they have. In Bernstein's words: 'From the moment the action begins, with the sound of a juke-box wailing behind the curtain, the ballet is strictly young wartime America, 1944.'[7] The servicemen compete for the attention of two girls, and attempt to impress them with their dancing prowess, individually demonstrating their skills in a galop, a waltz and a danzón. Robbins himself danced the role of the third sailor, his choreography perfectly matching the rhythmic complexity and dynamic energy of Bernstein's music, a moment that foreshadowed one of their later collaborations: 'the "Danzón" movement . . . stands out stylistically, providing a view of Bernstein's early tie to Latin musical traditions, a linkage that proved to have future implications for *West Side Story*'.[8] In *Fancy Free*, Bernstein and

Robbins, together with Oliver Smith, had produced an American masterpiece that spoke to the American people in a language that they understood
and related to, a language of music and dance that they would witness again
very soon in the trio's next work together: *On the Town*.

On the Town

There was perhaps an element of inevitability about Bernstein writing
music for Broadway, and following the success of their first collaboration, it was not long before it was suggested that Robbins, Smith and
Bernstein expand the story of their three sailors on twenty-four-hour
shore-leave into a full-scale musical. Not unexpectedly, ballet and dance
would feature prominently in the narrative, as the trio of friends travel
through New York searching for love and romance, but now with the
addition of songs to help propel the fast-moving story forward. To create
the libretto and lyrics, Bernstein recommended Adolph Green and Betty
Comden; Bernstein had known Green since late adolescence when they
met at summer camp in 1937, and had also played piano for the satirical
nightclub group The Revuers, of which Comden and Green were
members.[9] The team was completed by the producer George Abbott,
who provided the experience and knowledge that the young and fresh
colleagues needed to bring the musical to the stage (see Figure 2.1). Just
over seven months after *Fancy Free* had opened, *On the Town* premiered
to critical acclaim:

There can be no mistake about it: 'On the Town' is the freshest and most engaging
musical show to come this way since the golden day of 'Oklahoma!' Everything
about it is right ... [Bernstein] has written ballet music and songs, background
music and raucously tinny versions of the blues ... Mr. Bernstein has quite
understood the spirit of 'On the Town.'[10]

On the Town retains the trio of servicemen that had featured in *Fancy
Free*, but every other aspect of the tale is original, and on their trip through
the city the young men are waylaid by amorous women. The innocent
country boy of the three, Chip, is seduced by a rather insistent taxi-driver
called Hildy, and the clown of the group, Ozzie (played by Green), falls for
the anthropologist Claire (Comden). Gabey, the dreamer among the boys,
decides that he has to find Ivy Smith, who has been featured as
'Miss Turnstiles for June' on posters in the subway. He finds her in
Carnegie Hall, loses her again and, with the help of his friends and their

Figure 2.1 Writing *On the Town*: from left, Leonard Bernstein, Adolph Green; centre foreground, Betty Comden; right, Jerome Robbins. (Credit: Used with permission of Photofest, Inc.)

new-found sweethearts, is reunited with her just as the men have to return to their ship.

The energy and enthusiasm of the collaborators is embodied in Bernstein's music, and following the slow bluesy opening of 'I Feel Like I'm Not Out of Bed Yet', the three sailors burst onto the stage accompanied by the sound of syncopated urban jazz, reflecting the unbridled vivacity of the men as they descend on 'New York, New York'; their entrance is heralded with a fanfare to the city, a significant ascending motif that reappears at various points in the show, particularly in the dances. The driving rhythms with shifting accents and the dissonances of jazz harmonies encapsulate the constant hum of life in the city and the exhilaration and excitement of New York, especially as observed through the eyes of the visiting sailors. There is an edginess and restlessness that echoes the urban music of Copland and Gershwin. Further lively musical depictions can be heard at the end of the first half in 'Times Square Ballet', and in 'The Real Coney Island' towards the end of the show, in addition to featuring at other moments in the action; the Big Apple emerges almost as a protagonist in the story in its own right, displaying different characteristics at various points in the evening, but always portrayed in the language of American contemporary culture. As pointed out by Baber, 'the prevalence of jazz, from the opening of "New York, New York" through chase music and subway sequences that recall Gershwin's *An American in Paris*, leaves no doubt as to the verve and energy of the New York locale'.[11]

The rhythmic vitality of *On the Town* is not only derived from the syncopations of jazz, but also from instances of Latin American dances. The first is a brief but significant example, when we hear a very recognisable rhythm in the 'Conga Cabana'. This snippet of music had originally been composed by Bernstein for *The Peace*, and it would make another more significant appearance in *Wonderful Town*, as will be discussed below. The conga marks the change of scene into The Congacabana, a Latin nightclub where the sailors find themselves, together with Claire and Hildy. A nightclub singer wails 'I Wish I Was Dead', a number heard in a blues style in another establishment they had visited previously that night, but here transformed into a brisk beguine to suit the location. Having encountered Ivy earlier in the evening and arranged to meet her again, Gabey has been stood up, and with his mood rapidly descending, his shipmates and their new sweethearts attempt to cheer him up in the following ensemble number, 'Ya Got Me'. The Latin influence continues in this song, which is underpinned by an insistent rumba rhythm, and demonstrated flamboyantly in an exhilarating dance break derived from the vocal music.

The energy and dynamism of New York also extends to its inhabitants and is particularly present in the comedy songs that characterise the female protagonists. Claire sings a mock-operatic comic duet with Ozzie as they bemoan the fact that they both get 'Carried Away', and Ivy leads a female ensemble number in 'Carnegie Hall Pavane', which begins as a scalar vocal warm up, gradually shifting in styles until it 'provides a riotous flash point for the high–low fusions that define *On the Town*, invading the sacred space of "Carnegie Hall" with rousing swing rhythms and bluesy harmonies'.[12] Hildy has two songs that help to outline her very determined character: 'Come Up to My Place', where the objecting Chip is practically abducted in her cab, and 'I Can Cook Too', Hildy's solo seduction song as she lists her extensive attributes. Oja points out that 'the women usually had the last word in these songs, as they vigorously – sometimes raucously – breached the gender norms of their day'.[13] When heard separately from the metropolitan ladies, the men sound a little tamer, even when they are setting out their intentions for adventure in 'New York, New York'. In the song 'Gabey's Comin'', Chip and Ozzie advise their friend on how to go about picking up a date, but there is still an element of innocence in the pick-up lines they suggest.[14] Gabey's romantic tendencies are embodied in the ballads that he sings, 'Lonely Town' and 'Lucky to Be Me', the sentimental and somewhat nostalgic sound contrasting strongly with the strident metropolitan music of the women's numbers.

Bernstein, Comden, Green and Robbins had collaborated to create a fun and thrilling Broadway musical, but there was one specific dimension that lifted *On the Town* to a different level of theatre entertainment: the dances. The ballets that Robbins choreographed to Bernstein's music helped to move the story forward in a way that had only been observed in a small number of shows prior to 1944, including Rodgers and Hart's *On Your Toes* (1936), and *Oklahoma!* (1943) by Rodgers and Hammerstein, the second of which is frequently considered to be one of the first integrated musicals, with all the elements having equal importance in advancing the narrative.[15] *On the Town* contains eight discrete dance movements, all of which present important elements of the story: 'Presentation of Miss Turnstiles', 'High School Girls', 'Lonely Town Pas de Deux', 'Times Square Ballet', 'Subway Ride and Imaginary Coney Island', 'The Great Lover Displays Himself', 'Pas de Deux' and 'The Real Coney Island'.[16] However, Bernstein's background in highbrow composition led to a symphonic aspect in the dances,[17] and a complexity not previously heard within the musical theatre. There were also interconnections between the movements created by employment of recurring motifs that had already been heard in the songs, and which, in the manner of leitmotifs, had garnered some significance. These motifs linked the dances either to Gabey or to the city, perhaps the two real protagonists of the story. Two years after the opening of the show, Bernstein extracted three of the dances and published them for concert use as *On the Town: Three Dance Episodes*. In the original programme note, he stated: 'That these are, in their way, symphonic pieces rarely occurs to the audience actually attending the show, so well integrated are all the elements.'[18] Bernstein's music for *On the Town* blends classical and popular, highbrow and lowbrow, symphonic techniques and Broadway traditions, creating an eclectic mixture that is a feature of Bernstein's writing. Of course, *On the Town* was not just the end of Bernstein's journey to Broadway, but also the start of another, as he and his collaborators continued their adventures on the New York stage.

Nine years would pass before Bernstein would write the score for another show on Broadway, and in the interim, he composed for three other theatrical projects. The first of these, the ballet *Facsimile* (1946), was another collaboration with Jerome Robbins, while for the second, Bernstein contributed incidental music and songs to a 1950 production of *Peter Pan*. The last of these ventures was his opera of 1951/52, *Trouble in Tahiti*, for which Bernstein wrote both the libretto and the music. The seven scenes tell a tale of marital disharmony and distrust in the relationship between Sam and Dinah, possibly reflecting the troubled marriage of his own parents, but with a touch of jazz lightening the mood in the observations of a trio of singers, a Greek chorus commenting on the action. There is also another moment of Latin American influence, in Dinah's aria 'What a Movie!', which is based on rumba and beguine rhythms.

Wonderful Town

1952 saw Bernstein reunited with Comden and Green, working together to a very tight deadline, as they had less than five weeks to create the songs for *Wonderful Town*, a musical expansion of Jerome Chodorov and Joseph Fields' successful 1940 play *My Sister Eileen*. The writers had adapted their original work first for a movie version in 1942, starring Rosalind Russell in the central role of Ruth, and now they had crafted the libretto for a musical theatre production. The producers Robert Fryer and George Abbott had a contract for Miss Russell to reprise her role in the new version, but the contributions of their first-choice composer and lyricist had not been satisfactory, so the team from *On the Town* were brought in to complete the show, and furnish *Wonderful Town* with the musical numbers, before the contract expired. Although alterations were still being carried out through the try-outs in New Haven, the show opened to rave reviews at the Winter Garden on 26 February 1953: '"Wonderful Town," which opened there last evening, is the most uproarious and original musical carnival we have had since "Guys and Dolls" appeared in this neighborhood.'[19] One of the things that attracted Bernstein, Comden and Green to the project was the location, the action again set in New York, and more specifically in Greenwich Village, a district very close to the trio's heart where they had lived and performed in the late 1930s. As the show was to be set in 1935, this meant the creative team could indulge in a nostalgic excursion into the musical styles of their past, using specific sounds and genres to establish the period and inhabitants of the city. In the first song, 'Christopher Street', a tour guide points out the streets and characters of the area, as the music opens with a vamp made famous by the flamboyant New York 1930s pianist and bandleader Eddie Duchin, setting the scene and defining the era of the show. Following our introduction to a rather bohemian and chaotic side of New York City, we meet two sisters, Ruth and Eileen, arriving from Columbus, Ohio and feeling a little overwhelmed in this new urban location. Just as the male protagonists of *On the Town* were from out-of-town, so the girls are new to the bustling metropolis, and the ensuing clash of cultures forms an important thread in the show. The girls' first duet, 'Ohio', laments the hometown they have left behind, the lazy swung bass line reminiscent of a cowboy song, evoking a provincial 'country' sound that contrasts sharply with the preceding exhibition of city life that we have just witnessed.

Ruth and Eileen attempt to forge new lives for themselves in New York, as a journalist and an actress respectively, but neither are successful; Ruth's journalistic endeavours are rejected, and Eileen receives more propositions than job offers. We are introduced to other interesting residents, including the girls' landlord Mr Appopolous, an out of season professional footballer nicknamed The Wreck, a local drug-store manager called Frank Lippencott, and Bob Baker, an editor at the *Manhatter* who eventually wins Ruth's heart. The character songs and ballads are standard fare for Broadway, although there is frequently an intellectual element that lends an extra depth to the lyrics and the music. Ruth's first solo, 'One Hundred Easy Ways to Lose a Man', is an inventive set of instructions on how to scare away male attention, apparently based on Russell's instruction that the song should be 'da-da-da-da-*joke* da-da-da-da-*joke*'.[20] The comedic nature of the lyrics, which include a grammar lesson directed at an imaginary unfortunate suitor, combines with Bernstein's relaxed swing music, with occasional impertinent orchestral punctuation, to underline the sardonic facet of Ruth's character. The ballads 'A Little Bit in Love' and 'A Quiet Girl', sung by Eileen and Bob respectively, are gentle and simple songs, oases of genuine emotion amongst all the posturing and pretence that appear to dominate the lives of the city dwellers.

One particularly inventive moment comes in 'Conversation Piece', when the sisters are visited by Frank, Bob and Chick Clark, who is attempting to inveigle himself into Eileen's affections by providing Ruth with a job opportunity; the combination of callers results in a very awkward dinner party. The tension and unease of the situation is encapsulated perfectly in a heavy and melancholic vamp which is interrupted by various attempts to initiate polite conversation, all of which fizzle away leaving the orchestra to take over again. Eventually the tension is broken in a rather manic final section, as Eileen trills coloratura-like above the other singers, in a slightly hysterical manner.[21] The dramatic function of the music in this number was important to Bernstein: 'That's the kind of thing I like to do in the theatre. The background is pure theatre music, operating exclusively in theatre terms, not with an eye on Tin Pan Alley, and not to create a memorable tune, but something which is an integral part of the story';[22] this integration, such a significant aspect in *On the Town*, is absent from the majority of *Wonderful Town*. In the place of the earlier show's narrative ballets, we have a dance pantomime in 'Conquering New York', which depicts Ruth and Eileen's struggles in their first weeks in the city, as their attempts to find employment are met with rejection and dismissal. The only other distinct dance item is 'Ballet at the Village Vortex', a diegetic number which appears at the opening of the final scene and functions to establish the atmosphere in the club rather than moving the story forward. Other significant sections of dance music can be found in 'Swing!', 'Wrong Note Rag', 'Pass the Football', 'My Darlin' Eileen' and 'Conga!'. The first two of these numbers demonstrate different aspects of jazz: the contemporary 1930s rhythmic phenomenon in 'Swing', and earlier ragtime and novelty piano styles in 'Wrong Note Rag'. The final two songs in the list introduce pastiches of music from outside the city, indeed from outside the USA, that underline the diversity of New York, and its reputation as a melting pot of cultures and ethnicities. In 'My Darlin' Eileen' the younger sister is serenaded by a contingent of the NYPD in the style of an Irish jig, while 'Conga!' is the energetic final number in the first half. Ruth finally has a writing assignment, and is sent to interview the Brazilian navy cadets who are docked in the Brooklyn Navy Yard. The young sailors are more interested in dancing than talking, and despite Ruth's best efforts to garner their opinions on a wide range of American issues and personalities, an uproarious conga begins (which at least one cadet believes is an American dance, although another does point out that it is Cuban). As mentioned previously, the underlying vamp for this number is recycled music, as it had already appeared in *The Peace* and *On the Town*, but here it is expanded and combined with a cross-rhythmic vocal line, the dramatic interest maintained by the encyclopedic references to the 1930s in the lyrics, while the excitement is escalated by ascending key changes, until it seems that the whole of Greenwich Village has joined in the dance.

Olin Downes had this to say about Bernstein's contribution: 'On the purely musical side a composer and a phenomenal musician ... enriches his palette with many a pungent touch of dissonance and modern harmonic color, while yet keeping very clearly to the popular tone, the rhythmic vigor, the common human touch of our contemporaneous music of entertainment.'[23]

Following *Wonderful Town*, it was not long until Bernstein turned again to theatrical music, but this time for a different medium, as he created his one and only film score for Elia Kazan's 1954 *On the Waterfront*, starring Marlon Brando and Eva Marie Saint. There is an edginess and darkness to some of the music that Bernstein created for Kazan, reflecting the gritty nature of the story, as Terry (Brando) risks his life to take a stand against the crooked dockyard bosses in New York. There was more writing for the screen in 1955, although this time on a smaller scale, when Bernstein provided incidental music for a television production of Oscar Wilde's *Salome*, including a 'Dance of the Seven Veils'.[24] However, Bernstein had another encounter with Broadway between these two compositions, when he collaborated with Lillian Hellman on an adaptation of Jean Anouilh's play *The Lark*, based on the story of Joan of Arc. When the play opened in the Longacre Theatre on 17 November 1955, the audience were treated to the incidental choral music that Bernstein had crafted, utilising a seven-part a cappella ensemble, with some accompaniment from bells and hand drum; the songs were pre-recorded rather than performed live. The texts set were a mix of medieval French folk songs and the Roman Catholic liturgy, and Bernstein would later refashion the movements into his *Missa Brevis*.[25] This collaboration with Hellman occurred in the middle of another creative process involving the pair: the creation of *Candide*.

Candide

Bernstein's return to Broadway on 1 December 1956 was not a return to the urban sophistication of *On the Town* and *Wonderful Town*, but to the world of operetta; jazz and Tin Pan Alley were replaced by the nostalgic sounds of eighteenth- and nineteenth-century Europe. As the political atmosphere in the USA had become highly charged and vehemently anti-communist in the late 1940s, many of those who worked in the entertainment industry had found themselves under investigation, including Hellman herself. As a response to what became known as 'McCarthyism' – Senator Joseph McCarthy had been a prominent voice in the witch-hunt – Hellman settled upon Voltaire's 1759 novella *Candide* as a vehicle to protest the current situation. Although Bernstein was not called to testify before HUAC (the House Un-American Activities Committee), he had his own negative encounter with the political establishment when the US Justice Department refused to renew his passport in July 1953. The situation was only resolved when he gave an extended affidavit under oath confirming that he was not now nor had ever been a member of the Communist Party.[26] Bernstein joined the *Candide* project early in 1954, and he later qualified his reasons for agreeing to work on the production: 'Voltaire's satire is international. It throws light on all the dark places, whether European or American … Puritanical snobbery, phony moralism, inquisitorial attacks on the individual, brave-new-world optimism, essential superiority – aren't these all charges leveled against American society by our best thinkers? And they are also the charges made by Voltaire against his own society.'[27] Although Bernstein and Hellman were committed to the project, finding a lyricist to complete the creative team proved a complicated task. By the time *Candide* opened, lyric contributions had been made by John La Touche, Dorothy Parker, Richard Wilbur and Bernstein himself.[28] Despite the gravity of the original intentions, and what some considered to be a heavy-handed libretto created by Hellman, the score that Bernstein contributed contained some charming and light-hearted moments, as noted by the critic Brooks Atkinson, 'None of his previous theatre music has had the joyous variety, humor and richness of this score. It begins wittily. It parodies operatic music amusingly. But it also has a wealth of melody that compensates for the intellectual austerity of Voltaire's tale. While Candide is learning about life the hard way, Mr. Bernstein is obviously having a good time.'[29]

The story follows Candide on his picaresque journey around the globe as he attempts to find happiness in a world where the odds appear to be stacked against him. From our hero's optimistic beginnings in Westphalia with his teacher Pangloss, whose theories are embodied in 'The Best of All Possible Worlds', he travels to Lisbon, Paris, Buenos Aires, Eldorado and Venice, before returning to a now ruined Westphalia, having survived war, an inquisition, earthquakes, duels, slavery and drowning. Joining Candide at various points in this odyssey are his sweetheart Cunegonde, her brother Maximilian, an Old Lady, and a pessimist called Martin, together with a large cast of lesser characters. The variety of locations offered Bernstein the opportunity to employ a wide range of musical styles in skilful pastiches and parodies, including a Bach-like chorale ('Wedding Procession, Chorale and Battle Scene'), a rousing schottische in 'Bon Voyage', and a Straussian waltz in the 'Paris Waltz Scene'; we hear echoes of Bellini, Mozart, Gilbert and Sullivan, and twelve-tone music. However, even in his homage to operetta Bernstein still manages to indulge his predilection for Latin American dance rhythms. In the first scene in Buenos Aires we are presented with 'I Am Easily Assimilated', a rather anachronistic tango as the eighteenth-century setting is at least one hundred years too early for such a dance to be heard, but the colour that the music adds to the Old Lady's explanation of her apparent ability to thrive in any circumstances reflects perfectly her attitude to life: 'faking her way through a number of situations and cultures, she has survived by her ability to assimilate into any milieu'.[30] This song also contains one of the few dance breaks in the show, as the surrounding crowd is infected by the Old Lady's confident and tenacious spirit.

One of the most performed songs from *Candide* is Cunegonde's aria, 'Glitter and Be Gay', sung by Candide's betrothed as she is installed in a luxurious and bejewelled Paris boudoir, generously endowed by two gentlemen. She laments her current unvirtuous situation in a jewel song in the mould of Gounod, but with elements of a laughing song and just the hint of a brisk habanera. The florid coloratura writing which attracts so many sopranos to this show-piece aria demonstrates the influence of the operas that Bernstein had conducted,[31] and, as previously noted, had been briefly foreshadowed by Eileen's vocal histrionics in 'Conversation Piece'.

The dance forms that Bernstein employed, the waltzes, gavotte and schottische, have rhythmic identities of their own, but as *Candide* is comic operetta rather than musical comedy,[32] there is a paucity of dance in the show, excepting the section in 'I Am Easily Assimilated', and the separate dance item 'Paris Waltz Scene'. With the strident patterns of jazz and swing notably absent from Bernstein's score, the rhythmic vitality of *Candide* is rooted in the use of complex metres and shifting time signatures. These are first seen in the 'Overture' where the metre fluctuates between duple and triple time, a device also utilised in 'Pilgrim's Procession', 'Venice Gambling Scene', and to a lesser degree in 'Make Our Garden Grow'. Bernstein also employs quintuple and septuple time signatures, particularly in 'Oh Happy We' and 'Ballad of Eldorado', and frequently includes strong cross rhythms, seen in 'The Best of All Possible Worlds', 'Glitter and be Gay', 'Bon Voyage', and 'Paris Waltz Scene'. These techniques have the effect of distancing the music of *Candide* from Bernstein's earlier musical theatre scores and aligning it with his highbrow compositions and operatic ambitions, although still retaining a sense of humour in the unexpected twists and turns.

At the end of Voltaire's tale, and Hellman's libretto, a great many events have occurred, but after all the melodrama, the struggles, fights, deaths, abandonments and lies, after all the parodies and pastiches and rhythmic trickery comes one of the only moments of genuine emotion in 'Make Our

Garden Grow'.[33] The foolish optimism of the beginning of the show has matured into a more realistic expectation of the future, as the characters accept that this world is not the paradise they once believed it to be, and that their lives are not destined for perfection. Richard Wilbur's lyric takes its cue from Voltaire's final line 'mais il faut cultiver notre jardin',[34] and from a rising octave melodic motif heard scattered throughout the show that is associated with Cunegonde, Bernstein fashioned some of the most expressive choral music he ever wrote; as Crist articulates in her article considering the political atmosphere surrounding *Candide*: 'The grand and affecting style of "Make Our Garden Grow" casts aside Voltaire's studied skepticism to realise the composer's own humanistic credo … [Bernstein's] romantic faith in humanity and essential optimism resound throughout "Make Our Garden Grow", which celebrates absolute unanimity.'[35]

Despite all the sparkle and wit in Bernstein's score, it could not be reconciled with Hellman's bitingly satirical libretto, and the 1956 *Candide* was not a success, running for only seventy-three performances at the Martin Beck Theatre. However, Bernstein had already begun work on his next Broadway project and he had in fact been composing both scores in parallel. His new show would mark a return to collaborating with Jerome Robbins, and would open in New York less than eleven months later, changing musical theatre forever.

Notes

1. Humphrey Burton, *Leonard Bernstein* (New York: Doubleday, 1994), 11.
2. Burton, *Leonard Bernstein*, 9, 19–20.
3. Burton, *Leonard Bernstein*, 22–24. *Carmen* came in 1934, with subsequent summers seeing productions of Gilbert and Sullivan's *The Mikado* in 1935, and *HMS Pinafore* in 1936.
4. Burton, *Leonard Bernstein*, 23.
5. Robbins interviewed by Humphrey Burton, BBC Radio 3 *Composer of the Week*, 30 December 1996–3 January 1997.
6. John Martin, 'Ballet by Robbins Called Smash Hit', *New York Times*, 19 April 1944.
7. Quoted in the score foreword of Leonard Bernstein, *Fancy Free* (New York: Harms, 1950). Used by permission of The Leonard Bernstein Office, Inc.
8. Carol Oja, *Bernstein Meets Broadway: Collaborative Art in a Time of War* (New York: Oxford University Press, 2014), 36. In this book, Oja provides an excellent study of *On the Town*, especially its historical and cultural context.

9. Burton, *Leonard Bernstein*, 38–39, 102. Bernstein had also appeared on a recording with The Revuers in 1940, when he accompanied *The Girl with Two Left Feet* and *Joan Crawford Fan Club*. The two sketches were released on Musicraft as 'Night Life in New York' (Musicraft 1133–35, re-issued on CD in 1998 as *Leonard Bernstein – Wunderkind*, Pearl GEMS 0005).

10. Lewis Nichols, 'The Play', *New York Times*, 29 December 1940.

11. Katherine Baber, *Leonard Bernstein and the Language of Jazz* (Urbana: University of Illinois Press, 2019), 95.

12. Oja, *Bernstein Meets Broadway*, 253.

13. Oja, *Bernstein Meets Broadway*, 243.

14. This song was cut from the original Broadway production, much to the dismay of Bernstein, who lamented that the number contained thematic material that was central to the whole show (Robbins, quoted in Otis Guernsey, *Broadway Story and Song: Playwrights/Lyricists/Composers Discuss Their Hits* (New York: Dodd, Mead, 1985), 9). The song was later reinstated and appears in the published 1997 Boosey and Hawkes score.

15. For more information regarding integration in Broadway shows, see Paul R. Laird, 'Choreographers, Directors and the Fully Integrated Musical', in *The Cambridge Companion to the Musical*, 3rd ed., ed. William A. Everett and Paul R. Laird (Cambridge: Cambridge University Press, 2017), 264–80.

16. The first and last of these dance numbers do include a small amount of sung material, rather than being completely instrumental, but the lyric section of 'Presentation' is significant within the story, while in 'Real Coney Island' the diegetic vocal line helps to set the scene.

17. Although it had been completed in December 1942, Bernstein's *Jeremiah*, Symphony No.1 had premiered on 28 January 1944, only a matter of months before work began on *On the Town*.

18. Quoted in the score foreword of Leonard Bernstein, *On the Town: Three Dance Episodes* (New York: Amberson Enterprises, G. Schirmer, 1968). Used by permission of The Leonard Bernstein Office, Inc.

19. Brooks Atkinson, 'At the Theatre', *New York Times*, 26 February 1953, 22.

20. Adolph Green, quoted in '*Wonderful Town*: A Conversation with Comden and Green', *Prelude, Fugue & Riffs*, Fall 1994.

21. Eileen's interjections are also perhaps a glimpse of the vocal gymnastics demonstrated by Cunegonde later in *Candide*. This fact is also noted by Daniel Gundlach in '"Wär' Ich Doch Wieder Zuhaus!" – Nostalgie in *Wonderful Town*', in '. . . *wie die Stadt schön wird*', *Leonard Bernstein: Wonderful Town*, ed. Heiko Cullmann, Michael Heinemann and Andreas Eichhorn (Dresden: Thelem, 2017), 51.

22. Quoted in Stanley Green, *The World of Musical Comedy* (South Brunswick, NJ: A. S. Barnes, 1974), 292. Used by permission of The Leonard Bernstein Office, Inc.

23. Olin Downes, 'Wonderful Time: Bernstein's Musical is Brilliant Achievement', *New York Times*, 10 May 1953, Section 2, 7.

24. The incidental score is written for the unusual combination of electric guitar, harp, piano, percussion (four players), and off-stage singers; unpublished score in the Leonard Bernstein Collection in the Library of Congress.

25. In the programme note in the score of Leonard Bernstein, *Missa Brevis* (New York: Jalni Publications, 1988), Jack Gottlieb states that this reshaping was suggested by renowned choral director Robert Shaw, who had attended one of the first performances of *The Lark*. However, the idea already seems to have occurred to Bernstein, as he mentions in a letter to his brother written the day after the play began its try-outs in Boston in October 1955; reproduced in Nigel Simeone, *The Leonard Bernstein Letters* (New Haven and London: Yale University Press, 2013), 349.

26. The story is told is more detail in Barry Seldes, 'Bernstein and McCarthyism', 67–85 in *Leonard Bernstein and Washington, D.C.: Works, Politics, Performances*, ed. Daniel Abraham, Alicia Kopfstein-Penk and Andrew H. Weaver (Rochester: University of Rochester Press, 2020), 73–77; the affidavit itself is reproduced in Simeone, *Leonard Bernstein Letters*, 299–309.

27. Leonard Bernstein, 'Colloquy in Boston', *New York Times*, 18 November 1956, Section 2, 1, 3. Used by permission of The Leonard Bernstein Office, Inc.

28. Richard Wilbur joined the team as librettist in December 1955 and wrote the majority of the original lyrics; Burton, *Leonard Bernstein*, 257.

29. Brooks Atkinson, 'The Theatre: "Candide"', *New York Times*, 3 December 1956, 40.

30. Elizabeth A. Wells, West Side Story: *Cultural Perspectives on an American Musical* (Lanham, MD, Toronto and Plymouth UK: Scarecrow Press, 2011), 118.

31. During early 1955, Bernstein had conducted Maria Callas in Bellini's *La Sonnambula* at La Scala; Burton, *Leonard Bernstein*, 243.

32. Whatever *Candide* may have become in the years since its original production, through major revisions in 1972, 1982 and 1988 to the version that now sits more comfortably in the opera house than the theatre, it was described as a comic operetta in its first incarnation (Leonard Bernstein, Richard Wilbur, John La Touche, Dorothy Parker, Lillian Hellman, *Candide: A Comic Operetta Based on Voltaire's Satire* (New York: Random House, 1957)).

33. The other places that are free from parody and pastiche are 'It Must Be So' and the instrumental 'Eldorado'.

34. Voltaire, *Candide et Autres Contes* (Paris: Éditions Flammarion Gallimard, 1992), 108.

35. Elizabeth B. Crist, 'Mutual Responses in the Midst of an Era: Aaron Copland's *The Tender Land*, and Leonard Bernstein's *Candide*', *The Journal of Musicology*, 23, no. 4 (2006), 514.

3 | In Anticipation of *West Side Story*

The Confluence of Styles, Genres, and Influences in the Early Choreography of Jerome Robbins

PHOEBE RUMSEY

> I have tried to give you an accurate picture of myself – my selves. The evil, the good, the bad, the smiling, sneering, artistic, malicious, destructive, benevolent, rapacious, egotistical, sacrificing and selfish are all my selves . . . all me.
>
> – Jerry Rabinowitz, English 12, 1935[1]

Jerome Robbins's career prior to *West Side Story* was a balancing act between the vastly different worlds of concert ballet and Broadway musicals. Robbins's often Janus-faced artistic identity was created not out of random opportunities but because his way of working stemmed from a narrative investigation of movement that was forged in a unique time when ballet was modernizing and musical theatre was discovering the dramatic potential of dance. This chapter describes how Robbins (1918–1998) came to be a 'narrative artist' and how he did not emphatically choose between concert dance and Broadway but navigated between the two through the whole of his career. Owing to his innovative choreographic strategies and creative interpretations of the world around him, Robbins brought modes of communication from one artistic world to the other, generating an overtly mimetic and dramatic style in concert ballet and an athletic and punchy ballet style in musical theatre. In fact, this doubleness in Robbins's life extended throughout his career beyond *West Side Story* and helped to modernize (in his time) dance in both genres that has left a lasting impression. Notably, Robbins continually strove to exorcize his personal demons through concert dance and musical theatre, causing both joy and angst for the dancers and his collaborative partners. In the turbulent process, or perhaps in spite of it, he created some of the most lasting pieces of choreography in the repertoire of dance in the United States. This discussion traces Robbins's formative training years, early career, and then focuses on several foundational shows that set in motion his choreographic career along with lesser known creations that helped shape his mode of expression building up to *West Side Story*. Robbins's style, choreographic strategies, and ingenuities in *West Side Story* have a foundation in the material circumstances of his early career, helped along by key mentorships and collaborations with fellow artists both in ballet and musical theatre. I establish from the beginning how Robbins started out as many aspiring dancers do: cobbling together a variety of training schemes, odd jobs, and hustling for paid gigs. Along the way, I consider the tensions that continued to mount for Robbins between his personal life and his professional career and colour his way of working. Limitations of space prohibit a thorough investigation of Robbins's many successes, projects, and artistic relationships in the decade building up to *West Side Story*; however, I draw out a collection of primary threads that weave together to create the dance-driven storytelling that comes to full fruition in *West Side Story*.

There are many reasons, ranging from proximity to Manhattan to early artistic contacts and mentorships, why Jerome Robbins was able to experience and be involved in the New York performance scene from an early age. Jerome Robbins was born Jerome Wilson Rabinowitz on 11 October 1918 in New York City. He came from a lower-middle-class family that ran a corset company and lived in Weehawken, New Jersey. Growing up, Robbins had the advantage of piano lessons, a school with arts programs, and the opportunity to attend the cinema on weekends. In addition, his older sister Sonia pursued dance training and would invite him to watch her classes and be part of at-home rehearsals. Geographically, Robbins had the advantage of being a quick ferry ride away from a plethora of performance offerings in Manhattan, from Broadway musicals and plays, to a hotbed of avant-garde experimental artists practicing their craft, often outside for all to see. For amusement in his teen years, Robbins and his friends would seek out the strangest, most provocative work they could find in the city. Robbins constantly leaned on Sonia for support, encouragement, and help brainstorming future goals from a young age. Though Sonia wanted her own life and moved into the city to train as a dancer, Robbins, fiercely opportunistic from a young age, would constantly contact her for help and general advice.

While his family would have preferred Robbins enter the family business or pursue a more respectable and secure profession such as engineering or chemistry, his failing of several courses in his first year at New York University called for a reset of possible career trajectories. Robbins, who had a close relationship with his mother and a difficult relationship with his father, convinced his parents to let him try his hand at the various artistic endeavors he was interested in for one year. If his pursuits did not pan out, he agreed to return to the family business.[2] And so, after high school, at

Sonia's suggestion he auditioned for and was accepted into Senya Gluck Sandor's experimental modern dance company, where she was a member. Robbins was soon training and performing side by side with upcoming modern dance luminaries such as José Limón. Sandor was a unique mentor for Robbins as he was an unusual 'hybrid choreographer – ballet-trained, dedicated to modern dance, but also a veteran of Broadway, burlesque and vaudeville.'[3] In order to excel at his theatrical approach, Sandor encouraged Robbins to study ballet and take acting lessons on the side. Sandor provided a substantial amount of modern dance training and a variety of performance and social opportunities. Perhaps the most substantial job in Robbins's two-year engagement with the group was being part of the Yiddish Art Theatre's production of *The Brothers Ashkanazi*. Importantly, this show, choreographed by Sandor, had nine performances a week and was Robbins's first steady employment as a dancer. In this time Jerome Rabinowitz changed his name to one that was less Jewish sounding. The irony that this happened when he was learning more about his Jewish roots through working with a Yiddish company is not lost. In fact, the overt awareness of his Jewishness was something Robbins pulled away from in his early career.[4]

In this formative time two personal developments or basic character traits become clear – one practical, one artistic – that would go on to colour his early career. Firstly, Robbins was a resilient and relentless journeyman of the arts. He would seek out any creative employment opportunities he could find from puppetry to small tasks and backstage work that he would eagerly take on from anyone who was connected to the performing arts. He was extraordinarily determined and yet rarely got into projects the first time, second time, or at all. Recognizing that Robbins had to apply himself, press teachers for opportunities, and use considerable elbow grease to get even the chance to audition or try out ideas, brings a sense of ordinariness to someone who has often been exalted in dance and musical theatre history. His trials and tribulations also help explain the anxiety, self-doubt, and desperation he experienced early on; physicalized qualities that manifest at times in his movement style, such as seen in 'Cool' in *West Side Story*. Robbins's early archival papers include many letters to artistic directors, company managers, and fellow artists asking for opportunities to audition or pitch ideas.[5] Markedly, some of his early breaks in the dance world came from the need for male dancers in the profession.[6] For example, after only four ballet classes he was thrust into a partnering role with an independent professional ballerina who desperately needed a partner.[7]

Secondly, early on in his work with Sandor's company, and building on his experience in a variety of plays and operettas in high school, he began to be fascinated by the dramatic potential of the body. His interest in how to communicate through body language was consistently being deepened with every small project or nascent concept he was thinking and writing about. Deborah Jowitt, in *Jerome Robbins: His Life, His Theatre, His Dance*, explains that Sandor 'pushed dancers to think about their character's backgrounds and perform truthfully in the Stanislavskian sense.'[8] Sandor insisted the dancers understood 'the importance of theatrical credibility,' and Robbins absorbed this advice as he continued to pursue the development of narrative and character through his own movement.[9] The concept of believable characters stood in contrast to the pantomimic tendencies and stereotypical characters often found in ballet productions. Robbins's curiosity for realism would come to full actualization in *West Side Story*, where he consistently demanded truth and self-analysis from his performers.[10] In considering the fundamentals of performance, what began as general observations, informal performance ideas, and general curiosities about the ability of the moving body to carry plot, turned into a very particular 'intuitive knowledge.' This unique creative impulse strengthened when Robbins had the opportunity to spend four summers outside of New York at Camp Tamiment in his early twenties.

Camp Tamiment

Camp Tamiment was a Catskills-like resort in Pennsylvania, nestled amongst the Poconos Mountains, where people would come to relax, play, and get away from the stresses of the city. On the grounds of the resort was the relatively large Tamiment Playhouse, which seated approximately 1,200 people – roughly the size of a Broadway theatre. Max Leibman had been established as the director since 1933 and was tasked with the massive job of putting on a new musical or revue every week for ten weeks. Performers and entertainers of all sorts would come out to work at Tamiment. While the pay was minimal, it was a professional performance job and provided room and board. Robbins was thrilled to be hired as a performer in 1936 and not return to work at the corset factory. In *Jerome Robbins: A Life in Dance*, Wendy Lesser explains it was at Camp Tamiment where Robbins came to be a 'narrative artist.'[11] Several factors combine to give Robbins the space to develop this mode of creative expression.

To start, the advantage of employment at the summer resort was that established professionals would join in or headline the revues for the summer season. In this capacity, Robbins, who spent his first few summer contracts in the ensemble, was able to watch, emulate, work alongside, and eventually collaborate with some key people in the field including Leibman, Danny Kaye, Carol Channing, and Imogen Coca among others. He would study their style and timing and learn from their acting choices in rehearsal and unique physicalizations in performance. In his free time, he would play around with various bits of choreography for small groups and experiment with his own ideas inspired by the musical comedies he performed in. Lesser explains the key importance of Robbins's Tamiment experience: 'beyond the dance and performance experience, he was learning something about the essence of theatricality, and it was the comedians who really taught him this.'[12] In the development of musical theatre of the time, the form was becoming increasingly solidified as to its various conventions. As the genre became more prolific in the United States, established methods of constructing successful musical shows were taking shape. Various conventions, such as the pairing of characters, structuring narrative arcs, and inserting comic foils along the way became part of the essential toolbox of writers, composers, and directors of musical theatre. The process and experience of being a cast member in a new show every week, while intense, exposed the nuts and bolts of the form, and offered up a road map to Robbins's telling of a story in the musical theatre genre. He developed an innate sense of the performative gesture and how it worked to satisfy both the needs of plots and audience expectations. Considering the string of musical theatre offerings loaded with comedic bits and shenanigans that had circulated in Robbins's formative years over the past decade, including *Girl Crazy* (1930), *Anything Goes* (1933), *On Your Toes* (1936), *Me and My Girl* (1937), *The Boys from Syracuse* (1938), etc., there was a physical impulse and dramaturgical texture that became associated with Broadway musicals. Robbins was picking up on the many nuances of the form and how his own sense of movement could work in the genre.

In this musical theatre 'boot camp,' Robbins was included in the creation of a few short pieces that were sometimes included in the shows. He was always primed to learn a new skill, figure out lifts or partnering techniques, and help move rehearsals forward.[13] In this capacity, he became someone choreographers and directors wanted to work with – a creative problem solver (a role he would take on many times down the road on floundering shows to help out colleagues, mostly uncredited).[14] From his initial role as an ensemble member, towards the end of his four summers, he was often involved in the more formal choreography for the productions.[15] For someone who was extremely self-conscious and critical of himself from an early age, Tamiment offered a safe space to explore and experiment artistically and socially. In performance, Robbins had a physical exuberance and charm that was clever and appealing to watch and brought him the needed confidence to return to the city and audition for Broadway musicals and dance companies.[16]

A Taste of Broadway

When Robbins returned to the city, he proceeded to network with Broadway dancers, performers, choreographers, and directors he may have worked with at Tamiment. He went to every Broadway musical audition call for ensemble members and surprisingly (to him) had little luck. He was never quite able to shake his feelings of inadequacy, focusing often on his shortcomings and the growing paranoia that he would never get another opportunity. Eventually, he got into the chorus of *Great Lady* (1938), a Broadway musical with music by Frederick Loewe. This was followed by being in the ensemble of *Stars in Your Eyes* (1939) and *Keep off the Grass* (1940). His journals cry out with the frustrations and the hard work of being in the chorus and tell of the general woe of being in the background.[17] Despite his frustrations, the most key part of his chorus experiences is that George Balanchine, the rising star of the dance world, was the choreographer of *Great Lady* and *Keep off the Grass*. Robbins immediately identified the artistry in Balanchine, and closely followed his career trajectory and process and received some mentorship in return. Though Robbins's style would never be as minimal and classically derived as Balanchine's, the idea that he could dance and do choreography in both genres appealed to his creative impulse and obsessive desire to succeed on many levels. He turned his attention toward the ballet world in order to fulfill his desire to work and train amongst the best dancers.

Ballet Theatre

When Robbins heard Lucia Chase, a wealthy art lover, was set to invest in a new performance company called Ballet Theatre (which would go on to become the renowned American Ballet Theatre) Robbins was attuned to the opportunity this might present for him. True to form, he wrote letters seeking auditions with Ballet Theatre, tried to connect with some of the dancers in the company, and used his new status as an ensemble member in a Broadway show to give him a sense of legitimacy. During out of town try-outs for *Keep off the Grass*, when he heard the nascent Ballet Theatre were holding auditions he eagerly contacted the company managers. He wrote at the time, 'I am greatly interested in joining the company – but unfortu-nately I will be out of town at the time for two weeks . . .. I would gladly leave the show to join and rehearse for the fall season.'[18] This statement demonstrates his desire to be in the company given how quickly he would give up his Broadway gig. Eventually, after many attempts at contact and auditions, he got a job as a temporary summer intern in the company. Through a combination of fortunate breaks of being in the right place at the right time and doing the work required of him, Robbins was eventually offered a position in the company in the lower ranks. This was a very opportune moment for Robbins as he was able to take advantage of all the training and daily company classes traditionally offered in a ballet company and hone his skills. This increase in his technical aptitude was helped in large part by the opportunity he had to travel with the company to Mexico City for a four-month summer residency.

Still in his early twenties, Robbins felt for the first time in his anxiety-filled life that he had found a surrogate family in the company of ballet dancers in the new American company.[19] Robbins was happy, curious, and generally elated to be in Mexico City. He was at his most creative in this environment, thinking up poetry, scripts for plays, and ideas for choreog-raphy. While he was very closed off emotionally in some ways, he had an effusive and vivid internal dialogue about what he wanted to achieve as an artist. ('I will live to dance, eat to dance, sleep to dance.')[20] In this formative time Robbins was beginning to get a greater understanding of the classical form (much like Tamiment had taught him about musical comedy). This appreciation built on his early impressions from seeing Les Ballets Russes. These new companies, though operating on shoestring budgets, were modernizing the form with each premiere. They turned the page on the classic 'white ballets' filled with women in long layers of tulle and crinolines and began to experiment with form and style. Anxious to make the Ballet Theatre as formidable artistically as Les Ballets Russes that had toured in the USA as early as 1916, the company toured across America to many cities of all sizes. Of note, in his time as a dancer, Robbins had first-hand experiences of all the dramas, unfair treatment, body exhaustion, and shenanigans of touring.[21] Given this experience, one might suppose his treatment of his own dancers later on in his career would have been more understanding; however, it seemed the intensity fueled him to work harder and be even more self-critical, obscuring an established empathy for others. These ways of being in the world do in part go back to his childhood where his mother was brutally honest to him about every poem or story he would write.[22] In this capacity, he developed a very blatant sense of honesty which, like his mother's, was quite cruel. He writes in his diary, 'Sometimes I dream I am so mean I have to go to bed.'[23]

At Ballet Theatre, Robbins continued to hone his craft in the ensemble. He had already shown he had the grit to endure the brutally honest experience of casting within a large company. For example, when he failed to get cast as the understudy or even the second understudy for the title role in the ballet *Petrouchka* (which would become his favourite role) he writes, 'I went to [Fokine] and asked him if please could I just study it – he didn't have to spend any time with me, just let me come to rehearsals to watch and learn the role.'[24] In fact, this temerity paid off and he eventually stepped into the role, and would receive tremendous recognition for his interpretation of the part over the coming years. Refusing to take no for an answer was indeed his modus operandi. Thankfully amongst all this self-commanding and obsession, he continually took solace in exploring his surroundings on tour.

Taking in the moods and ambience of different towns across America was a great curiosity and delight for Robbins, and opened his mind to a broader feel for the United States. He would often tour around the various towns the company stopped in, whether it was Boston, Seattle, Atlanta, or New Orleans, among others. He was taking in what all these towns had to offer including jazz music and cultural offerings. Agnes de Mille, Martha Graham, and Katherine Dunham were among others who had ventured outside of New York or Hollywood, and were exploring what it meant to be American and how that could be interpreted on stage through movement.[25] Robbins describes the shift happening in the United States surrounding the status and acceptance of ballet, 'a democratic people's mark on the ballet is directly evidenced in its subject matter, its dancers, and the kind of audiences that attend it.'[26] The touring of Les Ballets Russes followed by Ballet Theatre, along with various other dance companies throughout America, had helped democratize the form, and with lower ticket prices allowed for greater accessibility. The cross-over of artists between the previously recognized 'lowbrow' musical theatres with the 'highbrow' classical ballet helped to level out hierarchies in performance and fostered more curiosity in the form from a wider range of people. The growing interest in ballet was reflected in musical theatre, and had been for a while, when you consider musicals such as *On Your Toes* (1936) or *I Married an Angel* (1938), both choreographed by George Balanchine. The inclusion of ballet in musicals was to become a substantial turn for the genre that would take firm hold for the next several decades. Robbins was to be part of this shift and, as developed on tour, already had his nascent ideas for a short ballet about three sailors visiting New York City.

Fancy Free and *On the Town*

Robbins was so eager to impress and officially start his career as a choreographer at Ballet Theatre with this potential new piece about sailors' shore leave that he continued to write letters and make pleas for the opportunity to put the ballet together formally with support from the company, rather than in his spare time. Once he finally gets a chance to rehearse his ballet, he writes in a letter to the company manager, promising, 'I'll dig in like crazy and the poor kids who work for me will not have felt a lash like mine.'[27] This statement exposes a culture of the artistic figure-head as disciplinarian. That Robbins felt, in order to pitch his idea, that he would also promise to work the dancers extremely hard is troublesome and is demonstrative of his growing desperation to carve out an artistic identity for himself. His eagerness to please and prove himself comes at a cost to his connection to dancers on an equal level (as one himself). At this point, there is already the development of an intensity of labor that comes to colour his process for the rest of his career.

Returning to the composition itself, Robbins explains much of his inspiration came from Paul Cadmus's 1934 painting *The Fleet's In!*; though he found it too crude.[28] Indeed, the painting of the scene of sailors' debauchery on shore leave caused quite a scandal when it came out. Robbins's *Fancy Free* seemed to make much effort to keep a youthful exuberance and curiosity to the characters and stays away from the raunchier ideas set forth in Cadmus's work. In fact, there is much more of a feeling of fellowship between the sailors. Lesser describes the camaraderie between the sailors as 'palpable,' and indeed it is this playfulness that is at the heart of the piece.[29] This quality is important to note for several reasons. Firstly, classical ballet at the time was experimenting with structure and form and these very forthright narrative or story telling qualities were not the norm in the new ballets. Secondly, the reservedness about the sexuality, he in fact embraces a year later in *Facsimile*.

The basic premise of *Fancy Free* is fairly simple: three sailors are on shore leave, they enjoy a fanciful night on the town pursuing women and good times. The men quickly come in contact with two women and the three men dance with them in a collection of duets. However, one man always is left out, or is found dancing alone. As a way of solving their dilemma the men hold a competition where each does a dance and the women choose the victor. Structurally, the unique strategy built into the piece is the odd number of performers. This unevenness is quite unusual in ballet, known for its many identical rows of swans, sylphs, etc., not to mention the conventional *pas de deux, quatre,* or *six.*[30] With the stage never seeming balanced, Robbins creates a jagged edginess to the moment that seems to be heading for a resolution, but never does. This effect creates a sense of anticipation or urgency and propels the piece forward, a strategy that carries through in *West Side Story*, in the opening prologue and elsewhere. Conversely, given Robbins's unshakable sense of disconnect with his peers and his own strict self-judgment, there is a tinge of sadness cast upon the one always being left out. Adding to the complexity in *Fancy Free*, the ballet is filled with canons, meaning, one dancer performs a move, which is then repeated by the next dancer and so on creating a sort of waterfall effect of the step occurring numerous times. Robbins did not invent this effect; however, his use of canons in *Fancy Free* adds a unique dimension as each sailor has an individual character as shown by how the move is interpreted with slight differences by each dancer. Markedly, as the canon is performed with an uneven number of dancers, and in combination with Bernstein's provocative score, the piece has a pulsing expectancy or promise that increases as the piece moves forward. Lesser explains the effect, 'This refusal to fall into neatly aligned symmetries and predictable matchups make the dance everlastingly interesting.'[31] Robbins's style has many moments of classical vocabulary juxtaposed with off-kilter shoulder, hips thrusts, and Latin stylings. There is no attempt to disguise the ballet elements, they appear as punctuation throughout. For example, in one of the early duets, *chassées* and *pas de bourrées* lead into a lift in *attitude* position, when only moments earlier the dancers had been doing a sharp snake hips-like section.[32] This obvious use of ballet moves alongside jazzy or invented steps becomes a signature of Robbins's style. Ballet audiences were unaccustomed to combinations of lyrical or romantic movement juxtaposed with more upbeat popular styles. The insertion of sharp, hot moves onto the concert ballet stage, not to mention the wearing of character shoes (heels) by the women launches *Fancy Free* into a league of its own. This insertion of more racy moves, seen in hip rolls, shoulder shimmies, and a more grounded sense of movement helped to modernize and sensualize the ethereal and lifted body posture of classical ballet. Overall, *Fancy Free*'s gestural and narrative style builds from moments of sheer virtuosity, tender silences, thrilling bravado, and a general salute to the comraderies of the three sailors, each with a distinct personality.

Fancy Free stood out amongst the ballet company's other offerings at the time and on 18 April 1944, the twenty-nine minute ballet was a near instant success. In its time *Fancy Free* offered a snapshot of New York City outside the doors of the theatre, or a postcard of the city for audiences on the company's extensive tours, and audiences and critics alike were very receptive. Reconsidered today, however, *Fancy Free* has its limitations, specifically surrounding the male–female stereotypes as well as the harassing actions of the men disguised as playful shenanigans. Lea Marshall, writing for *Dance Magazine* in 2019, suggests it may be time to retire *Fancy Free* from the repertoire. She explains, 'The ballet hasn't aged well, especially in the wake of #metoo. It's a study in rape culture.'[33] The pursuit of the women by the men, which involves hip thrusts aplenty, and a variety of grabs of body parts, though not championed in 1945, would likely be disapproved of in today's social climate and the suggestion of the repetition of the cycle at the end of the piece, despite the women being fed up with the men's antics, is also problematic.[34] The historical distance may offer an out for Robbins, and, considering he was choreographing for the *zeitgeist* of his time, the blame cannot rest entirely with him for the overt womanizing in the piece. Marshall, however, does not forgive this, noting, 'Robbins knew women don't relish this kind of behaviour from men. But he still made a comedy out of it.'[35]

***

Just over six months after the premiere of *Fancy Free*, essentially an intimate concert ballet piece, Robbins's concept became the inspiration for a Broadway musical. In a moment of unique collaboration, Betty Comden, Adolph Green, Leonard Bernstein, and Robbins teamed up to create *On the Town*, which premiered at the close of 1944. Robbins was deeply immersed in the whirlwind of creating a piece that would come to have many achievements on Broadway at the time, one of the most integral being the desegregation of the cast and crew and incorporation of a more diverse team on and off stage. This is particularly poignant in the hiring of Japanese dancer Sono Osato.[36]

The necessary changes in the transformation of the short ballet into a full-length musical, however, were illuminating to Robbins in regard to his aesthetics as a 'narrative artist.' When the piece was developed to an evening-length musical and directed by the renowned George Abbott, the most decisive element of the movement that was lost in the choreography was its 'free-floating timeless charm.'[37] The whimsical off-centeredness was squared up and most substantially, due to the conventions in the genre of musical theatre at the time (and often continuing today), there was a decided resolution to the piece in the final grouping of happy couples. The distinct conclusion to the musical drew away the ambiguity in the piece for Robbins. Moreover, Robbins was confronted with the decisive workings of a director and experienced a loss of the control he had cultivated in bringing *Fancy Free* to its feet. Abbott, a formidable talent with over a dozen Broadway shows under his belt, had a 'disciplined, forthright, pragmatic approach to directing' which did not mesh with Robbins's own singular way of working and brought much conflict in the run up to the opening.[38] Additionally, from a narrative point of view, and though he had been in several Broadway musicals himself, the introduction of singing seemed to shore up the grey areas of the characters' personalities and make them more black and white. For Robbins, the increasingly stereotypical characters removed any room for more individualized inter-pretations. As Lesser describes, 'the verbal obviousness crushes what was delicate and unspoken in dance.'[39]

The discordant experience for Robbins of joining of song and dance may have been instrumental in developing how he was to make a lasting impact in musical theatre. Robbins would continue to seek out moments where he could recapture the voiceless ballet quality, as is seen in the 'Prologue' of *West Side Story* or the 'Chavaleh Sequence' in *Fiddler on the Roof* (1964). Though the sounds and sensibilities of Broadway, including jazz and vernacular dance, was so influential to him, one of the basic tenets of ballet – story-telling through mimetic narrative – remained one of his key tools.

A Decade of Work

Fundamentally, with the success of *On the Town*, Robbins was able to share his time and artistic development between Broadway and ballet. Jowitt sums up the arrangement: 'the former subsidized the latter.'[40] *Fancy Free* received a prominent place in the Ballet Theatre repertoire, along with commissions for others, and his Broadway projects over the next ten years were in a constant flow. The diverse creative opportunities and challenges in both genres appealed to Robbins and having some financial security from his Broadway endeavors allowed him to do both. Robbins continued to develop his skills at bringing narratives to life through movement in a string of memorable musicals including: *Billion Dollar Baby* (1946), *High Button Shoes* (1947), *Look, Ma, I'm Dancing!* (1948), *Miss Liberty* (1949), *Call Me Madam* (1950), *The King and I* (1951), and *Peter Pan* (1954), where he assumed the role of director, after successfully co-directing *Look, Ma* with Abbott. As Robbins gained more experience on Broadway he began to work methodologically with the goal to have 'dances that made logical sense, supported dramatic intent, and provided a stylistic continuum from the Libretto.'[41] These goals sustained a string of mostly successful musicals and allowed for a productive and lucrative career for Robbins. Uniquely, it was his work in the ballet world, happening in tandem with his Broadway hits, that allowed him the freedom to experiment with deviations from the standard fare. In his ballet work he explored more ambiguous topics and aesthetic challenges of the form that would eventually fuse with the more popular styles he was using in musical theatre – a coming together that fully materializes in *West Side Story*.

The second ballet Robbins did for Ballet Theatre with Bernstein, before moving over to the newly formed New York City Ballet with Balanchine at the helm in 1949, was *Facsimile*. A brief glance at this three-person ballet gives some insight into Robbins and his process. While Robbins wanted a 'human aspect to emerge' in all his ballets he still was able to be much more abstract than in musicals.[42] Robbins used three dancers in the piece, one of them being himself. *Facsimile* has been called 'the first ballet about contemporary neuroses' by *New York Times* dance critic Anna Kisselgoff.[43] The ballet takes a much more urgent approach to a love triangle that is toyed with in moments in *Fancy Free*. Jowitt describes how Robbins was 'primarily intent on bringing out the superficiality of these people's lives and desires, the idleness that leads them into potentially harmful games.'[44] In an about face from his previous works, sexuality and eroticism are the modes of communication, laden with a sense of despondency and cruelty. *Facsimile* ends with the female dancer crying out 'Stop!' leaving an uneasy aura haunting the space (foreshadowing Maria's final cry at the end of *West Side Story*). John Martin describes the unlikeable characters in his review of the premiere, 'Without inner resources of any sort, they play around dangerously in the realm of psychological thrills. The argument of the piece is simply that Mr. Robbins doesn't approve of them.'[45] The erratic emotional realm created by the dancers, listed in the program as 'three insecure people,' does not come out again in Robbins's work until much later when he returns full time to the ballet world: in 1965 with American

Ballet Theatre, and in 1969 the New York City Ballet. I mention *Facsimile* because after its premiere, Robbins moves away from the exploration of neuroses or dysfunction, and does *Pas de Trois* (1947) and *Summer Day* (1947) before moving over to New York City Ballet. Even so, I suggest this physicalized leeriness, or depleted cynicism, and overt eroticism pulses within the visceral choreography in *West Side Story*, a quality not generally found in his more popular works and which can perhaps be traced to this moment of exploring the more corrupt or selfish aspects of humanity, some of which he may have seen in himself.[46]

Though Robbins retired from dancing in 1952, he continued creating work with the New York City Ballet. He made numerous very unusual ballets, including *Age of Anxiety* (1949) based on the poem by W. H. Auden and Bernstein's 1948 symphony of the same name, where the dancers wear fencing masks, and which explores reflections of the self and 'emotional emptiness,' and *The Guests* (1959) about inner and outer circles of society; both ballets can be seen to inhabit some of his own anxieties. In 1950, he created *The Cage*, about man-eating female insects, which is hailed as an experimental breakthrough in its non-human narrative, though generally discomforting in its complexities around sexual rites and initiations.[47] His interpretation of *Afternoon of a Faun* in 1953 is well-received, and praised for its dream-like quality and musicality. He does not return to the raw and troublesome world of *Facsimile* in ballet until later in his career, but a unique manifestation of physicalized anxieties and passions permeates his work in *West Side Story*.[48]

An Idea Long in the Making

West Side Story, originally titled *East Side Story*, had been an idea brewing between collaborators from as early as 1949. Robbins had pitched the idea of an updated *Romeo and Juliet* to his friends Arthur Laurents and Bernstein. Robbins was thinking through the different warring factions that could be pitted next to each other, perhaps Jewish and Catholic? Though the project was put aside, due to other commitments and the collaborators never coming to an agreement about the groups involved, the idea was never abandoned. As the story goes, newspaper headlines about juvenile delinquents sparring on US streets caught Robbins's attention. Jowitt describes, 'Robbins agreed … that ethnicity rather than religion should be the crux, and gangs, rather than families, the antagonists. The Jewish kids became Puerto Rican and the Italian gang a mix of European stock.'[49] When the group was able to get going on the project, work began on the musical.[50]

Robbins worked the dancers extraordinarily hard. He demanded constant soul-searching and full commitment to the physical and psychological demands of the show. Dancers tell tales of the harsh conditions of rehearsals, some bragging, others complaining. Robbins pit one group of dancers against the other so tensions were felt both on and off stage. His ability to physicalize the agitation, stress, anxiety, and adrenaline of the Jets and the Sharks, alongside the tenderness and passion of Tony and Maria, was unprecedented. As Chapter 14 in this volume will explore, Robbins championed the ensemble as physical story-tellers and created actable, intuitive, and raw movement, boldly juxtaposing ballet, jazz, and popular dances of the moment – a confluence of genres, but also of the complicated experiences disciplining his mind and body – to achieve all he desperately wanted in life.

***

Robbins's way of working stemmed from a narrative investigation of movement forged in a unique time when ballet was modernizing and musical theatre was discovering the dramatic potential of dance. As the years went by, the choreographer said he was more interested in a world 'where things are not named,' and his exploration of ballet's classical idioms became more abstract and profound.[51] His sister Sonia, Senya Gluck Sandor, Max Leibman, George Balanchine, Mikel Fokine, Leonard Bernstein, Betty Comden, Adolph Green, George Abbott, Arthur Laurents and others were mentors and collaborators who were part of Robbins's journey to what some say is his grandest accomplishment – *West Side Story*. Robbins engaged with people where he could; however, his anxiety and self-doubt pushed him to be more of an authoritarian over the work and he was decidedly not the easiest man to work with. What never changed, however, was his consistent awareness of the body in motion and the dramatic potential of dance. He astutely remarks at age twenty-seven:

And as the ballet and the theatre draw closer to each other, an exciting prospect opens in which not only musicals, but theatre pieces with vital ideals, will combine drama, dance and music, to the benefit of all three.[52]

Foretelling his work in *West Side Story* and eerily prophesying the creative intersections beyond his lifetime and into in the twenty-first century, Robbins's legacy lives on in the collaborations and complexities across musical theatre, ballet, and theatre today.

Notes

1. Jerome Robbins, 'My Selves: An Attempt to Express My Character as I See It by Jerry Rabinowitz, English 12' in Amanda Vaill's *Jerome Robbins, by Himself: Selections from His Letters, Journals, Drawings, Photographs, and an Unfinished Memoir* (New York: Alfred A. Knopf, 2019), 20.
2. Wendy Lesser, *Jerome Robbins: A Life in Dance* (New Haven, CT: Yale University Press, 2018), 7.
3. Amanda Vaill, 'A Biography in Brief,' Jeromerobbins.org, 2001. http://jeromerobbins.org/a-biography-in-brief/.
4. Robbins does not engage with his Jewishness in significant detail prior to *West Side Story*. He was keen to be assimilated amongst others, as was common for first generation youth at the time. Deborah Jowitt describes his fear of anti-Semitism, 'He had been brought up to believe to be a Jew meant to be in constant danger.' Jowitt, *Jerome Robbins: His Life, His Theater, His Dance* (New York: Simon & Schuster, 2004), 20. He returns to explore his Jewishness later in his career. For further information see Jowitt's Chapter 16, 'The Sixties – *Fiddler on the Roof*.'
5. See Amanda Vaill's *Jerome Robbins, by Himself* for the most recent collection of and information on Robbins's archival materials.
6. Robbins had the advantage of being white, which at the time was very much the casting norm on Broadway. Only as recently as 1933, five years before Robbins began working on New York stages, had a Black dancer (Buddy Bradley) performed on stage with white dancers, and that was in London, the fashion not yet acceptable on Broadway. For more on Bradley, as a choreographer and dancer, and the challenges of being a Black artist in the 1930s and 40s, see Chapter 21 in Marshall and Jean Stearns, *Jazz Dance: The Story of American Vernacular Dance* (New York: Da Capo Press, 1994), 160–69.
7. Vaill, *Jerome Robbins by Himself*, 31–33.
8. Jowitt, 18.
9. Ibid., 18.
10. See Dustyn Martincich's chapter in this collection (Chapter 14) for more on Robbins's creative process in *West Side Story*.
11. Lesser, 9.
12. Ibid., 9.
13. Excerpts from his diary outline his declaration of dance as his religion, see Vaill's *Jerome Robbins, by Himself*, 31.
14. *Wonderful Town* (1953) is one such show where Robbins helped out choreographer Donald Saddler with the more physical and athletic moments of the show.
15. Vaill, *Jerome Robbins, by Himself*, 22.
16. Lesser.

17. Vaill, *Jerome Robbins, by Himself.*

18. Excerpts from a letter titled 'To Company Management, Ballet Theatre' in Vaill's *Jerome Robbins, by Himself*, 44.

19. It is during his time with Sandor's company that Robbins reports in his diaries of his first homosexual experience. He does not openly discuss his sexuality and experiences and considerable anxiety builds up around the issue which would continue throughout his career. See Jowitt, 24.

20. Journal entry titled 'Journal 1939, October 28 4 A.M.,' Vaill, *Jerome Robbins, by Himself*, 41.

21. Vaill, *Jerome Robbins, by Himself.*

22. Lesser, 6.

23. Vaill, *Jerome Robbins, by Himself*, 9.

24. Diary excerpt 'Training, July 17, 1976' in Vaill, *Jerome Robbins, by Himself*, 60.

25. Dunham ventured outside of the United States entirely, bringing Caribbean and African influences to her work and training methods. For more on Dunham's contribution to dance in the United States and globally see Joanna Dee Das, *Katherine Dunham: Dance and the African Diaspora* (Oxford University Press, 2017).

26. Jerome Robbins, 'The Ballet Puts on Dungarees: A Choreographer Describes How Ballet Has Emerged from the Hothouse and Become America's People's Entertainment,' *The New York Times*, 14 October 1945: SM9.

27. Vaill, *Jerome Robbins, by Himself*, 71.

28. Lesser, 17.

29. Lesser, 21.

30. Two, four, six.

31. Lesser, 21.

32. From the ballet repertoire: a *chassée* is a traveling step where the body glides forward or to the side with knees bent and feet turned out. *Pas de bourrée* is a series of small steps generally used to link together steps. A lift in *attitude* is an overhead lift where the dancer lifted has one leg straight and one leg extended behind them in a bent position.

33. Lea Marshall, Op-Ed: 'Is It Time to Retire *Fancy Free?' Dance Magazine*, 19 April 2019, www.dancemagazine.com/fancy-free-ballet-2634991525.html. Accessed 30 July 2020.

34. Ibid.

35. Ibid.

36. For more on the diversifying of cast and crew in *On the Town* see Carol Oja's *Bernstein Meets Broadway: Collaborative Art in the Time of War* (New York: Oxford University Press, 2014).

37. Lesser, 25.

38. Barbara Wallace Grossman, 'Musical Theatre Directors' in *The Oxford Handbook of the American Musical*. Edited by Raymond Knapp, Mitchell Morris, and Stacy Wolf (Oxford: Oxford University Press, 2011), 283.

39. Lesser, 26.

40. Jowitt, 120.

41. Liza Gennaro, 'Evolution of Dance in the Golden Age of the American "Book Musical"' in *The Oxford Handbook of The American Musical*. Edited by Raymond Knapp, Mitchell Morris, and Stacy Wolf (Oxford: Oxford University Press, 2011), 52.

42. 'Jerome Robbins at New York City Ballet,' https://www.youtube.com/watch?v=Rigl9ejpuV4 Peter Martins. Accessed 24 August 2020.

43. Anna Kisselgoff, 'Jerome Robbins, 79 is Dead: A Giant of Ballet and Broadway,' *The New York Times*, 30 July 1998, A1.

44. Jowitt, 124.

45. John Martin, '*Facsimile* Ballet has its Premiere Here,' *The New York Times*, 25 October 1946: 36.

46. Robbins was a member of the Communist party in his early career, as were numerous artists at the time. Many of his colleagues were blacklisted and suffered the loss of opportunities and, thus, finances, while Robbins continued working and spent much time out of sight in Europe. When he was no longer unable to avoid testifying in front of the House Un-American Activities Committee (HUAC), he named many of his colleagues, a choice he thought was right at the time but came to plague him his entire life. He later claimed his choices involved not wanting his homosexuality made public; however, there is continued debate around his motives. As Greg Lawrence reports, in the words of Robbins's colleague James Mitchell, 'He was living in some kind of dream world. Who didn't know?' Lawrence, *Dance with Demons: The Life of Jerome Robbins* (New York: Putnam and Sons, 2001), Preface.

47. Lesser, 32. For more on *Age of Anxiety*, see Lesser, 28–38, and for *The Cage*, 56–68.

48. Additional ballets include: *Ballade* (1952), *Fanfare* (1953), and *The Concert* (1956). For a thorough chronology of all of Robbins's ballets and musicals see Vaill, *Jerome Robbins, by Himself*, 391–407.

49. Jowitt, 267.

50. For a thorough telling of the building and early days of *West Side Story*, see Elizabeth Wells's chapter, 'From *Gangway!* to Broadway: Genesis of the Musical' in Wells, *West Side Story: Cultural Perspectives on an American Musical* (Plymouth, UK: Scarecrow Press, Inc., 2011), 27–53.

51. www.nytimes.com/1998/07/30/theater/jerome-robbins-79-is-dead-giant-of-ballet-and-broadway.html

52. Jerome Robbins, 'The Ballet Puts on Dungarees,' 1945.

4 | Arthur Laurents before *West Side Story*

JOHN M. CLUM

During the twenty years between his graduation from Cornell University in 1937 and the opening of *West Side Story* twenty years later, Brooklyn-born Arthur Laurents had mixed success as a playwright.[1] Two of his plays (*The Bird Cage* and *A Clearing in the Woods*) didn't last a month; one (*Heartsong*), closed in Philadelphia. *Home of the Brave* lasted sixty performances, but did get sold to a Hollywood studio. Only *The Time of the Cuckoo* had a respectable run. The films for which he wrote screenplays during this period were not commercial or critical successes. Laurents's fame would come as book writer for the classic musicals *West Side Story*, *Gypsy*, and *La Cage aux Folles* (which he also directed), and as the writer of the screenplays for *The Way We Were* and *The Turning Point* in the 1970s.

Much of Laurents's good fortune, from getting a break as a writer for radio to working with famous Hollywood directors and actors during World War II, to his part in the creation of *West Side Story*, came from personal connections, particularly his friendship with director–choreographer Jerome Robbins, the initiating force in the making of *West Side Story*. This is not to denigrate Laurents's talent. He was a gifted writer who wisely took advantage of the opportunities that came his way.

Laurents was also a famously difficult person. Harold Clurman, who directed two of Laurents's Broadway plays, observed that in Laurents 'sensibility and a defensive aggressiveness are combined in precarious balance. The slightest rebuff, or what he suspects as one, makes him bitterly antagonistic; praise, encouragement, and affection melt him.'[2] Stephen Sondheim, who collaborated with Laurents on four musicals (*West Side Story*, *Gypsy*, *Anyone Can Whistle*, *Do I Hear a Waltz?*) recalls that 'Aplomb was not one of Arthur's chief virtues, and his tirades could be heard as far as Scranton.'[3]

Radio, Wartime Work, and Connections

Laurents moved back to New York after college and, while working at Bloomingdale's department store, took an evening course in writing radio drama taught by Bill Robson, a producer at CBS. Robson arranged for his network to buy *Now Playing, Tomorrow*, a script Laurents wrote for his class. The star of that first show was Shirley Booth who would star in Laurents's *Heartsong* and *The Time of the Cuckoo*. Listeners liked *Now Playing Tomorrow*, so until World War II Laurents had steady work writing for radio shows like *Lux Radio Theatre*.

For most young men, World War II put careers on hold. Laurents was lucky. At basic training at Fort Monmouth near the New Jersey shore, he befriended Bob Hoskins, who happened to be the son of a senior aide to Franklin D. Roosevelt. Thanks to Hoskins's well-placed father, Laurents was transferred to the US Army Pictorial Service, located in an old film studio in Astoria, Queens, where he was assigned to be a screenwriter of official Army training films as well as a writer of radio scripts for the Armed Forces. The director of his first film script was none other than George Cukor, one of the greatest directors of the studio era. Throughout the war, Laurents was fortunate to work with major Hollywood and Broadway talent while socializing at night with people in the New York theatre and dance world who would soon be in positions of power.[4]

Fraught Friendship: Laurents and Jerome Robbins

During Laurents's five years doing military work in Astoria, he had an affair with Ballet Theatre ballerina Nora Kaye[5] while also enjoying sex with a number of men. Through Kaye, he became friends with dancer–choreographer Jerome Robbins, whose 1944 ballet *Fancy Free* would later the same year be adapted into the musical *On the Town*, also with a score by Leonard Bernstein. Although Laurents at the time had no experience writing for the stage, Robbins had tried without success to convince Bernstein that his new friend should write the book for *On the Town*.[6] Through the next decade and a half, Laurents and Robbins would have a turbulent professional and social relationship that would eventually lead to Laurents's collaboration on *West Side Story* and *Gypsy*. Robbins found Laurents an agent and a producer for his first Broadway play, *Home of the Brave*, and, after the war, asked Laurents to write the book for a musical about a ballet dancer. Laurents turned in a draft whose central character was a ruthless, egotistical dancer modeled on Robbins himself. Robbins's biographer, Amanda Vaill, mused, 'What this says about Laurents's opinion of his friend Robbins is an interesting question.'[7] Eventually the writer pulled out of the project, which became the short-lived 1948 musical, *Look Ma, I'm Dancing*. Laurents's friendship with Robbins became somewhat strained when the director–choreographer betrayed friends in his testimony before the House Un-American Activities Committee in 1953,[8] Laurents recalls that Robbins said:

'I suppose I won't know for years whether I did the right thing.'
   'Oh, I can tell you right now,' I answered. 'You were a shit.'[9]

Throughout Laurents's memoirs, he attacks informers who betrayed their friends during the years of the Red Scare and blacklist. His 1995 play, *Jolson Sings Again*, is loosely based on the betrayal of another director–informer, Elia Kazan.

Despite Robbins's testimony to the House Un-American Activities Committee, Laurents remained friendly with Robbins, but their relationship unraveled because of Robbins's behavior during rehearsals for *West Side Story* and his insistence on more prominent billing than his colleagues received. Laurents later wrote of Bernstein's, Sondheim's and his anger at Robbins, 'The four of us had started the show together, created it together, had a wonderful time being together, but three of us weren't talking to Jerry. There was no pleasure in that; if anything, there was an additional load of resentment because he had caused the estrangement, he was why "together" had lost its meaning.'[10] Laurents would work with Robbins two years later on *Gypsy*, but their relationship was never the same. The surviving collaborators on *West Side Story*, Laurents and Stephen Sondheim, chose not to take part in Robbins's memorial service almost forty years later.

Broadway Debut: Home of the Brave

One crucial theme of *West Side Story* is prejudice. In the musical's original conception, *East Side Story*, the source of the intra-gang conflict was anti-Semitism, rather than bigotry against Puerto Ricans. Anti-Semitism is a theme that appears in *Home of the Brave* and in some of Laurents's later plays.

While Laurents was working in Astoria, he began the script that would become his first Broadway play, *Home of the Brave* (1945). The script was inspired by an experience Laurents had in basic training. At one barracks inspection, Laurents's friend Bob Hoskins punched a sergeant who complained about how badly 'the kikes' cleaned up the barracks. Hoskins wasn't Jewish but felt badly for his Jewish friend. A second impetus for the play was Laurents's new interest in psychoanalysis. During the five years Laurents was in the army, he became increasingly confused about his sexual orientation and behavior. His first psychiatrist believed that all his problems came from his homosexuality, which could and must be cured. Only years later with a more enlightened Hollywood psychiatrist did he become comfortable with his sexual orientation. However, the most powerful inspiration for *Home of the Brave* came from a photograph that landed on Laurents's desk of some GIs looking at the mutilated body of a comrade: 'That photograph haunted me. I pilfered it from the army files and kept it in my drawer. I didn't know why I knew it was a play but I did.'[11]

These three elements – the friend's reaction to an anti-Semitic slur, Laurents's inability to accept his sexual orientation, and the photograph – combined into the creation of *Home of the Brave*. The experience of writing for radio and film, which allow free movement in space and time, influenced the structure of *Home of the Brave* which, instead of being confined to one interior set, alternates between the present in an army hospital and the past on a Pacific Island. The central character is Peter Coen, a young recruit who is extremely self-conscious about his 'difference,' his Judaism. He tells the army psychiatrist, 'None of them are like me.'[12] His journey in the play is one of self-acceptance. When we first see Coen in the hospital, he is unable to walk, a result of a psychological trauma caused by the death of his closest friend, Finch, a young private from Arkansas. Through their wartime experience, they became so close that they planned to open a bar together after the war. Finch even joked about Coen marrying his sister. During a feud in a tense moment on an intelligence-gathering mission on a remote island overrun with Japanese, Finch barely stops himself from shouting an anti-Semitic slur. Coen, hyper-sensitive to such slights, feels betrayed by the only person he felt totally accepted him. Shortly after that, Finch is shot by a Japanese sniper. Coen and his fellow soldiers have to leave their wounded comrade to the incoming Japanese so that they can complete their crucial intelligence mission. Coen's subsequent paralysis is caused by a combination of anger over what he sees as Finch's betrayal and guilt over having to leave a wounded Finch to be tortured and killed by the Japanese.

From the outset, the psychiatrist knows that Coen's problem is at heart a societal problem, an inability to accept difference: 'That kid's crack-up goes back to a thousand million goddamn people being wrong ... They don't take a man for himself ... for what he is.'[13] The psychiatrist can only cure Coen's paralysis by the extreme tactic of shouting an anti-Semitic slur at him: 'You lousy yellow Jew bastard, get up and walk!'[14] Through therapy, Coen comes to realize that his sensitivity about anti-Semitism is based in great part on his own inability to accept his Jewishness – his difference. That sensitivity to anti-Semitism would lead to Laurents's interest in the first iteration of *West Side Story*, *East Side Story*.

It took decades for Laurents to accept that in *Home of the Brave*, he had not only dramatized his sensitivity about his Jewishness; he had also unintentionally projected his anxieties about his homosexuality onto Peter Coen. Laurents, born Levine, was sensitive enough about the prevailing anti-Semitism in America to change his last name in order to have a better chance of getting a job; however, his memoirs make clear that he was much more sensitive and confused about his sexual orientation. He was unable at the time to accept his homosexuality or to see that the primary relationship in *Home of the Brave* has a homoerotic element: 'Had I realized that it could be construed that way, I would have worked overtime to clean it out.'[15]

Home of the Brave demonstrated Laurents's ability to capture the language of young servicemen in tense situations. His ear for convincing colloquial dialogue would later serve him well in the creation of the teenage gang members in *West Side Story*. A 1949 film adaptation of the play (screenplay, Carl Foreman; director, Mark Robson), changed the central character from Jewish to African-American, thus making the key issue racism, not anti-Semitism, even though troops were racially segregated until 1948.

After many changes in directors and leading actors and multiple script revisions, Laurents's second stage play, *Heartsong* (1947), about a young couple dealing with abortion, closed in Philadelphia.[16] For the next few years, his base of operations would be Hollywood.

Hollywood and *Rope*

Laurents's first contract as a screenwriter for MGM earned him the generous sum of $2,500 a week. Working on his first assignment, the psychological melodrama *The Snake Pit* was a lesson in the pitfalls of screenwriting, including being forced to tack on an unbelievable happy ending and not receiving appropriate credit for his work. After collaborating on *The Snake Pit*, Laurents had two major screenwriting assignments during the late 1940s. The first was to adapt Patrick Hamilton's 1929 British stage play, *Rope*, for Alfred Hitchcock. The celebrated British director had hired his friend, actor Hume Cronyn, to write a treatment based on the play, then hired Laurents to Americanize the British dialogue. Laurents later insisted that even though Cronyn got screen credit for the adaptation, the final screenplay was his alone.[17]

Loosely based on the famous 1924 Leopold and Loeb murder case, the play and film depict two wealthy young men who murder a college friend, hide his body in a chest in the living room, then hold a dinner party in the same room. The crime is solved by a former teacher and friend who had taught the young men the Nietzschean concepts that led them to think that they were above conventional morality. Everyone who remembered the Leopold and Loeb murder of Bobby Franks knew that there was a sexual element in the killers' relationship. Patrick Hamilton's play is filled with innuendo that the two young men are sexually involved. Given the censorship in Britain at the time, such information could only be hinted at, never overtly presented verbally or physically. The same rule applied in Hollywood where any mention of 'sex perversion' was banned. Still, Laurents remembered how Hitchcock delighted in filling his film with homosexual intimations: 'At Warner Brothers studio in Burbank where *Rope* was shot, homosexuality was the unmentionable, known only as "it." "It" wasn't in the picture. No one was "one." Fascinating was how Hitchcock nevertheless made clear to me that he wanted "it" in the picture.'[18] The director knew that Laurents and the actors playing the murderous couple, Farley Granger (Laurents's housemate and lover at the time), and John Dall, were homosexual. Hitchcock's direction emphasizes the closeness of the murderers by keeping them together in the same frame through most of the film. Unfortunately, James Stewart is woefully miscast as the older friend who solves the case.

In Laurents's screenplay Brandon and Philip started a relationship in prep school and have stayed in contact even though Brandon went off to Harvard and Philip trained to be a concert pianist. Now they share an apartment in New York. The murder of their friend David seems to be a way to maintain a strained relationship. Brandon is the more dominant personality. Philip says at one point, 'You scare me. You always have – from the very first day in prep school. Part of your charm, I suppose.'[19] For Brandon the most exciting part of their crime is the dinner party they hold in the same room as the corpse. Their perverse guest list includes Janet, the victim's fiancée; Ken, her ex-boyfriend; and Janet's father. This gathering is for Brandon a delicious bit of theatre but Philip gets progressively drunk, frightened, and hostile. Laurents, living within Hollywood's policing of the closet and still deeply conflicted about his sexual orientation and his relationship with Granger, was the perfect writer to create an American version of Hamilton's dysfunctional gay couple.

Rope was not a box office success although film scholars and critics have over the years found much to praise in Hitchcock's direction and Laurents's screenplay. After *Rope*, Hitchcock repeatedly asked Laurents to adapt various properties for him but Laurents never found any of them congenial.

Caught

When Laurents was assigned to write the screenplay for *Caught* (1949), he understood that his job was to revise an adaptation of Libbie Block's novel, *Wild Calendar*. Director Max Ophüls had other ideas. Bristling from mistreatment at the hands of RKO Pictures owner Howard Hughes, Ophüls wanted to make a film that presented a negative portrayal of the eccentric mogul. He told Laurents, 'Make him an idiot! An egomaniac! Terrible to women! Also to men! Make him a fool! Make him die! Kill him off!'[20] Laurents used some elements of Block's novel about an unhappy marriage between a plain seventeen-year-old who marries her millionaire cousin but created an original story adding anecdotes he had heard about Hughes as well as common knowledge. In the novel, the woman, Maud, treats her older husband miserably. In the film, the husband is gratuitously cruel to his justifiably unhappy wife. Ironically, Robert Ryan, who would play the nasty character based on Hughes, and leading actress Barbara Bel Geddes were under contract to RKO, Hughes's studio. Hughes would not release them to be in the film unless some revisions were made in the script and he was allowed to see the daily footage.[21]

The film focuses on Leona Ames (Barbara Bel Geddes), a poor girl who wants a better life for herself. She scrapes some money together for a six-week course at a charm school and gets a job modeling clothes at a department store. A sleazy crypto-gay assistant to millionaire Smith Ohrig invites her to a party on a yacht where she will meet rich men. Before she ever gets to the party, Ohrig takes her for drinks, then makes a pass at her which she refuses. The next scene, a pivotal one, is at the office of Smith's psychiatrist. As he did in *Home of the Brave*, Laurents makes a psychiatrist his voice of wisdom. Smith has once again experienced the symptoms of a mild heart attack. His doctor knows that he only has these attacks when he doesn't get what he wants, in this case sex with Leona. When the doctor tells Smith that he shouldn't think of marrying her – he'll only destroy her – Smith perversely resolves to marry her and fires the doctor who tells him that he is only marrying 'to prove that no one has authority over you.'[22]

The doctor is right. The marriage is a disaster. Smith despises Leona from the outset and is seldom home. Leona leaves him, moves into a shabby Manhattan flat and gets a job as a receptionist in the lower East Side office of Larry Quinada (James Mason), an idealistic doctor who treats poor children. Larry came from a wealthy family that lost most of its fortune (thus explaining Mason's posh accent), and is now dedicated to healing poor children. Of course, Leona and the doctor fall in love. Even when he discovers that she is married and pregnant, he tries to save her from her hateful husband who says he will only divorce her if she will give him the child. Smith hates her but tries to hold on to her because he cannot lose: 'Only nice people lose.'

Laurents had one major problem in writing a logical screenplay out of this situation – divorce was not allowed in Hollywood films. The alternative in many films of the period involved murdering the husband. Laurents's somewhat bizarre ending dispatched the baby who dies after a premature birth thus robbing Smith of his hold on Leona. If *Rope* expressed Laurents's conflicted view of his homosexuality at the time, *Caught* allowed him to express his views of unbridled materialism. The film reflects Laurents's sympathy with the views of his left-wing Hollywood friends. Leona is torn between her desire for wealth and security, for which a high personal price must be paid, and the ideals of the good doctor who tells her: 'Money alone isn't security.' He tells her that she must decide how important money is to her as she chooses between a terrible marriage and him. At the end it is clear that she will be with the idealistic doctor. *Caught* earned less than a million dollars at the box office. While critics were not impressed at the time of the film's premiere, it has since been positively reappraised by admirers of Max Ophüls's work.

East Side Story

1949, the year *Caught* was filmed, was also the year the eight-year on and off gestation process of *West Side Story* began. Actor Montgomery Clift, Jerome Robbins's lover at the time, asked the choreographer to help him prepare to play Romeo. This led Robbins to think about the possibility of a modern-day interpretation of Shakespeare's classic. His 1949 ballet, *The Guests*, created for the New York City Ballet, was loosely based on the idea of star-crossed lovers from warring factions.[23] Robbins approached Arthur Laurents and Leonard Bernstein with the idea for *East Side Story*, a musical version of *Romeo and Juliet* with the Jews and Catholics as the warring factions. Bernstein first saw the story as worthy of grand opera treatment, but Laurents resisted: 'I want to make one thing clear before we go any further and that is that I'm not writing any fucking libretto for any goddamned Bernstein opera!'[24] Laurents also worried that the idea was too close to that of *Abie's Irish Rose* by Anne Nichols, which opened in 1922 and played for a record-breaking 2,327 performances as well as a record-breaking long-running national tour, movie (1928), and radio show (1942–1944). '"East Side Story" was *Abie's Irish Rose* set to music. I bowed out.'[25]

Back to Broadway: *The Bird Cage*

Between work on films, Laurents was writing his next Broadway play, *The Bird Cage*, which ran for only twenty-one performances in 1950. Like *Caught*, the play is a critique of capitalism and men who abuse power. The central character has no redeeming virtues to win an audience's sympathy or keep its interest. Wally Williams, emcee and half owner of a sleazy New York nightclub, only knows money, power and control. He has a long list of people he despises: his wife because the money that was supposed to come with the marriage never materialized; any girl who will not have sex with him; and his teenaged son because he isn't manly enough to have sex with the girl Wally provided for him. When his only supporter, the club pianist, talks back to him, Wally slams the lid of the piano keyboard on his hands. At the end, when Wally has lost control of the club and everyone has walked away, he sets fire to his tawdry little kingdom. Laurents has deftly captured the working-class patois of his characters but the play was too melodramatic to be successful.

The Time of the Cuckoo

In 1950, the Internal Security Act of 1950, known as the McCarran Act, was passed by Congress over President Harry Truman's veto. One of its edicts was that anyone deemed subversive would be denied a passport. Throughout the 1940s, both in New York and Hollywood, Laurents socialized with left-wing friends and even thought of himself as left-wing (he used this part of his past in his screenplay for his most famous film, *The Way We Were* [1973]). He shouldn't have been surprised to find that an anti-communist publication, *Red Channels*, listed him as one of 150 subversives in show business. Laurents's response was to get a passport as fast as he could and go to Europe on an extended sightseeing trip with Farley Granger and some leftist friends. Eventually to clear his name and be able to continue traveling freely, Laurents wrote a letter explaining his political views. The powers that be found his political philosophy so eccentric that they decided he couldn't possibly be a threat to national security.

Among the stops on his first Grand Tour with Farley Granger and friends was Venice, the inspiration and setting for Laurents's next play, *The Time of the Cuckoo*, which brought him together again with Shirley Booth, who had just had great success with William Inge's *Come Back, Little Sheba* on stage and on film. *The Time of the Cuckoo* presents a favourite topic of American authors from Nathaniel Hawthorne and Henry James to the present, the clash of Old World and New World sensibilities. The setting is a Venice *pensione* run by free-spirited Madame Fioria. One of her tenants is a 40ish 'fancy secretary' from New York, Leona Samish. Leona is socially outgoing but deeply lonely. Her parents died when she was sixteen, leaving her to support and care for her younger siblings. Now she is deeply conscious of being a single in a couples' world. She would love to have a romance, 'a wonderful mystical magical miracle,'[26] in Venice. Through a series of coincidences, Leona meets a Venetian shopkeeper, Renato Di Rossi, who takes an interest in her. While Renato is charming and offers the romantic adventure Leona wishes for, she cannot trust his motivation. Moreover, her American puritanism makes it difficult for her to be with a married man, even if his marriage is not a happy one. As Madame Fioria tells her, 'In Italy, there is not divorce, there is only discretion.'[27] Eventually, Leona's suspicions and her American materialism destroy any hope of a romance.

Through a young couple who also are staying in the *pensione* – Eddie, a young American artist and his wife, June – Laurents explores the dynamics of monogamous marriage and women who have no life outside of their marriage. Eddie is capable of having a life apart from his wife – his art, sex with Madame Fioria – and still love June. June endangers their marriage by wanting too much from a spouse, 'I have to be everything to someone I love.'[28] It is not clear at the end of the play how their marriage will survive. To the Italians, the Americans are children who prevent their own happiness as a result of their puritanism and materialism. At a crucial moment in the play, Leona says, 'It would be great if you could come here from America with nothing but a suitcase. But – you don't come over that way.'[29]

The Time of the Cuckoo had a respectable run of 263 performances. Laurents later confessed that the play 'was a moderate success that gave me moderate standing in the theatre.'[30] Shirley Booth understood the basic weakness in the play: 'In *The Time of the Cuckoo*, I played a woman who is very sorry for herself. It was one of my most difficult roles. I kept telling the author that the minute a character is sorry for herself, the audience won't be.'[31] The play was adapted by other writers into the film *Summertime* (1955), with Katherine Hepburn. Laurents had nothing good to say about the film adaptation after his screenplay was weakened by director David Lean and his star actress. It was also adapted into the ill-fated 1964 musical, *Do I Hear a Waltz?*, with book by Laurents, music by Richard Rodgers, and lyrics by Stephen Sondheim.

West Side Story Begins

While Laurents was in Hollywood working on *Summertime*, Leonard Bernstein was preparing for concerts at the Hollywood Bowl and Jerome Robbins was working on the film version of *The King and I* (he had choreographed the Broadway musical). Laurents and Bernstein had a poolside discussion about the Latino gang problem in Los Angeles, which quickly led them to think about turning *East Side Story* into *West Side Story* about gang warfare between whites and Puerto Ricans. Robbins was equally excited about the idea. However, all three had other projects. Laurents had some other screen assignments (*Anastasia*, based on the play by Marcel Maurette and an adaptation of Françoise Sagan's novel, *Bonjour Tristesse*), and was working on his next Broadway play, *A Clearing in the Woods*. Bernstein was working on *Candide* and Robbins was involved with the musical *Bells Are Ringing*, which he was slated to direct and choreograph (with Bob Fosse). Bernstein quickly realized that he couldn't write both music and lyrics, so Laurents arranged for his young friend Stephen Sondheim to meet with Bernstein. The rest is history.

Psychoanalysis and *A Clearing in the Woods*

In the process of his therapy with psychiatrist Judd Marmor, Laurents came to understand why he had been frightened of Farley Granger moving in with him: 'I was afraid that if he lived with me, he would know me.'[32] This expression of self-loathing echoes throughout *A Clearing in the Woods*, which opened in January 1957. Overcoming his own self-hatred, particularly because of his homosexuality, allowed Laurents to enjoy a relationship with Tom Hatcher begun in 1954, which lasted until Hatcher's death in 2006.[33]

In *A Clearing in the Woods*, Laurents attempted to 'soar above the confines of naturalistic theatre.'[34] The clearing that is the setting for the play is not a realistic location. Rather it is a psychological landscape where Virginia, the central character, comes to terms with her past and with herself. Virginia is a woman in her thirties who is in the throes of depression. Like Leona Samish, she is an executive secretary, about as far as a woman could then go in the corporate world. Virginia has been a failure in her relationships with men because she demands that they have the professional success she is not allowed. She has never fully expressed herself to the men in her life because if people truly knew her, they would not like her. In the clearing, Virginia has to confront those men. More important, she has to interact with versions of herself at different stages in her life: as a child, as a teenager, and as a young woman. Like Peter Coen in *Home of the Brave*, Virginia has to accept that she is not as different or special as she wanted to be. At the end, she tells her younger selves, 'Accepting you as you are means I can never be what I dreamed.' Their response is, 'An end to dreams isn't an end to hope.'[35]

A Clearing in the Woods was not successful because Laurents was too prosaic a writer to successfully create a poetic drama. He explains too much, repeats explanations too often. Laurents felt that Kim Stanley, an actress, he believed, 'whose brilliant acting talent was almost matched by her talent for self-extinction,'[36] never was able to communicate any of the humor necessary to make the audience sympathize with the character.[37] It isn't clear that another actress would have made much difference. As *New York Times* critic Brooks Atkinson accurately observed, 'Virginia is not an interesting woman.'[38] The play ran for only thirty-six performances.

Finally *West Side Story*

West Side Story went into production eight years after Laurents, Bernstein, and Robbins discussed the idea for *East Side Story*. Laurents and Bernstein were both smarting from the failures of *A Clearing in the Woods* and *Candide* and eager to create a new kind of Broadway musical.[39] Their first producer, Cheryl Crawford, backed out after failing to find backers interested in a dark musical with a cast of unknowns: She told the creators, 'We have *had* this whole school of ash can realism.'[40] After Stephen Sondheim told his good friend, producer Harold Prince, about their problems getting *West Side Story* produced, Prince and his producing partner

Robert Griffith took on the show, quickly found the funding, and set a September date for its opening at the Winter Garden Theatre.

According to Leonard Bernstein's biographer Meryle Secrest, the collaborators would discuss the musical's concept and overall shape:

Only after these discussions would he [Laurents] begin writing, 'to stay ahead of them,' he explained. 'For instance, Steve [Sondheim] had to take diction and character from the playwright; then he and Lenny would work on the songs. As for Jerry Robbins, he is part of [choreographer] Antony Tudor's literary tradition of choreography and would want to know what the dance was about, so I would write him a scenario.[41]

Laurents understood that, 'My task ... was to drive as eloquently and economically as possible to the musical moment, be it song, or dance, or both.'[42] This may be why *West Side Story* has less spoken dialogue than most musicals. Sondheim has stated, 'Of all the things I gleaned from working with Arthur, the most pointed was an awed respect for the book writer. ... The book writer is the source from which the songwriter ... takes character, diction, tone and style, and sometimes dialogue.'[43] Actually, there is more dialogue than Laurents or his colleagues originally intended. Laurents wrote a speech for Maria after Tony has been killed that Bernstein and Sondheim were supposed to turn into a song. Bernstein admitted that he never could find an effective way to set Maria's final lines: 'Everything sounded wrong. I made a difficult, painful, surgical decision not to set it at all.'[44] The musical ends with Laurents's words, not Bernstein's music.

West Side Story as Finale

While Laurents was justly proud of his work on *West Side Story*, he was not satisfied with the original production. He worked with Robbins directing the dialogue scenes but could not get the result he wanted with a cast of dancers who were not trained as actors. He thought, 'The music was magnificent but it was poorly sung and the acting if anything was non-existent.'[45] In 2009, at ninety-two years of age, Laurents took on the task of directing a revival of *West Side Story*. He was determined that 'the acting was going to be on a par with the ability to dance and sing.'[46] That production had a slightly longer run than the original production. At the end of his long career Laurents put his stamp on *West Side Story* as director as well as book writer. Nonetheless, although Jerome Robbins had been dead for eleven years, the posters and *Playbill* still contained the same box containing the statement 'Entire Production Directed and Choreographed by Jerome Robbins' that infuriated Laurents back in 1957.

Conclusion

Throughout his early career, Laurents the playwright was experimenting with new ways of structuring stage drama that reflected the free movement in time and space possible in radio drama and screenplays. This is evident in *Home of the Brave*, which moved back and forth from the present in a military hospital to the traumatic past on a Pacific island, to the symbolic setting and dreamlike quality of *A Clearing in the Woods*. One can see how Laurents could be drawn to musical theatre narratives, which move more freely in space and time than the typical one-set dramas of the period. Being a playwright drawn to formal experimentation, he was the perfect choice to create the book for what was certainly an experimental musical. Moreover, his years adapting novels and plays into film scripts gave him the experience necessary to translate *Romeo and Juliet* into a new medium. Laurents never had another play produced on Broadway. From *West Side Story* on, he would be primarily associated with musicals and screenplays.

Notes

1. Laurents became quite prolific as a playwright in the last twenty years of his life but he only had one more play produced on Broadway after 1957, *Invitation to a March* (1960). After *West Side Story*, he wrote the books for *Gypsy* (1959: music Jule Styne, lyrics, Stephen Sondheim) and *Anyone Can Whistle* (1964: music and lyrics, Stephen Sondheim), which he also directed, *Do I Hear a Waltz?* (1965: music Richard Rodgers, lyrics Stephen Sondheim), *Hallelujah Baby!* (1967: music Jule Styne, lyrics Betty Comden and Adolph Green). His later plays were produced by regional theatres, particularly the George Street Theatre in New Brunswick, New Jersey. For more detailed information and analyses of Laurents's work, see John M. Clum, *The Works of Arthur Laurents: Politics, Love and Betrayal* (Amherst, NY: Cambria Press, 2014).
2. Harold Clurman, *All People Are Famous (Instead of an Autobiography)* (New York: Harcourt, Brace, Jovanovich, 1974), 245.
3. Stephen Sondheim, *Finishing the Hat: Collected Lyrics, 1954–1981, with Attendant Comments, Principles, Heresies, Grudges, Whines, and Anecdotes* (New York: Virgin Books, 2010), 111.

4. Laurents chronicles his wartime experiences in his memoir: *Original Story by Arthur Laurents: A Memoir of Broadway and Hollywood* (New York: Applause Books, 2000), 13–25.
5. Nora Kaye later married choreographer–director Herbert Ross. Ross choreographed the musicals *I Can Get It for You Wholesale* (1961), which Laurents directed, and *Anyone Can Whistle* (1963), for which Laurents wrote the book and directed (Stephen Sondheim wrote the music and lyrics). Ross became a Hollywood director and helmed *The Turning Point* (1977), for which Laurents wrote the screenplay.
6. Bernstein's friends Betty Comden and Adolph Green wrote the book and lyrics.
7. Amanda Vaill, *Somewhere: The Life of Jerome Robbins* (New York: Broadway Books, 2006), 134.
8. The always ambitious Robbins was told that if he didn't testify, his homosexual affairs would be made public and his career would be threatened.
9. Laurents, *Original Story*, 332.
10. Laurents, *Original Story*, 365.
11. Laurents, *Original Story*, 49.
12. Arthur Laurents, *Home of the Brave*, in *Selected Plays of Arthur Laurents* (New York: Back Stage Books, 2005), 34. Further references to *Home of the Brave* are to this edition.
13. *Home of the Brave*, 32.
14. *Home of the Brave*, 79.
15. *Original Story*, 53.
16. Laurents chronicles the unhappy history of *Heartsong* and his relationship with novice producer Irene Mayer Selznick, daughter of Louis B. Mayer, the head of MGM and ex-wife of the Hollywood producer, David O. Selznick, in *Original Story*, pp. 65–77. According to Laurents, the decision to close in Philadelphia was his. *Heartsong* was Laurents's second project with Shirley Booth.
17. See *Original Story*, 27.
18. *Original Story*, 127.
19. Transcribed from *Rope*. Universal DVD (2005). The line is also included in the novelization of the film (no author credited but some websites attribute it to D. G. Ward), *Alfred Hitchcock's Rope* (New York: Dell, 1948).
20. *Original Story*, 141.
21. See *Original Story*, 142–43.
22. My quotations from *Caught* are transcribed from viewings of the film on YouTube.
23. See the description of *The Guests* in Vaill, *Somewhere*, 157–58.
24. Vaill, *Somewhere*, 251.
25. *Original Story*, 330.
26. Arthur Laurents, *The Time of the Cuckoo* (New York: Random House, 1953), 27. Further references to *The Time of the Cuckoo* are to this edition.

27. *The Time of the Cuckoo*, 85.

28. *The Time of the Cuckoo*, 81.

29. *The Time of the Cuckoo*, 107.

30. Arthur Laurents, *The Rest of the Story* (New York: Applause, 2012), chap. 2.

31. Jim Manago, *Love Is the Reason for It All: The Shirley Booth Story* (Albany, GA: Bear Manor Media, 2008), 106.

32. *Original Story*, 31.

33. Laurents met Hatcher in Los Angeles. Hatcher joined the playwright in New York and would have roles in Laurents's next two plays before becoming a successful real-estate developer.

34. Arthur Laurents, 'Preface' to *A Clearing in the Woods* (New York: Random House, 1957), vii. Further references to *A Clearing in the Woods* are to this edition.

35. *A Clearing in the Woods*, 168–69.

36. *Original Story*, 4.

37. See *Original Story*, 352.

38. *New York Theatre Critics Reviews, Volume 18* (New York: New York Theatre Critics Reviews, Inc., 1957), 396.

39. *Candide*, which ran concurrently with *A Clearing in the Woods*, only lasted seventy-three performances, though later revisions of the flawed script would lead to more successful revivals in theatres and opera houses as well as multiple recordings.

40. Vaill, *Somewhere*, 275.

41. Meryle Secrest, *Leonard Bernstein: A Life* (New York: Random House, 1994), 216.

42. *Original Story*, 350.

43. Sondheim, *Finishing the Hat*, 28.

44. Humphrey Burton, *Leonard Bernstein* (New York: Doubleday, 1994), 275. Used by permission of the Leonard Bernstein Office, Inc.

45. Laurents, *The Rest of the Story*, 13.

46. Arthur Laurents, *Mainly on Directing:* Gypsy, West Side Story, *and Other Musicals* (New York: Knopf, 2009), 159.

5 | Sondheim the Kid

STEVE SWAYNE

The Man and the Pen

Late on Tuesday evening, 4 October 1955, the opening night party for *Island of Goats* was underway. The play – an English adaptation of Ugo Betti's *Delitto all'isola delle capre* ('Crime on Goat-Island') – would close after all of seven performances. However the cast and crew felt that night, Stephen Sondheim, who did not attend the play's opening, had his own reasons for feeling downcast. His hoped-for professional debut as a composer–lyricist – *Saturday Night* (book by Julius Epstein based on a play by Julius and his twin brother, Philip) – had lost its main producer, Lemuel Ayers, who had died of leukemia two months earlier.

At the party, Sondheim felt somewhat out of place until he spied Arthur Laurents across the room. They had met some months earlier, when Laurents had attended an audition for a musical version of James M. Cain's 1937 book, *Serenade*. In his memoir, Laurents recounted Sondheim's rendition of songs from *Saturday Night*.[1] Sondheim had his own takeaway:

> I was invited [to the opening night party of *Island of Goats*] by Burt Shevelove, and I didn't know anyone there since Burt hadn't arrived yet. Then in the corner I spotted Arthur Laurents. I went over to make small talk and I asked him what he was doing and he said that he was just about to begin a musical of *Romeo and Juliet* with Leonard Bernstein and Jerry Robbins. I asked, just idly, 'Who's doing the lyrics?' and Arthur literally smote his forehead, which I think is the only time I've ever seen anybody literally smite his forehead, and he said, 'I never thought of you and I liked your lyrics very much. I didn't like your music, but I did like your lyrics a lot.' Arthur is nothing if not frank. So he invited me to meet and play for Bernstein, which I agreed to do because I thought it might be very glamorous to meet Lenny.[2]

Someone in the fall of 1955 might be forgiven for not knowing where Sondheim would land as a man of the theatre. In college he had written a radio play, music and lyrics for three different musicals, the book for two of those musicals, short stories and satire, music criticism, a piano sonata,

68

and the beginning of a novel. He had also earned acclaim for his abilities as an actor. The year after his graduation from Williams College found him completing a concertino for two pianos and a sonata for violin solo. He wrote a TV script for Jack Lemmon, then a budding young actor; between October 1953 and February 1954 he collaborated on eleven television scripts for the comedy series *Topper*. He had an apprenticeship of sorts with his mentor, Oscar Hammerstein II: two of the Williams musicals fulfilled half of the apprenticeship; a third, a musical based on P. L. Travers's *Mary Poppins*, failed to find its final form; neither did the fourth, *Climb High*. By early 1954 Sondheim had much to show from his efforts to write the book for a musical, but none of those efforts was polished enough to take the stage.

These scripts, sketches, and scores – nearly everything from 1946 to 1965 – are currently housed in the library and archives of the Wisconsin Historical Society.[3] These early materials have provided scholars and writers grist for popular and scholarly work, most notably Stephen Banfield's *Sondheim's Broadway Musicals* with its twenty-one pages on Sondheim's pre-*West Side Story* activities;[4] Meryle Secrest's *Stephen Sondheim: A Life*, which has a rich portrait of Sondheim's development;[5] and my own articles and book that trace the foundations of Sondheim's musicodramatic style.[6] To my knowledge, neither Banfield nor Secrest nor I have fully disentangled the composer from the lyricist nor fully explained reactions such as Laurents's.

Despite the plethora of scripts at Wisconsin, it is clear that Sondheim did not wish to be characterized as a writer of words. The 1965 biography that accompanies the Wisconsin finding guide talks about how

Sondheim's latest collaboration as a lyricist has been with Hammerstein's former partner, Richard Rodgers, for the musical *Do I Hear a Waltz?* (1965). Rodgers commented on Sondheim's style, 'It has a curious way of making people sing as if they were talking.'

Despite these attainments in writing lyrics, Sondheim has said that he does not especially enjoy writing them. Instead, he prefers to write music.[7]

In the first volume of his collected lyrics and the 'attendant comments, principles, heresies, grudges, whines and anecdotes' that go along with them, published forty-five years later, Sondheim returned to make the same point: that he was a composer first and foremost, and that meeting the composer for *West Side Story* only exacerbated his own desire to write for the musical stage. He said of the not-so-glamorous meeting with Bernstein that, notwithstanding his experience with Julius Epstein, working with Bernstein, Laurents, and Robbins was entirely different:

> To begin with, not only was I for the first time writing lyrics to someone else's music, the someone else was a legend verging on myth, whose score for *On the Town*, from the moment I'd heard it sizzling out of the orchestra pit when I was fourteen, had given me that rush of excitement you rarely get from musicals: a fresh individual and complex sound, a new kind of music.[8]

After recounting his audition for Bernstein, which reads as though the headstrong young man was in the presence of an inscrutable oracle, the eighty-year-old Sondheim tells the reader how the twenty-five-year-old Sondheim felt:

> I left with mixed feelings: I wanted to be asked to the party, I just didn't want to go. The fact was, and still is, that I enjoy writing music much more than lyrics . . . I had the good sense to discuss all this with Oscar and it was he who persuaded me that if I was offered the job, I should leap at it. . . . When Lenny phoned a week later and invited me to join the crew, I duly leapt.
>
> I have only two regrets about that decision. First, it tagged and then dogged me with the label 'lyricist,' so that when my music finally popped into the open two shows and five years later, I was dismissed by some as an overly ambitious pretender who should stick to his own side of the street. (The label has persisted to this day, though with less intensity.) [The second regret recounts Sondheim's feelings that the lyrics for *West Side Story* are too 'poetic,' to use Bernstein's word.][9]

The materials in Wisconsin provide the hard evidence of what Sondheim was doing from 1946 to the premiere of *West Side Story* in 1957. Two other more recent sources shine a light on the more affective aspects of this period in Sondheim's life. The two volumes of his lyrics buttress the opinion of Laurents and others who saw in these words a master at work. And two commercially available recordings, both titled *Sondheim Sings* and both released in 2005, serve as sonic witnesses, placing the astute listener alongside Laurents and others who heard Sondheim sing and play his songs. Together, these two sources make Laurents's assessment easier to comprehend: the lyrics rival those from the best in the business, while the music is not unlike Sondheim's description of Bernstein's music: 'a fresh individual and complex sound, a new kind of music.' And given that he did not have the profile that Bernstein the composer had, Sondheim the composer was more easily dismissed. One can imagine Bernstein parroting Laurents: 'I don't like your music, but I do like your lyrics a lot.'

'I liked your lyrics very much'

The audition that Laurents heard occurred around the time that Sondheim attended a gathering at lyricist E. Y. 'Yip' Harburg's apartment. Also there that afternoon were composers Burton Lane (*Finian's Rainbow*, 1947) and Harold Arlen (*House of Flowers*, 1954; 'The Man That Got Away' from the film *A Star Is Born* was released that year, although Judy Garland had recorded it the year before). Both Lane and Arlen 'played some stuff.' Then it was Sondheim's turn. He recalled that he played three numbers: 'a fast, a slow, and a fast.'

Harburg or someone said, 'This is the promising young composer.' And I got up and played ['Saturday Night'], and everybody applauded very loudly. And I played 'This Is Nice, Isn't It?,' and they applauded even more loudly. And I ended with this screaming 2/4, 'One Wonderful Day,' and they all cheered.

And I sat down, very pleased with myself, on the couch next to Harold Arlen. And he turned to me and he said – devastating me – 'You're afraid not to write a blockbuster, aren't you?' I wanted to go under the couch.[10]

A look at the lyrics for these three songs and others from *Saturday Night* – his first professional musical – show that, as a wordsmith, Sondheim was indeed writing blockbusters.

Sondheim patted himself on the back for his ability 'to imitate the Jewish Brooklynese of the Epstein brothers as if I'd been born in Greenpoint.'[11] The title song situates us in Jewish Brooklyn in its very first lines. Four guys are gathered at a home in Brooklyn. Ted is on the phone, trying to get a date with some woman; Ray bets that Ted will fail; Ray relates his opinion about Ted to Artie and offers up an alternate plan for the evening.

RAY
He's gonna get the axe from huh –
What would ya say to seein' a
Pitcha?

After apparently nixing the notion of seeing 'the combination [possibly a double feature] of Johnny Mack Brown and Bessie Love' at a nearby movie palace, Ray offers up another option that he found in the Sunday *New York Times*. Artie voices his disapproval in rather colourful terms:

RAY
Here's a revival of 'Ben Huh,'
Goes on at nine-fifteen at the
Cushman.

ARTIE
So when I got my mind on sex
Who gives a damn for Francis X.
Bushman?[12]

Dino, the fourth fellow at the house, plays a honky-tonk number on the piano, Artie strums a ukulele, and the ennui and desperation of the guys comes through in the sharpness of their dialogue in the form of Sondheim's lyrics.

As for Sondheim's characterization of 'Isn't It?' as a slow song, it might be more accurately described as a waltz, a dance that appears repeatedly in Sondheim's *oeuvre*. In fact, the materials in Wisconsin include two undated piano compositions, each named 'Waltz.' Both have the mien of French cabaret music with a whiff of Ravel thrown in. Given the character's (Helen) affectation of being from the South (she, too, is from Brooklyn), a waltz seems appropriate for her attempt to portray herself as a Southern belle. The lyric itself is fairly straightforward, containing just a few internal rhymes but organized around the last word in each stanza – 'band–demand–hand–grand' – while at the same time reminding us that this era features a red-hot stock market.

HELEN
Don't you think
We make natural partners?
Ah mean, like food and drink,
Or supply and demand?[13]

The 'screaming 2/4' – 'One Wonderful Day' – already exhibits wit and skill with its identity in the first two syllables. And in a song that revolves around the possibility of marriage, Sondheim sent up one of the best-known wedding melodies – the 'Bridal Chorus' from Wagner's *Lohengrin* – setting it to words that would be right at home in *Company*:

BOBBY
Don't do it, Gene.
Don't do it, Gene.
Love with a spouse is a household routine.
Then, when you're through,
What can you do?
Can't send a dame home
Who lives in the same home
As you![14]

A more positive take on marriage – one that, like 'Isn't It?' uses the stock market as a trope – comes in 'Love's A Bond.' As with other lyrics in *Saturday Night*, 'Love's A Bond' abounds in interior rhyme:

VOCALIST
Love's a bond that's pure.
Its dividends are sure.
This bond, if you get it,
Is stable and yet it
Will grow if you let it
Mature.[15]

Another song, 'Exhibit A,' conjures up the lawyerly disquisition that Fredrik lays out in *A Little Night Music* ('Now'). After detailing eight alphabetically organized 'exhibits,' A through H, that any enterprising young man will need to have at hand in order to have his way with his date by the end of the evening, including the scent of 'new pine' that will assist a fellow in getting his girl to become 'supine,' Bobby reviews the 'evidence':

BOBBY
A-B-C-D-E-F-G-H-I-
Rest my case![16]

Other lyrics from this same time period show a similar virtuosity and *joie de vivre*. The second volume of Sondheim's lyrics contains a sampling of birthday tributes, including two for Bernstein (1958 and 1988), one for Laurents (1998), and two for Harold Prince (1978 and 1993). The first Bernstein birthday lyric is a reworking of 'You're Only as Old as You Look,' a 1955 song that Sondheim wrote for Jerry Beaty, Mary Rodgers's first husband. The Bernstein version finds Sondheim twitting the birthday boy for his propensity to borrow other people's music; it also has a sequence where the rhymes are so closely assonant that one might be excused from hearing them initially as near or false rhymes, which Sondheim decried as 'the refuge of the destitute.'[17]

SS (Sondheim)
You've got more time to write more scores
Whether somebody else's or your scores,
'Cause you're only as old as you look
And you look four scores
Five
Why, you're practically alive. . . .

What great days have gone!
All the debuts, the bravos, the bombs!
And the time you took over the baton –
From Brahms.[18]

The original version of the song to Beaty opens *Sondheim Sings*, Volume II. Also on the CD is a birthday tribute he composed a year before titled 'A Star Is Born.' A clear nod to the Garland film of the same year, Sondheim fêted the birth of a classmate's daughter by regaling the infant's father – a Williams classmate and an avid movie and theatre buff – with an avalanche of references so dense that, in his volume, Sondheim felt the need to provide a glossary for some of the more than seventy actors, movies, and studios he invoked:

ss
Swanson sent a
Pale magenta
Mink-upholstered car,
Rita Gam
A silent Sam-
Ovar,
Oliv' de Havilland
Sent some gravel and
Half a ton of tile, cement and tar
To pave the driveway round the home of our star.[19]

This concatenation of names provides an early example of the list song in Sondheim's hands; later list songs include 'I'm Still Here' (*Follies*), 'Please Hello' (*Pacific Overtures*), and 'Putting It Together' (*Sunday in the Park with George*). And while it was written for a private audience – Charles Hollerith, Jr.; his wife, Catherine; and their newborn daughter, Catherine Louise – undoubtedly others in Sondheim's orbit at this time would have had opportunities to hear these songs.[20]

The scintillating wordplay found in *Saturday Night* and other contemporaneous songs and his emerging ability to define and describe character through his lyrics set Sondheim apart from other practitioners in his day. It is not by accident that Sondheim looked to Frank Loesser and *Guys and Dolls*, rather than Hammerstein or Alan Jay Lerner – *Brigadoon* (1947), *Love Life* (1948), and *Paint Your Wagon* (1951); *My Fair Lady* would come later (1956) – as a model for witty, acerbic, conversational lyrics at this moment in his career. The other men were poetic and romantic; Loesser was a wisecracking New Yorker.[21] And, like Sondheim, Loesser wrote his own music to his own lyrics. Except, unlike Loesser, nobody seemed drawn to Sondheim's music. The recordings give a hint as to why that might have been so. They open a window into Sondheim's piano technique. In a word: it was *formidable*.[22]

'I didn't like your music'

Although it was composed after *West Side Story*, 'Pretty Little Picture' (*A Funny Thing Happened on the Way to the Forum*, 1962; *Sondheim Sings*, Volume I: 1962–72) can illustrate what Sondheim might have sounded like when Laurents, Lane, Arlen, Bernstein, and others heard him sing his songs in the mid 1950s. For starters, the tempo of Sondheim's rendition (quarter note [q] = 120 to 126 bpm) is much faster than what has become the standard tempo, from Zero Mostel's performance to the present day (q = 106 bpm). Then Sondheim tossed off the Prokofievian 'wrong notes' as though there was no physical challenge whatsoever.[23] While there is an actual wrong note or two in his performance – for example, a G in the bass instead of an F at 1′ 43″ – the enthusiastic singing and playing, coupled with the fast tempo, result in a blockbuster performance.

One hears the same drive in his rendition of an early version of 'The Glamorous Life' (*A Little Night Music*, 1973). The piano playing sounds as though there is a second person sitting with him, but Sondheim executed both the piano playing and singing alone; the motoric accompaniment, the leaps into chords in the middle of the keyboard, and the shifts in meter are handled with vigor and aplomb. One hears an accomplished performer at work here, one for whom virtuosity seems to come with little effort.

I do not wish to oversell the pianistic facility found in the recordings. They represent only a selection of the recordings that Sondheim made, and one would presume that they were chosen for their fidelity to the songs and persuasiveness as performances. It is easy to imagine multiple takes of one song as he allowed the tape to roll, and those performances, filled with stops and starts and the inevitable clinkers, may one day yield their own thorough study. But these recordings give us a sense of what it must have been like to have been in the room where Sondheim, having spent the day preparing and practicing alone, auditioned his songs in order to interest potential producers and investors in his work.

In addition to the standalone songs 'You're Only as Old as You Look' and 'A Star Is Born,' *Sondheim Sings*, Volume II: 1946–60 has two songs from *Saturday Night*. The first, 'I Remember That,' is in 32-bar song form (here AA′BA″) with an 8-bar extension of the final A section. It also features a 28-bar verse in which Hank recollects meeting Celeste for the first time, getting all of the details wrong, and a 10-bar reprise of the verse by Celeste, who corrects Hank. Sondheim's playing closely resembles the published version, which is in the same key (C major) and, most importantly, contains the contrapuntal tenor voice in the piano part. In the introduction to the refrain, that voice sets up an oscillating figure that runs throughout the song; in the bridge, it traces a descending line that returns in the tag at the end; and this voice drives the modulation to the bridge, as the song moves to E major. In that transition to the bridge, the accompaniment also indicates that the left hand needs to cross over the right, which is playing the interior line at that point. This interior voice, preserved by the crossing of hands, resembles the piano writing in Rachmaninov, including in the second piano concerto – the first movement of which Sondheim performed[24] – and Sondheim has always been fond of counterpoint, which is evident in other moments in *Saturday Night*.

The melody for 'I Remember That' is more instrumental than vocal, with its repeated triadic arpeggiations climbing up the scale in the A sections: first C–E–G, then E–G–B, lastly G–B–D, all harmonized with a C major triad. And the tag features its own upward idea, as the melody, after hitting a high E, comes back down to a G as the stressed note, followed by an A and then a B, not unlike what one hears in the final A section of 'The Trolley Song,' sung by Judy Garland in *Meet Me in St. Louis* ten years earlier (1944; music and lyrics by Hugh Martin and Ralph Blane). All in all, it is an accomplished traditional song that has elements that make it challenging to sing, slightly more difficult to play than a standard lead sheet (the published score does not provide chord figures), and less immediately memorable than the songs of Irving Berlin and Jerome Kern, which this song, with its modulation in the bridge, seem to hold as its models.

Berlin was especially fond of double songs, beginning with 'Play a Simple Melody/Musical Demon' from his 1914 musical *Watch Your Step* and continuing through to his last completed musical ('Empty Pockets Filled with Love,' *Mr. President*, 1962) and to the last major revival he oversaw ('Old Fashioned Wedding,' *Annie Get Your Gun*, 1966). Closer to Sondheim's young adulthood – and its own bona fide phenomenon – was 'I Wonder Why/You're Just in Love' from Berlin's 1950 *Call Me*

Madam. The lovely, almost syrupy ballad sung by the male lead is touching, but once the real star of the show, Ethel Merman, cuts in with her jazzy counterpoint, the song enters a different stratosphere that is intensified when the two songs are sung in tandem. The song never failed to rouse the audience, and Merman and her male lead – one hesitates to call him a 'co-star' – often had to reprise the song as an instant encore.

'In No Time at All/A Moment with You' attempts to pay homage to this Berlin tradition, but it is a pale copy of what Berlin executed in 1950. Unlike the Merman showstopper, Sondheim's song has a single pace: 'Tempo di Fox Trot.' And the recording of Sondheim singing this song in 1954 doesn't fully realize the second song, making it difficult at this distance to determine how well the two lines work together. By the time the show was produced off-Broadway, the second 'song' became more of an echo of the first, taking over some of the wrong-note counterpoint in the piano part of the 1954 recording and setting that counterpoint to words.[25] And like 'I Remember That,' this song's bridge is a modulator's paradise, enharmonically going from D-flat major through F-sharp minor to E major and then to A major. The score retains the five-flat key signature as the music here is festooned with accidentals. Then a classic jazz tritone pivot sends the music from an A^{13} chord to an $E\text{-flat}^{13}$ chord, then through the dominant of the original key back home to D flat major. One can think of 'So in Love' (*Kiss Me, Kate*, 1948, Porter) or 'All the Things You Are' (*Very Warm for May*, 1939, Kern; book and lyrics by Hammerstein) for other examples of modulatory excess on Broadway that Sondheim would have known and admired.

The title song for *Saturday Night* takes modulation, counterpoint, and climbing melodies to a dizzying height.[26] After Dino's ragtime piano introduction in the key of B flat major, Artie strums three chords on his ukulele that place us on the doorstep of D-flat major. The first eight bars of the verse are in D-flat, but the second eight are jacked up to E-flat. They are followed by a harmonically unstable sixteen measures that, somewhat surprisingly, end with a return to E-flat major and the melody sitting on the sixth degree. Four measures in E-flat repeat the melodic figure that opened the verse, only to be cut short by Dino's honky-tonk piano, now thrown into D-flat instead of B-flat. It sets up Artie's three ukulele chords just fine ... and then the music continues without preparation in F major for the song's refrain (or 'burthen,' as Sondheim liked to call this section of a song, in homage to Kern).

The accompaniment thus far has had moments of contrast with the melody, but the refrain (a straight-up 32-bar song, in ABAC form) contains the same kind of interior tenor line that was so prominent in 'I Remember That.' Its true contrapuntal potential, however, is revealed in its second appearance. After a return to the beginning of the song, the D-flat/E-flat/ unstable harmonies/return to E-flat structure jumps to what is marked as the coda but is more a written-out version of the refrain repeat. This time, the snippet of the opening line of the verse is given its full eight bars (instead of four the first time), with the melody oscillating between $\hat{3}$ and $\hat{2}$ in E-flat, but midway the key changes to F, making the oscillation between $\hat{2}$ and $\hat{1}$. This static melody with a key change underneath is something Sondheim adopted from Ravel's Trio and String Quartet, deployed in the first movement of his piano sonata, and seen in the key change at the end of the bridge in 'Losing My Mind' (*Follies*). Here in 'Saturday Night,' with the music now in the key of the refrain, Sondheim pulls another compositional rabbit out of the hat: the melody of the A sections – which has the same stairstep quality found in 'I Remember That' – can be sung in canon at the unison with one bar separating each entrance, and the written-out repeat has four vocal lines as Ted, Ray, Artie, and Dino echo one another in lamenting their lonely plight on this particular Saturday night.

The stabbing wrong notes, the triadic and instrumental melodies, the insinuating contrapuntal lines, the modulatory harmonies, the energetic accompaniments: taken all together, Sondheim's songs exhibit an almost irrational exuberance, especially in comparison with what Loewe and Loesser and Berlin and Porter and Rodgers were offering on Broadway at the time. Only Arlen – Sondheim's favourite song composer – could come close to such musical audacity, and even he found it necessary to suggest to Sondheim that the young composer–lyricist tone down his exuberance.[27] Is it any surprise, then, that Laurents and others found Sondheim's music hard to digest? And Sondheim did little to help his cause by being such a polymath at the time. With Ayers's death and the subsequent shelving of *Saturday Night*, Sondheim would be known as a lyricist throughout the 1950s and for years thereafter.

Getting One's Goat

Sondheim knew in 1957 that, sooner or later, his music would arrive on Broadway, just as his lyrics had. And on Tuesday evening, 8 May 1962, when *A Funny Thing Happened on the Way to the Forum* opened, that day had arrived. It meant that Sondheim would receive his first professional reviews for his work as a composer as well as a lyricist. This is what he heard as someone read Howard Taubman's *New York Times* review aloud at the opening night party:

George Abbott, who has been around a long time but surely staged nothing for the forum mob, has forgotten nothing and remembered everything. He has engineered a gay funeral sequence to a relentlessly snappy march by Stephen Sondheim. [Abbott] has used mixed identities, swinging doors, kicks in the posterior, double takes and all the rest of the familiar paraphernalia with the merciless disingenuousness of a man who knows you will be defenseless.

Mr. Sondheim's songs are accessories to the pre-meditated offense. . . .[28]

Many talented hands fueled *Forum*'s run of 964 performances, and yet Sondheim's contribution to the show was virtually overlooked: *Forum* won the 1963 Tony Award for Best Musical; *Oliver!* won the Tony that year for Best Original Score; Sondheim was passed over in that category.

Arthur Laurents would give Sondheim a second chance as composer–lyricist with *Anyone Can Whistle* (1964); it closed after all of nine performances. Sondheim's heyday would have to wait until the 1970s, when he started becoming the doyen of American musical theatre with *Company*, yet for another decade his lyrics bested his music in the eyes of many critics. By 1980, there was no question about who Sondheim was: the premier composer–lyricist of the American musical. Time will tell, when Broadway's musical theatre history is recounted seventy years hence, whether Sondheim is seen as the GOAT ('greatest of all time'). Whatever that critical judgment is, his greatness, fleetingly acknowledged in the 1950s and early 1960s, is no longer in doubt. In the musical theatre pantheon, there will always be a place for him.

Notes

1. Arthur Laurents, *Original Story by Arthur Laurents: A Memoir of Broadway and Hollywood* (New York: Alfred A. Knopf, 2000), 334. Bernstein was originally enlisted as part of the creative team but left when Jerome Robbins insisted on returning to the *Romeo and Juliet* musical.
2. As quoted in Craig Zadan, *Sondheim & Co.*, 2nd ed., updated (New York: Harper & Row, 1989), 11–12.
3. For more on the Sondheim papers at Wisconsin and other theatre luminaries whose papers also reside there, see Mark Eden Horowitz, 'Early Signs of Talent: Wisconsin Archives Reveal Sondheim's Youthful Evolution,' *The Sondheim Review* 21, no. 2 (Spring 2015): 32–33.

4. Stephen Banfield, *Sondheim's Broadway Musicals* (Ann Arbor: University of Michigan Press, 1993), 11–31.

5. Meryle Secrest, *Stephen Sondheim: A Life* (New York: Alfred A. Knopf, 1998).

6. 'Music for the Theatre, the Young Copland, and the Younger Sondheim,' *American Music* 20, no. 1 (Spring 2002): 80–101 (looks at Sondheim's senior-year term papers on Ravel and Copland and the influence of their sound worlds on his); 'Sondheim's Piano Sonata' (his senior thesis), *Journal of the Royal Musical Association* 127 (2002): 258–304; 'Hindemith's Unexpected Grandson,' *Hindemith-Jahrbuch* 32 (2003): 215–34 (comparisons of Hindemith's style with the 1950 sonata, the Concertino for Two Pianos, 1951, and their choices of theatrical projects); *How Sondheim Found His Sound* (Ann Arbor: University of Michigan Press, 2005; paperback, 2007); and 'Williams College before, during, and after Sondheim,' in *Sondheim in Our Time and His* (New York: Oxford, 2022), 15–44.

7. Finding aid (typescript), Stephen Sondheim (1930–) Papers, 1946–1965, University of Wisconsin, U.S. Mss 66AN: 1.

8. Stephen Sondheim, *Finishing the Hat: Collected Lyrics (1954–1981) with Attendant Comments, Principles, Heresies, Grudges, Whines, and Anecdotes* (New York: Alfred A. Knopf, 2010), 25–26.

9. *Finishing the Hat*, 26.

10. Steven Robert Swayne, 'Hearing Sondheim's Voices,' PhD diss., University of California, Berkeley, 1999: 339.

11. Sondheim, *Finishing the Hat*, 4.

12. *Finishing the Hat*, 5. Sondheim placed an asterisk by the first 'huh' in the lyric and noted: 'Brooklynese – "her" without the final "r" sound.' F. Richard Pappas, an attorney representing Stephen Sondheim, authorized the quotations from Sondheim's lyrics that appear in this chapter.

13. *Finishing the Hat*, 8.

14. Sondheim, *Finishing the Hat*, 13.

15. Sondheim, *Finishing the Hat*, 8.

16. Sondheim, *Finishing the Hat*, 10.

17. Sondheim, *Finishing the Hat*, xxv–xxvii.

18. Stephen Sondheim, *Look, I Made a Hat: Collected Lyrics (1981–2011) with Attendant Comments, Amplifications, Dogmas, Harangues, Digressions, Anecdotes and Miscellany* (New York: Alfred A. Knopf, 2011), 410.

19. *Look, I Made a Hat*, 406. The glossary includes only half of those mentioned; Sondheim assumed that some remained famous enough in 2011 not to need additional information, such as Garland, Lucille Ball, Olivia de Havilland, and Gloria Swanson. Others not glossed include Claudette Colbert, Ricardo Montalban, Anthony Quinn, Roberto Rossellini, and Norma Shearer. Also not glossed is Alexis Smith, who would go on to star in *Follies* as Phyllis Stone.

20. For information on the *Sondheim Sings* recordings, see the inside back covers of the CD liner notes. For more on the Ryans' contributions to Sondheim, see

Secrest, 90 *et passim*. Ayers and Sondheim were groomsmen at the Ryans' wedding. D. D. was also the impetus for Kay Thompson to turn her cabaret song about a girl who lived in the penthouse of the Plaza Hotel into the *Eloise* series of books; see Douglas Martin, 'D. D. Ryan, Fashionable Godmother to "Eloise," Dies at 79,' *New York Times*, 29 July 2007, www.nytimes.com/2007/07/29/nyregion/29ryan.html, accessed 7 September 2020.

21. *Finishing the Hat*, 6.

22. See 'A Bowler Hat' (*Pacific Overtures*) for the French pronunciation (*Finishing the Hat*, 328).

23. For more on 'wrong notes' being Prokofievian, see Richard Bass, 'Prokofiev's Technique of Harmonic Displacement,' *Music Analysis*, 7, no. 2 (July 1988): 197–214. www.jstor.org/stable/854056, accessed 27 May 2021.

24. Sondheim: 'I liked playing the piano part of the first movement of the Rachmaninoff C Minor [Concerto, op. 18], which I played in high school, toured, and gave recitals in Pennsylvania.' Personal communication with the author, 20 November 2001.

25. Sondheim would have greater success with counterpoint songs in future musicals: see 'Now/Later/Soon' (*A Little Night Music*); the cut combination of 'Rain on the Roof'/'Ah, Paris!'/'Broadway Baby' (*Follies* and present in the vocal score); and, most successful of all, the quartet that sings 'You're Gonna Love Tomorrow'/'Love Will See Us through' (also from *Follies*).

26. The 2000 off-Broadway recording of 'Saturday Night' (on *Saturday Night*, Nonesuch 76902-2) is transcribed up a whole step from the published vocal score (*Saturday Night*, Hal Leonard, ISBN 0-7935-9576-2), which, while it has no publication date on it, was released in 1999. The score is marketed as 'vocal selections'; while it contains all of the songs from the musical, it does not contain the reprises of 'Saturday Night' and 'One Wonderful Day.' In my analysis, I will refer to the keys as they appear in the vocal score.

27. For Sondheim naming Arlen as his favorite composer, see *Finishing the Hat*, 222. Arlen had modest success on Broadway with *Bloomer Girl* (1944; 654 performances), *St. Louis Woman* (1946; 113 performances), *House of Flowers* (1954; 165 performances), and *Jamaica* (1956; 555 performances), but his star did not burn as brightly as the others mentioned here.

28. Howard Taubman, 'Theatre: "A Funny Thing Happened . . . ",' *New York Times*, 9 May 1962: 47.

6 | 'For a Small Fee in America'

Producing *West Side Story*

LAURA MACDONALD

In 1949 Jerome Robbins 'started looking for a producer and collaborators who'd be interested' in his idea for a contemporary *Romeo and Juliet*.[1] 'This was not easy. Producers were not at all interested in doing it,' he recalled decades later.[2] Even when producers were on board, they struggled to secure backers with additional funding. *West Side Story* was preceded on Broadway by the 1956 premieres of *My Fair Lady, The Most Happy Fella,* and *Bells Are Ringing* and was followed three months after its opening by *The Music Man* – hit musical comedies that conclude with a couple anticipating a future together, in contrast to *West Side Story*'s women grieving the deaths of their lovers due to gang violence. With no similarly unhappy ending earning well on Broadway at the time, it is unsurprising producers and backers were reluctant to support *West Side Story*.

This chapter examines the four producers who were attached to *West Side Story* on its way to Broadway – Cheryl Crawford, Roger L. Stevens, Robert E. Griffith, and Harold S. Prince – unpacking their relationships with each other and with the musical's creative team. While *West Side Story*'s creative team is well known for the innovation its members hoped to achieve with their lyric theatre collaboration, they were simultaneously keen to earn a profit. Two weeks after the musical opened, Arthur Laurents wrote to producer Roger L. Stevens, a real estate magnate, for advice on investing in real estate syndicates, and Stephen Sondheim kept Leonard Bernstein updated on the musical's profits while the composer was on a conducting tour.[3] The chapter will therefore also explore the ways this musical generated a profit, in particular its further circulation via national and international tours.

Though conversations and work on the musical developed over many years, producers and investors for *West Side Story* were recruited primarily in 1956 and 1957. The talent agent and producer Leland Hayward, and producer–authors Rodgers and Hammerstein, were among those who turned down the new musical. An audition for legendary Broadway producer George Abbott was particularly terrible. A nervous Bernstein played poorly and loudly, and, with Sondheim, 'sang like desperate frogs!' Laurents related to Robbins in a letter.[4] Abbott provided mixed feedback including his preference to lighten up the sombre musical. Though much of *West Side Story*'s development illustrates its creative team's desire to innovate musical theatre, that innovation was communicated to potential producers and investors through the traditional Broadway backers' audition. A producer's office or wealthy theatre afficionado's apartment were not the ideal venues for showcasing a musical drawing heavily on dance and dramatic music for its storytelling. *West Side Story*'s struggle to secure a producer and financing signaled the potential for new models of musical theatre development and pitches.

The Gambler and the Facilitator: Cheryl Crawford and Roger L. Stevens

The elder sister to three younger brothers, Cheryl Crawford (1902–1986) accumulated years of experience in sparring with boys. She was introduced to theatre as a child in Akron, Ohio where she lived with her upper-middle-class family. An avid reader who entertained audiences of her own, Crawford invented stories on her front porch based on prompts from the neighborhood children who delighted in her ability to construct a narrative.[5] She left the Midwest to major in drama at Smith College and spent a summer working for the Provincetown Players, during Susan Glaspell's tenure. Acting training with the Theatre Guild in New York City followed her college education so she could learn about professional theatre and pursue her goal of becoming a producer. 'Since [Theatre Guild executive director] Theresa Helburn was one of very few women, and certainly the most important one, in an executive position in the theatre, I hoped she would look on my ambition favorably, woman to woman,' Crawford recalls in her autobiography.[6] In 1926, after a year of training with Guild actors, Crawford began to establish herself professionally, as an actor, stage manager, director, and eventually producer.

'Sometimes I think a producer is a person who is absolutely unable to do anything else, who has a strong interest in all the arts but the talent for none of them and enough business sense to know that sometimes you must dare to go to the edge of disaster to achieve what you desire,' Crawford mused.[7] Musicals became her passion and she brought her business sense to the collaborations she facilitated. Crawford introduced German composer Kurt Weill, who wanted to work on an American subject, to the Pulitzer Prize-winning playwright Paul Green. Together they created the antiwar musical *Johnny Johnson* (1936), about an idealistic soldier who enlists to fight in the First World War. Disagreement between members of the creative team and a too-large theatre contributed to the musical's short run on Broadway.

Producing independently by the early 1940s and struggling after a string of failures, Crawford was recruited to co-produce at a summer stock theatre in New Jersey. She obtained permission from the Theatre Guild to produce a revival of *Porgy and Bess*, in New Jersey, and hired performers from the 1935 premiere as well as its conductor, Alexander Smallens. He and Crawford collaborated to streamline the work's recitative, to create greater flow and coherence. The production was such a hit that it transferred to Broadway early in 1942, went on tour, and returned to Broadway in 1943 and 1944. *Porgy and Bess* generated much needed income for Crawford and convinced her to focus on musicals. *One Touch of Venus* (1943), another Broadway collaboration with Weill, was followed by the musicals *Brigadoon* (1947), *Love Life* (1948) and *Paint Your Wagon* (1951).

Crawford's musicals were not always commercial hits, such as the short-lived *Flahooley* (1951), a satirical puppet musical. Her shows frequently revolve around opposing views – whether on war, capitalism, urban, suburban or pastoral life, or with *West Side Story*, on migration and assimilation. Crawford wanted *One Touch of Venus* to 'have social bearing and also be amusing,'[8] and similar potential would be a key element persuading her to develop *West Side Story*. Lehman Engel and Howard Kissel note how, 'Given the iconic status of the show, it is hard for us to understand the enormous gamble [*West Side Story*] posed.'[9] Barranger titled her biography *A Gambler's Instinct*, calling Crawford a 'woman of poker-playing instincts and gaming skills, the individual of courage and fortitude, the legendary risk-taker and penny-pincher who mastered the art (and gamesmanship) of producing on Broadway at mid-century.'[10] Bernstein offered *West Side Story* to Crawford in 1956 but she was unable to fund the entire $300,000 advance the production needed her to wager so she recruited Roger L. Stevens (1910–1998), with whom she had served on the board of the American National Theatre and Academy (ANTA), as co-producer.

Once on board, Crawford and Stevens explored the possibility of a Los Angeles out-of-town tryout for *West Side Story*. They corresponded with Edwin Lester, General Manager of the Los Angeles Civic Light Opera at the Philharmonic Auditorium. Copying Stevens on her letter to Robbins, Laurents, and Bernstein on 15 June 1956, Crawford's desire for an entertaining musical was clarified. 'We both feel that exciting as the show can be, it is no cinch and I think all of you realize that too, it has very few of the customary Broadway values of comedy and splash with three killings and music leaning to opera.'[11] She continued to share various concerns with Stevens over the summer, regarding the contract, profit sharing, advertising, and a play in development with a similar story. She also commissioned Sondheim to write a song and incidental music for N. Richard Nash's play *Girls of Summer*, opening later that year.

Lester followed up with Stevens at the end of 1956, praising the creative team's work but raising concerns over such a musical premiering at a Los Angeles venue owned by Temple Baptist Church:

Where a show has first been presented in New York and accepted there, it is not too much of a problem to make a few changes necessary for the piece to be palatable to the Church authorities, and such changes have never yet hurt any show that we've played because the basic values in the show were already established and the objectionable matter was not vital to success. But when you're doing a new show, to have to censor it before it is really born, may tend to destroy indigenous character.[12]

Less than a year after *West Side Story* opened on Broadway, its rival *The Music Man* launched its national tour with a six-week run at the Philharmonic as part of Lester's Civic Light Opera subscription series. *West Side Story* arrived in Los Angeles eighteen months after opening on Broadway, giving it plenty of time to generate positive media attention and word of mouth that would counter any church concerns.

Crawford relayed Lester's concerns to Robbins in the new year and floated Hartford as an alternative tryout. Crawford's devotion to the musical was unabated, despite the criticism she offered on form and structure: 'I re-read it very carefully and it's too good not to be great . . . Please know that I have lost none of my enthusiasm. I just want this to be the greatest it can and we shouldn't rush in only partially prepared.'[13] She explained that she had shared the script, giving it to

a very smart theatre guy to read, a man who was brought up in that kind of environment. He thought it had great promise but said one thing that I've been talking about too – that it doesn't have enough of the humor of these boys and girls. He said their original sense of fun and wit is incredible, that they have ways of expressing themselves that really rock your head back in surprise and laughter, that there is always one boy or girl who is a real clown and who entertains the others with his 'turns.' He suggested that we get in touch with someone in the Police Athletic League and spend a week observing these kids at work and play.[14]

Did Crawford's letter inspire Robbins? Within two months he was writing to his friend Tanaquil Le Clercq about a high school dance he had visited in Puerto Rican Harlem.[15] Laurents does not give Crawford any credit for advice on comedy, but in his memoir recalls, 'There was a need, I thought, for comedy relief which, by lessening tension, would increase the impact of the tragedy that followed. After getting nowhere with dramaturgical arguments, I invoked Shakespeare's use of clown.'[16] It may be a coincidence that Laurents and Crawford independently saw the potential for clowning in this musical, but given Laurents developed this comedy after Crawford's departure, it is difficult to read Crawford's letter to Robbins and not recall the number 'Gee, Officer Krupke' in which the Jet boys clown around, entertaining each other with their turns, as Crawford's friend suggested.[17]

Crawford wrote to Stevens in March 1957 before he traveled to England, discussing the production budget as well as the possible choice of the ANTA Playhouse (now August Wilson Theatre). She also emphasized, 'I will work hard to keep them at it.'[18] Despite her ongoing concerns and being busy with several plays, Crawford nevertheless enjoyed the creative team's milestones. 'Bit by bit I heard the score, wishing they would develop one great soaring ballad for it. Then one day Lenny phoned in great excitement: They had finished a wonderful new number. Sure enough, when I heard it at his apartment, I was delighted. The song was "Maria."'[19]

Barranger writes that, 'She remained enthusiastic until a backers' audition in April . . . during which none of the well-dressed potential investors opened his checkbook.'[20] Arts patron and co-producer of Crawford's *Brigadoon* and *Paint Your Wagon*, Bea Lawrence, hosted the discouraging audition at her apartment. Crawford recalled the evening two decades later:

Jerry presented a synopsis of the story as Lenny played the score with several singers. The reaction was less favorable than I had hoped. Indeed, I didn't believe anyone there was going to invest. Richard Rodgers and Oscar Hammerstein were present and felt that it would have to be cast with very youthful actors – and where were we going to find youngsters who could sing that score? I was discouraged, especially knowing that the production would cost more than any show I had ever produced.[21]

It had been nearly six years since her success with *Paint Your Wagon* and Crawford had weathered a string of flop plays; this latest musical needed to make money for her.

The creative team hoped to open the show in the spring of 1957 but were delayed due to Bernstein's conducting engagements, his work on *Candide* (1956), and the inability to cast a male lead. Months later, just before the

Broadway opening, *the New York Times* reported on the casting challenges Rodgers, Hammerstein, and Crawford had flagged, in an article titled 'Talent Dragnet.' According to reporter Murray Schumach, an eight-month search sent the *West Side Story* team to high schools, choirs, settlement schools, ballet companies, and nightclubs. Schumach explained how the new musical was combining the singing and dancing choruses that were separate in most musicals and noted the relative youth of the majority of the characters – 'almost the entire cast had to be young – and yet have the professionalism derived from experience.'[22]

The casting challenges highlight why backers' auditions, despite being an established industry practice, were unlikely to convince anyone to finance *West Side Story*. Robbins's biographer Deborah Jowitt is one of many who has emphasized the brevity of Arthur Laurents's script for the musical, 'Its passions rage primarily through song and dance,' she explains.[23] Beyond the beauty of Bernstein's sung melodies, much of the power of this show's music comes from the orchestration of its score, created in collaboration by Bernstein, Sid Ramin, and Irwin Kostal. Bernstein scholar Nigel Simeone explains, 'Bernstein began greatly expanding the orchestral contribution to a Broadway show in *On the Town* (1944), but in *West Side Story* the orchestra takes a pivotal role, becoming an integral part of the drama.'[24] Despite this expanded labor for orchestral music, work on orchestrations could only begin late in the production process, given a score must be completed prior to its orchestration. Similarly, while Robbins demanded eight weeks of rehearsal and assistants for both him and co-choreographer Peter Gennaro, the dances had yet to be created and could certainly not be easily showcased in Lawrence's living room even had they been ready in April of 1957. The format of a backers' audition could never contain, much less showcase, the innovations in Laurents's spare libretto with its explicit stage directions; Bernstein's songs alongside sophisticated, dramatic orchestrations; and Robbins's and Gennaro's fusion of ballet and Latin rhythms. The failure of the fundraising attempts predicted the evolution that would occur decades later in how investors are introduced to musical theatre material whose development they might fund.

It is no wonder that the discouraging audition spurred Crawford's recusal from the production; it was impossible for the material to express its potential through this kind of demonstration. Additionally, she wanted more than to excite audiences with songs and dances telling a contemporary story. Envisioning a sociological document explaining why kids were the way they were, she regularly sent memos to the creative team demanding rewrites and, 'Faulting the book for not tracing the socieoeconomic history of the neighborhood where the play took place.' Her proposed solution was to delineate 'how middle-class Wasp had given way to immigrant Jews to poor Negroes to motley mix.'[25]

Contemplating both the costs – $300,000 was *not* a small fee for this producer – and the casting requirements, she decided to pull out. Her exit strategy baffled some on the creative team. She wrote long, inflammatory memos to Laurents and Robbins, criticizing one man to the other. To Laurents she suggested the characters were under-developed, and that he make more of how upward mobility causes change to neighborhood demographics – something playwright Lorraine Hansberry would explore almost two years after *West Side Story* premiered, in *A Raisin in the Sun* (1959). Crawford believed that '[w]hat is happening to kids seems to be one of our most urgent problems today and although we've picked these special kids their desires and conflicts should be representative of more.'[26] She pressed Laurents for greater detail and further development, declaring, for example, 'I don't think any of the characters should be supernumerary or "group." Each should be part of a gallery of vivid and interesting kids with real stories.'[27]

Laurents responded that night, noting the depressing and discouraging atmosphere to which Crawford was contributing and that he was 'not interested in adding extreme detail – They never characterized anybody and I am bored to death with them.'[28] One of Laurents's stage directions nevertheless reinforced Crawford's belief, describing the Jets in the first scene as, 'an anthology of what is called American'[29] and recognizing they were representative of more than the events in the musical. Laurents ultimately provided specific details about each character. 'There were to be no anonymous chorus boys and girls; they all had names,' Jowitt describes. 'All were advised to figure out who they were, their family background, their day-to-day lives.'[30] Robbins famously asked the Jet and Shark actors not to socialize with each other, and the creative team eventually accomplished much of what Crawford suggested.

Crawford had gone to the edge of disaster with *West Side Story*, as she believed producers ought to, but ultimately reneged on her *West Side Story* wager because her own circumstances prevented her from achieving her goals. She announced her withdrawal to the creative team at a meeting in her office. 'Conflicting testimonies muddy the waters of what happened next. Harsh words were exchanged,' Barranger explains.[31] Laurents wanted to hurt Crawford so called her 'an immoral woman' and left with his collaborators.[32] Sondheim does not remember Crawford's involvement with any fondness, observing, 'West Side Story also exposed me to another, less reliable, kind of collaborator: the producer.' Overlooking her track record with musicals, he calls her 'a lady with a distinguished record of producing plays by Clifford Odets and Tennessee Williams' but laments that she announced her departure from the project just two months before rehearsals were scheduled to begin.[33]

In his memoir Laurents tries to understand why Crawford sent separate memos to him and Robbins, thinking she should have known the collaborators would keep one another informed. 'Could it be that this good, this moral Christian New Englander was not above being devious?' he wondered, demonstrating his limited knowledge of Crawford, a Midwesterner though she attended Smith College in Massachusetts. Decades later, when his colleagues were still grumbling about Crawford's departure, Robbins hung on to the facts: 'My version of Cheryl's withdrawal is very simple: she couldn't raise the money.'[34] Crawford had written to Robbins months before her withdrawal confirming, 'I want a hit possibly more than any of you so I don't want to muck this up rashly,' reinforcing perhaps both her passion for the project and her financial precarity.[35]

What the West Side Story creative team didn't know at the time of Crawford's withdrawal was that she had been subpoenaed by the House Un-American Activities Committee (HUAC). Robbins had already appeared before the committee in 1953 and decided to name names, a decision many of his colleagues credited as motivated by his desire to protect his career and prevent any public revelation of his homosexuality. Crawford, also homosexual, 'felt vulnerable, dispirited, and betrayed by her government,' Barranger notes. 'Not knowing what her legal expenses would be, she had no stomach for the super-expensive show about rival street gangs.'[36] Crawford's lawyer obtained the list of her political activities compiled by FBI and HUAC, and Crawford called the list of letters, lectures, presentations, and sponsorships 'petty and ridiculous.'[37] While the producer had friends and colleagues who were political, she had prioritized her theatre work over any political activity. She requested and received a postponement due to her work on a new play, and the hearing was postponed indefinitely.

Regardless of the HUAC subpoena and lack of capital, Crawford's dedication to West Side Story in the year she developed the musical undoubtedly helped the creative team to clarify what the show was and was not doing. 'She was hardly your conventional commercial producer,' Engel and Kissel suggest. 'The reason that she was the logical producer for West Side Story was that she had devoted her enormously successful career to producing plays and musicals of merit,' from Lerner and Loewe's *Brigadoon* to Kurt Weill's *One Touch of Venus*. 'How many other producers might take on such a serious project?'[38] While Crawford's autobiography includes the chapter 'Musical Adventures' that begins with a clear statement of her enthusiasm for them – 'There's magic in a good musical'[39] – Crawford makes no mention of *West Side Story* anywhere in the book. Barranger explains that Crawford 'counted *West Side Story* among the soaring blunders in a career rich in highs and lows.'[40] Upon the publication of her autobiography, Crawford wrote in *The New York Times* about the shows she didn't produce and that final meeting with the creative team in her office. 'I will always remember their unbelieving, angry faces as they walked out. Only Jerry stayed to shake my hand. I told Roger I was certain they would work harder than ever to prove me wrong. They sure did.'[41]

Leaving Crawford's office in the spring of 1957, the creative team sought consolation at a hotel bar, and Laurents placed a phone call to Stevens, who was in London and reassured the creative team. Sondheim explains,

> Roger reaffirmed his faith in the show and told Arthur not to worry. But Roger was primarily a fund-raiser, not a producer, not someone who could make and effect executive decisions about casting and stage management and set and costume design, who could supervise the advertising and arrange the booking and cope with the unions – all the grubby chores a producer has to attend to, and attend to well. For all his good will and financial acumen, we still needed a producer and it would be difficult, if not impossible, to find one on short notice who was free, competent and willing to take a chance with a show as daring and idiosyncratic as *West Side Story*.[42]

Historian Karen Heath concurs with Sondheim and notes 'As a musical theatre producer, Stevens was hands off; he was not interested in seeking the limelight, and he preferred to work quietly behind the scenes.'[43] She suggests Stevens followed a pattern in his career: 'he was always the man who could be relied on to take a risk and find the money to put on a promising show.'[44] By 1954 Stevens had doubled his investment in the Empire State Building after just three years of ownership as the leader of a syndicate that had bought the building in 1951.[45]

Stevens had 'a unique system for raising money,' *The New York Times* reported a year after *West Side Story* opened.[46] 'He offers a "package" of several shows to a small group of wealthy investors,' who may not even know what shows are in the package, but who had already made money in another business thanks to Stevens.[47] 'They feel a sense of obligation,' Stevens noted in the article, and he emphasized none of his money came from auditions or readings.[48] When Crawford departed *West Side Story*, Stevens 'set about arranging financing with the support of several of his real estate associates, plus a substantial investment of his own. The backers became limited partners in the West Side Story Company set up by the show's producers, Robert E. Griffith and Harold Prince.'[49] Some assumed they would take a loss on their *West Side Story* investment, but predicted it would be worth it, ensuring their eligibility to invest in future Harold S. Prince and Robert E. Griffith productions – the competent producers who were the next to join the production.

Harold S. Prince and Robert E. Griffith: Trying Out and Selling Out

In his 1974 memoir, *Contradictions: Notes on Twenty-Six Years in the Theatre*, Prince confirms 'Stevens had financed the formative years of that project. When Miss Crawford bowed out, Stephen Sondheim brought us in.'[50] The day Crawford withdrew from the production, Sondheim happened to receive a phone call from his friend, Prince, who was in Boston for the tryout of his new musical, *New Girl in Town*. Sondheim patiently listened to Prince unload his worries about the new show, then Sondheim 'told him that *West Side Story* had just gone down the drain and that my life was over.'[51] Prince asked for a copy of the script to consider with his producing partner, Griffith. They were on board after a quick trip back to New York to listen to the *West Side Story* score. The producing team agreed to take it on but only once *New Girl in Town* had opened in New York. Crawford surrendered her rights to Prince and Griffiths, and with new full-time producers in place, Stevens retained the billing, 'By arrangement with Roger L. Stevens.'

Sondheim interpreted Prince and Griffith's commitment to a single project at a time as 'an indication of what good producers they were.'[52] What Sondheim overlooks is the seed he had planted a year earlier that played a significant role in securing Prince and Griffith. Sondheim and Prince had established a friendship several years prior and they regularly compared notes as each man progressed in his career in New York. Sondheim joined the *West Side Story* project as lyricist in 1955 and, at some point in 1956, shared Bernstein's score with his friend Prince, swearing him to secrecy. Elizabeth Wells explains, 'Prince had to pretend that he had never heard it before, since Bernstein did not want anyone to hear the music before the show went into production.'[53] Prince therefore had an advantage in deciding to rescue the new musical; having secretly fallen in love with the score months earlier, its melodies lingered in his ear, persuading him of their appeal. Primarily a producer of musical comedies, Prince was recruited to Bernstein's dramatic score and a musical tragedy. He may have concluded that the audience buying tickets to his production of *The Pajama Game* might be similarly convinced to attend a dramatic musical.

West Side Story was Prince and Griffith's first venture without their *Pajama Game* (1954) and *Damn Yankees* (1955) co-producer Frederick Brisson. They shared years of experience working as assistants and stage managers for producer–director George Abbott. Griffith began his career as an actor, then shifted into stage management in the hope that directing work might follow. Mentoring and working with Prince in Abbott's office, Griffith thought producing might be fun. Theatre scholar Michael Schwartz suggests Griffith was unlike the many flamboyant or explosive personalities involved in musical theatre. '[H]is extensive experience as a stage manager for legendary director George Abbott, his ability to save significant production costs, and his singularly calm demeanour' set Griffith apart and helped him to succeed.[54] He was twenty-two years Prince's senior, and a shy introvert to the young and energetic Prince, but 'the two men, working out of a small office in Rockefeller Center and backstage, became close collaborators and friends.'[55]

What Prince and Griffith offered *West Side Story* was a sense of urgency, as Sondheim recalls: 'When Hal and Bobby came in on it, we all felt we had to make quick decisions and do whatever was required of us. We got very excited. With Cheryl, for all the enthusiasm, there was this feeling that we might not get into rehearsal on time. Suddenly there was this deadline right around the corner, only eight weeks away.'[56] In August 1957, after years of collaborative creation between Laurents, Robbins, Bernstein, and Sondheim, *West Side Story* headed to Washington DC (see Figure 6.1). Stevens wrote to Robbins following the premiere to congratulate him, 'on what I think is the greatest choreographical and directorial job that has ever been my pleasure to witness in the theatre.' Stevens praised him for conceiving the musical and for his success with casting: 'To me the only gamble in this production has been the problem of picking young people of star quality who would give the play the kind of magnetism it needed. You have solved all the problems admirably.'[57] He closed by noting, 'the word of mouth around New York is terrific.'[58]

The rave reviews and strong box office start in DC boded well for the next tryout in Philadelphia, where *West Side Story* was welcomed with a photo spread in the *Philadelphia Inquirer* magazine. Given the succession

Figure 6.1 *West Side Story* in rehearsal: Robert E. Griffith (producer), Hal Prince (producer), Jerome Robbins (director/choreographer), Stephen Sondheim (lyrics), Leonard Bernstein (composer), Arthur Laurents (book), Gerald Freedman (directorial assistant), Sylvia Drulie (production associate), and Oliver Smith (set design) watching. (Photo by Martha Swope © The New York Public Library for the Performing Arts.)

of producers and fundraising challenges, a photo of Bernstein featured a somewhat ironic caption suggesting, 'His *West Side* music is more straightforward and commercial' than his commercial failure *Candide*.[59] A photograph of Griffith and Prince was also included, trumpeting their track record: 'As co-producers of *The Pajama Game, Damn Yankees*, and *New Girl in Town*, they have never had a flop and from their past musical hits have grossed more than $10 million.'[60] Washington and Philadelphia were described as 'smash tryouts' in *Time* magazine shortly after the musical opened in New York, where the advance sale was estimated at $700,000.[61]

Stevens hosted the opening night party in New York. In a telegram to Bernstein sent that day, Stevens wrote: 'Thanks for your graciousness in remembering the dim dark days when it looked like everything was off. My faith was simple because with so many remarkable tunes the production just had to work.'[62] Less than a week later, Oscar Hammerstein sent his best wishes to Stevens, congratulating him 'on your courage in making the play possible. This is truly a great way to start off a new season.'[63] It did not take long for the producers and creative team to turn their focus away from their earlier struggles and the risks they had taken, to the returns they could now anticipate. A month after the opening on Broadway, Sondheim wrote to Bernstein, who was on a conducting tour of Israel, to update him on the state of the production. After reporting on the physical and vocal health of the cast and summarizing magazine critics' responses to the musical, Sondheim noted the songs from the musical being recorded by Jill Corey, Rosemary Clooney, and Vera Lynn.[64] Beyond the immediate box office revenue, Sondheim recognized the longer-term income he and Bernstein could look forward to earning.

Domestic and International Tours

Beyond Broadway revenue and covers of the musical's songs, national and international tours were also profitable. *West Side Story* toured to the United Kingdom with an all-American cast, opening in Manchester then London in late 1958. An American cast, including a young Michael Bennett as Baby John, also toured Europe. The national tour launched in Denver on 1 July 1959, four days after the Broadway production closed. Given the importance of Bernstein's music and its orchestration, *Variety* reported on plans for seven musicians to tour with the show and twenty additional musicians to be hired locally. The conductor and seven-member pit 'will be flown ahead of the company on each jump for longer rehearsals with the pickup musicians than would be permitted if they travelled by rail.'[65]

After a two-week tryout in Denver, the tour moved to Los Angeles for five weeks, San Francisco for six weeks, then on to Chicago where an extended run was anticipated. Undoubtedly aware of *The Music Man*'s eight-month head start in Chicago, Prince and Griffith splashed out on a colour ad in the Sunday edition of the *Chicago Tribune,* to announce the opening of the Erlanger Theatre box office.[66] Robbins visited Chicago to rehearse the touring company before the opening. Despite the advertising push and the director's check-up visit, *West Side Story* managed just a fraction of *Music Man*'s run in Chicago, running fourteen weeks. Six more stops throughout the Midwest and East coast in 1960 brought the tour back to Broadway where it ran through to the end of the year.

The groundbreaking musical's run of 732 performances, with a return engagement of 249 performances following a national tour, did not compare with one of the greatest commercial hits of the late 1950s, *My Fair Lady*, which had a record-breaking run of 2,717 performances. In hindsight Prince suggests he and his producing partners made a mistake with their treatment of the musical while it was still on Broadway. 'We calculated we had run out of our audience, so in a last-ditch effort to keep going until the road tour started, we lowered prices and initiated a two-for-the-price-of-one policy. Immediately we sold out; we had run out of one audience and *into* another. Ticket prices were too high even then for a substantial segment of our audience which indeed is interested in going to the theatre.'[67] Ticket pricing, he believes, must demonstrate an awareness of a show's different audiences in order to sustain longer runs, and the producing team had provided limited opportunities for lower income ticket buyers to experience *West Side Story* on stage prior to the more affordable film adaptation.

Conclusion

Reviewing *One Touch of Venus*, critic Ward Morehouse might have predicted Crawford's impact on *West Side Story*, more than a decade later: 'Cheryl Crawford has performed Broadway a service in bringing along a musical show that breaks sharply away from pattern and accepted routine.'[68] The backers' auditions Crawford and her collaborators had suffered were being scrutinized just a year after *West Side Story* opened, another routine the industry could break from. It is impossible for non-professionals to judge a musical's prospects from such auditions, journalist Murray Schumach suggested, and, 'the vast proportion of those who attend auditions have no intention of investing.'[69] Prince and Griffith produced *West Side Story* after producing three consecutive hit shows; Crawford's development of the musical had been preceded by multiple flop plays, and five years had passed since her modest success with the musical *Paint Your Wagon* (1951). Success does not always breed success in musical theatre, but Griffith and Prince's wealth from their trio of prior hits[70] insulated them against failure and attracted future investors.

Robbins, Laurents, and Sondheim reunited to work on *Gypsy* (1959), produced by David Merrick and Leland Hayward. Crawford and Robbins also reunited, when she recruited him to direct and co-produce with her the short-lived Broadway premiere of Brecht's *Mother Courage and Her Children* (1963). *Jennie* (1963), a vehicle for Mary Martin, and Tom Jones and Harvey Schmidt's *Celebration* in 1969, were Crawford's final musicals.

Despite their brief runs, she admitted in her autobiography, 'Down deep I am still addicted.'[71] Stevens continued to dabble in musical theatre producing, rescuing Bernstein in 1976 to produce *1600 Pennsylvania Avenue*. He hosted the musical's Washington tryout, as Chairman of the Kennedy Center, hoping for the hit the floundering Center needed, but the new musical was a flop. A year later, 'The nostalgia-driven *Annie* (1977) served to redeem both Stevens's reputation and the Kennedy Center's finances,' Heath explains.[72]

Griffith and Prince produced *Fiorello!* (1959) and *Tenderloin* (1960), followed by a flop play, *A Call on Kuprin* (1961). Griffith died suddenly of a heart attack two weeks after the play opened. Prince earned his first directing credit the following year on *A Family Affair* and gradually added more directing to his producing agenda. He partnered with Robbins again, producing *Fiddler on the Roof* (1964), and sustained a long, productive relationship directing and/or producing many of Sondheim's musicals. Speaking to industry stakeholders at a conference organized by Broadway Across America in 2016, Prince insisted on a division between investors and producers and emphasized the impact of careful budgeting and the subsidy from 175 investors on his hit shows. He reported that *West Side Story* had to date returned 1,521 percent on its original investment.[73]

Notes

1. 'Landmark Symposium: *West Side Story*,' *The Dramatists Guild Quarterly*, 22, no. 3 (1985), 11.
2. 'Landmark Symposium,' 11.
3. Stephen Sondheim, Letter to Leonard Bernstein, 23 October 1957, Box 52, Leonard Bernstein Collection, Music Division, Library of Congress, Washington, DC; Arthur Laurents, Letter to Roger Stevens, 10 October 1957, Box 43, Folder 2. Roger L. Stevens papers, 1863–2002, Music Division, Library of Congress, Washington, DC.
4. Quoted in Deborah Jowitt, *Jerome Robbins: His Life, His Theater, His Dance* (New York: Simon and Schuster, 2004), 272.
5. Cheryl Crawford, *One Naked Individual: My Fifty Years in the Theatre* (Indianapolis: Bobbs-Merrill, 1977), 6–9.
6. Crawford, *One Naked Individual*, 28.
7. Crawford, *One Naked Individual*, 4.
8. Crawford, *One Naked Individual*, 116–17.
9. Lehman Engel and Howard Kissel, *Words with Music: Creating the Broadway Musical Libretto* (New York: Applause Theatre & Cinema Books, 2006), 365.

10. Milly S. Barranger, *A Gambler's Instinct: The Story of Broadway Producer Cheryl Crawford* (Carbondale, IL: Southern Illinois University Press, 2010), xii.

11. Cheryl Crawford, Letter to Jerome Robbins, Arthur Laurents and Leonard Bernstein (Roger Stevens cc'd), 15 June 1956, Box 43, Folder 2. Roger L. Stevens papers, 1863–2002, Music Division, Library of Congress, Washington, DC.

12. Edwin Lester, Letter to Roger L. Stevens, 26 December 1956 Box 43, Folder 2. Roger L. Stevens papers, 1863–2002, Music Division, Library of Congress, Washington, DC.

13. Cheryl Crawford, Letter to Jerome Robbins, 3 January 1957, Box 43, Folder 2. Roger L. Stevens papers, 1863–2002, Music Division, Library of Congress, Washington, DC.

14. Crawford, Letter to Jerome Robbins, 3 January 1957.

15. Quoted in Jowitt, *Jerome Robbins*, 275.

16. Arthur Laurents, *Original Story by Arthur Laurents: A Memoir of Broadway and Hollywood* (New York: Knopf, 2000), 350.

17. Cheryl Crawford, 'Who Would Want to See a Play about an Unhappy Salesman?' *The New York Times*, 20 March 1977, 73.

18. Cheryl Crawford, Letter to Roger L. Stevens, 13 March 1957, Box 43, Folder 2. Roger L. Stevens papers, 1863–2002, Music Division, Library of Congress, Washington, DC.

19. Crawford, 'Who Would Want?', 73.

20. Barranger, *A Gambler's Instinct*, 172.

21. Cheryl Crawford, 'Who Would Want?', 73.

22. Murray Schumach, 'Talent Dragnet,' *The New York Times*, 22 September 1957, 135.

23. Jowitt, *Jerome Robbins*, 269.

24. Nigel Simeone, *Leonard Bernstein*: West Side Story (Farnham, Surrey: Ashgate, 2009), 84.

25. Laurents, *Original Story*, 328.

26. Cheryl Crawford, Letter to Arthur Laurents, 11 April, Box 43, Folder 2. Roger L. Stevens papers, 1863–2002, Music Division, Library of Congress, Washington, DC.

27. Crawford, Letter to Arthur Laurents, 11 April 1957.

28. Arthur Laurents, Letter to Cheryl Crawford, 11 April 1957, Box 43, Folder 2. Roger L. Stevens papers, 1863–2002, Music Division, Library of Congress, Washington, DC.

29. Arthur Laurents and Stephen Sondheim, *West Side Story* (London: Heinemann, 1972), 11.

30. Jowitt, *Jerome Robbins*, 275.

31. Barranger, *A Gambler's Instinct*, 172.

32. Laurents, *Original Story*, 328.

33. Stephen Sondheim, *Finishing the Hat: Collected Lyrics (1954–1981)* (New York: Knopf, 2010), 29.

34. Quoted in 'Landmark Symposium,' 17.

35. Crawford, Letter to Jerome Robbins, 3 January 1957.

36. Barranger, *A Gambler's Instinct*, 172.

37. Crawford, *One Naked Individual*, 255.

38. Engel and Kissel, *Words with Music*, 365.

39. Crawford, *One Naked Individual*, 163.

40. Barranger, *A Gambler's Instinct*, 172.

41. Cheryl Crawford, 'Who Would Want?', 73.

42. Sondheim, *Finishing the Hat*, 29.

43. Karen Patricia Heath, 'Roger L. Stevens: The Great Facilitator,' *The Palgrave Handbook of Musical Theatre Producers*, ed. Laura MacDonald and William A. Everett (New York: Palgrave Macmillan, 2017), 207.

44. Heath, 'Roger L. Stevens,' 208.

45. Eric Pace, 'Roger L. Stevens, Real Estate Magnate, Producer and Fund-Raiser, Is Dead at 87,' *The New York Times*, 4 February 1998, 9.

46. Murray Schumach, 'Again the Angels Flutter Over Broadway,' *The New York Times*, 28 September 1958, 28.

47. Schumach, 'Again the Angels,' 28.

48. Quoted in Schumach, 'Again the Angels,' 28.

49. Heath, 'Roger L. Stevens,' 209.

50. Hal Prince, *Contradictions: Notes on Twenty-Six Years in the Theatre* (New York: Dodd, Mead & Company, 1974), 29.

51. Sondheim, *Finishing the Hat*, 30.

52. Sondheim, *Finishing the Hat*, 30.

53. Elizabeth A. Wells, West Side Story: *Cultural Perspectives on an American Musical* (Lanham, MD: Scarecrow Press, 2010), 37.

54. Michael Schwartz, 'The Nice One: The Productions of Robert Griffith,' *The Palgrave Handbook of Musical Theatre Producers*, 191.

55. Carol Ilson, *Harold Prince: From* Pajama Game *to* Phantom of the Opera (Ann Arbor, MI: UMI Research Press, 1989), 8.

56. Quoted in 'Landmark Symposium: West Side Story,' 19.

57. Roger Stevens, Letter to Jerome Robbins, 22 August 1957, Box 43, Folder 2. Roger L. Stevens papers, 1863–2002, Music Division, Library of Congress, Washington, DC.

58. Roger Stevens, Letter to Jerome Robbins, 22 August 1957.

59. 'Rough Time for All in a Tough Musical,' *Philadelphia Inquirer Magazine*, 1 September 1957, 106–08. Museum of the City of New York, *West Side Story* papers, 108.

60. 'Rough Time for All in a Tough Musical,' *Philadelphia Inquirer Magazine*, 108.

61. 'New Musical in Manhattan,' *Time*, October 1957, 48–49. Museum of the City of New York, *West Side Story* papers, 48.

62. Leonard Bernstein and Nigel Simeone, *The Leonard Bernstein Letters* (New Haven: Yale University Press, 2013), 383.

63. Oscar Hammerstein II, Letter to Roger L. Stevens, 1 October 1957, Box 43, Folder 2. Roger L. Stevens papers, 1863–2002, Music Division, Library of Congress, Washington, DC.

64. Stephen Sondheim, Letter to Leonard Bernstein, 23 October 1957.

65. '"Story" a Heavy Tourer; Company Tooters Will Plane to Rehearsals,' *Variety*, 215, no. 2 (June 1959), 71.

66. '"Story" Resumes Tour, "Music" Will Follow,' *Variety*, 217, no. 2 (December 1959), 69.

67. Prince, *Contradictions*, 39–40.

68. Quoted in Barranger, *A Gambler's Instinct*, 78.

69. Schumach, 'Again the Angels,' 28.

70. '"Pajama"–"Yankees" $2,000,000 Profit,' *Variety*, 203, no. 5 (July 1956), 1, 63.

71. Crawford, *One Naked Individual*, 182.

72. Heath, 'Roger L. Stevens,' 211.

73. Hal Prince, 'Broadway Needs Producers, Not Just Investors,' *American Theatre*, 25 October 2016, www.americantheatre.org/2016/10/25/broadway-needs-producers-not-just-investors/ (accessed 26 September 2022).

PART II

The Work Itself and Its Context

7 | The Score

Creation, Orchestration, Unification, and Analysis

PAUL R. LAIRD

No Broadway team setting out to write songs and music for a show – not even Leonard Bernstein and Stephen Sondheim – can decide to compose an iconic score. Only posterity accords such status, when the music and lyrics remain ubiquitous for later generations. Numerous scores from the 1940s through the 1960s are iconic – *Oklahoma!* (1943), *South Pacific* (1949), *Guys and Dolls* (1950), *My Fair Lady* (1956), *The Sound of Music* (1959), and *Fiddler on the Roof* (1964), to name several – their popularity driven by successful original cast albums, film versions, and songs that have remained well known outside of productions. Certainly, these three conditions exist for *West Side Story*. The original cast album is still famous, what Nigel Simeone calls ' . . . the most enduring representation of the show in its "original" form . . . '[1] After the musical played on Broadway for over two years – interrupted by a national tour – it was seen as a memorable, artistic show with ground-breaking use of dance and a score that featured unusually effective musico-dramatic unification. The guarantee of its future came from the first, spectacularly successful film (United Artists, 1961), which won ten Academy Awards and grossed $44,061,777 worldwide.[2] Several songs in the score are still popular, especially 'Maria', 'Tonight', and 'Somewhere'. These three factors, plus the work's effective modern retelling of *Romeo and Juliet* and its striking commentary on racism in the United States, have helped keep the work current. *West Side Story* artistically shines a bright light on some serious problems in the United States and calls upon its citizens to be better versions of themselves, a challenge that retains as much resonance today as it had in 1957. The property's appeal has been enhanced by Steven Spielberg's 2021 film version, which features an intelligent, sensitive rendering of the music.

In this chapter we focus on the score – music and lyrics – that lies at any show's heart, but in *West Side Story* the importance of dance raises music to an even more significant position. Unlike the case in most Broadway scores, Bernstein the songwriter wrote the dance music. Bernstein's hand in *West Side Story* also included the orchestration, in which he supervised the efforts of Sid Ramin and Irwin Kostal. Then, as if the composer were not already sufficiently encumbered, Bernstein also played a major role in teaching the challenging music to the cast. With Stephen Sondheim, he formed a memorable song-writing team that combined Bernstein's melodic and rhythmic invention with Sondheim's mastery of language and rhyme. The lyricist aired his dislike for some of his work for *West Side Story*, but he did not dampen the world's enthusiasm for the show's score.[3] This chapter approaches *West Side Story*'s score from four different angles: its creation, orchestrations, Bernstein's efforts to unify the work through musical associations, and description of individual numbers. Important sources on the show's score include books by Nigel Simeone, Elizabeth A. Wells, and chapters in books by Joseph P. Swain, Geoffrey Block, Katherine Baber, Helen Smith, and Paul R. Laird.[4]

Creation

Seeds for the *West Side Story* score were sown in Bernstein's earlier collaborations with Jerome Robbins. In 1943–44, they created the sparkling ballet *Fancy Free*, a humorous look at three sailors on leave in New York City. Its similarity with *West Side Story* comes in the use of various social dances in both choreography and music along with jazz and blues references, but *Fancy Free* includes only swing references while Bernstein accessed later jazz styles in *West Side Story*.[5] The two collaborators joined forces with Betty Comden, Adolph Green, and George Abbott to develop the Broadway musical *On the Town*, which opened on 28 December 1944 and, like *Fancy Free*, demonstrated how effectively the artists could reference popular culture in wartime America.[6] Robbins and Bernstein collaborated on the ballet *Facsimile* in 1947, a serious, introspective work that did not land with audiences, who were probably hoping for a repeat of *Fancy Free*'s high spirits. In subsequent years, Robbins choreographed Bernstein's Symphony No. 2, *The Age of Anxiety* (1950), and provided uncredited choreography to his music in *Wonderful Town* (1953).[7] By the time they collaborated on *West Side Story*, Bernstein understood intuitively what Robbins wanted from music to inspire movements and the choreographer had a deep knowledge of Bernstein's musical style and affective range.

It is not only the works that Bernstein wrote for choreography by Robbins that foreshadow his music for *West Side Story*. His ability to compose a melody that would fit into a score for musical theatre dates back to his Symphony No. 1, *Jeremiah* (1942), heard in the second movement, 'Profanation'. Beginning seven measures before rehearsal 20, one hears a lyrical, compelling theme in mixed meters. With appropriate text, the melody would fit into a scene featuring Tony and Maria. Bernstein's Symphony No. 2, *The Age of Anxiety* (1949), foreshadows *West Side Story* in the 'Masque' with aspects of bop in both solo piano and orchestra, every bit as evocative as the composer's references to cool jazz and bop in 'Cool'. The gritty score to *West Side Story* includes dissonant harmonies, syncopations, and cross-rhythms, such as in the 'Prologue' and 'The Rumble', similar to what one hears often in Bernstein's film score to *On the Waterfront*. This music effectively underscores urban life in the 1950s, an association described in detail by Anthony Bushard.[8] The film also includes music for lovers that resembles 'Tonight' and 'Somewhere'. Bernstein's use of Latin musical tropes in *West Side Story* also appeared earlier in his output, including the 'Danzon' [*sic*] variation from *Fancy Free* and *Conchtown* (1941), a sketch for a ballet that became the song 'America'.

Robbins conceived the idea of updating *Romeo and Juliet* in January 1949 and interested Bernstein and playwright Arthur Laurents in the project.[9] Laurents sent the composer a draft of four scenes for *East Side Story* (focusing on Jewish/Catholic tensions) in May, but work stalled and they abandoned the project for six years. In 1955, Laurents and Bernstein pitched another idea to Robbins, but he held out for an adaptation of *Romeo and Juliet*.[10] In August 1955, the two writers realized that the show's plot could involve youth gangs in New York City, an idea that Robbins liked, and progress resumed. Bernstein planned to write the lyrics, but with simultaneous work on *Candide*, guest conducting, and his television shows for *Omnibus*, he needed assistance. Laurents had a young friend, Stephen Sondheim, whom he suggested as a possible lyricist. Bernstein and Sondheim hit it off, sharing their love for difficult word puzzles when they reached a creative impasse. Sondheim wanted to write music, not just lyrics, but his mentor Oscar Hammerstein II and agent Flora Roberts advised him to work with such Broadway successes as Bernstein, Laurents, and Robbins.[11] Sondheim and Bernstein began as co-lyricists; the composer later allowed his collaborator full credit. Extensive work began between the four men about November 1955 and lasted until March 1956, when Bernstein concentrated on *Candide* before it opened in December. Progress ceased on *West Side Story* for about a year, but most of the Act 1 music had been written.

Candide closed in February 1957, the month that the collaborators resumed work on *West Side Story*. Some of Bernstein's music travelled between the two scores; for example, the material that became the songs 'One Hand, One Heart' and 'Gee, Officer Krupke' started in *Candide*.[12]

Work on music for Act 2 continued into the summer. Auditions occurred in the spring and rehearsals lasted from June to August; Simeone shows the score's state before rehearsals with a list of numbers from perhaps May.[13] The score changed considerably during rehearsals, but the music was pretty much set before they opened in Washington, DC on 19 August. Bernstein and Sondheim wrote their last song, 'Something's Coming', in early August, when the collaborators determined that Tony needed a song that would define his character.[14]

Robbins allowed that the romantic leads might be singers but insisted that the remainder of the cast be dancers first.[15] Bernstein did not spare the performers with his score, which was more difficult to sing than the typical Broadway fare of the 1950s. Bernstein (and perhaps Sondheim)[16] helped alleviate the challenge by aiding in teaching the cast material like the vocal intricacies of the 'Tonight' (Quintet) and 'A Boy Like That'. Carol Lawrence, who played Maria, reports that Bernstein ' ... would work with each of us on an individual basis for hours ... ',[17] and Chita Rivera, the original Anita, has also recalled working personally with Bernstein on 'A Boy Like That': ' ... he taught me *how* to hit those notes ... '[18] The composer did this while continuing to provide needed revisions and new music, and while working on the show's orchestrations with Sid Ramin and Irwin Kostal.

Orchestrations

Bernstein asked his friend Sid Ramin to help him with the show's orchestrations on 20 June 1957.[19] Bernstein was five months older; they had met in their Boston neighbourhood at about age 12, bonding over their love for music. In their teens, Ramin for a time studied piano and music theory with Bernstein, and later music theory, especially related to jazz, starting in March 1937 when Bernstein was a student at Harvard.[20] Ramin spent World War II in the US Army scoring music for instrumental ensembles and then entered the field after the war, becoming a leading arranger for radio, television, and recordings. He orchestrated occasionally for theatre when called into projects by friends, assisting for example with Bernstein's score for *Wonderful Town* (1953), pulled in by Robert 'Red' Ginzler, his collaborator in arranging music for Milton Berle's television show. Ramin was wary of Bernstein's invitation to work on *West Side Story* because he doubted that he could adequately cope with Bernstein's classical influences. Ramin asked Irwin Kostal if he might be interested in joining the team.

Kostal was similarly a successful arranger of commercial music, but he had also studied classical scores. Bernstein welcomed Kostal, and the three met for the first time on 26 June. The credit line for the show reads 'Orchestrations by Leonard Bernstein with Sid Ramin and Irwin Kostal', a process executed through what Ramin described as 'pre-orchestration' and 'post-orchestration' meetings. For each number that Bernstein wrote, the three men looked through the piano/vocal score, discussing possibilities and noting places where he provided instrumental suggestions. Ramin has called the scores and instructions that the composer provided them ' ... the most complete and detailed he ever worked with in the theater'.[21] Ramin and Kostal would then prepare an orchestrated draft for Bernstein, who ' ... literally proofread what we wrote'.[22] Bernstein reviewed their work in detail, as may be seen in numerous manuscripts in the Sid Ramin Papers at the Columbia University Archive. All of the scores are written in the hands of Ramin and Kostal and most include Bernstein's changes in red and green pencil. Two drafts that are especially revelatory are of 'America' and 'The Rumble', manuscripts that are smaller than most of the scores and appear to be earlier versions with copious marking in the composer's hand.[23] Kostal remembered Bernstein's great interest in the process: 'He took keen delight in his own creativity and jumped for joy whenever Sid or I added a little originality of our own. He sometimes would look at one of our scores and say, "Who said orchestration couldn't be creative?"'[24]

One of the most important aspects of orchestrating for a show is deciding what instruments to use. Bernstein's contract for *West Side Story* stated that there would be twenty-six to thirty musicians; the final number was twenty-eight.[25] Extant documentation shows Bernstein trying out various possibilities of twenty-eight instrumentalists; the final configuration included: a wide palette of reed sounds with the unusual provision for bassoon only in the fifth reed book, played by Bernstein's friend Sanford Sharoff (a friend from their student days at Curtis); seven brass instruments for a score full of jazz references and loud, violent moments in the dances; parts for two percussionists, one handling the trap set and the other playing a plethora of other instruments, including numerous Latin sounds; keyboard; guitarist; and a string section without violas.[26]

In a musical like *West Side Story*, where the goal was an organic whole in service of story and characterization, the orchestration must contribute to that process. There are three basic soundscapes: (1) the Jets, based on various types of modern jazz and irregular rhythms and dissonances of twentieth-century concert music, often heard in brass, saxophones, and appropriate percussion; (2) the Sharks with various types of Latin music, dominated by winds and appropriate percussion instruments; and (3) Tony and Maria with rich use of strings, woodwinds for colour, and muted brass. These soundscapes pervade songs and dances associated with these characters, as may be seen in this brief review of the score. The 'Prologue' offers the Jets soundscape with prominent use of saxophones, brass, double bass, piano, and sinister sounds from pitched drums. The 'Jet Song' features similar accompaniment, but 'Something's Coming' carries a more subtle effect. In this, Tony's 'I Want' song, one hears an approximation of a big band but more use of strings, a combination of the first and third soundscapes. An example of specific word-painting by the orchestra occurs under the text 'The air is humming ... ' (OCR57, track 2, 1'56"), accompanied by tremolo in the first four violin parts and harmonics in the other three. The 'Dance at the Gym' includes a contrast of soundscapes: the first in the opening 'Blues' to accompany the Jets dancing, the second dominating the 'Mambo' and the gentle 'Cha-Cha'. The 'Meeting Scene', 'Maria', and 'Balcony Scene' mostly evoke the third soundscape, but perhaps because Tony's lover is Hispanic, Bernstein also introduced elements of Latin music: for example, the *tresillo* rhythm in 'Maria' played by bassoon, electric guitar, and string bass; and the pulsating eighth notes of a beguine rhythm in strings and woodwinds in 'Tonight'. 'America' offers the Latin soundscape with appropriate percussion. The orchestra reacts to such lines as 'tropical breezes' (OCR57, track 6, 0'26") and 'tropic diseases' (0'45") and provides sarcastic laughter supporting Anita in staccato eighth notes in two flutes, B-flat clarinet, bassoon, all of the brass, trap set, and piano (1'42"). 'Cool', marked 'Solid and boppy', is in the Jets soundscape with muted brass, restrained use of woodwinds, vibraphone, and trap set when imitating cool jazz and more of a bop big band in the aggressive moments. 'One Hand, One Heart' returns to the soundscape intended for the lovers with touching use of the orchestra in the underscoring. Orchestration in the 'Tonight' (Quintet) includes material from all three soundscapes describing various characters as they sing. For example, the music for the gangs constitutes a complex march accompanied by brief fanfare interjections in the brass, a bass line in 3/4 in the low strings, and staccato eighth notes in woodwind and upper strings. Just before Anita enters at 1'07", ascending lip smears in alto and tenor saxophone underscore her anticipation of a romantic rendezvous with Bernardo. When Tony at 1'25" begins his solo verse of 'Tonight', aspects of the accompaniment are reminiscent of what one hears in the earlier 'Balcony Scene', but the pulsating rhythm played in several instruments is different, built instead from syncopations and off-beats. 'The Rumble', which concludes Act 1, returns to the violence of the gang world with a harshness that is striking in a Broadway musical and pushes the pit orchestra to its limits. Here Bernstein approaches some of the most violent music that he ever wrote, like the 'Din-Torah' from Symphony No. 3, *Kaddish*, and shocking moments from *On the Waterfront*.

'I Feel Pretty' opens Act 2 with striking contrast to 'The Rumble'. Strings and high woodwinds carry a heavy load here, with trumpets for emphasis and some Iberian/flamenco sounds: Spanish guitar, castanets, tambourine, and onstage clapping. The 'Ballet Sequence' includes 'Somewhere', in which the accompaniment returns to the third soundscape, but the segment also draws from 'Maria', the 'Cha-Cha', 'Prologue', and 'The Rumble', referencing other soundscapes. Bernstein placed 'Gee, Officer Krupke' in a unique soundscape for the show, identified by the rubric 'Fast, vaudeville style'. The song's accompaniment includes an oom-pah pattern in strings, piano, and percussion with the vocal melody sometimes doubled and harmonized in thirds and punctuated by moments of full orchestra and slapstick effects. The final song is the double number 'A Boy Like That/I Have a Love', another collision between soundscapes. Anita has spent the show surrounded with Latin music, but as she tears into Maria the music is reminiscent of 'The Rumble' with similar dissonance and rhythmic irregularity. The orchestration offers deep sonorities: three bass clarinets, bassoon, seven muted brass instruments growling low in their ranges, and *marcato* strings. A distinctive moment occurs in the song's B section as various instruments double Anita's vocal line – bassoon, and later flute, violin, and cello – driving her to the climax of her line on the words 'heart' and 'smart' (OCR57, track 14, 0'40"-0'42"). When Maria interrupts Anita at 1'09", the soprano is doubled by flute and three violins – not unlike her typical soundscape – but Anita's accompaniment with lighter scoring continues as they sing in counterpoint. The heavier scoring returns for a moment just before 1'47" as Maria stops her friend with the words 'You should know better … ' The accompaniment of 'I Have a Love' is similar to what sounds in Maria's solo sections of the 'Balcony Scene', pulsating with restrained syncopations or long chords in woodwinds and strings or doubling the melody. Instruments state snippets of her melody during long notes at the ends of phrases, like horn 1 at 0'28" (OCR57, track 15). The orchestra effectively supports the number's climax and Maria's final duet with Anita. The 'Taunting Scene' resides within Anita's usual soundscape based on Latin music. The show's finale is a lightly scored version of the close of the 'Ballet Sequence', a restrained close for a show where the orchestra often provides considerable dramatic punch.

Musico-Dramatic Unification in the Score

The notion of a musical idea returning to underline a textual or dramatic association when words have been set by a composer is a venerable practice. It was an important part of Renaissance madrigals and motets and continued throughout the Baroque, assuming a structural significance in nineteenth-century opera in Wagner's systematic use of leitmotifs, which made the orchestra a powerful force in plot development. Broadway composers occasionally used such unifying devices in their scores in the first half of the twentieth century. Geoffrey Block, for example, has described Jerome Kern's use of the perfect fourth to describe the Mississippi River and tie together a number of the songs in *Show Boat* (1927).[27] Reprises of songs at dramatically appropriate moments were common, but greater concern for systematic manipulation of musical motives was a rare feature in Broadway musicals before *West Side Story*, even in the scores by Rodgers and Hammerstein, writers lauded for their level of integration between music and plot. Jim Lovensheimer, for example, has demonstrated musical association between the music for Emile de Becque and Nellie Forbush in *South Pacific*, but the association forms little more than an interesting sidelight to the score as a whole, certainly not as prominent as some of the repeated motives in *West Side Story*.[28] Kurt Weill, however, coming from a conservatory-trained background, tended to use leitmotifs in his Broadway works, such as *Johnny Johnson* (1936) and *Lady in the Dark* (1941).[29]

Bernstein's Broadway scores always included efforts at musico-dramatic unification. Jerome Robbins remembers the composer's disappointment when 'Gabey's Coming' was cut from *On the Town* because he had made material from that song prominent in the score, as has been demonstrated by Helen Smith.[30] She has also shown the prominence of the perfect fifth and fourth in *Wonderful Town* in the songs 'A Little Bit in Love', 'A Quiet Girl', 'Conversation Piece', 'Conquering the City', and 'What a Waste'.[31] The show also features motivic repetitions at dramatically important moments, such as music from 'Ohio' in the introduction to 'What a Waste' when Baker sings 'Why did you ever leave Ohio?' Smith and others have made similar points about *Trouble in Tahiti* and *Candide*. Bernstein tended to make comparable efforts in his concert music; indeed, Jack Gottlieb, in the first extended study of Bernstein's musical style, stated: ' . . . it can be said that he actually composes with intervals as his main source materials'.[32] Given these factors, it is strange that Bernstein once stated, concerning his apparently careful efforts to unify the score of *West Side Story*, 'I didn't do all this on purpose.'[33]

Is this possible? Simeone states: ' . . . this apparent motivic or intervallic consistency [in *West Side Story*] was never a planned decision on Bernstein's part and it seems simply to have evolved as one of the work's defining musical characteristics'.[34] The author cites several pieces of evidence: the 'haphazard way' that Broadway scores tend to be assembled, a reminiscence from Irwin Kostal about how Bernstein discovered the repeated intervals and motives during a rehearsal break, Ramin's confirmation of this anecdote, and Stephen Sondheim's statement that he pointed out to the composer the many tritones he used in the songs.[35] These conversations all came after the vast majority of the score had been written. In what Simeone describes as a later document,[36] Bernstein jotted down nine leitmotifs from *West Side Story* (Library of Congress 1079/19; see Example 7.1), perhaps proof for himself of these unifying elements. (Of the nine motives Bernstein provides, some are repeated in the score more than others, as will be shown below.) Simeone might be correct that Bernstein did not plan the recurring motives in the score, but it is tempting to suggest that the composer at some earlier point knew what he was doing. As noted above, this is how the man worked. All of his musicals were written in the same piecemeal way with his collaborators: songs and dances composed, revised, sometimes replaced, and then perhaps re-inserted elsewhere in the score. However, each of the shows demonstrates some sense of musico-dramatic unity. It would not be surprising if Bernstein at some point realized that he was using the tritone prominently in *West Side Story*, inspiring him to continue. Maybe he was surprised to note the extent of his motivic unification when speaking to Kostal and Ramin at that rehearsal, but would a musician like Bernstein have missed the prominence of the tritone in the openings of both 'Maria' and 'Cool'? Geoffrey Block simply ignores Bernstein's suggestion that he didn't intend the score's sense of unity and notes that the first songs that Bernstein drafted were 'Maria' and 'Somewhere', both featuring prominent motives in the score.[37]

The tritone is ubiquitous, appearing in the opening phrases of 'Maria', 'Blues', 'Cha-Cha', 'Cool', 'Something's Coming', and in the motive that Jack Gottlieb compares to a shofar call, the rising perfect fourth followed by the tritone heard often in the 'Prologue', 'The Rumble', and elsewhere. (This motive at one point carried the text 'This turf is ours!') The tritone makes many other appearances, from the clearly significant such as when F♯ sounds against the C major chord at the show's end, to tiny moments such as when one hears a tritone between the voice and bass line in the vamps that open each verse of 'Gee, Officer Krupke'. The tritone seems to be related to gang violence and the volcanic love that Tony and Maria

Example 7.1 Page of leitmotifs for *West Side Story* that Bernstein wrote at some point, including: (1) the 'shofar call' that sounds often in 'Prologue' and 'The Rumble' and sometimes opens the show; (2) first melodic motive in the 'Prologue', which also appears in B section of the 'Jet Song'; (3) rhythmic diminution of (2) heard in 'Prologue' and 'The Rumble'; (4) opening of 'Maria' with tritone ('Maria' motive) as the first interval; (5) opening of 'Cool', also with tritone as first interval; (6) opening of verse of 'Tonight' from the 'Balcony Scene'; (7) opening of chorus of 'Tonight'; (8) bass ostinato from 'Cha-Cha'; and (9) opening ostinato from 'Something's Coming'. (Library of Congress, Leonard Bernstein Collection, 1079/19. Typeset version produced by Adrian Hartsough.)

share. The perfect fourth, besides opening the 'shofar call', also appears prominently in the opening of 'Something's Coming', 'Tonight' – both the 'Balcony Scene' (see Example 7.2) and 'Tonight' (Quintet) – 'America', and

Example 7.2 'Balcony Scene', mm. 51–54, with opening ascending perfect fourth in the melody and beguine rhythms in eighth notes of the right hand

Example 7.3 'Ballet Sequence', mm. 86–89, 'Somewhere', with opening ascending minor seventh in melody and various accompanimental voices

the 'Taunting Scene'.[38] Another interval that plays a significant role is the evocative minor seventh that opens 'Somewhere' (see Example 7.3), which also helps close the 'Balcony Scene' (foreshadowing the 'Ballet Sequence'), and 'Somewhere' recurs in the final scene. The ascending minor seventh is also heard in the 'Cool' fugue subject and on the words '*I love* him' in 'I Have a Love'. Another recurring element is the short–long rhythmic pattern that sets the title word in 'Somewhere'. Short–long rhythms, with the first note of various lengths, pervade the 'Ballet Sequence' (see Example 7.4) and elsewhere, for example often heard on the word 'pretty' in 'I Feel Pretty'. Joseph P. Swain notes that hemiola effects recur in the score, including in the 'Prologue', 'Jet Song', 'Something's Coming', 'America', and the 'Taunting Music'.[39]

Melodic and rhythmic motives are not the only elements that help unify Bernstein's score. As is usually the case in his works, *West Side Story* is an eclectic mixture of styles, with influences from various types of jazz and Latin music being especially significant, both prominent in American urban life in

Example 7.4 'Ballet Sequence', mm. 45–54, 'Transition to Scherzo', with various evocations of short–long rhythms, later heard in title text of 'Somewhere'

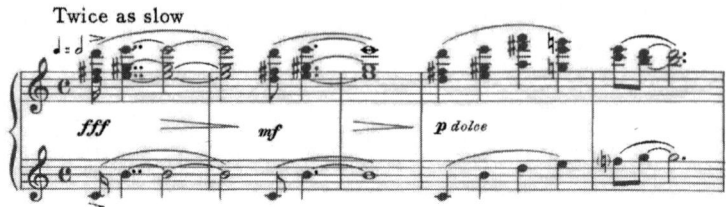

the late 1950s. Katherine Baber has written persuasively about the sounds of modern jazz in the show, noting that Bernstein's blend of bop and cool jazz would have been heard as what some called 'crime jazz' because of their associations with *film noir* soundtracks, such as Elmer Bernstein's score for *The Sweet Smell of Success* (1957) and Henry Mancini's *A Touch of Evil* (1958).[40] Jazz helps establish the affect for gang violence and would have sounded strikingly different from typical Broadway fare. One hears influence from bop in the 'Prologue', 'Jet Song', louder sections of 'Cool', and 'The Rumble', and much of the remainder of 'Cool' is a musical pun on the style. It was in keeping with the tendency of musicians in the United States that Bernstein made few distinctions between various types of 'Latin music', applying an Afro-Cuban *rumba* rhythm in 'Maria', a Puerto Rican *tempo di seis* and an allegedly Mexican *huapango* in 'America', the Cuban mambo and cha-cha in 'Dance at the Gym', and what could be described as an Aragonese *jota* in 'I Feel Pretty'. Elizabeth A. Wells provides a varied look at Hispanic elements in *West Side Story*, including the music, in her West Side Story: *Cultural Perspectives on an American Musical*.[41]

Individual Numbers

Consideration of individual songs and numbers will include a summary of what preceded that musical placement in the show and an overview of distinctive musical and lyrical qualities. Nigel Simeone in his *Leonard*

Bernstein: West Side Story provides the most coverage in one volume of how the show developed in terms of numbers that were removed and changed.[42] Numbers cut from the show, such as 'Mix!' and 'Like Everybody Else', will not be considered unless they were replaced by other songs. In addition to the musical examples provided in this chapter, the reader will be directed to tracks and time indices on the 1957 and 2009 original cast recordings (OCR57 and OCR09) or Bernstein's 1984 studio recording (SR).[43]

'Prologue'

The opening scene was finalized late in the show's development. At one point, it was to occur in the Jets' hideout. The violent songs 'Mix!' and 'This Turf Is Ours!' were intended for later in the scene.[44] The music now heard in the 'Prologue' and 'Jet Song' appears in other guises in manuscripts.[45] There was indecision as to whether or not the show should open with the 'shofar-call', as does OCR57 (tr. 1); it does not appear in the published piano/vocal or orchestral scores.[46] The motive pervades the 'Prologue', such as the strong unison statement at 1′55″. The number's affect is edgy, building to chaos at 3′27″ when the gangs fight before the police arrive. The 'Prologue' includes the following distinctive ideas or moments: a preponderance of major/minor triads; ties between the eighth notes and downbeats in 6/8, disguising the meter (e.g., 0′07″); frequent eighth-note duplets and ties to further disrupt the beat; the iconic finger snaps (0′14″); a wide-ranging theme (see Example 7.5) describing the Jets heard first in the alto saxophone (0′17″) that includes blues thirds (C♯/C-natural) and sets the text 'You're never alone . . . ' in the 'Jet Song'; menacing sounds from pitched drums (e.g., 0′47″); a move to 2/4 (2′03″) with numerous 'shofar calls' as the gang battle starts; a jazz walking bass line (2′13″) and thickening texture as the violence increases; an exciting, descending motive that ends in a tritone in trumpets and woodwinds (2′36″); wild, imitative material in the brass (2′45″); re-introduction of the walking bass with a triadic motive in the mallet percussion (2′56″); and unpredictable rhythms and staccato notes (3′14″) with thickening texture leading to long, accented notes with flutter-tonguing as Bernardo pierces Arab's ear (3′25″), preceding a frenzied recapitulation of earlier material as the police enter.

'Jet Song'

Music for this song existed in earlier versions of the first scene.[47] On OCR57, it is a continuation of the 'Prologue', with which it shares thematic material, but the song follows dialogue in the show. 'Jet Song' is an AA′BA

Example 7.5 'Prologue', mm. 9–17, with a wide-ranging theme starting in anacrusis to m. 4 also heard in the B section of the 'Jet Song' and blues third C-natural in m. 17

Example 7.6 'Jet Song', mm. 28–35, with melody in triple meter against syncopations in the right hand and bass line in 6/8

tune, first sung by Riff; the A′ bears considerable variety. The vocal line in the A sections is in 3/4, but Bernstein's bass line is in 6/8 and the remainder of the accompaniment is syncopated (see Example 7.6). The B melody is the alto saxophone line heard early in the 'Prologue' (tr. 1, 0′17″) and in this song's introduction. Measures 100–116 in the piano/vocal score, where the Jets sing about the dance that night, is not on OCR57 but heard on the SR (1/tr. 2, 1′29″ff). (This section later sounds in the 'Blues' from the 'Dance at

Example 7.7 'Jet Song', mm. 190–199, with *tresillo* rhythm in the vocal line and walking jazz bass like that heard in sections of 'Prologue'

the Gym', as will be stated below.) After Riff leaves, the remainder of the gang sings the song and repeats the final BA, but with a different affect. Sondheim's lyrics to this point mostly declare how great it is to be a Jet, but here they become more confrontational, and Bernstein's music follows suit. The final B section (OCR57, tr. 1, 5′27″ff) is in 6/8 with the accompaniment mostly in two, featuring dissonant chords (major/minor triads with added minor and major sixths); the last A section (5′36″ff) changes to 2/4 with the walking bass from the 'Prologue' (see Example 7.7) and the vocal rhythms changed from quarter notes to a *tresillo* (3+3+2).

'Something's Coming'

This was the last song written for the show, designed to make Tony less of a 'euphoric dreamer'.[48] Sondheim suggested a song in a propulsive 2/4 like 'The Trolley Song' from *Meet Me in St Louis*.[49] In a letter to his wife, Bernstein admitted that he had complicated the meter. The song includes other rhythmic intricacies, including a hemiola in the 3/4 ostinato (OCR57, tr. 2, 0′00″) and numerous cross-accents in 2/4 sections (e.g., 0′22″). The opening verse is ABAB and the refrain is CDCDECDE with a coda based on A. Sondheim's use of short questions, references like 'cannonballing' and a baseball metaphor, and poetic evocations provide Tony with a variety of feelings not heard from other Jets. As Simeone notes, Bernstein's setting includes numerous melodic and harmonic tritones and lowered sevenths in the melody, also heard in the 'Jet Song'.[50] The most fetching lowered seventh in 'Something's Coming' is Tony's last long C-natural (2′16″), producing a minor seventh over the bass that evokes 'Somewhere', and a concluding dominant seventh chord, as though the song fails to end.

'Dance at the Gym'

An early version of this scene took place in a nightclub called the Crystal Cave,[51] but apparently the show's creators then realized that these young people could not have entered such an establishment. Bernstein wrote dances for the nightclub that he abandoned: 'First Mambo', 'Version B (mambo)', and 'Huapango'.[52] Among sketches for the scene (Library of Congress, Bernstein Collection, Folder 1077/12), one finds most of the music for the 'Dance at the Gym', sometimes under other names. For example, the show's 'Mambo' appears as 'Fast Mambo (Merengue)' and an 'Atom Bomb Mambo' became part of the dance (OCR09, tr. 4, 2′43″ff). The opening 'Blues' in 'Dance at the Gym' starts as the bridal shop scene concludes, when Maria starts to whirl to a musical hint from 'Something's Coming', followed by undulating triplets in 12/8 based in chromatically adjacent triads (0′00″). The scene changes and a section marked 'Rocky' ensues (0′18″), the 12/8 mimicking a swinging 4/4. Bernstein retains the sliding between adjacent triads and places blues notes over a strong bass line, setting the abovenamed segment from 'Jet Song' as the Jets dance with their girlfriends. The Sharks enter and Glad Hand, the emcee, proposes a meeting dance for which Bernstein provided a 'Promenade' (SR, 1/5) marked 'Tempo di Paso Doble', a cheesy moment with four-square rhythms and tinny orchestration. Everyone quickly grabs their usual partners and launches into the 'Mambo' (OCR09, 1′36″), a competitive dance between the gangs based in the soundscape of the Sharks. It opens with an explosion of Latin percussion, followed by frenetic music block-scored for the sound of a Latin big band, but with strings (besides bass) functioning alongside the woodwinds. Bernstein introduces the omnipresent tritone in the brass, first in the trombones (2′06″), complemented by the surrounding chromaticism. There are exciting solos for trombone 1 (3′13″ff, joined by horns at 3′20″) and trumpet in D (3′27″). Block-scoring returns with earlier material and the 'Mambo' fades after Tony and Maria see each other (over tritones in the orchestra), introducing the 'Cha-Cha' (4′08″). Woodwinds, muted trumpets, and strings playing pizzicato and harmonics offer the melody to 'Maria', *staccato* over a Latin accompaniment; Bernstein layers in additional

Example 7.8 'Meeting Scene', mm. 1-8, with tritone and 'Maria' motive heard four times in ascending eighth notes of mm. 2–5

instruments for the repeat of A (4′34″). The B section is fuller with the violins now arco, leading directly into the 'Meeting Scene', where the 'Maria' motive dominates in strings, vibraphone, celesta, and high wood-winds in the underscoring (see Example 7.8). The scene ends with a return of the 'Promenade', now scored more fully, and a 'Jump' (SR, 1/9) scored for a small combo.

'Maria'

Bernstein wrote a version of this song before Sondheim joined the project. Tony knows only Maria's name and glories in its sound and his feelings. As Simeone notes, the song's opening is one of the few recitatives in the score (OCR57, tr. 5, 0′00).[53] On OCR57, Larry Kert is joined by off-stage voices, not the case on OCR09, where the song is a solo throughout. Bernstein avoids the tritone in the recitative, so once the lyrical 'Moderato con anima' begins (0′34″), one cannot miss the striking interval that punctuates 'Maria'. We have heard this motive many times in the 'Dance at the Gym', statements that help lead to this satisfying moment. Despite the

Example 7.9 'Maria', mm. 9-14, with *tresillo* in bass line and A' as a tritone over E-flat in bass in mm. 9, 10, and 12

song's fame, its charm remains with its winning melody, convincing use of speech rhythms, and the *tresillo* rhythm from the *rumba* in the bass (see Example 7.9). As Tony keeps repeating her name (1'24"ff), Bernstein wrote a B-flat' for two measures, with a simplified *ossia* part that most singers use. José Carreras realized the high note gloriously on the SR, but otherwise on the recording struggles too much with the English text.

'Balcony Scene'

An update of *Romeo and Juliet* requires a balcony scene – here on a fire-escape – but what music to use with it was a matter of debate. An early page with Bernstein's lyrics indicates that 'Somewhere' was intended for the scene,[54] and Folder 1079/8 in the LC Bernstein Collection includes music from 'Somewhere' with 'Balcony' crossed out on the cover. 'One Hand, One Heart' also at one point was in the scene, as may be seen in Folder 1078/10, where the title 'Balcony Scene' also has been deleted. Bernstein and Sondheim derived this version of 'Tonight' (Folder 1079/17, dated 4 July 1957) from the 'Tonight' (Quintet).[55] The scene follows immediately after 'Maria', the music of which continues as underscoring. Shortly after Maria starts singing the verse (OCR57, tr. 5, 0'05"), a beguine rhythm starts (see Example 7.2, eighth note pattern in the second line), which becomes the song's heartbeat. The verse is lyrical, wide in range, with occasional orchestral doubling of the vocal line. The lovers are in a brief, fully fledged duet by the verse's end, and kiss passionately as the orchestra prepares the refrain (0'47"), a carefully constructed AA'BA with fetching modulations. After the refrain, the orchestra settles downward from B-flat major to A for their duet (1'54"), sung in octaves, still propelled by the beguine rhythms (2'12"). Maria goes into her family's apartment for a moment and Bernstein descends one more half-step to A-flat major for Tony's brief solo; the underscoring for their ensuing dialogue is not on OCR57. It does appear on the SR (1/11, 4'58"); Bernstein references the opening motive of 'Somewhere' often in the orchestration. On OCR57, their final, brief duet starts at 3'13", again sung in octaves. 'Somewhere' sounds once again in the orchestra as they hold their final note, ending with the 'Maria' motive.

'America'

Aaron Copland perhaps spurred Bernstein's interest in Mexican music. The younger musician arranged Copland's *El Salón México* in 1941, and the same year wrote his own movement, *Conchtown*, as a possible ballet; later that music became 'America'. The opening section, a *seis* (OCR57, tr. 6, 0'00"), is the score's only imitation of Puerto Rican music. A *seis* is an accompanied vocal work with lines of eight syllables ('America' here includes some nine-syllable lines),[56] but Bernstein omitted the genre's usual instrumental interludes. The *seis* leads directly into the *huapango* (1'14"), a fast, Mexican dance that tends to mix 3/4, 6/8, and 2/4. Bernstein provides a similarly complicated mixture with some *alla breve* rhythms, quarter-note and half-note triplets, and a *tresillo* in the song's opening section (see Example 7.10), as Wells notes, but that is in the *seis*.[57] Rosalia fondly remembers her home's beauty, but Anita mocks her with images of the island's sickness, storms, poverty, and violence, references that Puerto Ricans have often criticized. The orchestration cleverly supports points made by both women in the *seis*. In the *huapango*, instead of combining meters, Bernstein alternates continuously between 3/4 and 6/8. As Simeone has noted, 'it is not one of the most musically demanding numbers in the show ... ',[58] but 'America' is mesmerizing and fluid, the key shifting effortlessly between C major and A-flat major as Anita and her friends mock Rosalia and praise life in the continental United States. Sondheim's

Example 7.10 'America', mm. 5–12, with combination of half-note and quarter-note triplets, *tresillo* in a clave rhythm (bass line), and *alla breve* (m. 7, voice)

lyrics are witty and effective, if at times difficult to understand with the fast music. The orchestration in this number crackles with excitement with well-placed Latin percussion and other delightful moments.

'Cool'

'Cool' is ready proof of the sophistication of Bernstein's score when compared to typical Broadway fare in the 1950s. Its affect and orchestration are based upon a musical pun related to cool jazz. In contrast to the aggressive sounds of bop, cool jazz included such instruments as vibraphone, flute, French horn, and subtle use of saxophones and muted trumpets. The Jets are nervous about the rumble that night and Riff wants to focus their energy, a spectacular dance opportunity. The song's melody (OCR57, tr. 7, 0′10″) opens with a tritone, but not on an accented beat as in 'Maria'. 'Cool' is a 32-bar song, ABAB′, for which Sondheim provided an appropriate text with delightful internal rhymes. What follows is a memorable jazz fugue. As Simeone notes, the first four notes of the subject strongly resemble famous passages of Beethoven's *Grosse Fuge*.[59] The subject sounds in long notes from muted trumpet (with dotted rhythms from the vibraphone) and surprisingly nearly forms a twelve-tone row. The countersubject enters (1′20″), with more

Example 7.11 'One Hand, One Heart', mm. 112–116, with 'Maria' motive stated four times in eighth notes in the third stave

swinging dotted rhythms in the vibraphone while the subject in whole notes passes to the trombone. As the exciting fugue progresses, Robbins's dance moves present excited youths trying to restrain themselves. Their energy bursts forth at 2′51″, when Bernstein turns his pit orchestra into a bop big band. The Jets sing the final AB′ as the number returns to its cool roots.

'One Hand, One Heart'

Bernstein originally wrote this melody for *Candide*. Its first placement in *West Side Story*, as noted above, was in the balcony scene, where Simeone believes it was to follow 'Somewhere'.[60] During rehearsals, the creators moved the tune to the mock wedding in the bridal shop, prompting a new version dated 4 July 1957 (Folder 1078/9). The melody was in dotted half notes; Sondheim prevailed upon Bernstein to break those values into some shorter notes to accommodate additional words. The folder includes a lead sheet with the new lyrics. Here the 'Cha-Cha' underscores Tony and Maria imagining meeting each other's parents, and music later heard with 'Somewhere' underscores their vows. 'One Hand, One Heart' is a slow waltz, with an elegant melody that revolves around the third degree of the scale. There are blues intervals of a lowered seventh ('now we *start*') just before the climax (OCR57, tr. 8, 1′01″ff) and a lowered third ('Even death', 1′13″) prior to the conclusion. The lovers repeat the song's second half, singing more counterpoint. Not surprisingly, the 'Maria' tritone sounds in the accompaniment, such as at the song's conclusion. (See Example 7.11 for an example.)

Example 7.12 'Tonight' (Quintet), mm. 1–9, with changing meters, triple meter outlined by the ascending bass ostinato, and bitonal use of C and E major

'Tonight' (Quintet)

Originally intended to be sung by Riff, Bernardo, Tony, Maria, and Anita, by the time the show premiered in New York the gangs sang with their leaders.[61] Although it was no longer a true quintet, Bernstein's operatic model remained clear with five vocal lines heard individually and combined towards the end. The 'Tonight' (Quintet) immediately follows 'One Hand, One Heart', perhaps the show's most jarring musical juxtaposition. The number's level of dissonance, metric complexity, and cross-accents foreshadow the violent music heard in 'The Rumble'. As the number opens, Bernstein apposes C and E major and a bass ostinato in a clear triple meter against march rhythms in alternating 4/4 and 2/4 measures (see Example 7.12), later with occasional 3/8 bars. The gangs alternate, singing in a low range, their lines sounding in E minor with many lowered sevenths and frequently dissonant with the accompaniment. The vocal parts shift to a pitch center of A with more lowered sevenths and some C-naturals (OCR57, tr. 9, 0′42″), with the orchestra now projecting A and F major. When Anita makes her entrance (1′07″), Bernstein returns to C and

E major and the opening accompaniment, but a sexy saxophone entrance greets her as she anticipates a passionate evening with Bernardo. When Tony enters with 'Tonight' as heard earlier (1'25"), the composer recalls the beguine rhythms and uses less dissonance. Tony sings the whole chorus followed by an orchestral statement of the opening march material in A and F major. Riff meets Tony (2'23") singing the gang melody (now in E-flat and G major/minor), reminding Tony to attend the rumble. When Maria enters (2'40"), Bernstein has formed a trio; quickly all five parts come together, an extraordinary moment in the Broadway repertory. A few more modulations occur to accommodate the melody that Tony and Maria sing together (3'05"), with the other three active parts creating an exhilarating, dense texture. Dissonance continues as the accompaniment sounds both D and E-flat chords against the prevailing C major.

'The Rumble'

The song 'Mix!' got moved here after being deleted from the first scene,[62] but the gang fight became a ballet. Bernstein logically returned to material from 'The Prologue', but it has been stripped of any of the innocence or youthful enthusiasm heard early in the opening number. Tritones, triads with added tones, and striking orchestration abound in 'The Rumble'. There are many of the 'shofar calls' sounding in a variety of textures, including in the dense, opening 50 seconds (OCR57, tr. 10) and in cat-and-mouse imitative material as Riff and Bernardo jockey for position in their knife fight (0'51"ff), a segment that builds to a shattering climax with the same motive when Bernardo kills Riff (1'24"). The remainder of the segment minutely follows the action on stage, demonstrating Bernstein's close collaboration with Robbins.

'I Feel Pretty'

'The Rumble' closes Act 1. Following an intermission, the 'Entr'acte, is 'I Feel Pretty', the instrumental selection continuing directly into the song. Laurents did not think that the number belonged in the show and Sondheim has expressed distaste for his own work because he places sophisticated English rhymes in the mouth of a Puerto Rican girl whose first language is Spanish.[63] As Simeone states, however, audiences love the song and there is a dramatic reason for its presence in the show.[64] The audience saw the rumble and its deadly results; Maria has yet to learn about the fight. A young woman, dizzy with her first love, just might play around with her friends before seeing the man that she loves, and those friends might tease her when they believe that her lover is Chino, a Shark. 'I Feel Pretty', therefore, helps fill out Maria's character and provides some humour, which this show needs. For the music, Bernstein seems to have referenced Iberian models (OCR57, tr. 11). In a fast three, 'I Feel Pretty' is a waltz but also resembles an Aragonese *jota*, an identification buoyed by the use of castanets and ornamentation in Maria's vocal line redolent of flamenco (e.g., the triplet on 'tonight' at 0′16″). When her three friends tease her, they suggest that Maria believes herself to be in Spain. Sondheim was right, of course, that a real Maria probably could not conceive these rhymes, but musical theatre audiences often are willing to make dramatic allowances for enjoyable songs.

'Ballet Sequence'

Given the significance of dance in *West Side Story*, one almost expects a dream ballet. Manuscript evidence indicates that finding the scene's form and content was a difficult task for both Bernstein and Robbins, as Simeone details.[65] The scene came together quite late, even after orchestrations were well in hand, because there is material in the orchestral manuscript 'New Intro to Ballet Sequence' that failed to remain in the scene.[66] The segment's emotional range is notable, as is the number of other themes from the show that Bernstein works into it. The opening 'Under Dialogue' (some of it heard on SR) accompanies Tony's anguished explanation of the rumble to Maria. Marked 'Allegro agitato', it is a development of the 'Maria' motive over insistent percussion. An ascending half-step dominates the accompaniment as Tony sings (OCR57, tr. 12, 0′00″) that they will flee, joined by Maria as they hope for a place that offers them freedom. As they run (0′20″ff), there is further development of the 'Maria' motive and material from the 'Cha-Cha'. A strong statement of the 'Somewhere' motive (0′35″) opens the 'Transition to Scherzo' followed by a succession of short–long rhythms – related to both the 'Maria' and 'Somewhere' motives – leading into the playful 'Scherzo' (1′07″ff), where cast members from both sides dreamily dance together. The music is based on similar material. 'Somewhere' follows (2′36″), sung by a member of the ensemble. It is a simple, refined melody built from several ideas, proceeding with compelling inevitability because of its regular phrase structures and various sequences. The contrapuntal accompaniment includes satisfying, rising minor sevenths and imitation. The 'Procession and Nightmare' (4′47″ff) opens with the 'Somewhere' melody against 'I Have a Love', a combination that recurs in the 'Finale'. This is the first time the audience hears any of Maria's last song. Orchestral material from the

Example 7.13 'Ballet Sequence', mm. 84–88 of 'Procession and Nightmare', with 'Somewhere' motive stated three times in mm. 86–88 and F sounding in mm. 86–87 as root of the chord

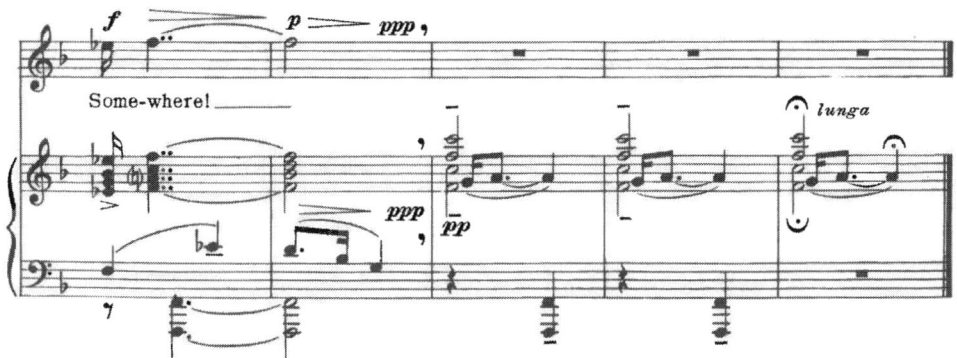

'Scherzo' follows (5′42″ff) but played more urgently. Bernstein further transforms it for the nightmare, briefly reprising music from 'The Rumble' (6′18″). Tony and Maria conclude the scene (6′42″) singing material from 'Somewhere'. The three final measures in the orchestra (7′11″ff) are like those that close the show (see Example 7.13), but the two entrances in the bass on second beats of the first two 2/4 bars in the passage are the root of an F major chord rather than a tritone away, which is how the show ends. For a brief moment, the lovers are safe and fulfilled, ending a ballet, during which they are understood to have consummated their relationship.

'Gee, Officer Krupke'

As reported above, Bernstein wrote this music for *Candide*; Burton notes that it was for the scene in Venice.[67] Creators of *West Side Story* added this song for the Jets during rehearsals. Laurents thought the second act needed the relief, but Sondheim suggested that the positions of 'Cool' and 'Krupke' should be reversed, which is what happened in the 1961 film.[68] Bernstein marked the number 'Fast, vaudeville style', setting up the song's mocking tone and slapstick effects in the orchestration. Sondheim's lyrics provide useful social commentary on how society deals with juvenile delinquents.

'A Boy Like That/I Have a Love'

The show's two most operatic numbers are the 'Tonight' (Quintet) and this double song, which went through a long process of development, as Simeone describes.[69] Anita comes to Maria for comfort and discovers

Example 7.14 'I Have a Love', mm. 1–9, with movement from conjunct to disjunct motion in the melodic line

that she has been with Bernardo's killer. She tears into Maria, singing low in her range for much of a violent song filled with dissonance. As noted above, the orchestral accompaniment is redolent of 'The Rumble'. The first two measures in the orchestra function as a ritornello that sounds between each of Anita's phrases in the AABA form, but the instrumental interjection is only one measure before the B section, as if Anita is so enraged that she cannot wait to sing (OCR57, tr. 14, 0′31″). Maria interrupts her (1′01″ff), quickly rising to an A-flat″, but then defending herself, singing Anita's music in a lower range. As Anita starts to repeat her song in counterpoint (1′20″), Maria moves to the opening motive of 'I Have a Love', repeated numerous times as she parries Anita's thrusts. Maria ends the duet soon after she reaches a B-flat″ (1′48″) and then tells her friend, 'You should know better!' 'I Have a Love' (OCR57, tr. 15) ensues, opening in an innocent G major and moving quickly from conjunct motion to cover a larger range with skips (see Example 7.14) and effective modulations like those heard in 'Tonight'. Once Maria holds a G′ on 'life' (1′24″), now in E minor, Anita has been won over. Following an orchestral climax, they sing a contrapuntal duet (1′38″ff), signalling Anita's willingness to try to help Tony and Maria.

Example 7.15 'Finale', mm. 24–28, with 'Somewhere' rhythmic motive stated three times in mm. 26–28, resolving to C major triad and tritone F♯ stated in bass in mm. 26–27

'Taunting Scene'

Anita goes to the drugstore to give Tony a message, but the Jets detain her, taunt her, and have begun to assault her when Doc breaks it up. This recorded music sounds from the jukebox and is based on music from Anita's soundscape: the 'Mambo' and material derived from 'America', the latter deconstructed and combined with unfamiliar elements.

'Finale'

Bernstein wanted music in place of Maria's final speech when she holds the gun. He stated: 'I don't know how many times I tried to musicalize that. It cries out for music.'[70] Despite his statement, however, no such sketches survive and the most dramatic moment in the show is spoken without underscoring. Earlier in the scene, Maria sings some of 'Somewhere', briefly joined by Tony before he dies. Material from 'Somewhere' accompanies Maria bidding farewell to him. She then excoriates the gangs as she threatens everyone with the gun, but finally she collapses. To conclude the scene during the procession as the gangs carry off Tony's body, Bernstein used music from the end of the 'Ballet Sequence', a contrapuntal treatment of 'I Have a Love' and material from 'Somewhere'. As noted above, the show's last three measures are based on how the 'Ballet Sequence' ends, but Bernstein now combines C major (with the rising major second from 'Somewhere' resolving from D to E) joined by a jarring F♯ in the bass, stated only the first two times in the original show (see Example 7.15). The final measure includes just the C major triad with the rising major second ending on the third of the chord. Bernstein added the tritone to the chord root C′ with the F♯ in the bass to the last measure in the Symphonic Dances from *West Side Story*, in his 1984 studio recording, and in the 1994 orchestral score. Most of the written finale appears on the OCR57 (tr. 16) and on the SR.

Conclusion

Created for a show that explored new ground on Broadway, the score for *West Side Story* was also unusual for its time with its very wide range of influences and the consistently high level of inspiration heard in the music. It includes unforgettable melodies and lyrics that strongly add to the definition of characters and dramatic situations. The dance music, written by Bernstein counter to the usual Broadway practice of hiring a dance arranger, is more original than the arrangements of songs heard in most contemporary shows. Numbers are unified by motives that often recur elsewhere in the score, making the music a major force in *West Side Story*'s sense of organic wholeness. The orchestrations translate the music into three dominant soundscapes that help tie together different scenes involving similar characters and situations. A fine monument to the music's effectiveness is the orchestral work Symphonic Dances from *West Side Story* that Bernstein worked on with Ramin and Kostal in 1961. Numbers do not appear in the suite in show order, allowing one to hear the music without lyrics and out of dramatic context, where the score's power remains undiminished, a tribute to the striking creativity that Bernstein brought to his most famous work.

Notes

1. Nigel Simeone, *Leonard Bernstein: West Side Story* (Farnham, Surrey: Ashgate, 2009), 137.
2. www.imdb.com/title/tt0055614/ (accessed 28 February 2020).
3. Sondheim describes his dislike for the show's lyrics in his *Finishing the Hat: Collected Lyrics (1954–1981) with Attendant Comments, Principles, Heresies, Grudges, Whines and Anecdotes* (New York: Alfred A. Knopf, 2010), 26ff. His embarrassment had to do with the 'poetic' lyrics that he wrote for Tony and Maria, calling them 'maundering' (p. 26) and for the complicated rhymes that he wrote for Maria to sing in 'I Feel Pretty', considered below.

4. Simeone, *Leonard Bernstein:* West Side Story; Elizabeth A. Wells, West Side Story: *Cultural Perspectives on an American Musical* (Lanham, MD: The Scarecrow Press, Inc., 2011); Joseph P. Swain, *The Broadway Musical: A Critical and Musical Survey*, 2nd ed., Revised and Expanded (Lanham, MD: Scarecrow Press, Inc., 2002), 221–64; Geoffrey Block, *Enchanted Evenings: The Broadway Musical from* Show Boat *to Sondheim*, 1st ed. (New York and Oxford: Oxford University Press, 1997), 245–73; Katherine Baber, *Leonard Bernstein and the Language of Jazz* (Urbana, Chicago, and Springfield: University of Illinois Press, 2019), 155–84; Helen Smith, *There's A Place for Us: The Musical Theatre Works of Leonard Bernstein* (Farnham, UK: Ashgate, 2011), 139–69; and Paul R. Laird, West Side Story, Gypsy, *and the Art of Broadway Orchestration* (London and New York: Abingdon/Routledge, 2022), 76–134.

5. For consideration of the music of *Fancy Free*, see: Paul R. Laird and Hsun Lin, *Leonard Bernstein: A Research and Information Guide*, 2nd ed., Routledge Music Bibliographies (New York: Routledge, 2015), 36–39.

6. Carol J. Oja covers both *Fancy Free* and *On the Town* from several angles in: *Bernstein Meets Broadway: Collaborative Art in a Time of War* (New York: Oxford University Press, 2014). For a study that covers *Fancy Free* in detail, see: Sophie Redfern, *Bernstein and Robbins: The Early Ballets*, Eastman Studies in Music (Rochester: University of Rochester Press, 2021).

7. For material on Robbins's ballet to Bernstein's Symphony No. 2, *The Age of Anxiety*, see: Wendy Lesser, *Jerome Robbins: A Life in Dance*, Jewish Lives (New Haven and London: Yale University Press, 2018), 28–32. For mention of the uncredited work that Robbins did for *Wonderful Town*, see: Humphrey Burton, *Leonard Bernstein* (New York: Doubleday, 1994), 225.

8. For a comparison of the scores of *On the Waterfront* and *West Side Story*, see: Anthony Bushard, *Leonard Bernstein's* On the Waterfront: *A Film Score Guide* (Lanham, MD: The Scarecrow Press, Inc., 2013), 53–58.

9. Most of the material concerning the creation of *West Side Story* appears in numerous sources.

10. Burton, *Leonard Bernstein*, 248.

11. Meryle Secrest, *Stephen Sondheim: A Life* (New York: Alfred A. Knopf, 1998), 112.

12. Burton, *Leonard Bernstein*, 269.

13. Simeone, *Leonard Bernstein:* West Side Story, 51–52.

14. Bernstein described the composition of 'Something's Coming' in a letter to Felicia Bernstein written on 8 August 1957; see: Nigel Simeone, ed., *The Leonard Bernstein Letters* (New Haven and London: Yale University Press, 2013), 366.

15. Robbins stated this in a letter to Bernstein and Laurents, dated 18 October 1955. See: Simeone, *Leonard Bernstein Letters*, 346–49, esp. 348–49.

16. There is a famous photograph of Sondheim at the piano at a rehearsal, but the show's lyricist has stated that he 'played almost nothing for the rehearsals . . .'

(Simeone, *Leonard Bernstein:* West Side Story, 51). The photo appears in Block, *Enchanted Evenings*, 250.

17. Carol Lawrence, *Carol Lawrence: The Backstage Story* (New York: McGraw Hill, 1990), 46.

18. 'A Place for Us: 50 Years of *West Side* Story' (NPR 2007), presented by Scott Simon, National Public Radio, 26 September 2007, quoted in Simeone, *Leonard Bernstein:* West Side Story, 50–51.

19. Simeone, *Leonard Bernstein:* West Side Story, 89.

20. Simeone, *Leonard Bernstein Letters*, 4–9, 14.

21. Allen Shawm, *Leonard Bernstein: All-American Musician*, Jewish Lives (New Haven and London: Yale University Press, 2014), 149.

22. Steven Suskin, *The Sound of Broadway Music: A Book of Orchestrators & Orchestrations* (New York: Oxford University Press, 2009), 74.

23. Columbia University Archive, Sid Ramin Papers, Flatbox 702. For detailed consideration of two manuscript drafts of orchestration for 'America', see: Laird, West Side Story, 99–107.

24. Suskin, *The Sound of Broadway Music*, 63.

25. Simeone, *Leonard Bernstein:* West Side Story, 86–87.

26. The complete scoring is as follows: Reed I: Piccolo, Flute, Alto Saxophone, Clarinet in B-flat, Bass Clarinet; Reed II: Clarinet in E-flat, Clarinet in B-flat, Bass Clarinet; Reed III: Piccolo, Flute, Oboe, English Horn, Tenor Saxophone, Baritone Saxophone, Clarinet in B-flat, Bass Clarinet; Reed IV: Piccolo, Flute, Soprano Saxophone, Bass Saxophone, Clarinet in B-flat, Bass Clarinet; Reed V: Bassoon; 2 Horns in F; 3 Trumpets in B-flat (2nd doubling Trumpet in D); 2 Trombones; Percussion (2 players): Traps, Timpani, Vibraphone, 4 Pitched Drums, Guiro, Xylophone, 3 Bongos, 3 Cowbells, Conga, Timbales, Snare Drum, Police Whistle, Gourd, 2 Suspended Cymbals, Castanets, Maracas, Finger Cymbals, Tambourines, Small Maracas, Glockenspiel, Woodblock, Chimes, Triangle, Temple Blocks, Chimes, Tam-tam, Ratchet, Slide Whistle; Piano/Celesta; Electric Guitar/Spanish Guitar/Mandolin; Violin I–VII; Cello I–IV; and Contrabass.

27. Block, *Enchanted Evenings*, 28–31.

28. Jim Lovensheimer, South Pacific: *Paradise Rewritten* (New York: Oxford University Press, 2010), 125–26.

29. For discussion of Weill's use of leitmotifs in these two shows, see: bruce d. mcclung and Paul R. Laird, 'Musical Sophistication on Broadway: Kurt Weill and Leonard Bernstein', in *The Cambridge Companion to the Musical*, 3rd ed., ed. William A. Everett and Paul R. Laird (Cambridge: Cambridge University Press, 2017), 232–33.

30. See: Otis Guernsey, *Broadway Song and Story: Playwrights/Lyricists/Composers Discuss their Hits* (New York: Dodd, Mead, and Co., 1985), 9–10 and Smith, *There's A Place for Us*, 18–24.

31. Smith, *There's A Place for Us*, 95–97.

32. Jack Gottlieb, 'The Music of Leonard Bernstein: A Study of Melodic Manipulations' (DMA document, University of Illinois, 1964), 19.

33. Mel Gussow, '*West Side Story*: The Beginnings of Something Great', *The New York Times*, 21 October 1990, H5. Used by permission of the Leonard Bernstein Office, Inc.

34. Simeone, *Leonard Bernstein:* West Side Story, 80.

35. Simeone, *Leonard Bernstein:* West Side Story, 80–81.

36. Simeone, *Leonard Bernstein:* West Side Story, 80.

37. Block, *Enchanted Evenings*, 250.

38. Simeone, *Leonard Bernstein:* West Side Story, 81–82.

39. Swain, *The Broadway Musical*, 227–31.

40. Baber, *Leonard Bernstein and the Language of Jazz*, 159.

41. Wells, West Side Story: *Cultural Perspectives*, 99–140.

42. Simeone, *Leonard Bernstein:* West Side Story.

43. Recordings: Leonard Bernstein and Stephen Sondheim, *West Side Story*, Original Broadway Cast, CD [1957] (Columbia CK 32603, 1973); Leonard Bernstein and Stephen Sondheim, *West Side Story*, The New Broadway Cast Recording, CD (Sony Masterworks Broadway 88697–53085–2, 2009); Leonard Bernstein and Stephen Sondheim, *Leonard Bernstein Conducts* West Side Story, 2 CDs (Deutsche Grammophon 415 253–2, 1985).

44. Simeone, *Leonard Bernstein:* West Side Story, 55–57.

45. Simeone, *Leonard Bernstein:* West Side Story, 60–61.

46. Piano/vocal score: Leonard Bernstein and Stephen Sondheim, *West Side Story* (New York: G. Schirmer, Inc., and Chappell & Co., Inc., 1957, 1959). Orchestral score: Leonard Bernstein and Stephen Sondheim, *West Side Story* ([New York]: Jalni Publications, Inc. and Boosey & Hawkes, 1994).

47. Simeone, *Leonard Bernstein:* West Side Story, 61.

48. Simeone, ed., *Leonard Bernstein Letters*, 366. Leonard Bernstein © Amberson Holdings LLC, Used by permission of The Leonard Bernstein Office, Inc.

49. Stephen Sondheim in conversation with Jeremy Sams, National Theatre, London, 1 June 1993, quoted in Simeone, *Leonard Bernstein:* West Side Story, 62.

50. Simeone, *Leonard Bernstein:* West Side Story, 96.

51. Simeone, *Leonard Bernstein:* West Side Story, 57.

52. Simeone, *Leonard Bernstein:* West Side Story, 57–59.

53. Simeone, *Leonard Bernstein:* West Side Story, 98.

54. Simeone, *Leonard Bernstein:* West Side Story, 63.

55. Simeone, *Leonard Bernstein:* West Side Story, 64.

56. Jorge Duany, 'Popular Music in Puerto Rico: Toward an Anthropology of *Salsa*', *Latin American Music Review* 5, no. 2 (1984): 190.

57. Wells, West Side Story: *Cultural Perspectives*, 24.

58. Simeone, *Leonard Bernstein:* West Side Story, 102.

59. Simeone, *Leonard Bernstein:* West Side Story, 102.

60. Simeone, *Leonard Bernstein: West Side Story*, 103.

61. Simeone, *Leonard Bernstein: West Side Story*, 104.

62. Simeone, *Leonard Bernstein: West Side Story*, 68.

63. Arthur Laurents, *Original Story* (New York: Alfred A. Knopf, 2000), 351. Sondheim described his conversation with Broadway lyricist Sheldon Harnick, who pointed out this problem with 'I Feel Pretty', much to Sondheim's embarrassment. See his *Finishing the Hat* (2010), 48.

64. Simeone, *Leonard Bernstein: West Side Story*, 107.

65. Simeone, *Leonard Bernstein: West Side Story*, 68–70.

66. Simeone, *Leonard Bernstein: West Side Story*, 70. The manuscript is in Volume 2 of Flatbox 266 in the Sid Ramin Papers.

67. Burton, *Leonard Bernstein*, 269.

68. Simeone, *Leonard Bernstein: West Side Story*, 70–71.

69. Simeone, *Leonard Bernstein: West Side Story*, 71–73.

70. Quoted in: Gussow, "*West Side Story*". Used by permission of The Leonard Bernstein Office, Inc.

8 | Un-Gendering 'Somewhere'

Women's Agency and Redemption in *West Side Story*

KATHERINE BABER

In the 2019 revival of *West Side Story* in Manchester, directed by Sarah Frankcom, the character Anybodys steps forward and sings the iconic opening phrases of 'Somewhere':

There's a place for us,
Somewhere a place for us.

Anybodys and the cast gather to sing of a peaceful place in the 'open air,' the antithesis of the cramped urban grid they occupy, and a time for learning and caring, the opposite of their experience so far. In addition to Stephen Sondheim's lyrics and the song's appearance in the middle of a 'dream ballet,' the music Leonard Bernstein crafted for this moment reminds the listener that this place is imagined. The melody begins with a leap up of a minor seventh, which provides neither a comfortable landing nor the impetus to continue up to the octave. The rest of the verse then flows from this gesture that reaches but ultimately falls short, only for the singer to try again and keep trying. In turn, the chorus provides no conclusion, ending with the incremental step up of a major second on each of the words 'someday, somehow, somewhere.' By the end of the act, this loose melodic thread is still hanging. With Bernardo, Riff, and Tony dead, we do not hear a final song from Maria or a closing chorus. Instead, we hear a reprise of 'Somewhere' from the orchestra, ending on the major second interval, repeated three times ('someday, somehow, somewhere') as the Jets and Sharks process offstage, together carrying Tony's body. It seems that Bernstein was out of songs, done in by the challenge of scoring a musical that ends in a tragedy.[1] Or perhaps he recognized that he and his collaborators had already made their point.

Music critics and scholars seem to agree that 'Somewhere' is the heart of *West Side Story*, the carrier of its 'message,' but what that message might be is open to interpretation. Bernstein called his shot when he wrote 'an out-and-out plea for racial tolerance' across his copy of *Romeo and Juliet*.[2] The first drafts of the adaptation by Arthur Laurents took place on New York's East Side and centered on a religious conflict between Catholic and Jewish gangs. Jerome Robbins, as director and choreographer, was concerned with the challenges faced by young people from immigrant families. The characters wound up united by class and generation but riven by race. The 1961 film version solidified the analogies to the Civil Rights movement and subsequent productions have introduced disability as an organizing theme, critiqued the original text's stereotyping of Puerto Rican and Latinx communities, introduced a bilingual book and lyrics, and turned the mirror on violence, poverty, and xenophobia in America. What all these interpretations share is the recognition that the central dynamic of the musical is the push and pull between exclusion and inclusion. 'Somewhere' tells us is that this is a story about the importance of belonging. In response, Frankcom's choice to have Anybodys sing 'Somewhere' – rather than the anonymous girl of the original, or the boy soprano of Arthur Laurents's 2009 revival – asks us to consider what happens when we read that message through the lens of gender.

In order to read (that is, to interpret) *West Side Story* in a feminist way, we must recognize the unfinished nature of its project. The journey to, or creation of, a place to belong as described in 'Somewhere' is not yet accomplished by the musical's end, but it is perhaps within reach: 'Hold my hand and we're halfway there.' The narrative and characterizations – as expressed through songs, dances, and score – suggest a way forward and that redemptive path, I would argue, is gendered. Or, if we pay attention to Anybodys as a character, and consider also the roles of performer and spectator, the belonging we seek is *un-gendered*. To reach 'Somewhere,' we must step outside the confines of normative masculinity and femininity, each of which comes with its own reductive and destructive strictures.

Beginning with and returning to 'Somewhere' in this chapter also functions as a comment on methodology. When we listen to the score, read the book, attend a revival, or watch the film, we are only 'halfway there.' Although authorial intent is notoriously difficult to untangle in the collaborative medium of the musical, decoding the problems of masculinity and femininity embedded in the text of *West Side Story* is necessary to reading its message. How the middle-class, mainstream audiences of the original production understood gender roles in the socio-political landscape of the 1950s is crucial to this pursuit. Likewise, the performers of the work, and perceptions of those performers, multiply its potential meanings. And without giving in to a presentist critique, the responses of spectators from then to now also matters. As Stacy Wolf demonstrates with her project 'to look and hear from a lesbian point of view,' the meanings of a given work are always assembled from a combination of text, context, and spectator.[3] While this chapter is not primarily concerned with the spectator's uses of the musical, as Wolf is, a feminist reading needs all three facets of analysis, including the perspectives of what is often described as 'fandom.' This is particularly true in the case of Anybodys, a character whose embodiment and interpretation have evolved in the decades since the premiere in ways that are crucial to our understanding of *West Side Story*.

In addition, any feminist reading of *West Side Story* must be intersectional. Having migrated from Kimberlé Crenshaw's landmark work in legal studies to other fields, intersectionality is a broadly construed and continually evolving methodology in antiracist, feminist analyses.[4] It is also a useful tool in complicating the history of this musical in particular. What attending to race-and-gender reveals is that, in their efforts to create a universalized message about 'prejudice of different kinds,' Bernstein, Laurents, Robbins, and Sondheim landed on a colourblind moral that was gendered as feminine, even as the narrative arc depends on the musical styles and performances of women of colour.[5] The Sharks are nominally Puerto Rican, a category that includes Afro-Latinx people, but cultural specificity and diversity were not goals of the original production team. Still, Black and Latinx women have always been formidable, although limited, presences in the musical. Chita Rivera (whose father was Puerto Rican) originated the role of Anita and when Rita Moreno (born in Puerto Rico) took over in the role in the film adaptation, she became the first Latina to win an Oscar. African-American soprano Reri Grist played Consuelo in the original production and also performed 'Somewhere' from the pit during the live production and on the Broadway cast recording.

However, while reproducing stereotypes remains a hazard of every revival, reading *West Side Story* affords an opportunity to examine the 'intercategorical complexity' of the various identities at play. As Jennifer C. Nash explains, this strain of analysis uses categories of identity (e.g. race, ethnicity, class, gender) in a contingent fashion, in order to reveal the relationships between them and expose the inequalities such categories perpetuate.[6] Crenshaw and others affirm that attending to identity can 'reveal how power works in diffuse and differentiated ways through the creation and deployment of overlapping identity categories.'[7] In this practical vein, casting has become an area where the critical analysis of the text connects to the work of social justice. The women carry the moral of the story, so it matters that we have seen Ariana DeBose (whose father is Afro-Puerto Rican) as Anita in Steven Spielberg's 2021 film adaptation. On a textual level, if the message of the musical is that intolerance kills, then looking at and listening to the intersection of race and gender tells us that racial violence is not just the doing of white supremacy, but is aided and abetted by what we now call 'toxic masculinity' and by restrictive gender roles that limit the agency of women of colour to the affective realm.

Much Ado about Masculinity

Within the frame of *West Side Story*, as in postwar American society, anxieties about race and gender are mutually reinforcing. Not only are the Sharks and Jets embroiled in a racialized conflict over territory, but as teenagers they also struggle to define and defend their 'manhood.' Together, the score, choreography, and the lyrics emphasize belonging as the crux of the matter. As Riff reminds the Jets, 'when you're a Jet, you're a Jet all the way, from your first cigarette to your last dying day.' They are each other's chosen family, 'never alone' and 'never disconnected.' They are also brothers in arms, on the defense against the Sharks and often using militarized language. Robbins's choreography embodies both the belonging and the aggressiveness in densely packed formations, lunges and prowling, and athletic leaps. Even the violence is choreographed, in cooperation with the music, which draws heavily on the then contemporary styles of bebop and cool. The words used to describe jazz where it appears in the outlines – brutal and violent – suggest the music as embodying, in and of itself, the characteristics of conflict.[8] And that conflict is not only racially coded, via the association with jazz, but is also an explicitly male domain. As Wells notes, the 'Prologue' and later 'The Rumble' are 'ritualistic tableaux in which male energy, male behaviors, and male street values are reified.'[9] In a similar way, the music, lyrics, and choreography of 'Cool' demonstrate that for these boys on the cusp of adulthood, maintaining their masculinity is like walking a tightrope.

The Jets, ultimately, do not keep their cool and in the show's deceptively boisterous 11 o'clock number, 'Gee, Officer Krupke,' they explain to themselves and to the audience that their hoodlum status is a failure of 'domestic containment.'[10] In ascribing their troubles, albeit jokingly, to a 'social disease,' the Jets turn our gaze to systemic issues. As the representative youth, Action is bounced from Krupke the police officer, to a judge, to a psychologist, and finally to a social worker who recommends 'a year in the pen,' presumably starting the cycle over again. Most of the song focuses on the deficits of the Jets' home lives, and alcohol and drug abuse figure prominently in this disordered domestic scene (grandpa is 'always plas-tered' and grandma 'pushes tea'). However, it is the inability to correctly perform gender roles that drives the verse home: 'my sister wears a mustache, my brother wears a dress. Goodness gracious, that's why I'm a mess.' The social contract of the 1950s placed the burden of forming a proper adult masculinity on the mother. As Elaine Tyler May explains, 'mothers who neglected their children bred criminals; mothers who over-indulged their sons turned them into passive, weak, and effeminate "perverts."'[11] In the 2009 cast recording, Curtis Holbrook lisps the final words of the stanza, 'that's why I'm a mess,' signifying what sort of 'sickness' we should presume Action has.

In order to belong, at least to one another, the Jets must both affirm their whiteness, counter to the Sharks, and prove their masculinity by rejecting the feminine. Little wonder, then, that they constantly dismiss their girl-friends, Graziella and Velma, and the gender non-conforming Anybodys. Moreover, when we realize that this virulent form of white masculinity is a driving force throughout the musical, it seems inevitable that the tragic ending is guaranteed by the rape of Anita, a woman of colour. It is also worth noting that the sexual violence was not demanded by the source material. Killing Bernardo as the Tybalt figure was dictated by Shakespeare's text, but the 'taunting' of Anita is an invention for the musical. That said, the authors' decisions should be considered in light of the fact that for them, the threat of being diagnosed as 'sociologically sick' was very real, given that all of them were gay and Jewish – two communities often under suspicion.

Miscegenation, Assimilation, and the Feminine Other

The Jet Girls and the Shark Girls are different sides of the same coin. They are young, but striving for an adult stylishness, and they challenge the authority of the boys they run with. Before the War Council at Doc's store, Graziella sasses Riff and Diesel as they attempt to dismiss them: 'I and Velma ain't kid stuff, neither.'[12] Similarly, Anita warns Bernardo, 'I am an American girl now. I don't wait.' When he responds with a nostalgic invocation of Puerto Rico, where women know their place, her retort undercuts his masculinity: 'Back home, little boys don't have war councils.'[13] With their roles conditioned by gender *and* race, the girls represent two related concepts that complicate the theme of belonging: the desire to assimilate and the fear of miscegenation.

Although the parts for the Jet Girls are small, with no music of their own, they do have a symbolic impact. *Romeo and Juliet* is a story about inter-marriage and adapting it to a 1950s context updated that tribalism to fit current racist and xenophobic taboos. The fear of miscegenation is clearest in the 'get together dance' as moderated by Glad Hand, which produces exactly that outcome – Shark Boys with Jet Girls and vice versa. As described in the stage directions: 'There is a moment of tenseness, then Bernardo reaches across the Jet Girl opposite for Anita's hand.' The 1961 film adaptation, which addresses racism even more directly than the musical, heightens this moment. The statuesque blonde Carole D'Andrea as Velma stops opposite George Chakris's Bernardo and it is she who recoils, offended. Throughout the swing era, desegregated dance floors, like the one at the Savoy in Harlem, had produced anxious commentary.[14] On this 1950s dance floor, white girls are used to confirm that any inter-action between Jets and Sharks other than fighting is unacceptable.

On the other side, there is Maria, more naïve than Graziella or Velma, but crucially a temptation to a white man. According to Wells, Maria is a figure familiar from the exotic operas and operettas of the nineteenth century as 'an exotic, ethnically differentiated character who woos – or despite her chaste passivity, attracts – a white male tenor, often to his demise.'[15] Indeed, Tony and Maria's romance does get the white male tenor (or leading man) killed. Given that Bernstein's stated goal was to make a point about racism, and the racial dynamics encoded in the music, dancing, and characterizations, it is plausible to read this inter-gang romance as an analogy to miscegenation. Notably, the serenade 'Maria' is composed out of the dissonant tritone interval that unifies the score as a whole and which is fundamentally unsettled, as an interval that splits the octave in equal halves. Although the interval resolves in this number, it emphasizes Tony's yearning and foreshadows that in captivating him, Maria has become a destabilizing force within the score and the narrative. Though she is a milder personality than Anita, Maria is no less dangerous as a magnetic feminine Other.

We never see enough of Tony and Maria's romance to know the basis of their attraction, but her appeal to the audience at least is made clear in 'I Feel Pretty.' At the same time, the song functions as a container for Maria, confining her to the realm of the affective. Where we might have expected an 'I want' song from her, we have instead a song that simply states how she feels: pretty, witty, gay, charming. The fast triple meter that indicates both waltz and an Aragonese *jota* (two charming dances), the flamenco-inspired flourishes and castanets all add to her exotic allure while the largely strophic form and the straightforward harmonies keep her expression simple. This is also one of the few songs where the tritone interval is not present, perhaps indicating that Bernstein wanted the song to be uncomplicated. Moreover, Sondheim's later admission that the rhymes he gave Maria in the song were too sophisticated for her is revealing. Rather than clever, Maria is meant to be straightforward, as Laurents confirms in the dialogue. When they meet, Tony asks if she is joking, meaning deceiving him, and she responds: 'I have not yet learned how to joke that way.'[16] Although naïve, the power of her feelings and those she evokes in Tony lead the hero to his doom.

Anita, on the other hand, is a force in her own right and gives voice to the strategic move that also preoccupied the musical's creators: assimilation. Andrea Most has provided an overview of the assimilation narrative and its prevalence among the music theatre works of Jewish-American creators. Those earlier narratives, like *Abie's Irish Rose* (1922), were common enough for Bernstein, Laurents, and Robbins to be worried about repeating a cliché. In response, they moved *East Side Story* to the Upper West Side and shuffled the ethnicities involved. As they take the place of the Jewish gang/Capulets, there is a marked tendency to acculturate among the Shark Girls. When we first see Anita, remaking Maria's dress in the bridal shop, she is described as a Puerto Rican girl wearing a flashy dress that is an 'unsuccessful attempt at movie-star-American.'[17] In a similar vein, Consuelo is described as having 'patently' bleached blonde hair. These efforts to assimilate are characterized as deliberate and perhaps overdone – not just American, but 'movie-star' American.

The issue of assimilation comes to a head as Bernardo and the Sharks depart for the War Council. When Anita insists on her Americanness, Bernardo mocks her by addressing her in Spanish and with all of her saint and matrilineal names – 'Anita Josefina Teresita ... Beatriz del Carmen Marguerita, etcetera, etcetera' – a naming practice one might downplay or curtail as part of acculturating.[18] He is crudely illustrating that she is a first-generation immigrant, as opposed to the second- or third-generation Jets. Bernardo and Anita recognize the same problems, but their reactions to the Jets are conditioned by their gender roles: beating them versus joining them.[19]

Anita and the Shark girls are positioned as cultural mediators and 'America' is Anita's argument for assimilation. Working on a lyrical and musical level, it creates a cosmopolitan, hybridized style that captures the mixing of communities. Rather than a faithful evocation of any particular Puerto Rican genre, it is a mashup of the Mexican *huapango* (from which the song takes its characteristic cross-rhythms), the Puerto Rican *seis*, and the *seis de bomba* (the origin of the verbal rejoinders from Anita and the other girls).[20] In addition, these folkloric traits are blended with the blues, a brassy orchestration more characteristic of Latin jazz, and the Broadway vernacular. The slow prelude captures the 'spirit, if not the letter, of the *seis*,' with its gentle syncopations and orchestration featuring Spanish guitar, guiro, and claves, as Rosalia sings about the beauty of Puerto Rico.[21] But when Anita takes over the melody, she inserts a prominent blue note as she declares: 'I like the island Manhattan. Smoke on your pipe and put that in!' This slang expression and bluesy turn usher in the chorus which touts the benefits of living in the US. Doubling down on the role of women as cultural mediators, both film adaptations gender the disagreement, with Bernardo and the boys opposing Anita and the girls, emphasizing the resistance of race to assimilation. The future is only alright 'if you're all white' in America. The women, their perspective, see more social freedoms and economic opportunities.

Even within the original text of the musical, the conflict is immutable, only yielding a little in the final, unspoken moments of the 'Somewhere' reprise. We could read Anita's fate as determined by the tragic arc, but that would ignore the confluence of race and gender that we have already seen in the characterization of the Jets, the use of the Jet Girls as a device, and in Maria's role. Anita is a type of exoticized female lead related to Maria, but still distinctive. In operatic terms, Anita is a Carmen-like figure whereas Maria is more like the demure Micaëla. According to Elizabeth Wood, characters and singers like Anita, Chita Rivera, and Rita Moreno are a threat to white patriarchy as 'renegade figures of unbridled sexual passion: gypsy and Jew as the exotic, feminized, non-Western Other, the object of the male gaze whose return of the gaze with teasing defiance, scorn, or indifference enhances her allure for male desire.'[22] 'Teasing defiance' captures Anita's attitude toward Bernardo and the flashy choreography and costuming that attends almost every iteration of 'America' is certainly alluring. The parallels to *Carmen* would have been clear to the collaborators, all of whom were familiar with opera.

Although initially intended as a parallel to Juliet's nurse in Shakespeare's play, Anita's role here is also embedded as part of a secondary romantic couple as dictated by the demands of opera, operetta, and musicals. As a result, there were some difficulties in defining her character, since she was neither significantly older like Juliet's maid (or Aunt Eller in *Oklahoma!*) nor a peer like Rosaline (or Ado Annie). Given the struggles, when Robbins wrote to Bernstein and Laurents on 18 October 1955, he was afraid that Anita would fall into cliché as 'the typical downbeat blues torch-bearing 2nd character,' citing Julie in *Show Boat* (1927). As a result, Robbins predicted, 'the audience will know that somewhere a "my man done left me" blues is coming up for her.'[23] In this comment, Robbins clearly reads Anita as a woman of colour. Julie is passing at the beginning of *Show Boat* but is later revealed to have 'Negro blood' and it is that miscegenation that puts her narrative on a tragic course. The torch song 'Can't Help Lovin' Dat Man' provides the audience with their first hint that Julie is a 'tragic mulatta' figure when Queenie, the Mammy figure of the musical, recognizes it. The blues singers and characters Robbins was thinking of, as well as those whom Bernstein most admired, like Billie Holiday, were Black women.[24] In turn, Anita and her version of femininity draw expressive power from these voices.

Small changes to Anita's character (lowering her age) and the avoidance of the blues (for the most part) in her musical characterization helped avoid the cliché Robbins feared. However, there was no easy solution to the threat Anita posed to the social order, whether the collaborators were conscious of it or not. Of course, Maria's message to Tony has to go astray, as does the messenger Friar Lawrence sends in *Romeo and Juliet*, and the expediencies of musical theatre meant the messenger had to come from among the existing cast. Anita is close at hand and in terms of her own character development, perhaps recognizes that Maria's goal and her own desire to belong in America are sufficiently aligned. The sexual violence she experiences, however, is not called for by the plot. It is a consequence of the demands of race and gender that intersect in her person and the legacy of the unruly women of colour who are her theatrical ancestors. Extending the work of Susan McClary and Nelly Furman on the figure of Carmen, Wood proposes that such voices can be heard 'Sapphonically,' as a 'rupture and escape from patriarchal order,' an order that insists that 'runaway female desire, Carmen's "rebel bird", must be captured, caged, crushed.'[25] This is doubly true for Black women in America, like Julie, who dare to express their desires. Ironically, it is Anita, with her faith in the assimilation narrative of 'America,' who becomes the most forceful example of its failure. However, the invocation of the 'Sapphonic' points to the way out of the racial trap that *West Side Story* exposes and it does so through two women's emotional relationship with each other.

The Redemptive (Colourblind) Feminine

The song complex of 'A Boy Like That' and 'I Have a Love' sits uneasily within *West Side Story* for many reasons. The discomfort makes sense narratively: Anita has just lost her love and Maria is striving to keep hers alive. Although appropriate to the situation, the wild contrasts in mood and style can be awkward to hear – particularly Maria's operatic exclamation 'Oh no, Anita, no!' (Performances by Kiri Te Kanawa and Cecilia Bartoli have made clear the dramatic potential in this line specifically.) Indeed, that cry, the duet in counterpoint that follows, and later the *parlando* transition, seem to come from a different world than the songs on either side. The jagged rhythms and contours of 'A Boy Like That' are aggressive and Anita's scansion is awkward. According to Wolf this disorder emphasizes both her fury and that English is her second language.[26] Relatedly, Wells hears Anita's music as part and parcel of the Hispanicization of the Shark Girls.[27] These are both valid interpretations, but the passage would still be musically unsettling even if the language were more fluent. Moreover, this passage has none of the folkloric influences of 'America,' rather it embodies the jazz-based, modernist violence of the 'Prologue' or 'The Rumble.' Anita is adopting what has been, throughout this musical, a masculine style and that cooption is just one of the ways that this pair of songs destabilizes the patriarchal forces driving the narrative.

On the surface, Anita and Maria argue about Tony's fate, but they also negotiate the relationship between the redemptive feminine and the assimilation narrative. In a striking reversal, driven by her recent experience, Anita rejects the notion of integrating into American culture, warning Maria: 'stick to your own kind.' The 2009 revival reinforced this sentiment by having Anita return to Spanish for 'A Boy Like That.' Maria initially argues back in Spanish, before switching to English to reprimand Anita: 'You should know better. You were in love, or so you said.' After struggling to be heard by Anita throughout 'A Boy Like That,' Maria now has her attention and can deepen what Wolf describes as her 'pedagogy of emotion' in the second song, 'I Have a Love.'[28] This pair of songs 'develops an emotional shift, a change brought about by one woman's influence on another' and is as 'intensely homosocial' as the rest of the musical has been.[29] In this moment, the balance tilts from the masculine kinship of the Jets toward these two women. In Wolf's reading, Anita and Maria's extended duet 'upends the heterosexual romance entirely, altering and feminizing the affective organization of the musical by linking the two women in intensely grounded affiliation and mutual understanding.'[30] Wells also focuses on their shared place in a violent, masculine world in which this argument between two women represents 'the only successful and rational mediation of conflict in the entire work.'[31] Wolf hears this kind of female duet as disrupting the heterosexual drive of the musical whereas Wells hears it as offering up the traditional redemptive role for women, at least temporarily. The latter reading is much closer to the conscious decision-making of the authors, in which the survival of 'Juliet' was a key decision.[32] The nature of Maria's persuasion bears further investigation, then, as do the narrative results.

According to Wells's reading, which she acknowledges is just one possibility, 'I Have a Love' grounds redeeming femininity in whiteness. When Maria shifts to the language of opera, she ushers in a slower, more moderate ballad, which Wells hears as closer to 'classical' style (notoriously the realm of dead, white men). The result is that 'both women have shed their ethnic identity by the end of the number.'[33] Wells sees this as one of the tragedies of the show. The women's wisdom becomes increasingly central to the narrative, but to 'convey the horror of a men's world ... they also must abjure their ethnic allegiances, a primary source of their spirit and group identity.'[34] This scene hijacks Anita's own self-professed drive toward Americanization, dictating conformity instead of the hybridity of 'America' as the terms of inclusion.

However, another interpretation is evident in the drafting process and ultimately in the score: 'I Have a Love' proposes colourblindness as the solution to the problem of belonging. In as much as Robbins was searching for contemporary touchstones, the collaborators were also seeking to present a universalized theme. The desire to address intolerance in America was always present, even as the cast of characters shifted from early outlines, through scene lists and drafts of the book. As he wrote in his copy of *Romeo and Juliet*, Bernstein had in mind 'racial intolerance,' but also a specific setting at Passover/Easter and a Catholic vs. Jewish conflict.[35] These first thoughts in response to Shakespeare's text reveal the ways in which ethnicity, religion, and race were overlapping concepts for him and his contemporaries. One early outline also proposed a scene at a 'festival, possibly Chinese,' which together with Anita's proposed last name (Ellis, as in the island) demonstrates how the collaborators were attempting to capture the diversity of New York's immigrant community.[36] Another early outline, even closer to the Shakespeare and in which both principals still die, Juliet takes her poison and wanders the streets deliriously. The authors propose that 'as she walks through the streets it's as though – from what we see and hear – she is walking through alleys of prejudice of different kinds.'[37] These attempts to generalize about prejudice depend on what George Lipsitz calls the supposed 'universal interchangeability' of categories of identity.[38] Only this leveling of difference could allow for the solution offered in 'Somewhere,' a song in which prejudice disappears because people simply let go of such differences, including race.

In its formulation of utopia, 'Somewhere' imagines a colourblind America and 'I Have a Love' lays out the path to that vision. However, colourblind logic has often been used to shore up racist structures, perpetuating racial inequality, because its side-effect is to affirm whiteness as the un-marked 'normal.' According to Lipsitz, 'the appeal to colorblindness is a claim with no content. It is a proclamation without a program, a pronouncement without a plan of action.'[39] Lipsitz's definition of colourblindness certainly applies to the logic of 'Somewhere' and 'I Have a Love.' The lyrics, for instance – 'peace and quiet and open air' – indicate only that this idyllic place, free from discrimination, is not a city. The definition of 'somewhere' is so unmarked as to be practically anywhere suburban, exurban, or rural. However, whether one hears these songs as an evocation of classical music (*pace* Wells), as a ballad in the Broadway vernacular, or some of both, the unmarked norm at work is white. It is worth noting that the first performance of 'Somewhere' was *literally* colourblind as Reri Grist sang anonymously from the orchestra pit. Laurents perhaps also tipped his hand in 2009 by having Anita switch to English as well for the duet portion of 'I Have a Love,' which vocalizes the unstated assumption that 'universal' belonging is English speaking. However, departing from Lipsitz, I would argue that in the case of *West Side Story*, this colourblindness is not empty of content, rather it overflows with *affective* content.

If we return to Wolf's idea of 'emotional pedagogy' and look carefully at the score, 'I Have a Love' takes up the themes of 'Somewhere' and completes its work. In terms of melodic content, both songs lack the unsettling tritone present in the rest of the musical. Both have simple melodies and lighter orchestrations featuring the warmth of the string section. The two songs also share organizing intervals and 'I Have a Love' manages to resolve the more open-ended structure of 'Somewhere.' The opening phrase, 'I have a love and it's all that I have,' repeats a step up from F to G (with some embellishment), recalling the major second interval of 'someday, somehow, somewhere.' In addition, the minor seventh leap that opened 'Somewhere' reappears with the words 'I love him.' The difference is that after Anita is persuaded to join the melody, they finally land the octave leap that 'Somewhere' never accomplished. This gesture is a triumphant conclusion that accompanies the words: 'Your love is your life.' The way to a colourblind utopia is, quite literally, to love enough. For Maria to love Tony enough not to care about their differences. For Anita to love Maria enough to do as she asks. The redemptive feminine *is* the plan of action.

Of course, this plan of action is not enough. The resolve of these two women of colour is ultimately overpowered by violent masculinity. As Wells puts it, 'their responses to these atrocities are the loss of faith, the loss of compassion, and the loss of the redemptive feminine.'[40] Because the women's agency is limited to the affective realm – their persuasion is based in emotion and so is the solution they propose – their ability to bend the narrative arc is limited. Moreover, they are bound by gender *and* race. What Devon W. Carbado describes as 'colorblind intersectionality' does not work for women of colour; only white women can stand in for 'all women.'[41] Perhaps the most disturbing aspect of the tragedy, then, is that only after colourblindness fails as an option and Maria has experienced sufficient pain and suffering is her challenge to the racist, patriarchal social order enough to move them. She forces everyone – both gangs, Doc, the police – to hear her by holding them all at gunpoint as she stands over Tony's body. At this point, the authors of *West Side Story* deliberately chose to leave their Juliet alive and there is the smallest indication that Maria's words may have landed, as both Sharks and Jets carry Tony's body offstage behind her. But we still have a long way to go from this procession to 'Somewhere.'

Conclusion: Un-Gendering *West Side Story*

What Anita's and Maria's fates demonstrate is that the problems of race, gender, and sexuality are inextricable. A colourblind solution fails in part because, in attempting to move past race as an issue, it does not attempt to dislodge the restrictive norms of gender roles and compulsive heterosexuality that also bind the characters. In analyses by Wolf and Wood, alternative readings of musicals and operas, as well as alternative ways of listening to performers, can give voice to otherwise unexpressed identities and even suggest alternate endings. In addition, the text of *West Side Story* itself may suggest such a queer reading in the person of Anybodys, the character who almost saves the day. It is Anybodys who warns the Jets that Chino is stalking Tony with a gun and it is Anybodys who succeeds in finding Tony just before the end. Not listening to Anybodys in that moment seals Tony's fate – too far gone in grief to heed the warning, he instead yells for Chino to come shoot him. Continually rejected for refusing to abide by gender norms, it is Anybodys who proves herself the most resilient character. The name also suggests that a universal message might be embodied by the character, both within the text of the musical and in its afterlife.

In the case of the show's leading women, their performances can be read as embodying a lesbian sensibility. According to Wolf, any woman who defies gender norms can appear lesbian because 'culturally dominant, "commonsense" understandings of femininity weave heterosexuality into femininity'.[42] Examples of this 'commonsense understanding,' like the expectation that women serve as mediators or the idea of the redemptive feminine, are key elements of *West Side Story*. A lesbian reading is particularly apt for Anita, whose likeness to Carmen, as discussed before, makes her not only a threat to the masculine of authority of the Sharks and the Jets alike, but also a danger to the heterosexual structure of the musical as a whole. The latter is a feat, fundamentally, of performance rather than authorial intent.

Wolf's lesbian interpretation of 'A Boy Like That/I Have a Love' draws on Wood's scholarship and her own analysis of two seminal performances. The different vocal qualities of Rivera and Carol Lawrence contribute to the effect of the shift in emotional timbre halfway through the number. As heard in the original Broadway recording: 'The last section transforms a song of conflict and conversation into an expression of love as they join together musically – Rivera's thick, rough-edged belt and Lawrence's clear, plaintive soprano – and sing their agreement to each other with the same notes that the (heterosexual) lovers sang to each other earlier.'[43] In Wolf's reading, the intimacy this scene produces alters the terms of the musical and audiences certainly feel more sympathy for both women in this moment than for anyone else, thanks in large part to Rivera's and Lawrence's complementary abilities and performance choices. And to the extent that this song pair lives on in performance, other singers have the opportunity to embody different emotional realities, gender expressions, and sexualities. Indeed, the afterlife of *West Side Story* began fairly quickly, not just with the film adaptation, but also with jazz recordings based on the score, the suite of dances Bernstein excerpted and arranged (Symphonic Dances from *West Side Story*), and concert and cabaret performances of the songs.

One performance that offers up something like an alternate ending for the characters can be heard in a concert given by Carol Burnett and Julie Andrews at Carnegie Hall in 1962. Throughout the evening, which was also broadcast on CBS, Carol's and Julie's performances 'repetitively underline how they complement, harmonize, and complete one another,' which taken together can position the two, implicitly, as a butch-femme couple. In Wolf's reading, 'Carol is Julie's "other" much more so than any man with whom Julie performed.'[44] Their rendition of 'A Boy Like That/I Have a Love' comes at the end of a Broadway medley in which they cover a broad swath of repertoire, 'singing songs representative of the various epochs or eras, if you will, as they were handed down through the ages and into history,' as Julie archly suggests. (Carol's response: 'What?') In their performance of 'I Have a Love,' the grainy timbre of Carol's voice displaces the typical male role as counterbalance to Julie's clear coloratura. As a result, we hear two women within the kind of romantic, symmetrical frame that had previously been the territory of (presumed) heterosexual romantic pairs.[45] Notably, the medley for Carol and Julie stops at this point, not because they are out of Broadway history but because their relationship has reached its emotional end-point. If the medley and the program as a whole are about demonstrating their affinity, the two could not be closer than at this moment.

In a similar vein to these lesbian readings of Anita and Maria, the character of Anybodys invites queer listening practices and identifications among fans of the musical. Described in the book as a tomboy, Anybodys can also be understood as a transgender boy or a non-binary person. As Wells points out, the yearning for belonging and normalcy expressed in 'Somewhere' is perhaps most perfectly embodied by Anybodys: 'Although we can clearly see what is required for the other characters to escape – for Puerto Ricans and whites to stop fighting, for Tony and Maria to run away – the metaphor of an incomplete or possible escape suits Anybodys more closely. There is, in fact, no solution to her dilemma of not fitting in anywhere.'[46] One significant story beat, however, does allow Anybodys belonging as a Jet. Having delivered the crucial news that Chino is after Tony, Anybodys finally gets an assignment on behalf of the gang. Before they go their separate ways, Action says: 'Ya done good, buddy boy.' Anybodys responds: 'Thanks, daddy-o.'[47] This moment of acceptance, affirming the role Anybodys has wanted throughout the show, stands in stark contrast to Tony's dismissal later. As Anybodys attempts to get him to safety, he yells: 'You're a girl: be a girl! Beat it!'[48] His rejection attempts to put Anybodys back in place as a girl, but the writers of the musical recognized that their character was not 'like any other girl on earth' – as lyrics from a cut song 'Like Everybody Else' confirm. Whereas A-Rab and Baby John want to be taller or older, Anybodys' predicament is profound: 'Why can't I be male?' Removed almost as quickly as it was added in August of 1957, during the show's out-of-town trial in Washington, DC, the song nonetheless opened a window to another reading of Anybodys, the traces of which still remain in the dialogue and action of the book.

The casting of iris menas, a transgender non-binary actor, in the role of Anybodys in the 2021 film adaptation of *West Side Story* highlights the importance of the character to transgender representation. Likewise, Tony Kushner's small but significant adaptations in the script confront Anybodys' problem more directly than other versions. Most striking is the clear trauma inflicted shortly before 'Gee, Officer Krupke' in another violent confrontation with a fellow Jet. A-Rab says he can verify that Anybodys is a girl because he pantsed them. Anybodys' response is defiant and comes with fists: 'I ain't no goddamn girl!' (A similar fight in earlier versions stemmed from an insult to Anybodys' sister instead.) It was never a stretch to read Anybodys as transgender, given that the book for the musical and the 1957 film script both eventually recognize the character's gender identity and expression. The act of a fellow Jet affirming Anybodys' true self – 'buddy boy' – resonates with other affirmations like correct pronoun usage. This reading has been widely adopted by fandom as 'head-canon' for Anybodys – what the text might not confirm, but what a fan assumes to be true. Even the 1950s descriptor 'tomboy' can be translated into contemporary notions about the possibilities of gender identity and expression beyond the binary. Kushner's script shifts the audience toward the realization that Anybodys is trans before there was a word for it and menas's performance hints that his acceptance may have come too late. Having only recently moved from outsider to insider, he is capable of understanding that others who are marginalized are also at risk. Indeed, immediately after the affirmation of 'buddy boy,' he runs into Anita on her way into the drugstore and warns her quietly but urgently: 'leave.'

The queerness of Anybodys is part of what makes them perhaps the closest to a universal character in *West Side Story*. The name Anybodys rings true, as does Sarah Frankcom's decision to have them sing 'Somewhere' and deliver the musical's message. While Spielberg and Kushner did not recapitulate Frankcom's choice, they also chose a different performer for 'Somewhere' in a move meant to universalize its message. They created a role for Rita Moreno as Valentina, the Puerto Rican widow of Doc who now runs the drugstore and shelters Tony. Like Anybodys she stands between categories. She at least somewhat rejects assimilation: 'I married a gringo. He (Riff) thinks that makes me a gringa, which it don't and I ain't.' But she is in turn rejected by Anita who, after the older woman interrupts the Jets' assault, calls her a traitor and rejects her help: 'yo no soy tu hija!' Valentina's version of 'Somewhere' reads like a prayer, one rooted in her own past and concerned for the future of the next generation, spanning the generational divide in the hope of breaking down others.

In writing a musical about immigrant youth in New York City, the authors of *West Side Story* confronted intertwined anxieties about sexuality, gender, and race. As a tragedy, it challenged the standards of American musical theatre and fundamentally changed the genre. However, the slim hope of belonging offered at the end of the musical effectively retreads a colourblind, assimilative (or integrationist) path taken by Civil Rights advocates and opponents of progress alike. This deferred redemption of the Sharks and the Jets is also gendered – it both depends on the imagination of women like Anita and Maria and produces their suffering. However, we can still imagine a path to 'Somewhere' out of the ending of *West Side Story* (an invitation Bernstein hands us in the score) if we look to the work of performers and spectators. If we recognize the interplay of gender, sexuality, ethnicity, and race we can consider solutions (read: performances and political actions) that undo multiple restrictions or offer multiple ways of belonging. We might also, as invited by the character of Anybodys, expand our ideas about gender beyond the binary and un-gender our vision of 'Somewhere,' making it a space that welcomes multiplicity and complexity. Belonging is not just a 'boy thing' or a 'girl thing' – it's for anybody and everybody.

Notes

1. Elizabeth A. Wells, *West Side Story: Cultural Perspectives on an American Musical* (Lanham, MD: Scarecrow Press, 2011), 160.
2. 'West Side Story: Birth of a Classic,' www.loc.gov/exhibits/westsidestory/westsidestory-exhibit.html, accessed 28 May 2022. Used by permission of The Leonard Bernstein Office, Inc.
3. Stacy Wolf, *A Problem like Maria: Gender and Sexuality in the American Musical* (Ann Arbor: University of Michigan Press, 2002), 4–5.
4. For Crenshaw's reflection on intersectionality and the evolution of critical race theory see: Kimberlé Williams Crenshaw, 'Unmasking Colorblindness in the Law: Lessons from the Formation of Critical Race Theory,' in *Seeing Race Again: Countering Colorblindness across the Disciplines*, edited by Kimberlé Williams Crenshaw, Luke Charles Harris, Daniel Martinez HoSang, and George Lipsitz (Berkeley: University of California Press, 2019). For a summary of the evolution of the term in feminist studies see: Sumi Cho, Kimberlé Williams Crenshaw, and Leslie McCall, 'Toward a Field of Intersectionality Studies: Theory, Applications, and Praxis,' *Signs* 38/4 (Summer 2013): 785–810, 785–88.
5. Typescript outline (1955), box 73, folder 10, Leonard Bernstein Collection (hereafter LBC), Library of Congress.
6. Jennifer C. Nash, 'Re-Thinking Intersectionality,' *Feminist Review* 89 (2008): 1–15.
7. Cho, Crenshaw, and McCall, 797.

8. Katherine Baber, *Leonard Bernstein and the Language of Jazz* (Urbana: University of Illinois Press, 2019), 162.

9. Wells, 143.

10. May's term for the social and domestic restrictions placed on women postwar references Secretary of State George F. Kennan's strategy of containment regarding the Soviet Union. Elaine Tyler May, *Homeward Bound: American Families in the Cold War Era* (New York: Basic Books, 2008; orig. 1988), 16–18.

11. May, 96.

12. WSS script, 49.

13. WSS script, 41.

14. Baber, 83–84.

15. Wells, 144.

16. WSS script, 25.

17. Version B, box 73, folder 10, LBC. For Andrea Most's study of assimilation in the United States by Jewish-American creators of Broadway musicals, see her *Making Americans: Jews and the Broadway Musical* (Cambridge, MA: Harvard University Press, 2004).

18. WSS script, 38.

19. Baber, 177–78.

20. Wells, 124–25.

21. Wells, 124.

22. Elizabeth Wood, 'Sapphonics,' in *Queering the Pitch: The New Gay and Lesbian Musicology*, 2nd edition (New York: Routledge, 2006; 1994), 43.

23. Letter from Robbins to Bernstein and Laurents (18 October 1955), box 73, folder 10, LBC.

24. Baber, 89.

25. Wood, 44.

26. Wolf, *Changed for Good: A Feminist History of the Broadway Musical* (New York: Oxford University Press, 2011), 46.

27. Wells, 154–55.

28. Wolf, *Changed for Good*, 47.

29. Wolf, *Changed for Good*, 49.

30. Wolf, *Changed for Good*, 50.

31. Wells, 154.

32. Three draft scripts exist for *West Side Story*, one in which the double-death at the ending of *Romeo and Juliet* is preserved, one in which both lovers survive, and one that matches the eventual ending. Script Versions A, B, and C, box 73, folder 10, LBC.

33. Wells, 155.

34. Wells, 155.

35. Annotated copy of *Romeo and Juliet*, box 73, folder 10, LBC.

36. 'Gang Bang' outline, box 73, folder 10, LBC.

37. Romeo and Juliet outline – 2 acts, box 73, folder 10, LBC.

38. George Lipsitz, 'The Sounds of Silence: How Race Neutrality Preserves White Supremacy,' in *Seeing Race Again: Countering Colorblindness across the Disciplines*, edited by Kimberlé Williams Crenshaw, Luke Charles Harris, Daniel Martinez HoSang, and George Lipsitz (Berkeley: University of California Press, 2019), 40.

39. Lipsitz, 24.

40. Wells, 155.

41. Devon W. Carbado, Colorblind Intersectionality,' in *'Seeing Race Again: Countering Colorblindness across the Disciplines*, edited by Kimberlé Williams Crenshaw, Luke Charles Harris, Daniel Martinez HoSang, and George Lipsitz (Berkeley: University of California Press, 2019), 210.

42. Wolf, *A Problem like Maria*, 41.

43. Wolf, *Changed for Good*, 48.

44. Wolf, *A Problem Like Maria*, 133.

45. Wood, 36–37.

46. Wells, 165.

47. WSS script, 103.

48. WSS script, 115.

Adapting *Romeo and Juliet*

JANE BARNETTE

As a dramaturg who specialises in adaptations for the stage, when I consider *West Side Story*, I do so in light of its source, *Romeo and Juliet*. There are several different ways to focus dramaturgical work for theatrical adaptations, depending on the specific needs of the work in question.[1] Although the entirety of any dramaturgical approach for *West Side Story* ultimately depends on the approach taken by the director and creative team behind a particular production, I nevertheless ground my initial research in questions central to adapturgy itself. Here, I examine the 'spirit of the source', as well as the pleasures available for spectators familiar with the source material. Finally, I question the geography of adaptation – how questions of time and space figure into comparisons between the texts as well as their production histories.

The Spirit of the Source

While the search for a singular original source is foolish, especially when considering adaptations of Shakespeare's work, shifting the question from a desire to pinpoint an origin to *the spirit of the source* allows for a more nuanced understanding of the core story being adapted. We know that *Romeo and Juliet*, like every other play attributed to Shakespeare, was itself an adaptation, but we may also discern the core elements that audiences and readers associate with *Romeo and Juliet* in order to see how they are later adapted by others.[2] At the crux of William Shakespeare's play is the concept of 'star-crossed lovers', a theatrical trope often associated with the improvisational sketches of the Italian *commedia dell'arte*. Whereas *commedia* sketches include young lovers, their love story is merely the fodder for the primary focus, which typically centres on the comic ways that their fathers' servants attempt to disrupt or trick the lovers out of (or into) trouble. Not only does Shakespeare transform this story from comic to tragic, then, but he also shifts the focus from the parents and their servants to the young lovers themselves.

In so doing, the nature of how exactly the lovers are 'star-crossed' becomes that much more significant, for in order for a tragedy to work, audiences must understand the risks and stakes involved that inevitably lead to the tragic ending. What did it mean, then, for Romeo to be 'star-crossed' with Juliet? And how does that idea – the spirit of the source – translate into the lovers at the core of *West Side Story*? In order to explore this carefully, I want to consider both the 'star' and the 'crossed' part of the story's essence separately, before analysing the notion of 'star-crossed' altogether.

As literary critic J. W. Draper acknowledged in the early twentieth century, '*Romeo and Juliet* is a tissue of improbable coincidence' – nearly every event that leads to the tragic ending appears to occur by accident, if we do not fully consider the impact of the stars, or fate itself.[3] We take the phrase 'star-cross'd lovers' from the Prologue itself and it is Romeo who muses that 'Some consequence, yet hanging in the stars, / Shall bitterly begin [its] fearful date / With this night's revels' just before he departs for the Capulet party where he will meet Juliet (I.iv.107–09). References to the stars, heavens, fortune, and fate abound throughout the play, which is not surprising when we recall that 'the sixteenth century generally accepted astrology as a science'.[4] Combined with the belief that the human body was ruled by 'humours' or bodily fluids that required balancing for optimal function, analysis of human behaviour in Shakespeare's era involved the predictive practice of astrologists with that of proto-doctors who 'read' their patients' humours as a means of categorising and predicting the opportunities and obstacles they would encounter. Thus, humans with an excess of bile (the choleric) were associated with the element of fire, and therefore influenced by the signs of Leo, Aries, and Sagittarius; those with an excess of blood (the sanguine) followed the signs of Aquarius, Gemini, and Libra, which are connected to the element of air. For those connected to the element of water, with an excess of phlegm, their ruling signs were Scorpio, Pisces, and Cancer, while the excess of black bile corresponded with humans ruled by Capricorn, Taurus, and Virgo.

Through the lens of this categorical system, an adaptation dramaturg might trace the connective threads between different humours and astrological signs with their corresponding characters in the source, while also noting how (and whether) these same designations hold true in the adaptation. The particular adapturgical interest here is whether (or how) this overall concept of Fortune drives the choices that characters make, given the tendencies predicted by the astrology and humours that influence them most. For example, Juliet's cousin Tybalt 'is clearly of the choleric or wrathful type' – he admits as much himself when he refers to his 'wilful choler' (I.v.91), and after he is slain by Romeo, Benvolio notes Tybalt's 'unruly spleen' which is 'deaf to peace' (III.i.162, 163).[5] While his counterpart in the musical does not reference choleric metaphors directly, Maria's brother Bernardo is introduced in the stage directions as being 'handsome, proud, fluid', with 'a chip on his sardonic shoulder'.[6] His protectiveness over his young sister sharpens when she shows interest in Tony, whom he calls a 'Polack' several times, including the moment that escalates the rumble at the end of Act 1, when Bernardo reaches for his knife, which eventually leads to him killing Riff.[7] Thus, both the source and the adapted characters exhibit the hot tempers and rash actions of choleric types.

Equally important to the spirit of the source is the second part of this phrase, how they are 'crossed.' In Shakespeare's play, the Prologue establishes that the Montagues and the Capulets have an 'ancient grudge,' but there is no further exposition to explain the feud, nor do theatre historians have reason to believe that it would have been a question raised by Shakespeare's audiences. We simply accept that these two families and their employees do not associate with each other. For those who yearn for specificity of origin, it is possible that Shakespeare's reference to these two families has historical (and poetic) precedents with Dante's *Divine Comedy*, since in the *Purgatorio* he references a feud between the Montecchi and the Cappelletti, or Montagues and Capulets. While scholars have typically accepted the idea that Shakespeare did not read (or was not influenced directly by) Dante, this short reference is nevertheless intriguing, because it implies that the two families were 'also caught up in the Ghibelline versus Guelph factionalism'.[8] These factions represented a rivalry from the twelfth and thirteenth centuries between support for the Pope and support for the Emperor, resulting in civil war during much of the late Middle Ages throughout Italy.[9]

The question of how the lovers' families are 'cross'd' gained complexity when the creative team of Robbins, Bernstein, and Laurents began to tackle their adaptation in the mid twentieth century. Following the instinct of performance scholar Brian Eugenio Herrera to refer to *West Side Story*'s origin narrative as 'legend,' in recognition that 'the veracity of any particular account is less important than the generally shared belief in the actual narrative,' from most accounts it was Robbins who first landed on the idea of translating the crossing from warring families to religious cultures at odds when he conceived of *East Side Story* in 1949.[10] In this case, the way the stars aligned in Robbins's concept was through the timing of Easter and Passover, and the crossing was to be between Catholics and Jews who lived on the Lower East Side of New York City. However, once playwright Arthur Laurents was recruited to join the team, his recognition of the direct parallels between this adaptation and the 1920s smash-hit play *Abie's Irish Rose* quickly ended the excitement, leading the team to look for other parallels that would communicate the spirit of the source in a way that translated for twentieth-century audiences. Six years later, when the stars aligned such that 'Laurents and Bernstein bumped into each other by chance at the Beverly Hills Hotel', they were compelled to discuss the project again, and could not ignore a newspaper headline about 'Gang Riots on Olvera Street', citing warfare between Mexican American and white gangs in Los Angeles.[11]

Because these collaborators were committed (above all else) to creating a musical version of Shakespeare's tragedy, and because they recognized their Broadway audiences would be far less likely to embrace a story about California Mexicans than immigrants coming to New York, they translated the gang rivalry into a plausible scenario Laurents could better imagine: 'I knew firsthand [about] Puerto Ricans and Negroes and immigrants who had become Americans.'[12] Thus, the crossing of the stars was adapted from Italian families with a centuries-old rivalry to two youth gangs competing for territory as well as the right to be seen as American. If we are to accept the theory that the feud between the Montagues and Capulets developed from factionalism related to the political and religious conflict between the Holy Roman Empire and the Catholic Church, it seems that the musical team's initial translation of 'star-cross'd' as Jews in conflict with Catholics would make a more direct match, insofar as it would retain the religious (and, related to some extent, political) factions vying for power. However, in shifting the emphasis away from religion, Laurents, Robbins, and Bernstein seized on a theme that was arguably more authentic for US audiences: the question of how we define American-ness, especially as it relates to immigration, race, and ethnicity.

Palimpsestuous Pleasures

One can hardly discern the nature of American-ness – that is, what it means to be an American – without employing the concept of a palimpsest. A palimpsest is a piece of artwork or writing that has several layers, and onlookers can discern parts of what was created or written before underneath the top layer. Most often used to refer to a manuscript or section of writing, a palimpsest both recycles previously written-upon material (papyrus or paper, usually) and does not entirely efface what existed before it. The trace or residue of history is crucial to the concept of palimpsests, and while in some ways the same could be said of any nationality, given the history of the USA (and especially that of New York City), palimpsestuousness has particular resonance for American identity. The ultimate goal of assimilation is to erase the trace of one's previous identity, taking on the target culture such that no layers of difference might be seen – and yet, especially with regard to racial identity, we cannot define one without the other.[13]

This is especially true of Puerto Rican-ness, in part due to the multiplicity of race found there, combined with the easily overlooked fact that it too is part of the USA. 'Since Puerto Ricans are a differently racialized people,' as cultural historian Frances Negrón-Muntaner explains, 'and some are indistinguishable from whites or African Americans (as coded in Hollywood cinema), *boricua* ethnic specificity [has] to be easily seen and heard.'[14] In other words, it must be performed, or layered on top of what is initially seen, as if adding a layer to a palimpsest. To be sure, this need to perform *boricua* (as Negrón-Muntaner argues) invites traumatic practices such as the use of brownface for Bernardo (played by George Chakiris on film – the same actor who had played the leader of the Jets onstage), but within the field of adaptation studies, it is the very ability to see beneath the top layer that provides pleasure for spectators.

To have a palimpsestuous pleasure, then, is to see at once the adapted choice *and* the residue of the source. It is this delight of recognition, of discerning the links between source and adaptation, that creates this response. For audiences of *West Side Story*, the palimpsests exist in several different ways of seeing the performance – for our purposes here, I will focus primarily on the ways that the characters of the musical are palimpsests that allow rewarding glimpses of Shakespeare's play to peek through at strategic moments.

From the outset, it is clear that the adults are far more prevalent in *Romeo and Juliet* than they are in *West Side Story* – although the focus in both shows is on the lovers and their friends, all adolescents in the contexts of their times, the lovers' parents remain unseen throughout the musical. Nor does Juliet's counterpart have a Nurse as confidante – indeed, one of the most impactful changes made through adaptation was to transform the confidante role from elder to peer. While all adaptation processes hinge on practicality considerations – in this case, Robbins needed a female lead dancer – these decisions are never made based on expediency alone; thematic consequences are part of the creative process as well. By creating the character of Anita to replace the Nurse, and pairing her with Maria's brother Bernardo, the leader of the Sharks (and therefore an adaptation of Tybalt), the writers make possible several significant changes that occur in the second act of *West Side Story*, as it deviates from Shakespeare's play.

Rather than staging her own death in an ultimately unsuccessful plan to create the exit strategy for her to run away with Romeo, as Juliet does, Maria does not pretend to die. The extraordinary string of bad fortune that befalls Romeo (due, as we have discussed, not to chance alone but to fate written in the stars) culminates when Friar John fails to share Juliet's secret with him, and instead Romeo believes his servant's claim that his beloved has killed herself. In contrast, the Tybalt character that Romeo kills for revenge in the musical is not only the killer of his best friend (Riff), he is further entangled into the story by being Anita's boyfriend and Maria's brother. Bernardo's death understandably enrages Anita, but when she tries to warn Maria that Tony is a murderer, she quickly learns that Maria has forgiven Tony. 'A boy like that who'd kill your brother, / Forget that boy and find another!' Anita sings, but Maria remains unconvinced.[15] After Officer Schrank arrives to question Maria, she asks her best friend to deliver a message to Tony whom she is supposed to meet at the drugstore.

Reluctantly, Anita agrees and goes to the drugstore with the intention of updating Tony as Maria requested. However, her encounter with the Jets there changes her mind: Tony's friends proceed to taunt her mercilessly, culminating in a 'wild, savage dance, with epithets hurled at Anita, who is encircled and driven by the whole pack'.[16] After she falls down in the corner, the Jets lift up Baby John and drop him on top of her, implying the spectre of sexual assault, which is interrupted only as Tony's mentor and confidante Doc arrives and insists, '*Stop it!*' Shaken and dishevelled, Anita purposefully lies to the gang, telling them that after learning about Bernardo's murder, Chino has killed Maria. This is the final straw that leads to Tony running into the streets, inviting Chino to 'COME ON: get me too!'[17]

Whereas I do not suggest that viewers of this scene glimpse the Nurse role peeking out from underneath Anita's character, there is a palimpsest here that brings pleasure. The gamble that Anita takes in telling her lie recalls the gamble Juliet takes when she follows Friar Laurence's advice, allowing her to feign her death with his sleeping potion. In both cases, the female characters defy the fate their community thrusts upon them: Anita refuses to allow the Jets' disrespect for her (and murder of her boyfriend) stand without recourse; Juliet refuses to allow her parents to force her into a marriage with Paris. In effect, both women's decisions confront and dismantle the very real consequences they would otherwise face of losing agency over their bodies and violating their morals, allowing them to assert a path forward that aligns ethically with what they believe is right. Thus, the palimpsestuous pleasure in this instance recalls the combination of dread that spectators feel when they see that Anita and Juliet are cornered, only to be replaced with a tragic sense of relief when they carve out another path, albeit one that audiences predict will not end happily.

Other opportunities for appreciating the palimpsestuous layers exist when we compare the supporting characters – the question of how Doc replaces Friar Laurence, for example, allows for a useful comparison between the roles of mentors who are secular versus those based in the Church – but I maintain that the most effective and crucial of these alterations to characters is that of Anita for the Nurse. It is up to characters, after all, to move the plot forward, based on the choices they make and the consequences and obstacles they face. However, any analysis of theatrical adaptation would be remiss to overlook the role of geography in the story.

Geographies of Adaptation

All stories – whether experienced as readers, listeners, or spectators – take up space. The space they occupy might be imaginary for the duration of our experience with a story, or we might first read (and imagine) the world of the story before seeing it on the screen or the stage. Because in live performance we have the option of creating a sense of space using both three-dimensionality and projected imagery or suggested depth with scrims and tricks of stage lighting, questions of geography as they apply to scenography are fundamental to theatrical adaptation dramaturgy. Especially when tasked with creating the fantastic or impossible onstage (through special effects, sleight of hand, symbolism, or puppetry, for example), the specific choices that are both indicated in the adapted script as well as those taken by designers for full productions of the adaptation are productive portals for dramaturgical analysis.

Of all the settings we might associate with *Romeo and Juliet*, the one expectation that audiences likely share is that of Juliet's balcony. 'The balcony scene', as it is frequently called, occurs in the second act, although it is not the only time where the lovers' speech indicates that they are either above or below each other. While the likelihood of a three-dimensional balcony appearing onstage during Shakespeare's lifetime is virtually nonexistent, it is not a stretch to suggest the creative team for *West Side Story* would have imagined one as they considered the crucial elements of the source.[18] Regardless of its actual presence onstage, the *sense* of a balcony – namely the verticality it provides, and the corresponding symbols it provokes for readers/spectators – must be considered central to the story and theme of *Romeo and Juliet*. Part of this is textual, not surprisingly for Shakespeare. Consider Juliet's concern that Romeo has climbed up to see her: 'The orchard walls are high and hard to climb, / And the place death, considering who thou art' (II.ii.63–64). As literary scholar David Bevington suggests, 'The vertical separation between Juliet's window and the orchard or garden below lends itself to recurrent visual images of ascent and descent, aspiration and despondency.'[19] Not only is Shakespeare foreshadowing the fall that inevitably awaits the young lovers, he is also calling upon the Biblical worldview that medieval stages made literal – early Renaissance stages retained the depictions of heaven and hell in their ceilings and trap doors or discovery spaces.

Rather than a general auguring of doom, Shakespeare offers specific signposts for what will befall them with Juliet's words after Romeo has descended from her window: 'O God I have an ill-divining soul, / Methinks I see thee, now thou art so low, / As one dead in the bottom of a tomb' (III. v.54–56). The tomb is the other most significant space of action for *Romeo and Juliet*, as the location of both her feigned death and actual suicide. In a study of the Elizabethan staging of the tomb, theatre historian Leslie Thomson argues:

> The movement from the [balcony scene] at the fictional window of Juliet's bed chamber, to the scenes on the stage level in Juliet's chamber and later in the tomb is a physical movement from high to low: metaphorically a half-turn on Fortune's wheel. But while taken literally the dialogue describes this downward movement, the pervasive wordplay implies elevation, inviting the audience to perceive not funeral but marriage, not death but life.[20]

The verticality of movement – both the literal climbing up and down and the conceptual references to high and low – reinforces the spirit of the source, calling upon well-known medieval iconography of fortune as a wheel ('stars') as well as the oxymoronic references to love and happiness that occur alongside stage action of death ('crossed'). Moreover, this 'theatrical conflict – words contradicting actions' emphasises the transcendent theme of this play, urging audiences to believe, as Romeo and Juliet do, that death has no power to end true love.[21]

In contrast, what is vertical in Shakespeare's play becomes horizontal in *West Side Story*. While upon initial inspection observers might point to the parallels between the balcony scene and Tony's use of the fire escape outside Maria's bedroom (see Figure 9.1), when considering the musical as a whole, the importance of the streets quickly outweighs that of the fire escape. Unlike most mid century musicals, *West Side Story* does not begin with an overture but rather features a dance prologue that establishes the conflict between the two gangs. In part because it was so innovative, this opening scene remains one of the most iconic for spectators: beyond the movement-based exposition it provides, the prologue communicates the territorial protection of urban space that motivates gang warfare.[22]

In translating the spirit of the source from the transcendent power of fortune/fate to a sociological question about belonging and terrain, the musical collaborators move our focus from divine or sublime concerns about the nature of the universe to earthly notions grounded in conflict created from human prejudice. Thus, while the fire escape scene in Act 1 does have the effect of mirroring the balcony scene (allowing for palimpsestuous pleasure), we also cannot help but recognise the practicality and

Figure 9.1 Tony and Maria on the fire escape in a *West Side Story* production at Starlight Theatre, Kansas City, MO. (Photo credit: Starlight Theatre, Kansas City, MO)

ubiquity of fire escapes – they provide a short-hand for urban spaces, especially in New York.[23] Our reception of those moments, then, is less about ascending the stairs than about escaping down them, and ultimately this scene reinforces the grounded, horizontal nature of geography throughout the musical.

To return to the scene where Anita goes to the drugstore to deliver Maria's message (2.4), although there is a sense of verticality insofar as Tony and Doc are in the cellar, below ground level, the conflict remains horizontal and the dialogue reinforces the ground-level concerns around which the adapted story revolves. In a pointed moment of wordplay, Anita asks the Jets, 'Will you let me pass?' as she attempts to get by them so that she can descend into the cellar to find Tony. Snowboy, however, retorts 'She's too dark to pass.'[24] While clever, unlike Shakespeare's wordplay of oxymorons and foreshadowing metaphors, Laurents speaks plainly to Americans, based in understanding colourism – for some, it may even call up a recognition of US racial history and the infamous 'one-drop' basis for segregation and slavery.[25] Moreover, her request – to pass – emphasises horizontal movement, both literally and metaphorically: the desire of immigrants to blend in, to walk among whiteness, as well as her practical desire to cross the stage.

The original scenic design of *West Side Story* reinforces this horizontal tendency – on several occasions, the 'set flies away and the stage goes dark', leaving actors alone onstage and bringing to mind the bleak bareness of deserted streets and alleys without surrounding foliage.[26] These moments are not meant to be literal as much as expressionistic representations of the primary characters' psyches – for example, in 2.5 when this happens, it is just after Doc tells Tony Anita's lie, that Chino has killed Maria. Tony runs out of the cellar, and as he does the surroundings disappear, leaving him to call for Chino in a blackout. When the next scene begins, 'the lights come up to reveal the same set we saw at the beginning of Act One – but it is now jagged with shadows. Tony stands in the emptiness, calling, whirling around as a figure darts out of the shadows and then runs off again.'[27] The 'emptiness' here evokes what Tony feels, believing that his love has been murdered because of his own misdeeds, but it also reinforces the overall despondency of a world without upward mobility, where the options for success are not about climbing the social ladder, but about mere survival.

There are earlier instances when the set disappears in the musical to express happier emotions – the first time occurs in 1.5 just before the hopeful duet 'Tonight' – after Maria's line, 'All the world is only you and me!' the 'buildings, the world fade away, leaving them suspended in space.'[28] The promise of this song is reinforced by the stage directions, indicating their suspension, as if they are floating above the ground, unaffected by the rules of gravity (or fate). And yet, with the exception of Tony's brief ascent of the fire escape for this encounter, for the majority of the show the movement and use of space remains on the street level. As the lovers sing, 'Today the world was just an address, / A place for me to live in, / No better than all right, / But here you are / And what was just a world is a star / Tonight!' In Sondheim's lyrics we have one of the clearest adaptations of Shakespeare's play, with a chorus that explicitly recalls the spirit of the source, repeating the phrase 'And what was just a world is a star' throughout the optimistic song.

The world they reference is the subject of the most iconic use of geography to communicate adapturgy in 'Somewhere' (2.1), the song that follows Maria's discovery of Tony after the rumble, knowing that he has killed her brother and yet, miraculously, she insists that he stay with her and not turn himself in. 'We'll be all right. I know it', Tony offers. 'We're really together now.' Yet Maria corrects him: 'But it's not us! It's everything around us!' Tony's suggestion, then, to 'find some place where nothing can get to us' erupts into him singing, 'Somewhere there's got to be some place for you and for me.' This moment is reinforced by Oliver Smith's scenic design when once again the 'walls of the apartment begin to move off' and 'the two lovers begin to run, battering against the walls of the city'. Their escape works, 'and sud-denly – they are in a world of space and air and sun'. For this brief interlude – during Robbins's dream ballet sequence – the horizontal nature of space is no longer that of the heaviness of gravity or the barren streets. It is the expanse of nature, of 'joy and pleasure and warmth', as the stage directions indicate, and the horizon begins to be one of possibility instead of limits.[29] In order for these crossed-lovers to exist happily, the adapters suggest, the world itself has to change. Indeed, as Shakespearean scholar Irene G. Dash claims, 'this emphasis on place in *West Side Story*, specifically on America, reiterates the importance not only of America, but also of New York'.[30] This focus is further driven home by recognising that the Jets are introduced in the stage directions as 'an anthology of what is called "American"', as well as the unforgettable song, 'America', sung by Anita, Rosalia, and the Shark Girls.[31] In this adaptation, then, the lovers are world-crossed instead of star-crossed.

Crossing Genres

The couple's optimism is crucial for us to believe they are truly in love, and for spectators to have a sliver of hope that they might be able to succeed, against all odds. But those odds – whether grounded in sociology or foretold by the stars – must always be looming, in order for these stories to remain tragedies. In his recollection of creating *West Side Story*, Leonard Bernstein noted that the exact nature of the subject matter they would choose for their version of *Romeo and Juliet* was 'all much less important than the bigger idea of making a musical that tells a tragic story in musical-comedy terms'.[32] The challenge of 'using only musical-comedy techniques, never falling into the "operatic" trap', as Bernstein put it, was considerable, because it had not been done before.[33]

What are the essentials for tragedy? Definitions for this genre have shifted with contemporary playwriting, but as of the mid twentieth century when this musical premiered, Western theatre-makers would likely rely upon a combination of Aristotle's *Poetics* with Arthur Miller's 'Tragedy of the Common Man'. Both theories of tragedy assert that audiences must identify with the tragic hero, but Miller maintains that the focus should be on the working- or middle-class person rather than (as previous centuries had insisted) one of noble rank.[34] Whereas it is clear that the collaborators achieved an adaptation that 'spoke to bias in contemporary culture – ethnic bias, racial bias, and perhaps economic bias',[35] what is less clear is whether the play upon which they based their experiment was itself a tragedy in the first place.

To suggest doubt about the genre of *Romeo and Juliet* is not meant to underplay the tragic nature of their love or ultimate demise. To the contrary, for most scholars, there is no doubt that this is one of Shakespeare's tragedies, specifically a love tragedy that features two heroes instead of one.[36] Instead, I want to draw attention to the necessity of *hamartia* as well as *anagnorisis* in tragedies, following Aristotle. In order to create the possibility for *catharsis*, he suggests, the hero(es) must make a tragic error (*hamartia*) and have recognition of doing so (*anagnorisis*).[37] What fatal mistake do Romeo and Juliet make? To fall in love when their families are at odds? Is it Romeo's revenge killing of Tybalt? Ultimately, they rely on others to communicate vital information and to offer their escape – this is where they falter, for Juliet's death ruse does not work. However, these are not their decisions or actions; nor do (or should) they recognise them as such.

In both the source and the adaptation, it is society that fails the lovers rather than their own actions that directly trigger the tragic ending. Far beyond the reality of their 'crossed' natures, which are also outside of their direct influence, in both instances the young lovers are obstructed by forces beyond their control. As Friar Laurence tells Juliet, when she wakens from the sleeping potion, 'A greater power than we can contradict / Hath thwarted our intents' (V.iii. 153–54). Similarly, upon Tony's death Maria exclaims, 'WE ALL KILLED HIM.'[38] While the friar points to fate (or God's will) as the reason the plans failed, and Maria's accusation includes all of us and society more broadly, in both cases the stories also demonstrate the failure of adults to protect adolescents from these dangers. If Juliet were not forced into marriage by her parents, she never would have considered suicide. Had Tony's so-called friends not harassed and attempted to assault Anita, she would not have spoken the fatal lie. Surprisingly, in both cases, a striking message against patriarchal control emerges: in the Renaissance play, it is more literal and can be traced to Capulet's role as Juliet's father; in the twentieth-century musical, it is more generally the atmosphere of 'prejudice and hatred engendered around them'.[39] Further, although it is Juliet's father's rule that she upholds, with regard to a tragic error, both the Nurse and Anita 'lose their moral compass as they attempt to save Juliet/ Maria'.[40] However, neither character is given room onstage to acknowledge their error, and so arguably the tragedy is incomplete.

Through considering the process and product of adaptation here, what has been achieved is ultimately my goal with any subject of adapturgy: to refresh the spectators' (and my own) vision of the source, so that they (and I) might see it anew. The comparative explicitness of Anita's peril, as one example, helps contemporary audiences understand the stakes for Juliet as she considers her fate if she weds Paris. And the palimpsest works in both directions: through recognising what Juliet dreads and ultimately takes her own life to avoid, an audience's appreciation for Maria's refusal to abandon Tony even after he has killed her brother is also strengthened. For, while it is accurate to attest that this musical stands on its own and can be appreciated and enjoyed without exploring its source, by examining the spirit of the source, the palimpsestuous pleasures, and the geographies of adaptation, a new understanding of both the adaptation and the source emerges.

Notes

1. For more about adaptation dramaturgy, see: Jane Barnette, *Adapturgy: The Dramaturg's Art and Theatrical Adaptation* (Carbondale: Southern Illinois University Press, 2018).

2. Shakespeare was inspired by *The Tragicall Historye of Romeus and Juliet* (1562), by English poet Arthur Brooke. Brooke's poem was itself a 'free paraphrase' of an Italian poem about the lovers by Bandello. 'Arthur Brooke Biography', www.canadianshakespeares.ca/folio/Sources/romeusandjuliet.pdf (accessed 18 September 2020).
3. J. W. Draper, 'Shakespeare's "Star-Crossed Lovers"', *The Review of English Studies* 15, no. 57 (January 1939): 16–34; 16.
4. Draper, 'Shakespeare's "Star-Crossed Lovers"', 20.
5. Draper, 'Shakespeare's "Star-Crossed Lovers"', 22.
6. *Romeo and Juliet and West Side Story* (New York: Dell Publishing, 1965), 137. All subsequent quotations taken from this book.
7. Bernardo says, 'Come on, you yellow-bellied Polack bas—' just before Riff lunges at him at the end of the first act (scene 9). He also calls Tony this epithet in scene 5, 'And Chino makes half what the Polack makes – the Polack is American!' (*Romeo and Juliet and West Side Story*, 193 and 165, respectively.)
8. 'Dante and Shakespeare: A Tale of Montagues and Capulets' in *Secrets of Inferno* blog, 17 November 2013. https://secretsofinferno.wordpress.com/2013/11/17/dante-and-shakespeare-a-tale-of-montagues-and-capulets/ (accessed 18 September 2020).
9. *Catholic Encyclopedia*, s.v. 'Guelphs and Ghibellines', https://en.wikisource.org/wiki/Catholic_Encyclopedia (1913)/Guelphs_and_Ghibellines (accessed 18 September 2020).
10. Brian Eugenio Herrera, 'Compiling *West Side Story*'s Parahistories, 1949–2009', *Theatre Journal* 64, no. 2 (May 2012): 231–47; 233, n. 15.
11. Herrera, 'Compiling *West Side Story*'s Parahistories', 235.
12. Arthur Laurents, *Mainly on Directing*: Gypsy, West Side Story, *and Other Musicals* (New York: Alfred A. Knopf, 2009), 337–38, quoted in Herrera, 'Compiling *West Side Story*'s Parahistories', 235.
13. Further, 'woven into the musical are comments on the political atmosphere of the times', especially in the wake of the HUAC investigations, in which Jerome Robbins took part, testifying about his short stint in the American Communist Party, while identifying others. The pressure to assimilate was always present for Robbins's generation, but these investigations heightened the cost of assimilationism. Irene G. Dash, *Shakespeare and the American Musical* (Bloomington: Indiana University Press, 2010), 93.
14. Frances Negrón-Muntaner, *Boricua Pop: Puerto Ricans and the Latinization of American Culture* (New York: New York University Press, 2004), 66.
15. *Romeo and Juliet and West Side Story*, 212.
16. *Romeo and Juliet and West Side Story*, 219.
17. *Romeo and Juliet and West Side Story*, 221.
18. Not only were balconies virtually nonexistent in sixteenth-century (or earlier) Verona, but the Elizabethan stage where *Romeo and Juliet* would be produced was also notoriously limited in scenic elements. See Leslie Thomson, '"With

patient ears attend": Romeo and Juliet on the Elizabethan Stage,' *Studies in Philology* 92, no. 2 (Spring 1995): 230–47.

19. David Bevington, *Action is Eloquence* (Cambridge, MA: Harvard University Press, 1984), 111.

20. Thomson, '"With patient ears attend"', 237.

21. Thomson, '"With patient ears attend"', 246.

22. *West Side Story* also culminates as it begins, in the streets of the city.

23. Additionally, the use of the fire escape underscores the vision that Laurents had for the adaptation, insofar as it relates to the danger of fires, an appropriate metaphor for the erotic heat that the playwright sought to amplify between Maria and Tony (Herrera, 'Compiling *West Side Story*'s Parahistories', 242).

24. *Romeo and Juliet and West Side Story*, 217.

25. Although never officially federal law, the 'one-drop rule' remained an 'American cultural definition of blacks' for much of the twentieth century – it references the notion that any person with one Black ancestor could be considered Black. See: F. James Davis, 'Who is Black? One Nation's Definition,' *Frontline*, PBS.org, www.pbs.org/wgbh/pages/frontline/shows/jefferson/mixed/onedrop.html (accessed 18 September 2020).

26. *Romeo and Juliet and West Side Story*, 221.

27. *Romeo and Juliet and West Side Story*, 221.

28. *Romeo and Juliet and West Side Story*, 161.

29. *Romeo and Juliet and West Side Story*, 201.

30. Dash, *Shakespeare and the American Musical*, 77–121; 102.

31. *Romeo and Juliet and West Side Story*, 137.

32. Leonard Bernstein, 'Excerpts from a *West Side Story* log,' in Leonard Bernstein, *Findings* (New York: Simon and Schuster, 1982), 144. Quoted in Dash, *Shakespeare and the American* Musical, 77. Used by permission of The Leonard Bernstein Office, Inc.

33. While tragic events certainly occurred in previous musicals that also included comedy, such as in *South Pacific* (1949) and *The King and I* (1951), as an adaptation of *Romeo and Juliet*, *West Side Story* was unusual insofar as it transformed a tragedy with three murders into musical theatre, with very little in the way of comic relief.

34. With the resurgence of interest in the ancient world that drove neoclassical theory, seventeenth-century authors wilfully misinterpreted Aristotle's reference to noble character to mean nobility or noble rank, rather than a description of morality.

35. Dash, *Shakespeare and the American Musical*, 115.

36. For more on Shakespeare's dual tragic heroes, see Catherine Bates, 'Shakespeare's tragedies of love', in *The Cambridge Companion to Shakespearean Tragedy*, 2nd edition, ed. Claire McEachern (Cambridge: Cambridge University Press, 2013), 195–217.

37. The translation of *hamartia* to mean 'tragic error' (and not 'tragic flaw') is crucial here – not only does the Greek word come from *hamartanein* ('to miss the mark'), but within the larger field of analysis, we must focus on actions rather than temperament alone. On this distinction, see: Isabel Hyde, 'The Tragic Flaw: Is it a Tragic Error?', *The Modern Language Review* 58, no. 3 (July 1963): 321–25.

38. *Romeo and Juliet and West Side Story*, 223.

39. Norris Houghton, 'Introduction', *Romeo and Juliet and West Side Story*, 7–14; 13.

40. Dash, *Shakespeare and the American Musical*, 119.

10 | *West Side Story* and the Hispanic Problem

ERNESTO ACEVEDO-MUÑOZ

For millions of theatre, music, film, and television fans the words 'West Side Story' are forever entangled with perceptions and representations of US Latinx cultures like no other art product in the history of 'American' media.[1] Since Leonard Bernstein, Arthur Laurents, Jerome Robbins, and Stephen Sondheim premiered *West Side Story* in 1957 it has become a filter, a set of eyeglasses through which US Latinxs and Puerto Ricans have been codified for mainstream audiences. Frances Negrón-Muntaner has referred to *West Side Story* as 'the Puerto Rican *Birth of a Nation*: a blatant, seminal . . . valorized, aestheticized eruption into the (American) national "consciousness."' In other words, *West Side Story* has been seen by many social critics and academics as a sort of 'trauma' for the Puerto Rican diaspora.[2]

Paradoxically, it has also been identified by many Puerto Rican, Newyorican, and Latinx performers in all media as a motivation and a door into the arts. Performers from Rita Moreno to Jennifer López to Lin-Manuel Miranda have cited *West Side Story* as an instrumental and inspirational step in their paths to professional careers.[3] I have argued elsewhere that the instinct to 'burn' *West Side Story* because of its perpetuation of stereotypes is shortsighted: it misses the historical and political context through which the Latinx experience of *West Side Story* can be seen as rebellious and subversive. From the revision of the 'America' lyrics to more accurately represent the disappointment of Bernardo and the Sharks vis-à-vis racism, discrimination, harassment, and lack of economic opportunity, to Maria's usurpation of the 'Miss America' title, to the ironic rendition of the hymn '(America) My Country, 'Tis of Thee,' and other references, *West Side Story* offers many conspicuous instances of criticism, resistance, and debunking of various 'American' myths.[4] The fact that most of that criticism is channeled through the Puerto Rican Sharks, and well-grounded in the Puerto Rican mid century 'immigrant' experience, allows for a reading of *West Side Story* as somewhat subversive in the landscape of 1950s and 1960s US popular culture. The argument, typical in sociological debates, that *West Side Story* offers no alternative to the representation of Puerto

Ricans/Latinx than that of finger-snapping, knife-wielding, juvenile delinquents is myopic and fails to account for the genuine, if limited social commentary that the text offers in context.[5]

But while the representation of immigrant, Latinx/Puerto Rican characters and attitudes can be debated as ranging from abject to progressive, it is the history of casting the Sharks in the most visible versions of *West Side Story* – Broadway 1957, the 1961 film, and prominent revivals – where more problematic issues arise. Historically, the casting of principal performers in *West Side Story* tends to favor a pattern that arguably privileges ethnically white – Anglo, Caucasian, and European types – for certain roles while reserving background and/or smaller parts for visibly more 'ethnic' actors. This pattern, which extends to the TV show *Glee* (2009–2015), was only visibly subverted in the 2020 Broadway revival. The controversial production though, directed by Ivo van Hove, went on hiatus on 15 March 2020 after only a few months due to the Coronavirus pandemic. The shift to a Puerto Rican focus, after the aborted 'East Side Story' idea, brings the Hispanic cultural debate into focus.[6] This chapter considers primarily issues of Puerto Rican/Latinx representation and casting in the original 1957 Broadway show and the 1961 film directed by Robert Wise with Jerome Robbins, while briefly commenting on other productions, including the 2020 Broadway revival, directed by Ivo van Hove, and the 2021 film, directed by Steven Spielberg.

'In America now . . . '

Negrón-Muntaner addressed the issue that the original film was not 'about' Puerto Ricans, that it was never intended to be 'real,' and that it does not 'seem real to Puerto Rican spectators.'[7] She argues that *West Side Story* is 'the most cohesive product of American culture to "hail" Puerto Ricans as Puerto Rican-Americans. Puerto Rican spectators have not been able to resist the command to turn around and respond to the film's shameful hailing,' she writes.[8] In spite of the argument that the Sharks are depicted mainly as criminals, it is clearly the Jets who begin the cycle of violence that places the Sharks on their path to criminality. In the prologue that sets up the film's first act, the spectator is introduced first to Riff, leader of the Jets, who refers to his gang as 'juvenile delinquents,' and later to Bernardo, leader of the Sharks. Bernardo is harassed without visible provocation apart from his 'otherness.' Later at the 'war council' it is confirmed that it was the Jets who 'jumped' Bernardo the first day he moved to the neighborhood.

Criminality and lawlessness are not initially associated with the so-called 'immigrants,' but rather with the perceived 'natives.' Lieutenant Schrank and Officer Krupke are continuously represented as operating 'outside' the law in trying to make deals with the Jets. But police are also the common enemy, and the only truce between Sharks and Jets appears as a rebellious gesture against these corrupt authority figures.

In contrast to the lawlessness of the 'natives' and the impotence of 'the Law,' the Sharks (especially 'their girls') are productive, law abiding, and bound by ties that constitute them within some sense of community. Maria, Anita, Rosalia, and Consuelo all work in the bridal shop and appear to live in the same building. They speak Spanish to one another occasionally, trust each other, and visit one another. There is no real reference to 'home' or community around any one of the active Jets; they are amorphous as far as social or national identity is concerned, with the exception of the term 'natives.' Tony is also explicitly finished with his gang life; he works (which provokes the scorn of the gang) and tells Maria that he goes to church. In contrast, Riff lives with Tony's family and he explains the Jets' dire domestic situations in 'Gee, Officer Krupke': drugs, alcohol, abuse.[9]

As comical as the number is, it stands in great contrast to what we know about the Sharks and their community. In the film, Bernardo and Maria live with their parents and people know them and respect them in their building. We know that Maria has a caring, loving relationship with her parents, as evidenced in their exchange at the fire escape during the 'Tonight' duet. Although parents are absent from the immediate space of the narrative action, we know that Maria's parents are just off-screen. It is also evident that Maria has been brought up properly, in an environment that encourages work and Catholicism, itself an important identity symbol for many Puerto Ricans. Besides the Shark women, we know that Chino also works, and the movie suggests that Maria's parents own the neighborhood bodega. Moreover, the only 'domestic' space represented in the film is Maria's family apartment in the 'Puerto Rican' neighborhood. There is a sense of community already built around the space shared by the characters and it is one of diversity and integration, however unwanted for the assorted 'whites.' In the prologue sequence we see two prophetic signs opposite each other, one stating 'KEEP OFF' and the other 'SE HABLA ESPAÑOL.' These suggest the inevitable integration of this neighborhood and the acknowledgment of the Puerto Rican/Latinx presence. The Jets are just an assortment of what Lt. Schrank calls 'immigrant scum,' with no distinct cultural backgrounds. (Tony is referred to as 'a Polack.') With no 'home' other than the streets, no 'family' other than the gang, no social ambitions other than reclaiming their indistinct 'turf,' the Jets are, by far, the group with no discernible cultural or social identity.

The block, the building, and the apartment where Maria and Bernardo live with their parents constitute the only 'home' seen in *West Side Story*. In the 1961 movie there are six important sequences that take place in the apartment and its immediate surroundings, more than any other space. These are: Bernardo, Anita, and Maria after the dance at the gym; Tony and Maria on the fire escape where she speaks to her father through the window; the 'America' number sung on the rooftop of the same building; Tony and Maria's utopic 'I want' song, 'Somewhere,' and the lovemaking scene; Maria and Anita's confrontation in the 'A Boy Like That/I Have a Love' duet; and Lt. Schrank's interview with Maria after the fatal rumble. This unique domestic space is somewhat problematic in the absence of parental figures, its 'colourful' design and the featuring of a shrine to the Virgin Mary in Maria's bedroom, expanding on certain stereotypes about Latinos. It is, however, the only domestic space seen in the film, but one where some signs of cultural identity can be glimpsed: a bowl of tropical fruit on the table, a guitar propped up against a corner, a combined dining/living room area. Besides the 'colour,' food, music, and references to family and Catholicism as cultural identity signs, there is a fleeting yet clear image of a small Puerto Rican flag along with the US flag visible on top of a television set. The two flags together call Schrank's attention and he stops for a moment, to observe. The Puerto Rican flag shows up occasionally in films or television where a Puerto Rican presence is implied, especially in New York settings. What is far less common is to see the Puerto Rican flag together with the US flag, though that is the official Commonwealth of Puerto Rico constitutional practice. Media representations of Puerto Ricans rarely acknowledge Puerto Rico's unusual political relationship with the USA. Extending Bernardo's retort to Anita during the 'America' argument, 'Puerto Rico is *in* America now' – slightly revised from the show – and referring to the constitutional status of the territory in 'Commonwealth' with the USA, Maria's family, in all evidence, is adjusted to this new status and welcoming of their 'US–Puerto Rican' political and social (if not ethnic/cultural) identity.

Puerto Ricans have been US citizens since 1917, and the 'Commonwealth' status was made constitutional by referendum and ratified by the US Congress in 1952. As US citizens, Puerto Rican 'migration' to the US mainland began in earnest in the 1920s and continued to grow over the next three decades. Between 1950 and 1960 some 470,000 Puerto Ricans (around 20 percent of the Island's population) came to the USA, mostly to New York City, but also to places like Philadelphia, Chicago, and Boston.[10] This migratory wave peaked around 1953/54 coinciding with Maria's arrival – and with Bernstein, Robbins, and Laurents seriously beginning to give shape to *West Side Story*. Nevertheless, it is the definition of Maria's family as 'US Puerto Ricans' that is most significant, giving them, more than any other characters in the film, a sense of identity; a problematic hyphenated identity, but to a certain extent, 'real.' Maria's family is one of 'good' immigrants and good Americans: hard-working, law-abiding, church-going, and respectful of Puerto Rico's political and constitutional relationship to the United States, however awkward that status might be. The phrase 'Puerto Rico is *in* America now' that Bernardo recites to Anita with ironic gusto acquires a double significance. On one hand, it acknowledges Puerto Rico's new political status that surrounds directly the temporal context; on the other, it emphasizes Bernardo's slippery, sardonic definition of that status. As the 'counterpoint' of 'America' effectively foregrounds, 'Puerto Rico is *in* America now,' but Puerto Ricans remain trapped between unofficial second-class citizenship, and the need to assimilate culturally.

'Will you let me pass?'

Within the improbable narrative world of *West Side Story*, the focus on Puerto Ricans has been well documented and criticized. Not only were all four creators of the show Jewish New Yorkers, but Sondheim himself acknowledged that he was not qualified to write for these characters: 'I can't do this show . . . ' he is reported to have said. 'I've never been that poor and I've never even *known* a Puerto Rican.'[11] And yet in the process of the movie adaptation, Sondheim and screenwriter Ernest Lehman made a significant number of changes to the lyrics and format of the song 'America,' transforming it into an 'argument' oscillating between definitions and revisions of the immigrant experience and the fallacy of 'the American dream.'

Besides the fact that nobody in Puerto Rico refers to the USA as 'America' (more likely *Estados Unidos*, or 'New York,' as synecdoche for the USA), the film version of the song significantly softens up the prejudiced content that led to such criticism during the initial stage run.[12] The biggest change is the reworking of the song structure from an argument between four of the girls (Rosalia, the one favorable to Puerto Rico, Anita and the others to 'America') into a gender-divided counterpoint where the boys, led by Bernardo, and the girls, led by Anita, discuss passionately the immigrant experience from two well-defined and completely opposite points of view. In the stage version the song 'America' is emphatic in its lampooning of Puerto Rico as an underdeveloped, poverty-stricken, over-populated, violence-infested, and disease-riddled country, in contrast to the material advantages of the 'American' experience.

The film version of 'America' sharply emphasizes the social disadvantages, the ethnic and racial prejudice, and even the violence to which the immigrant is exposed. The 'Americanization of Anita' is ridiculed by Bernardo and the Sharks as a sign of weakness as he quips, 'Look, instead of a shampoo, she's been brainwashed ... and now she's queer for Uncle Sam.' The prologue to the musical number is faithful in the adaptation, affirming Bernardo's disappointment at the contradictions between his naïve immigrant desires ('We came eager, with our hearts open ...') and the cruel reality of prejudice ('Lice! Cockroaches!'). But that is as far as the stage version goes, so it is meaningful that the film version goes to such efforts to dramatize Bernardo's disillusionment, and then later to give him the final word; agreeing in no uncertain terms with Bernardo's miserable prophesy of 'America' ('Everywhere grime in America ... Terrible time in America'). The movie's gender counterpoint emphasizes the women's shallow view of 'assimilation' as something strictly related to conspicuous consumption: it suggests that *being* American means to spend notably on consumer goods. The men, however, have a decidedly dystopian, more realistic view of a significant portion of the immigrant experience in the USA.

Surely the result is imperfect, yet nothing short of subversive, especially since Anita, the most vocal champion of the 'America' experience, later recants her previously cheery 'Americanization.' After the traumatic attempted rape perpetrated against her by the Jets, Anita's near-final words serve as a real redemption for her character: 'Bernardo was right ... If one of you was bleeding in the street, I'd walk by and spit on you!' She delivers the false news about Maria's death saying 'I have a message for your *American* buddy' pronouncing the adjective 'American' as if it were an insult. Anita realizes that 'Bernardo was right' about the fallacy of the American dream, even if it takes the experience of sexual violence to come to this realization. While the Sharks are certainly portrayed as patriarchal and infected with stereotypically 'Latin' machismo, they are also evidently affectionate (especially Bernardo with Maria and Anita), while the Jets are consistently and plainly misogynistic ('... Whadda we poopin' around wit' dumb broads?'). The Jets' women,

Anybodys, Graziella, and Velma, are treated in an openly hostile manner. This pattern reaches its most violent manifestation in the racially and sexually charged assault against Anita.

Anita's attempt to make peace, prompted by Maria's desire to escape with Tony 'Somewhere' (against Anita's warning, 'you'll meet another boy tomorrow, one of your own kind, stick to your own kind') leads to what is the most violent scene in both versions. By contrast most of the fight action between the gangs is 'stylized' dancing rather than stunt fighting. Even the killings of Riff and Bernardo, one arguably accidental, the other swiftly brief, are notorious for their lack of graphic violence. But Anita's confrontation with the Jets at Doc's candy store is verbally and dramatically aggressive. While trying to reach Doc and Tony, Anita is harassed by the Jets with racial epithets and cruel stereotypes ('Spic! Lyin' Spic!').

The screenplay and libretto describe the rest of the scene graphically, referring to the Jets as animals, as if they were attacking wolves or dogs:

> The taunting breaks out into a *wild, savage* DANCE, with epithets hurled at Anita, who is encircled and driven by the whole *pack*. At the peak she is shoved and falls in a corner. The Jets lift Baby John up high and drop him on top of her ...[13] (My emphasis.)

Ultimately, for Anita as much as Bernardo, the phrase 'terrible time in America' turns out to be a prophetic, emphatic truth. Subversive for its 1957/1961 contexts, the progressive discourse in *West Side Story* is subtle yet persistent, and never as violent as in the assault against Anita.

Moreover, Maria's desire to usurp the 'Miss America' title is itself an act of resistance against the ultimate celebration of white female Americana. The idea of an 'ethnic' Miss America in the 1950s is nothing short of unthinkable. Criticism of 'I Feel Pretty' points to it as a sign of Maria's submission to the gaze of a white man: she only becomes visible when desired by Tony. Yet arguably she is also showing an unusual sign of subjectivity. She rebels against patriarchal assumptions ('Why did my brother bring me here? To Marry Chino. When I look at Chino nothing happens') and expresses her desire to 'touch excitement.' Granted, she falls in love with the first man she sees outside of the immediate work and domestic spaces. Yet, the 'choice' of Tony is her only expression of sexual desire and agency. 'I Feel Pretty' and the Miss America claim extend the manifestation of Maria's subjectivity and expand on the consistent questions about Puerto Rican 'Americanness.'

Another important reference to the Puerto Rican 'problem' is the Sharks' whistled rendition of Samuel Francis Smith's 1831 '(America) My country 'tis of thee . . . .' Upon being banned by Lt. Schrank from Doc's candy store the Sharks' farewell statement is the whistled phrase from the song invoking the lyrics 'My country 'tis of thee/sweet land of liberty/of thee I sing . . . ' The last note is rendered in a lowering turn, as if it was deflating, subverting the fallacious lyrics. Like Maria's claim to the Miss America title, the Sharks' appropriation of this other 'America' song comes across as an act of rebellion with its ironic use of a cultural symbol whose lyrics insist on the 'native' profile of the 'real' American: ' . . . Land where my fathers died [. . .] My native country thee . . . ' With these three visions and revisions of the word 'America,' Anita, Maria, Bernardo, and the Sharks are constantly calling our attention to the dystopia of *this* immigrant experience.

'It was like putting mud . . . '

The history of *West Side Story* and its relationship to Puerto Ricans and Latinxs in the USA continues to be controversial. Even if context allows for a reading against the grain that puts Puerto Rican characters in a progressive light, as I argue, more effort went into getting the music right than the casting. Some 'Newyorican' context was to be provided by Bernstein's musical choices. As Elizabeth Wells has demonstrated, the many colours of Latin rhythms, Afro-Cuban jazz, the influence of Xavier Cugat, Dámaso Pérez Prado, and the 'mambo craze' of the 1950s all found their way into Bernstein's score.[14] The ease of travel between New York and San Juan allowed Bernstein to fly south to the Island and do some research there. The prominent Newyorican musician, composer, and band director Bobby Sanabria released the album *West Side Story Reimagined* in 2018. It unearthed inspiration from samba, mambo, Mexican, and even strong Afro-Caribbean intersections lying just under the surface of Bernstein's score, though many of these had already been partially adopted into the city's musical soundscape.[15]

The casting practices for the original 1957 Broadway production of *West Side Story*, however, set the pattern for the persistent racial and ethnic hierarchization of principal roles that has been associated with *West Side Story* since 1957. The original run featured two actors of Puerto Rican descent in prominent roles: Jaime Sánchez as Chino, and Chita Rivera as Anita. Sánchez would go on to a long career in theatre, films, and television. Rivera, a 'Newyorican,' was already a Broadway veteran who was married to 'Jet' Tony Mordente. That Anita, the show's designated 'Latin spitfire' stereotype, should be played by a performer with real Puerto Rican ancestry became the norm, especially in contrast to the casting of Maria. Carol Lawrence, who played Maria in the first run and the 1960 revival, was Italian American. She showed up at her first audition 'heavily made up and bejeweled in an attempt to look like a Puerto Rican Juliet.' But Robbins would not have it and instructed her to clean up and then come back.[16] She won the role after numerous auditions and callbacks, and aside from a heavily 'accented' speech and singing pattern, the Maria/Anita contrast in make-up, costume, and even movement – given that Maria's is largely a non-dancing part – was clearly established. Since then, the female actors identified with Maria (especially Natalie Wood) would continue to fall into the 'whiter' category, associated with her modesty and lack of sexual experience, in contrast to Anita's 'spitfire' persona. With Chita Rivera on Broadway and Rita Moreno in the 1961 movie the Maria/Anita dichotomy became most visible.

During its Broadway run, Hollywood producer Harold Mirisch saw the show, purchased the film rights, and began developing the project for United Artists.[17] Natalie Wood was one of the last actors cast for the film in August 1960. Rita Moreno had tested for Anita as early as January. With more tests and screen credit negotiations extending for months, Moreno was signed up as Anita in late July 1960.[18] Moreno was an established character actor in countless 'barefoot princess' parts going back to 1950. But she had played important featured roles in the movie version of *The King and I* (1956), for which Jerome Robbins had recreated his Broadway choreography, and especially *Singin' in the Rain* (1952) where, as 'Zelda Zanders,' co-director Gene Kelly gave her the only non-ethnic part of her early career. Paradoxically, and in contrast to the 'whitening' of the role of Maria (on stage and film) Moreno, the 'Spanish Elizabeth Taylor' was not dark enough to play Anita.[19]

Besides having to fake a heavy accent, all the 'Sharks' in the cast – assorted white actors and a handful of Latinx dancers – were required to don 'brownface' makeup. In a 2017 interview with NPR, Moreno described the makeup as 'extremely dark . . . It was like putting mud on my face.' The story, which Moreno has told in numerous interviews and retold in her 2013 memoir, is further elaborated in the interview. Moreno says that she explained to the make-up man that Puerto Ricans came in a wide array of colours: fair, light brown, 'Taíno' bronze, black. 'Why do we all have to be the same colour?' The man replied, according to Moreno, 'What are you, a racist?'[20] Precisely because Puerto Ricans are not easily identifiable due to our broad racial diversity, Negrón-Muntaner argues that Puerto Rican 'ethnic specificity had to be easily seen and heard.'[21] This need led to the imposition of 'extremely dark' make-up and the uniform thick accents on all actors. These practices were especially conspicuous in George Chakiris as 'Bernardo,' a Greek American who had played 'Riff' in the London production in 1959, and Joanne Miya, a Japanese American, as 'Francisca,' who recalls how she had to 'pass' for Puerto Rican in her audition.[22] And while the 'Sharks' are presumably a mix of 'Newyoricans' born in New York, and recently arrived migrants (like Maria), the accent, along with the 'brownface' was adopted by the producers and imposed on the performers in a form of 'drag' or 'masquerade' designed to avoid any 'ethnic misreading' of their identity.[23]

In spring 1960 the film producers were considering some actors for the part of Maria who had 'ethnic' acting experience, or even Latinx heritage. A standout on the list was Susan Kohner, daughter of Mexican actress Lupita Tovar, who had played the troubled 'passing' teen 'Sarah Jane' in Douglas Sirk's 1959 remake of *Imitation of Life*.[24] But the producers, nervous about a largely unknown cast, hired Natalie Wood. Wood had a long career as a child actor from the 1940s, later specializing in *ingénues* at the brink of sexual awakening, and she had the right experience. Furthermore, she had name recognition and, like Carol Lawrence before her, she was of white European ancestry. In the context of 1950s and '60s Hollywood, Maria and Tony's romance could be interracial only in 'drag' but not in reality. While the other Sharks were required to apply 'extremely dark' makeup (even the fairly light-skinned Moreno), Wood was allowed to 'pass' for Puerto Rican without such impositions. As a typical Latin 'spit-fire,' Anita's persona also comes imbued with sexuality – a slightly different version of the 'barefoot princess' she had been playing since the early 1950s. That stereotype has been mapped out by many scholars, most recently Priscilla Peña Ovalle. 'Hollywood's depiction of racialized female sexuality,' writes Peña Ovalle, was 'a version of femininity that signified looseness or "excessive" female sexuality through hoop earrings, long and wild hair, an off-the shoulder blouse, and bad attitude.'[25] By contrast, the recently transplanted Maria, in her white dress and her *ingénue* manner, is unequivocally characterized as virginal, a disparity further emphasized by the casting of a white actor as Maria.

The 1980 Broadway revival, directed by Jerome Robbins himself, under-scored this pattern in a rather paradoxical way. A contemporary article published in the *New York Times* described the two characters in typical terms. 'The one is ethereal, fawnlike. The other is a little firecracker, sizzling and popping on stage and off.'[26] Needless to say, the article was referring respectively to the roles of Maria and Anita. Tellingly, the role of Maria went to the Puerto Rican actress Jossie de Guzmán, who was made to dye her hair several shades darker than her natural light brown and have 'her pale skin' darkened. But the compromise of a Puerto Rican actress playing the 'ethereal, fawnlike' Maria – even in 'brownface' – appeared to complicate the implied sexual contrast associated with the characters. Debbie Allen, an African American dancer and choreographer, was cast as Anita. In the black-and-white photograph accompanying the article the skin tone contrast is even more dramatic. But the author goes further in the 'type-casting' of Anita: he describes Allen's outfit for the interview as 'a fox jacket with free-swinging skins, a knit dress in fire-engine red and shiny cowboy boots to match.' While that description could fit a 42nd Street sex worker circa 1980, no such description of de Guzmán followed. Instead, aligning again actress and character, the author wrote of de Guzmán '[s]he is deeply religious, like the girl whose role she plays.'[27]

The next major revival on Broadway ran 748 performances from 2009 to 2011. Directed by then ninety-one-year-old Arthur Laurents, the production featured an attempt to further acknowledge and contextualize the Puerto Rican culture purportedly at the core of the show. Lin-Manuel Miranda, a Newyorican known at the time as the Tony award-winning composer and lyricist of the hit show *In the Heights* (off-Broadway 2005), was engaged to translate and adapt certain lyrics and dialogue into Spanish, in a search for more authentic flavour. 'A Boy Like That,' one of the dramatic high points of the show, with the fatal lyrics 'Stick to your own kind,' was one of the translated songs. But audience response was luke-warm, and the lyrics went back to their original (accented) English after only a few months.[28] Casting was also revised to hire all Latinx actors for the Shark parts. Karen Olivo, a Broadway veteran whose credits included *Rent* (1996) and *In the Heights*, won a Tony Award for the role of Anita. Olivo is a Bronx native from a multi-ethnic Puerto Rican–Dominican family. The role of Maria went to Josefina Scaglione, an Argentinian musical theatre actress of Italian descent. According to an article in the *Wall Street Journal*, Laurents was unable to find a suitable Maria – among the thousands of Latinx performers auditioning for parts – leading to his casting of Scaglione.[29] She was a Broadway rookie who had appeared in Argentinian productions of *Cinderella* and *Hairspray*. It is telling that Laurents could not find the 'right' Maria and the final choice confirmed the historic trend: Scaglione's fair skin, light straight hair, and green eyes were a visible contrast to Olivo's brown skin, wavy dark hair, and dark brown eyes.

In its third season, the Fox television show *Glee* (2009–2015) featured a story line around a production of *West Side Story*. The casting of Maria itself became a dramatic hook; the white star of the 'glee' club, Rachel Berry (Lea Michele) and the African American diva, Mercedes Jones (Amber Riley) auditioned and competed for the role. After much embellished suspense and various 'sing offs' the role went to Rachel, by white default casting. The co-directors declared Mercedes a 'risky' choice, presumably because of the implications of miscegenation brought by her pairing with a white Tony. More importantly, the role of Anita went – by 'brown' default – to Santana López, the only openly Latina character in the main cast of *Glee*. Santana was played by Naya Rivera, born in Los Angeles to a multi-ethnic family with Puerto Rican and African American ancestry. As I have argued elsewhere, the most notable element in the *Glee* narrative arc is that Santana/Rivera is never seen auditioning for the part of Anita. While casting Maria became the narrative cliff-hanger of several episodes, it appeared that Santana López was the *only* choice for Anita.[30] In one scene, Santana and Rachel are rehearsing the duet 'A Boy Like That/I Have a Love' in a dark limbo set. That scene comes near the end of the show, with Anita in mourning and Maria in her nightgown after sexually consummating her relationship with Tony. But in the *Glee* intersection, Santana appears in a low cut, sleeveless, fire-engine red dress topped with a red rose in her hair, while Maria appears in the white dress ('the only one there in white . . . ') as seen, presumably, in the 'Dance at the Gym' scene. Once again, the contrast drawn between Anita's type and Maria's visibly whiter, more demure fashion, conforms to the historic pattern: 'one sassy, sexy and brown,' the other 'virginal, modest, and white.'[31] The alignment of whiteness with modesty ('ethereal, fawnlike') and brownness with the 'spitfire' stereotype ('racialized sexuality') is firmly upheld for *Glee*'s twenty-first-century teen/tween audiences.

'Getting it right'

In the volatile cultural wars of the Trump years, it is hardly a coincidence that in the 2020s *West Side Story* saw a major Broadway revival and a Steven Spielberg remake of the film.[32] The Broadway production, a 're-imagining' by Belgian avant-garde director Ivo van Hove, featured a multi-ethnic cast that included Newyorican soprano Shereen Pimentel as Maria, and first-generation Colombian American Yesenia Ayala, as Anita. In an atypical role reversal, Pimentel's Maria was the one with the slightly darker skin and wavy hair, while Ayala has lighter skin and straight hair. Moreover, van Hove's version, set in contemporary times, made the 'Jets' a more racially diverse gang than the original assorted whites of every other historic production, in a nod to its twenty-first-century setting. The 'Sharks,' meanwhile, retained their predominantly Latinx – if not exclusively Puerto Rican – ethnic composition. Arguably, the diversification of the 'Jets' represented an acknowledgment of evolving US demographics. The incorporation of a multi-media design, including live video feed from backstage, and 'Jumbotron' style CCTV displays of main action on stage, attempted to create the urgency of a social media livestream. The production eliminated the song 'I Feel Pretty' and the 'Somewhere' ballet, allowing it to run in 100 minutes without an intermission. Van Hove replaced Robbins's choreography – with its balletic motifs – and substituted it with a more defined 'street dance' style by Anne Teresa De Keersmaeker. Not all the critics were impressed, but some emphasized the background of the Trump war on immigration and police violence as a fitting context for the revival, pointing to its formal sense of urgency as a political statement. In fact, van Hove's production expressly underscored the ways in which the original social and political message of *West Side Story*, however naïve or muddled originally, could be brought to the contemporary surface with an innovative approach that otherwise left its core message intact.[33] In a cover story in the *New York Times Magazine*, Sasha Weiss wrote: '[s]o many of the contentious issues of contemporary life – poverty, immigration, gender discrimination and dysphoria, sexual violence, police brutality – are written into the play from the very first scene . . . "it's all there."'[34]

While van Hove's revival was still playing on Broadway, Steven Spielberg's remake of the film was in post-production. Rumors about the 'pet project' by the distinguished director had circulated for years. The trade journals finally broke the news in early 2018, while 'buzz' features about casting calls and speculation about Spielberg's approach began appearing in the media shortly thereafter.[35] Aware of the controversy about representation that has followed many productions, Spielberg pledged to engage Puerto Rican actors, singers, and advisors. Screenwriter Tony Kushner (*Angels in America*, 1991) rewrote the character of 'Doc' as a woman named 'Valentina' and Spielberg cast Rita Moreno in the part, with executive producer credit. Spielberg's pledge to 'get it right' came to the foreground in a townhall meeting with Kushner at the University of Puerto Rico on 14 December 2018. The room was filled to capacity with students and faculty from the Theatre Department. When asked by UPR Professor Isel Rodríguez to address how they would 'represent Puerto Ricans,' Kushner first flubbed his answer (miscrediting the offensive lyrics '... let it sink back in the ocean' to the stage show) before passing the question on to Spielberg. In a video of the exchange posted on Facebook, Spielberg answered:

The reason we're here ... The reason we've hired so many Puerto Rican singers and dancers and actors, is so they can help guide us to represent Puerto Rico in a way that will make all of you and all of us proud ... It's absolutely important to ensure the authenticity ... including props, signage, dialect ... We can only go to the experts ... That is going to give a lot of credibility to the 'Sharks,' to the Puerto Rican community.[36]

But some at the townhall remained skeptical. No production of *West Side Story* contextualizes the Puerto Rican migration vis-à-vis economic conditions in the US territory; people migrate out of necessity, not contempt for the Island, as the 'America' lyrics suggest. *The Hollywood Reporter* quoted Rodríguez: 'No one leaves this Island without sobbing. Three hundred thousand people left after (hurricane) Maria and the scene at the airport was like a funeral.'[37]

Another reason Spielberg and his team were in Puerto Rico was to conduct auditions with local talent. But none of the actors who auditioned through the local talent agent landed any major parts in the film, despite Spielberg's pledge. Puerto Rican actress, singer, and dancer, Ana Isabelle, a veteran of youth shows on the Telemundo network, was cast as Rosalia – the vocal dissenter in the original 'America' version. Casting expanded to Latinx hubs in the USA including New York, Miami, and Los Angeles. The role of Maria went to Rachel Zegler, a Colombian American high school student from New Jersey. She answered the open casting calls that reportedly attracted 30,000 aspirants. The role of Anita went to Ariana DeBose, also a Latina with an Afro-Puerto Rican father, with Broadway experience (*Bring It On*, 2011; *Pippin*, 2014; *Hamilton*, 2015; *Summer*, 2017). Purposely or not, this casting repeats the pattern of a 'darker' Anita, curly hair included, in contrast to a Maria who is visibly lighter skinned and with straight hair.

Superficial as the casting distinctions may seem, the Spielberg pledge to 'get it right' did extend to important details of context, setting, atmosphere, and historical accuracy to the Puerto Rican experience. As early as 2018 the production engaged the services of Prospero Latino, a strategic consulting firm on US Latinx issues. The firm went on to establish a 'Community Advisory Board' to offer advice and strategies to ensure a more equitable and truthful representation of the Puerto Rican/Newyorican community in the 1950s. The Board included academics, cultural critics, historians, musicians, and members of various communities, in an effort to 'integrate historically and culturally authentic elements in every aspect of the production' and to 'hear the voices' of cultural stakeholders. Its purpose was to fairly represent 'the history of the Puerto Rican diaspora, Latin music, Hispanics in the arts, and the LGBTQIA+ community . . . '[38]

Prominent members included Bobby Sanabria, the Newyorican jazz musician and band leader, known for his extensive work on the 'Latin' roots of the *West Side Story* score that resulted in the Grammy-nominated album *West Side Story Reimagined*. Sanabria was one of the people consulted extensively by screenwriter Tony Kushner to help him access a better understanding of the cultural context of *West Side Story* and the impact of the Puerto Rican diaspora in New York in the 1950s. Also on the Board was Dr. Virginia Sánchez-Korrol, Professor of Puerto Rican and Latino Studies at Brooklyn College. One of the founders of the Center for Puerto Rican Studies and a distinguished historian of the Puerto Rican diaspora, Sánchez-Korrol was a main consultant on the project. She too advised the producers on set, looking at everything from diction to posture, to the look of the neighborhood. The filmmakers, she says, wanted to 'get everything right.'[39] The Board met with members of the cast and crew and confirmed the efforts made at authenticity: costumes, setting, music, etc. Even details of art direction were revised to better reflect Puerto Rican sentiments in 1950s New York, including graffiti references to important political and historical figures like Pedro Albizu Campos and Eugenio María de Hostos.

Delayed for release during the Coronavirus pandemic, Spielberg's version of *West Side Story* was finally released in theatres on 7 December 2021, to overwhelmingly positive reviews. While there were some naysayers in smaller publications, prominent critics from the *Washington Post*, the San Francisco *Chronicle*, the *Hollywood Reporter*, the *New York Times*, and many media organizations praised the new adaptation for its more rounded representation of the Puerto Rican characters, its fidelity to the look of 'the Barrio' in the 1950s, its emphasis on the conflicts brought up by gentrification, and its diverse casting. But the film was also a disappointment at the box office, failing to reach the audiences that its $100 million budget anticipated. Nevertheless, the Academy of Motion Pictures honored the film with seven Oscar nominations, including Best Picture and Director. The standout (and stand-alone) winner at the Oscars on 27 March 2022 was, as expected, Ariana DeBose winning Best Supporting Actress as Anita, making her the second Latinx woman (after

Rita Moreno in the same role sixty years earlier) and the first openly gay woman of colour to win the Oscar. In her emotional, gracious acceptance speech DeBose reworded lyrics from the libretto to reclaim *West Side Story* as an anthem of inclusion, concluding, 'there is, indeed, a place for us.'

The effort to 'get it right' in these contemporary approaches to *West Side Story* is particularly conspicuous in the context of Trump's 'America,' but also logical. As I have argued, the edgy, rebellious social critique that *West Side Story* offers is visible in any close reading of the text(s); its portrait of 'America' a lot less passive than critics have acknowledged. A political reading of *West Side Story* does not neutralize the stereotypes about Latinx and Puerto Ricans, the inequities in gender relations, and problems of race, class, homophobia, etc. Nonetheless, the political edge and social critique, as Ivo van Hove said, 'is all there.' The last word should go to Anita herself. On Bernardo's condemnation of a 'terrible time in America,' it is Anita who concludes, 'Bernardo was right.'

Notes

1. An earlier version of a segment of this chapter was previously published in Acevedo-Muñoz, *West Side Story as Cinema: The Making and Impact of an American Masterpiece* (Lawrence: University Press of Kansas, 2013).
2. Frances Negrón-Muntaner, *Boricua Pop: Puerto Ricans and the Latinization of American Culture* (New York: New York University Press, 2004), 58–61.
3. Acevedo-Muñoz, *West Side Story*, 152–55; Anthony Breznican, 'West Side Glory,' *Vanity Fair*, April 2020, 107.
4. Acevedo-Muñoz, *West Side Story*, 155–67.
5. Alberto Sandoval-Sánchez, *José, Can You See: Latinos On and Off Broadway* (Madison: University of Wisconsin Press, 1999), 62–82.
6. Keith Garebian, *The Making of* West Side Story (Oakville, ON: Mosaic Press, 2000), 29–31; Arthur Laurents, *Original Story by Arthur Laurents* (New York: Applause, 2000), 338.
7. Negrón-Muntaner, 84.
8. Ibid., 85.
9. Arthur Laurents, *West Side Story* (New York: Dell, 1965), 207.
10. José Vázquez Calzada, *La población de Puerto Rico y su trayectoria histórica* (San Juan: Escuela Graduada de Salud Pública, Universidad de Puerto Rico, 1988), 286.
11. Garebian, 37.
12. Ibid., 134–37.

13. Ernest Lehman, *West Side Story*, screenplay (MGM Home Entertainment, 2003), 117–19. Arthur Laurents, *West Side Story*, 217–19.

14. Elizabeth Wells, *West Side Story: Cultural Perspectives on an American Musical* (Lanham, MD: Scarecrow Press, 2011), 32–33.

15. Bobby Sanabria interview with Maria Hinojosa. NPR's Latino USA, 26 September 2018.

16. Garebian, 110.

17. Walter Mirisch, *I Thought We Were Making Movies, not History* (Madison: University of Wisconsin Press, 2008), 114–15.

18. Acevedo-Muñoz, *West Side Story*, 36, 39.

19. *Rita Moreno: A Memoir* (New York: Celebra, 2013), 87; 96.

20. *In the Thick* podcast. NPR, 10 January 2017.

21. Negrón-Muntaner, *Boricua Pop*, 66.

22. Joanne Miya, 'Passing for Puerto Rican,' in *Our Stories: Jets & Sharks Then and Now*, ed. Robert Banas (Denver, CO: Outskirts Press, 2011), 223.

23. Negrón-Muntaner, *Boricua Pop*, 67.

24. Acevedo-Muñoz, *West Side Story*, 38.

25. Peña Ovalle, 'Rita Moreno's Hair,' in Caparoso Konzett, ed., *Hollywood at the Intersection of Race and Identity* (New Brunswick, NJ: Rutgers University Press, 2019), 31. See also Priscilla Peña Ovalle, *Dance and the Hollywood Latina: Race, Sex, and Stardom* (New Brunswick, NJ: Rutgers University Press, 2011), 105–06.

26. Nan Robertson, 'Maria and Anita in *West Side Story*,' *The New York Times*, 22 February 1980, C-4.

27. Ibid.

28. Acevedo-Muñoz, *West Side Story*, 146.

29. Ellen Gamerman, 'I've Just Met a Girl Named Josefina,' *The Wall Street Journal*, 9 January 2009.

30. Acevedo-Muñoz. 'Everything *Glee* in "America": Context, Race, and Identity Politics in the *Glee* Appropriation of *West Side Story*,' in Caparoso Konzett, ed., *Hollywood at the Intersection of Race and Identity*, 256–57.

31. Ibid., 259–60.

32. Matt Donnelly and Brent Lang, 'Fox Feels the Pressure from Disney as Film Flops Mount,' *Variety*, 13 August 2019.

33. Adam Feldman, *TimeOut New York*; Ben Brantley, *New York Times*; David Rooney, *The Hollywood Reporter*. All appeared 20 February 2020.

34. Sasha Weiss, 'How "West Side Story" Was Reborn,' *The New York Times Magazine*, 20 January 2020 (Cover story, p. 3).

35. Patricia Guadalupe, 'Many Latinos Loved *West Side Story* but not the Stereotypes. Can New film Version get it Right?' *Culture Matters*, NBC Latino, 17 April 2018. See also, Raúl Reyes, 'A New "Maria?" Latino Actors Audition, Hope for Role in *West Side Story* Remake,' *Culture Matters*, NBC Latino, 30 April 2018.

36. The video, posted by Mario Alegre Femenías, a Puerto Rican film critic, can be viewed here: https://m.facebook.com/story.php?story_fbid=1015656 9184585549&id=739660548.

37. Seth Abramovitch, 'Spielberg Met with Puerto Ricans about "West Side Story" Concerns,' *The Hollywood Reporter*, 15 January 2019.

38. Letter from the *West Side Story* Creative team to members of the Community Advisory Board, 6 June 2019.

39. Community Advisory Board meeting held via Zoom, 28 May 2020.

11

West Side Story and the Intersections of Class,
Colourism, and Racism

ERICA K. ARGYROPOULOS

Leonard Bernstein always feared his legacy would be that of 'the composer of *West Side Story*.'[1] Doubtless he had already enjoyed celebrity stature long before the show; Bernstein had been hurled into the upper echelons of society as a young man. After stepping down from the post of Music Director of the New York Philharmonic in 1969, the Maestro continued to hobnob with the likes of the Kennedys, Andy Warhol, and the Jewish progressive music set in New York. Bernstein's collaborators in the show that secured his place in music history, though perhaps not as famous as Bernstein himself, were all highly successful in their respective fields and thus could be found socializing in similar circles. In fact, at least three of the four would be in attendance at the infamous soirée that inspired Tom Wolfe's controversial essay, 'Radical Chic: That Party at Lenny's' (1970): a scathing indictment of classism and racism among elite liberals, as well as the decadence of white privilege.[2] In examining the essay alongside the ways in which class and race intersect in *West Side Story*, one sees reflected clearly both the progressive spirit of the collaborators and what could be called their colonialist and commercial sensibilities; indeed, just as today, we must remember that prejudices often hide behind education and self-professed leftism.

Broadway and the 'Culture Industry'

One could assert that Bernstein bemoaned his predicted legacy because he long yearned for not just commercial but also critical success as a composer of concert music and opera. Long before Bernstein's entrance on the scene, however, Broadway was dominated by late capitalist economic considerations not unlike those in other sectors of industry. Certainly, Bernstein and his collaborators pushed boundaries in innovative and unprecedented ways. Ultimately, however, they were still subject to the ambitions of their financial backers, and thus limited in the way all music is when the creators are paid commodities and music their product.[3] As one of America's most emblematic forms of musical entertainment, Broadway is thoroughly embedded in what Max Horkheimer and Theodor Adorno dubbed the 'Culture Industry.' Briefly put, this refers to a society that is totally economically driven, where cultural 'products' undergo increasing levels of reification, boosted by the mass media.[4] Adorno argued repeatedly throughout his career that in late capitalist society nothing is held sacrosanct and above fetishization; the approach to 'manufacturing' arts, theatre, film, literature, and other cultural idioms is no longer distinguishable from the means by which products are kept stocked on grocery shelves.[5] Much like the multitude of brands that grow increasingly similar based on consumer taste, music and other arts are fetishized in the name of the free market. Tin Pan Alley, for example, churned out a constant barrage of songs not unlike goods traveling down a factory conveyor belt, often in the process exploiting musical styles developed by people of colour. Speedy proliferation and delivery of songs were often more important than artistic quality. Such an approach, as Horkheimer and Adorno argue convincingly, is also an exhibition of the thought values encouraged by the greater establishment and their emotional manipulation of society. By streamlining American culture, conformity, superficiality, and standardization in all other areas of society are bolstered; the mass media consequently reinforces the continued production of art by saturating our society with its product to increase the appeal further still.[6] Those who extol the virtues of the free market argue that it creates more choices; in fact, the 'Culture Industry' can produce a self-reinforcing system of limited choices and standardization, traits that often define authoritarian societies.

Class and the Creators

To be sure, the collaborators who created *West Side Story* all enjoyed high social status and the trappings of wealth; they also, however, were genuinely committed to bringing about social change through their work. The political beliefs of the three older men – Robbins, Bernstein, and Laurents – were far enough left that the career of each was affected to some extent by McCarthyism. From the outset, however, *West Side Story* was perhaps limited by the 'Culture Industry' and the manner in which the latter shaped the men's own values concerning class and race. Regardless of this potential influence and the musical's commercial success, the collaborators were truly groundbreaking in confronting important social issues of the times: particularly in a realm of the arts often reserved for light-hearted entertainment and the many conformist tropes encouraged by the 'Culture Industry.' The notion of a Broadway musical that depicted youth gangs and the violence they caused along with the hatred and racism that brought about their formation was subversive in 1957. The show's creators did wrestle with strictures posed by their financiers, determined to preserve the artistic integrity of the show. Its unusual and violent nature made it difficult for head producer Cheryl Crawford to raise money, and in April 1957 she pulled out of the project. (See Laura MacDonald's chapter on the show's producers for more on this [Chapter 6].) The social, musical, and dramatic significance of *West Side Story* make plain that its creators were intent on a new approach to the musical in which controversial social issues were not just clever gimmicks for shock value; indeed, they were being centered for one of the first times in Broadway history.[7] No work, however, should be above scrutiny, nor should its creators.[8] *West Side Story* has been performed all over the world for decades, and continues to be embraced globally as a masterpiece. As long as this work remains such an important part of the repertory – and given the show's inherently serious nature – scholars must resist the temptation to ignore those elements that can be criticized.

In 1970, journalist Tom Wolfe was ready to take the creators of the show to task in a controversy that directly confronts the issues of class and white privilege. Three of the collaborators – Bernstein, with Jerome Robbins and Stephen Sondheim guilty by association – received a thorough literary mauling that year in his 'Radical Chic,' a prescient essay that has remained relevant, all the more so in the era of Black Lives Matter and George Floyd. Bernstein, with his A-list attendees as accessories, is lambasted for his classism, casual racism, and shocking tone deafness concerning the extent of his white privilege. Bernstein was hosting a benefit soirée for the legal aid of several prominent Black Panthers. Wolfe introduces the concept of 'radical chic,' a term coined by the author to describe the way in which rich socialites and celebrities collect social issues to champion not with sincere conviction, but because it adds to their socially progressive credentials and helps them climb the social ladder. While he does not use the term itself, the author refers implicitly to what writer Teju Cole dubbed the 'White Savior Industrial Complex,' a systemic aspect of capitalist society in which Black people are reified for the emotional gratification of the white saviour. Not unlike the charges made by Wolfe against Bernstein, Cole argues: 'The White Savior Industrial Complex is not about justice. It is about having a big emotional experience that validates privilege.'[9] Perhaps with good reason, Wolfe indeed considered Bernstein to be part of that very problem, savagely lampooning the musician for suggesting that he had known discrimination similar to that experienced by Black Panther leader Don Cox. Bernstein asked Cox how he felt being in his luxurious penthouse: 'When you walk into this house, into this building . . . you must feel infuriated!' Cox felt 'embarrassed' but assured Bernstein, 'I don't get uptight about all that . . ., ' then relating how recently he exited ' . . . the courthouse in Queens and there was this off-duty pig going by . . . see . . . and he gives me the finger. That's the pig's way of letting you know he's got his eye on you.' Cox admitted that made him angry, causing Bernstein to respond, 'God, . . . most of the people in this room have had a problem about being unwanted!'[10] Wolfe's portrait of Bernstein is devastating: A famous, rich white man who believed himself capable of understanding the feeling of rejection that Don Cox would have felt in that situation, probably because he was Jewish and gay and had known prejudice, but unable at that moment to accept how different his life experiences were to those of Cox.

We cannot separate such snapshots of Bernstein the man from Bernstein the composer, Jewish musical champion, and conductor who primarily led performances of works by his fellow white composers. In addressing these complex biographical constructions, we initially come across far more questions than answers. The significance, however, begins when we actively confront and decolonize history while remaining sensitive to the challenges Jewish American composers such as Bernstein faced. To be sure, he understood prejudice well as both a gay man and first-generation American Jew coming of age during the Holocaust – nonetheless, he enjoyed a degree of privilege his colleagues of colour did not.

In similarly poor taste to his conversation with Don Cox and decades prior, Bernstein had dedicated his Harvard undergraduate thesis to racial elements in American music, assigning these works in their unadulterated form to an inferior stage of development and lauding the multiculturalism and what he considered sophisticated use of jazz as realized by the likes of Copland and Gershwin. Given his undergraduate thesis at Harvard, Bernstein clearly considered himself an 'expert' on the 'natural development' of multiculturalism in music: regrettably, he persisted in confusing forced assimilation, assumed authorship, and uncredited cultural appropriation with promoting a diverse picture of the 'American dream' – allegedly accessible to all.[11] At best, Bernstein's thesis, written at the age of 20, was haughty and dismissive of colleagues of colour who possessed similar merit and musical training, such as William Grant Still; at worst, the ideas assumed superiority and outright entitlement to assert ownership over elevating Black music to a perhaps 'high art' form as heard in music by Copland and others.

In examining Bernstein's magnum opus, how do such issues of class, colourism, and racism intersect? In what ways did the collaborators' subtle racism manifest in *West Side Story*? Did Bernstein engage in cultural appropriation of Latinx and African American musical materials? These are all questions that must be addressed in any critical analysis of the work.

Class, Colourism, and Racism in *West Side Story*

In many regards, *West Side Story* is centered on issues of class, and this was indeed always the intention, from the days in which Bernstein, Robbins, and Laurents entertained the idea of an 'East Side Story,' which was to be based on rival Irish Catholic and Jewish immigrants on New York's Lower East Side. In essence, this would represent the ethnic struggle between two white outgroups who both experienced discrimination, with the Catholic populace still enjoying more privilege than their Jewish counterparts. Eventually, the idea evolved into the Jets (Polish or Eastern European whites) and the Sharks (Puerto Ricans). From the outset, the Latinx gang is assigned the more menacing name, with 'Sharks' conjuring gruesome images of dangerous predators ready to attack at any moment. It is impossible to know whether the naming of the gangs itself was an unconscious expression of racism; however, it is among other aspects of the show that could have been more culturally sensitive.

In terms of casting, however, there were more insidious forces at work, particularly in the 1961 film version. There has been much discussion over the years about the decision to cast Carol Lawrence, a white woman, in the role of Maria for the original stage rendition. Did the creative team simply defer to their own racist colourblindness? Did they intend for Maria to represent a lighter-skinned Puerto Rican who would therefore appear more desirable and more chaste? When we compare Maria and the darker-skinned Anita, their characters are almost opposites. Where Maria is naïve and virginal, Anita is portrayed as sex-crazed and sassy. When the Jets meet Maria near the end of the show after Chino has killed Tony, they are deferential; when they encounter Anita at the drugstore where she has come to deliver a message to Tony from Maria, they sexually assault her, implying that she was 'asking for it.' While this was likely meant as a harsh criticism of sexual violence, when seen in the context of a greater narrative, one wonders if Anita's darker skin tone was – consciously or unconsciously – correlated to her characterization.[12]

While Bernstein had little involvement in the film version of *West Side Story*, the set was rife with colourism. The filmmakers insisted that Rita Moreno, the Latinx performer who played Anita, wear brownface along with her castmates, Natalie Wood and George Chakiris. Moreno has shared the treatment to which she had been subjected:

We all had the same color makeup, it was a very different time ... I remember saying to the makeup man one day, because it was like putting mud on my face, it was really dark and I'm a fairly fair Hispanic, and I said to the makeup man one day 'My God! Why do we all have to be the same color? Puerto Ricans are French and Spanish ... ' And it's true, we are very many different colors, we're Taino Indian, we are Black some of us. And the makeup man actually said to me, 'What? Are you a racist?' I was so flabbergasted that I couldn't come back with an answer.[13]

It is important to note that the show's original collaborators were not involved in the decision to use brownface, but this was indeed the culture that surrounded the show. Those who made the film recruited a very white cast, which can also be said about the original Broadway production.

What about the lyrical and literary content of the show? Is it inherently racist? In fact, just as in the case of radical chic, the collaborators almost certainly intended to express the injustice that the immigrant faced. Class is represented, not inaccurately, as being tied to colour. We see the honest working-class man in Doc; the menacing, racist police officer in Officer Krupke; and the leadership of the white supremacist system is represented by the white detective, Lt. Schrank. As the show progresses, Schrank makes clear that he holds in higher regard the white European immigrant children who make up the Jets. This too demonstrates an important social truth: there is a racial hierarchy in the country in which one's relative proximity to whiteness determines social status and general worth as a human being. In *West Side Story*, even amongst gang members, white criminals are treated with more humanity. There is a sense in the detective's conversations with the Jets that perhaps not all hope is lost for the white gang; the Latinx one, however, must be taken down immediately. The detective appeals to race and colour when he attempts to join forces with the white gang members. As Ernesto Acevedo-Muñoz demonstrates in Chapter 10 in this volume, it is actually the Puerto Ricans for whom family life seems to be more important in the show, and the Jets seem to be more devoted to juvenile delinquency.

The creators of *West Side Story* also likely believed that utilizing jazz and Latinx musical materials gave the show a tolerant, internationalist flavor.

Musical tropes from Spanish-speaking cultures also were significant in American popular culture of the 1950s and Bernstein had already shown a fondness for them in earlier compositions, although never to the same extent as in this score. Without consulting with any people of colour in this process – and especially knowing the attitude Bernstein expressed so provocatively in his thesis – using these materials is more akin to cultural appropriation than cultural appreciation, part of a long line of white composers using elements of jazz, blues, various types of Latinx music, and stylistic borrowings from elsewhere in the world. This mining of musical styles from cultural groups who often form a despised 'Other' in American society is assisted by copyright laws, which allow pieces of music to be protected but not musical styles. What attitude then do the *West Side Story* collaborators express in what is arguably the Puerto Ricans' most celebrated moment in the show: 'America'? It can be interpreted as an anthem of American exceptionalism, a moment in which some of the Puerto Ricans themselves castigate their own homeland while others remember it fondly. (The differences between the way that the song plays in the stage version and in both films is significant here, because on stage one woman defends Puerto Rico while the remainder celebrate their intended assimilation. In the films, 'America' is an argument between the women who praise New York and the men who criticize their treatment by whites and pine for their homeland.) Is it an opportunity for Sondheim to have a laugh at American ignorance about Puerto Rico and its people? It can be seen as that and as a paean to American exceptionalism, just as the benefit for the Black Panthers was driven by both genuine care and class-driven ignorance.

When Oppression Meets Oppression

While Bernstein was often well meaning and sincere in fighting overt racism and white nationalist violence, like the majority of comfortable white people of his time, he was perhaps unaware of the covert ways in which he enjoyed the benefits of white supremacy. He whitewashed his own closeted queer-ness, pitting that identity and his own Jewishness (which he celebrated) against the more powerful prejudices with which African Americans strug-gled. Even in his grand vision for the development of an Israeli national music amidst his early encounters with the Jewish state, he imagined that Israeli composers would be wise to appropriate vernacular music from the Palestinian population and that of other neighboring Arab countries; in doing so, they too could reach 'high art' in crafting an 'authentic' national music that 'honored' diversity.[14] Bernstein was known to use his platform as a celebrity and respected intellectual to elevate his Jewish peers while sometimes showing less interest in the musical accomplishments of people of colour, certainly the case in his Harvard thesis. While Bernstein was genuinely interested in the Black Panthers receiving a fair trial, for example, his engaging of the Panthers in 'Radical Chic' perhaps reveals a rich white man's delusional savior complex. Bernstein appears to have marveled at these African American men as cultural curiosities and controversial social commodities. In the safety of his bubble of enlightened privilege, he felt qualified to engage the Panthers in conversation about complex issues of race and Black culture, believing he was providing solidarity as a progressive authority, above reproach as a fellow victim of fanatical prejudice.

Looking back on the era of *West Side Story*, much has changed, but even more has stayed the same when it comes to the treatment of people of colour, often significantly impacted by classism. Where is the line between reification of people in the 'Culture Industry' and in that of society at large? Increased standardization of culture only serves to preserve class and racial divides and can be a step towards intolerance. Today, even US Presidents are celebrities, hiding behind an image both crafted and leveraged by the 'Culture Industry'; they can be found hosting podcasts with rock stars, appearing on *Saturday Night Live*, and filling arenas for the purpose of political theatre. In the quest for social justice, we must be ready to confront our history, including some of its greatest cultural treasures. We can have empathy for the creators of *West Side Story*, who all experienced discrimination because they were Jewish and gay. Yet, like many white liberals then and now, at times they were blind to their own classism and racism, even as they genuinely believed they were allies to the poor and people of colour. As Martin Luther King, Jr. stated in his 'Letter from a Birmingham Jail': 'Shallow understanding from people of good will is more frustrating than absolute misunderstanding from people of ill will. Lukewarm acceptance is much more bewildering than outright rejection.'[15] We can enjoy and celebrate works such as *West Side Story* while also publicly recognizing potentially insidious messaging and confronting it.

Notes

1. Bernstein stated this often, including in an interview with Paul R. Laird in Washington, DC, on 15 March 1982. Used by permission of The Leonard Bernstein Office, Inc.

2. Tom Wolfe, 'Radical Chic: That Party at Lenny's,' *New York Magazine*, 8 June 1970. https://nymag.com/news/features/46170/. Accessed 18 June 2021. Wolfe republished the essay in: *Radical Chic and Mau-Mauing the Flak Catchers* (New York: Farrar, Straus and Giroux, 1970; reprint: New York: Bantam Books, 1999).

3. In Marxist economic theory, a product is a finished good intended to be sold, while commodities represent the raw materials used to create the product.

4. Max Horkheimer and Theodor Adorno, 'The Culture Industry: Enlightenment as Mass Deception,' in Gunzelin Schmidd Noerr, ed., *Dialectic of Enlightenment: Philosophical Fragments* (Stanford, CA: Stanford University Press, 2002), 94–146.

5. It is important to note that as significant as Adorno is in theorizing the detrimental impact of mass media in late-stage capitalism upon the arts and therefore the oppressed, he was also blinded by his own unconscious racial biases, reflected in his polemical views on jazz, for example. For a nuanced discussion of Adorno's criticism of jazz, see: Fumi Okiji, *Jazz as Critique: Adorno and Black Expression Revisited* (Stanford, CA: Stanford University Press, 2018).

6. When Adorno emigrated to the USA, he briefly worked for a radio broadcaster. He was angered by the simplistic, erroneous manner in which they approached educating the public in music; further, he was disturbed that media companies conducted continual marketing research to further mold the music to the will of the masses, undermining artistic integrity. To Adorno, this was nothing short of brainwashing the public to adopt commercial tastes laden with the values and ideas that ultimately reinforce conformity and uphold class and racial division. The German émigré had seen the power of mass media to shift society as a professor under the Nazi regime and did not want to see the music industry weaponized, as was Goebbels's film industry.

7. Rodgers and Hammerstein paved the way for *West Side Story* in this regard with shows such as *South Pacific*, which opened eight years prior.

8. In the era of McCarthyism, the creators would likely have been forced to avoid including material that may have more accurately reflected their personal views. Yet it is important to recognize that they must still be held accountable as the ultimate authors of the show. With music history saturated with infrequently challenged white supremacy, we must go beyond the common explanation that these works were a product of their time. We often stop short of saying what that 'time' was like for members of the lower class, immigrants, and people of colour.

9. Teju Cole @tejucole (8 March 2012), Twitter post, http://twitter.com/tejucole. Accessed 19 January 2022.

10. Wolfe, 'Radical Chic'.

11. Leonard Bernstein 'The Absorption of Racial Elements into American Music,' Harvard Thesis, 1939. Published in: Leonard Bernstein, *Findings* (New York: Simon and Schuster, 1982), 36–99. For a useful contextualization of Bernstein's thesis, see: Geoffrey Block, 'Bernstein's Senior Thesis at Harvard: The Roots of a Lifelong Search to Discover an American Identity,' *College Music Symposium* 48 (2008): 52–68.

12. The racist trope of the woman of colour who is sexually promiscuous has long existed, not unlike the sexual vilification of the Jews as sexual predators intent on raping 'Aryan' women. Here, the show's creators show the dominant group as the aggressors, likely an intentional statement regarding the savagery of the white race against people of colour.

13. Rita Moreno, 'The Many Accents of Rita Moreno,' 10 January 2017, *In the Thick* (podcast). www.latinorebels.com/2017/01/10/the-many-accents-of-rita-moreno-podcast/. Accessed 19 January 2022.

14. For a consideration of Bernstein's work in Israel and his efforts to foster native Israeli composers, see: Erica K. Argyropoulos, 'Conducting Culture: Leonard Bernstein, The Israel Philharmonic Orchestra, and the Negotiation of Jewish American Identity, 1947–1967' (PhD dissertation, University of Kansas, 2015).

15. Martin Luther King Jr., 'Letter from a Birmingham Jail,' 16 April 1963. www.africa.upenn.edu/Articles_Gen/Letter_Birmingham.html. Accessed 28 June 2021.

12

The Real Gang History of New York

ELIZABETH A. WELLS

When *West Side Story* opened in 1957, it was received by audiences and critics alike as a thoroughly modern musical, a stylistic departure from even Bernstein's own idiosyncratic works like *On the Town* and *Wonderful Town*. It was also seen as diametrically opposed to another of the year's hit musicals, Meredith Willson's *The Music Man*. Indeed, the race for the Tony Awards was largely between that show and *West Side Story*, each of which put forward a distinct vision of American culture. Whereas *The Music Man* celebrated the home-grown and small-town, *West Side Story* told the tale of warring hoodlum factions in Manhattan's city streets.[1] As such, Bernstein's work did not lull audiences into a sense of harmony and patriotism, but instead forced them to confront some of the biggest challenges in American culture during the 1950s.

Some of those challenges, like poverty and immigration, had been covered extensively in earlier musicals. Juvenile delinquency, however, was a new topic: although very well covered in other kinds of entertainment media,[2] it had so far gone unmentioned on Broadway. In *West Side Story*, audiences saw depicted on stage what was regularly reported in the *New York Times*, and although stylised and reified in high art, the content was still shocking for its original milieu. Contemporary audiences may find juvenile delinquents wearing jackets and ties and dancing in balletic moves almost quaint by comparison with modern gang culture, but at the time there was no other musical reference for these kinds of characters, making the depiction seem strikingly realistic. The creators of *West Side Story* set the bar for telling stories of juvenile delinquency on the Broadway stage – and, by including them, chose to depict a social issue of immediate relevance to their audiences. Our understanding of the musical, then, must include the context of the 1950s and its cultural debates. Not content with exploring just one pressing sociocultural issue, *West Side Story* also deals with the mid century scourges of communism and fascism. In this light, we can see that the musical's creators were unafraid to tackle high-priority national and international sociocultural problems; this willingness may have contributed to *West Side Story*'s popularity.

In the late 1950s, Broadway audiences might have been accustomed to seeing lawlessness portrayed by tricksters like Ali Hakim and Judd in *Oklahoma!*, Joey in *Pal Joey*, or Sky Masterson and his compatriots in *Guys and Dolls*. Nothing about these characters, however, would have made audiences take them seriously as criminals. Then came *West Side Story*. The audience was confronted in the first moments of the show by particularly vicious episodes of gang warfare that included knives, fistfights, and the intervention of the police. There was no question that these were not the youth of musicals past, but a new breed of tough, unapologetic gangsters whom audiences would be afraid to pass on the street. The sheer aggression of the first scene was mirrored in its musical score: one critic went so far as to call it 'a mugging set to music'.[3] Violence is violence, even when danced and sung, and right from the start these youths were the most violent that Broadway audiences had ever seen.

Although depictions of youth culture and delinquency formed much of popular entertainment in the decades that followed, in 1957 the gangs of *West Side Story* were particularly topical. Stories of young people committing crimes were featured every day in the *New York Times*, on the cover of *Time* magazine, and in other major news outlets. Although many of the crimes were minor, much of American society felt that this was one of the most pressing social problems facing large cities, and – increasingly – suburbs and small towns. Popular books like *Other People's Children* warned parents from all walks of life that their children were not immune to the dangers of youth criminality.[4] However, cities were the centres of youth delinquency. Immigration, first by Italian and Irish newcomers, and later by Puerto Ricans, had changed the ethnic mix of Manhattan, and gangs were often formed around national identities rather than strictly by city territory. Particularly threatening were the children of immigrants, who after the war had more money, more leisure time, and less supervision from working parents. Although the media often blamed working mothers for the problems of 'latch-key' kids, it was in fact a number of complex causes that led to New York City's largest challenge in decades. Nor was it an exclusively male issue: the rise of urban girl gangs and female offenders also frightened the American public. 'Victory Girls', who had sexual encounters blamelessly with ex-servicemen, were amongst the problem groups in a culture whose sexual morality was starting to loosen. Women taking back their sexual agency would eventually lead to the feminist movement and the sexual revolution of the 1960s. When *West Side Story* first premiered, however, 'loose' women who no longer cared to be reprimanded – and some who also turned to crime – were yet another source of national anxiety.

West Side Story is therefore completely in tune with what audiences would have been reading about, and perhaps seeing, on the city streets. Two gangs, one ethnically mixed and the other Puerto Rican, were in constant battle over territory, while their girlfriends played active or supporting roles. The musical's opening 'Jet Song' highlights that belonging to a particular gang was critical to the juvenile delinquent identity. 'From your first cigarette to your last dying day', as Riff explains, gang membership was the most defining feature of these young people's lives. When Riff tries to encourage Tony to leave his job at Doc's candy store, making it impossible for Tony to achieve social mobility, he does so on the basis of gang loyalty. For the 1950s, this was largely how young people, and particularly those who were poor and delinquent, organised their lives. *West Side Story*'s depictions of gang politics could not have been more current, especially given the public outcry at the time against delinquent behaviour.

It is worth noting, however, that by 1957 juvenile delinquency had been a hot topic for at least a decade. In the 1940s, off-duty servicemen battled with so-called 'Zoot Suit'-wearing young Mexican-American men as they argued over racial issues and wartime tensions. It was at this point that the American political and judicial systems first became heavily involved with juvenile delinquency treatment and prevention. The 1943 documentary *Youth in Crisis* features delinquents rioting in the streets, and the film's producers (as well as those invested in quelling juvenile delinquency) predicted that by the mid 1950s (when *West Side Story* was being written) all youth would be delinquent.[5]

J. Edgar Hoover led the charge in the '40s, with a special focus on female offenders. In his mind, the end of the war had brought about a decline in morality, and he was particularly concerned about Victory Girls and girl gangs. In *West Side Story* the character of Anybodys, the jeans-wearing tomboy who wants to join the Jets, could be a figure from Hoover's nightmares. Although she is not sexually attractive to the Jets (they have Graziella and Velma for that), she is told to 'go walk the streets' like her sister; the fact Anybodys was added later in the writing period suggests a deliberate nod to the perceived threat of female delinquency. A cut number from the show places Anybodys in the limelight with two other Jet gang members. In it, she wants to be male, presumably because she can fight (something the Jets will not allow her to do) and become equal with the males in the gang. That it is she who precipitates the ending of the show, with her search for Chino and subsequent warning for the Jets, shows that the inclusion of this new female role was both deliberate and important.[6]

The end of the war meant teens had more time on their hands, and the resulting youth culture was blurred with delinquency in both the public mind and by government agencies. A series of Senate committees debated the issue. Many sociologists and criminology experts ran studies to determine how and why youth were turning to crime. By the 1950s, the problem had not been solved, but one of the major culprits had been identified: mass media, in particular the crime comic book. Psychologist Frederick Wertham published a widely read book in 1954 entitled *Seduction of the Innocent*.[7] In it, he blamed crime comic books for the rise of youth delinquency. A long series of battles ensued within the publishing industry and juvenile delinquency experts regarding the banning of comic books. In one of the drug store scenes in *West Side Story*, Baby John is reading such a comic book. It would be surprising if this were not a direct nod to the well-documented war on comic books. The publication of *The Seduction of the Innocent* caused a public panic over juvenile delinquency, which peaked between 1954 and 1956, exactly the years when the authors were putting the finishing touches on the musical and after Wertham's publication. Although the problem of gang warfare on city streets was by now at least a decade old, it remained both topical and urgent. The creators of *West Side Story* had hit on a minor miracle. Although youth crime did not increase during these years of panic, the nature of the crimes was escalating. In the 1940s and early '50s, youth crime consisted primarily of minor sexual offences, stealing, and jacking cars. However, in 1954 four Brooklyn gang members murdered a vagrant, setting off newfound alarm bells amongst the middle class as to how dangerous these teenage gangs could be. *West Side Story* responded without pulling punches. Three murders are portrayed onstage, a record for a musical maintained for decades after its premiere.

Although musical theatre had never featured such depictions of young criminals, they were mainstays of other entertainment media. The cultural urgency of the juvenile delinquency movement had spawned a number of artistic renderings of youth culture, and audiences were eating them up. Films like *Rebel without a Cause* gave Americans a kind of prurient look at juveniles (although here Marlon Brando was less a teenager than a young adult) who wreaked havoc on otherwise law-abiding citizens, painting teenagers as misunderstood outsiders who only needed to fit in. This depiction was both romantic and frightening, a combination which seemed to appeal particularly to young audiences. Indeed, as the juvenile delinquency panic peaked in the mid 1950s, over sixty films with this theme were produced and distributed to a demographic that was increasingly young and who had the finances and time to consume this particular brand of culture.[8] Although some films, like the *Beach Party* series, painted teenagers as insipid but fun-loving oafs, most of these movies lured audiences in with the dangers and intrigue of juvenile delinquency in America. Everyone from *Time* magazine to Hollywood saw a real advantage to telling these stories, and it is impossible to imagine that the original audiences for *West Side Story* remained oblivious.

Indeed, concern about juvenile delinquency extended far beyond the arts and entertainment industries. Every day in the *New York Times* during this mid 1950s period, story after story included the antics and problems of juvenile delinquents. They were the major cultural phenomenon of their time. When Leonard Bernstein and Arthur Laurents met poolside in Los Angeles, they discussed a project which had started out life as 'East Side Story' – a tale of warring Catholics and Jews. Seeing a newspaper headline about Mexican gangs fighting in California redirected their failing project to the slums of Manhattan. For the first time, Bernstein reports, he could hear the rhythms and imagine the music of New York's streets, and they reframed the conflict to include Puerto Ricans and 'Whites'.[9]

Although depictions of juvenile delinquency were extensive, the most prominent artistic rendering was the 1954 novel *Blackboard Jungle* by fledgling author Evan Hunter.[10] The story follows a young, naïve teacher, Richard Dadier, who after graduating with an English degree takes up a teaching position at an inner-city trade school in New York. Like *West Side Story*'s characters, his students come from different cultural backgrounds, but they all share an aggressively negative opinion of teachers and school. Puerto Ricans and African Americans are heavily featured in *Blackboard Jungle* (although the arch-villain turns out to be white) and to Laurents and Bernstein this racial mix must have seemed more up-to-the-minute than the tensions between religious factions on the East Side. One character in *Blackboard Jungle*, played by Sidney Poitier in the 1955 MGM film version, finds himself by the end of the story and stands up for the beleaguered teacher. However, apart from this minor epiphany, the novel and subsequent film version paint a picture of animalistic and barbaric teens with no redeeming qualities, who rape, vandalise, and steal in equal measure.

Although the novel was clearly an artistic representation of the new delinquency problem, the film version sought to inform as well as entertain. At the beginning of the movie, before the title sequence, came a stark message for viewers:

We, in the United States, are fortunate to have a school system that is a tribute to our communities and to our faith in American youth. Today we are concerned with juvenile delinquency – its causes – and its effects. We are especially concerned when this delinquency boils over into our schools. The scenes and incidents depicted here are fictional. However, we believe that public awareness is a first step toward a remedy for any problem. It is in this spirit and with this faith that BLACKBOARD JUNGLE was produced.

By presenting the film as a quasi-documentary, this warning label led audiences to expect a morality tale of the highest importance. The fact that the film was released less than a year after the novel was published also suggests that problem was timely and urgent.

At a time when the movie industry was losing viewers to television at a significant rate, audiences flocked to see *Blackboard Jungle*. The film was a massive hit, grossing $9 million worldwide. Educators debated its realism and the depiction of ill-prepared teachers and overcrowding in city schools. Polls suggested that audiences found the film realistic and felt that it drew attention to real problems. Schools fought back, issuing statements protesting that nothing like this was going on in their particular district. However, for the general public, *Blackboard Jungle* accurately represented their worst fears about teens, schools, and delinquency.

The creators of *West Side Story* saw the film, although they may or may not have read the novel. The movie's influence is clear in their portrayal of teen characters, from the way they speak to their general attitude. The students in the *Blackboard Jungle* novel call their teacher Dadier 'Daddy-O', a moniker that comes up in the musical as well. The novel's authors were very careful to portray the characters as realistically as possible, at least in comparison to other popular media. There is no love story in *Blackboard Jungle*, and neither the film nor the novel features warring factions, which are crucial to a modern-day Romeo and Juliet story. However, the up-to-the-minute urgency and realism of both versions of *Blackboard Jungle* were hugely important to *West Side Story*'s creators.

Apparently, the musical's creative team took this all very seriously. Intent on bringing the tale to light in the most realistic – albeit artistic – way possible, Robbins visited real dances at gyms to see the way young people danced and acted.[11] One dash of realism that made it into rehearsals was the use of flowers worn in trouser cuffs. When tried in the dance studio, however, the flowers made for total chaos, and that idea was quickly jettisoned. It is likely that Robbins (and perhaps some of his collaborators) trolled the streets at night trying to get a better sense of youth culture. At one point, he even proposed auditioning talented street kids for the musical's dance roles. The idea never got much traction, given that his demands challenged already seasoned professional dancers and actors. It is worth noting that, during this time period of massive closeted gay activity, gang members often posed as gay to attract men looking for sex. Once lured in, they would roll these men for money or beat them up. By observing gang members, the closeted Robbins put himself at some risk for the sake of authenticity.

Ironically, the producers and creators of *West Side Story* did not take the usual film studio approach of luring young people into seeing their musical. Based on the musical genres Bernstein chose to include, it is clear that target audiences were instead middle-class and middle-aged. Elvis Presley was one of the most important musical figures of the time, and the bane of parents and juvenile delinquency experts alike. With his gyrating hips, his slicked-back hair, and his links to African American music, Presley was the number-one icon for a generation of rebellious teenagers. If Bernstein was going to make a realistic musical about youth culture, he would have taken rock and roll as his model and Presley as his muse. Bernstein was well aware of rock music; it was everywhere. Even the film version of *Blackboard Jungle* presents its opening credits against a backdrop of 'Rock around the Clock' by Bill Haley and the Comets.

Although the Latin American music that pervades *West Side Story* could be a nod to the ethnic mix of Manhattan's west side, Hollywood preferred to use more romantic and traditional music for stories of juvenile delinquency. In *Blackboard Jungle*, the opening credits are the only time we hear rock music. The rest of the score uses standard Hollywood markers of danger or excitement that would be just as appropriate in an action movie or romantic drama. The movie even occasionally dips into jazz – definitely not the music of the young – to reach out to its primarily middle-aged audience. The teachers, representing an older generation, listen to jazz; there is a tragic scene in both the film and novel featuring the destruction of a teacher's beloved jazz vinyl collection by the recalcitrant teens.

There is no hint of the rock aesthetic in *West Side Story*. In retrospect, it is a surprising choice. Other musicals of the era, like *Bye Bye Birdie* (1960) or the British *Expresso Bongo* (1958), include scenes featuring young rockers. Instead, in *West Side Story*, the 'Dance at the Gym' is set, of all things, to a mambo, although the 'Blues' section may have been closer to what young people listened to.[12] This music did not belong to the young. It belonged to their parents. It was the music of the highbrow 'long-haired' listener attracted by Bernstein's classical cachet. The musical's operatic aspirations and dissonant score offered other attractions to that kind of listener. The Latin jazz sensation that had hit the American middle class was by now well established, so much so that it was featured in later films like *Dirty Dancing* where older adults learn Latin dances on summer vacations in the Catskills. Latin dance clubs already had a large, devoted audience, as did Latin jazz recordings, and Latin music was often explicitly connected to musical theatre.

The so-called 'modernity' of the *West Side Story* score, then, was not that it presented up-to-the-minute commentary on youth culture, but that it reified middle-aged culture in a way that made those audiences feel that they were really 'with it'. Indeed, the depiction of juvenile delinquency in film and literature began to bleed into mainstream culture. The youth were not just disappointing adults, they were leading them. The focus changed: instead of asking teenagers to explain themselves, American society began looking to youth for cultural leadership. *West Side Story* could well have appealed to young people, given its subject matter and key themes. From a musical perspective, however, it was a story of youth culture aimed at an adult population.

Gang life, which inspired *West Side Story*, loomed large in the zeitgeist of mid 1950s America. Its effects on cultural trends influenced the white, middle-class audiences that made up *West Side Story*'s primary audience. That parallel makes the creative team's choice of subject matter all the more fascinating. In his *American Cool: Constructing a Twentieth-Century Emotional Style*, author Peter N. Stearns traces America's relationship with emotion from the nineteenth into the mid twentieth century. As Americans moved from traditional ideas about emotional openness to a more consumerised, commodified culture, the idea of 'cool', as crystallised in the musical's song by the same name, makes the work very much of its time. Stearns describes how the expression of emotions, especially anger, was becoming ungainly for the mid twentieth-century American. Heroes like Superman do not deal with emotions. Dr. Spock, the famed child-rearing expert, warned against allowing children to express anger, and anger in the workplace was particularly frowned upon. As Stearns writes, 'New levels of concern about anger and aggression followed in part from perceptions of heightened crime, including juvenile delinquency, and the untrammeled aggression in Nazism and then renewed world war.'[13] Seeing gangs as echoes of Storm Troopers was particularly frightening for

Americans, especially the Jewish middle-class audiences flocking to see *West Side Story*.

If we look at the song 'Cool', we see an interesting combination of complexity and emotion. The lyrics read, 'Boy, boy, crazy boy, keep cool, boy. Got a rocket in your pocket, keep cooly-cool boy. Don't get hot, 'cause man you've got some high times ahead. Take it slow, and Daddy-O you can live it up and die in bed.' Accompanying these words is the cool jazz style that we have come to associate with the Jets. By contrast, the dance scene features a fugue, the score's densest and most complicated music. The scene is choreographically complex and ripe with repressed frustration and anxiety. The fugue's convoluted musical texture warns that the worst thing these teenagers can do is give in to their natural tendency toward aggression. They must remain 'cool'. The conflict between expression and repression was hugely topical, echoed in the business world of the 1950s and '60s where sensitivity training was introduced to defuse angry clients.[14] *West Side Story*'s characters are tragically flawed not just because they are delinquent or underprivileged, but because they cannot control their anger.

No character in *West Side Story* is innocent of anger. Bernardo's tragic murder comes when Tony, who has come to the rumble to stop the violence, is overwhelmed with rage. His momentary fall from pacifist to killer is what drives the story, and Shakespeare's conflict becomes Laurents's momentum. Similarly, Tony believes Maria is dead because of Anita, who is furious after her attempted rape by the Jets in Doc's candy store. She warns them that she would spit on them in the street if she saw them dying and tells them to let Tony know that Maria is dead. Laurents was particularly proud of this moment. In Shakespeare's version, everything turned on a simple misunderstanding. In *West Side Story*, the fall was caused by racism and misogyny. If Anita had not been attacked and lashed out in self-defence, the story would have ended very differently. The relationship between the gangs and the police is also fuelled by uncontrolled anger on all sides. Policeman Schrank taunts gang members in the candy store, hoping that their rage will make them slip up and tell him where the rumble will be. His own anger over his inability to bring peace to the streets results in a diatribe about unruly Puerto Ricans. Anger is always boiling below the surface, with tragic consequences.

An interesting corollary to anger management and charges of fascism was the concern that juvenile delinquency was linked to left-wing ideology, particularly communism.[15] During the era of House Un-American Activities Committee (HUAC) inquests and the blacklisting of artists in Hollywood and beyond, the threat of communism was extremely serious. Jerome Robbins informed on some of his colleagues during this period, mostly for fear that he would be outed as gay at a time when queerness was as reviled as communism – or more so. Bernstein had communist leanings, as did most of the creators of *West Side Story*, at least early in their careers. As Barry Seldes has revealed, Bernstein once had his passport renewal denied because his past ties to the communist party had put him on a government watch list.[16] The popular fear that communism had infiltrated American values through delinquency gave the quest for their mutual eradication special urgency. As James Gilbert writes, 'A poll taken by the Roper organization in 1959 suggested that delinquency was viewed more seriously than open-air testing of atomic weapons or school segregation or political corruption.'[17] By 1960, the musical was in its first revival, and the film version would be released a year later, in 1961. Audiences and creative team alike would have known that juvenile delinquency was not just any topical subject: it was *the* topical subject of the late 1950s.

The musical draws an additional fine line between using juvenile delinquency as subject matter and analysing it as a social problem. Nowhere is this line drawn more clearly than in the show's hit song, 'Gee, Officer Krupke'. For one thing, the song criticises the real-life strategy of giving police more authority to crack down on youth crime. For another, it directly addresses the problems faced by members of the establishment as they attempt to deal with delinquency. The song comes in the musical's 11 O'Clock position: traditionally, songs in this slot are showstoppers featuring the principal cast members. It could be argued that the gangs themselves are the principals, not the stereotypical lovers Tony and Maria, making 'Gee, Officer Krupke' an 11 O'Clock number in truth. Regardless, the song was a moment that savvy audiences would have anticipated all evening.

Less experienced audience members might have been surprised by a comic song in the midst of tragedy. However, 'Gee, Officer Krupke' did the work of an 11 O'Clock number by stopping the show every night without fail. It also became one of show's hit songs, especially in Britain, where youth delinquency was on the rise. The song satirises different interventions meant to solve juvenile delinquency in a series of skits performed by the teenage gang members. This vaudevillian approach to a serious social problem may seem a little unorthodox, even disrespectful. However, audiences welcomed the funny moment as a break from the story's tragic plot, just as a society saturated with the seriousness of juvenile delinquency would have welcomed its lighthearted send-up.

The song addressed recent work in predicting and treating juvenile delinquency, along with the social work and judicial systems. The gang members agree that none of these solutions is going to work. After acting out scenes in which the teens would normally find some kind of respite from their troubled lives, the Jets fire off a list of possible causes for their friend's delinquency: the trouble is not in his genes, his head, or society, but that he has a 'social disease'. In the 1950s, this meant a sexually transmitted infection. The play on words between 'social disease' and 'social work', the problem and its would-be solution, was a very funny but pointed slam by the creators against a system that had failed to curb youth delinquency.

At the end of the song, the teen gang members finally turn to the police officer and say, 'Gee, Officer Krupke, Krup you'. In *Blackboard Jungle*, the final show-down between teacher and students occurs because the most difficult of the students finally fires off a considered ending for 'Krupke' of 'fuck you' at teacher Richard Dadier. This precipitates a scuffle-turned-knife-fight in which Dadier is wounded and the young juvenile who has supported him comes to his defence. As could be expected in mid 1950s, this line in the film was changed to something less incendiary. However, a teenager saying 'fuck you' to an authority figure seems be a critical tipping point; both *Blackboard Jungle*'s author and *West Side Story*'s creators use such a moment to demonstrate the complete breakdown of moral and social order.

'Gee, Officer Krupke' presents the Jets with an opportunity to own their own delinquency. Their unwillingness to conform, to behave, gives them a sense of purpose – yet it robs them of any acceptance in society. The positioning of the teens in *West Side Story* as misunderstood outsiders would have appealed to audiences, since the Jets and Sharks need to emerge as sympathetic characters in order for us to care what happens to them. They cannot be two-dimensional villains: if they were written that way, the plot would not work and their attitude shift after Tony's death would make no sense. Indeed, the portrayal of youth gangs in this musical is not just a reflection of what was in the papers, but a plea from the creators to understand and to accept these youths in a way that the rest of the social order did not. The fact that the teens express themselves through song and dance shows that they are special. The adults of *West Side Story* are confined to the real world. The teenagers alone can tap into the magic of musical theatre and share it with us. If we are to care about them enough to share these magical moments, they have to be portrayed as authentic. At the same time that this subtle shift towards sympathy was occurring in audience members, society at large began to lose some of its fear of youth culture. Although adults were initially worried that youth would take over popular culture entirely (and it could be argued that they did), in the early 1960s adults started turning to youth as beacons of change and ambassadors of a new way of life.

In the 1950s, however, youth culture was still a scourge on the nation's good name. What seemed to bother adults most about their teens turning to crime, or at least a new youth culture, was not the delinquency. Of greater concern was that these young people were crossing class lines, turning to lower-class morals and styles. This applied to everything from sexual openness to wearing jeans. Even the language they adopted was seen as being 'below' middle-class standards. A little crime was one thing. Challenging the class system was quite another. Some of this awareness may have spilled over into the approach that the creators took to the work. Sondheim, who had grown up in privilege among Manhattan's artsy set, claimed that he had never met a Puerto Rican. This was likely true for most of the creators, whose experience with other classes would have been limited to the hired help in their homes. Bernstein (like most of the team) had a staff of domestic help, mostly from Latin America. Robbins did the choreography for the Jets, but asked Peter Gennaro to do choreography for the Sharks. Ostensibly, this was because it was one of Gennaro's areas of special expertise. One wonders, though, if it was also considered 'below' Robbins to learn about or engage with Puerto Rican culture and the popular Latin dances. After all, *West Side Story* was meant to be a work of high art, even if the subject matter was from the streets.

In the late 1950s, as a social programme, producer Harold Prince's office offered free *West Side Story* matinee tickets to young people in New York under the supervision of social workers. Students interviewed after seeing the show commented on how much they liked the music and dancing (even though it would have seemed anachronistic), and they even mentioned *Blackboard Jungle* in their commentary on the musical's themes. There was no sense that the creators had been off the mark in portraying these young people. Yet the teenagers had no idea why they were taken to see the show. They did not see themselves as delinquent; they saw themselves as normal.

This may be the most fascinating aspect of *West Side Story*'s gang members: that the youth in the musical are meant not to represent some strange and terrifying 'other'. The delinquent youth of the 1950s may have been other people's children, but they were still American children. They were the product of the very society that feared them. And, in time, their culture came to influence the mainstream – adults emulated delinquent youth. The divide became less of a wall and more of a mirror: even in 1957,

West Side Story depicted gang members as teenagers whose rebellion made them outsiders, but who could be saved by renouncing that inner anger. Every character in the musical is flawed, and although the teenagers can sing and dance their frustration, it bubbles up just as often in the adults. The audience feels it in the pulse of Latin rhythms and the intensity of the score, in the approaching train wreck of the dénouement. When the story ends in a scene of tragic catharsis, every character, every audience member is changed, young and old alike. The boundary between delinquent youth and fearful society disappears.

The creators and producers, all Jewish, mostly closeted gays, artists made outsiders in a period of conformity, must have identified with their delinquent protagonists. Like the homosocial and tight relationships amongst real-life gang members, so these Broadway artists would have seemed like a subculture unto themselves. The fact that Robbins had to rehearse the dancers to create animosity between the Jet and Shark actors lends credence to the idea that we are all misunderstood, damaged individuals who are taught to hate. Surely audiences of the era, whose relationships to the musical styles made them feel young, were meant to feel sympathy for the teenaged characters. However, this sense of connection challenged the bitter divide of 'us vs them' that underscored the approach to juvenile delinquency in the 1950s.

The musical's bittersweet ballad 'Somewhere' asks us all to imagine a world where people can be themselves, accepted and free. Perhaps this was what the creators were picturing when they put together a musical to represent their own complex identities, as both gay, Jewish, and 'other' as artists, and perhaps this is what audiences secretly desired when sat down to watch. Art has the capacity to challenge prejudice, and we all have the capacity to change our perception of others. In the end, the distinctions between gang members and adults seem trivial in the face of loss. Perhaps the tragedy was necessary to clarify what truly matters. Perhaps we are all outsiders in one way or another.

Perhaps we are the gangs of *West Side Story*.

Notes

1. For more on the comparison of these two musicals and what they say about American culture, see Carol J. Oja, '*West Side Story* and *The Music Man*: whiteness, immigration and race in the US during the late 1950s', *Studies in Musical Theatre* 3, no. 1 (August 2009): 13–30.

2. For more on juvenile delinquency and *West Side Story*, see Elizabeth A. Wells, West Side Story: *Cultural Perspectives on an American Musical* (Lanham, MD: Scarecrow, 2011), 189–216.

3. Frank Farrell, *New York World Telegram*, 27 September 1957.

4. Anna Judge Veters Levy, *Other People's Children* (New York: Ronald Press Co., 1956).

5. Peter N. Stearns, *American Cool: Constructing a 20th Century Emotional Style* (New York: New York University Press, 1994), 29.

6. For more on the female characters, and Anybodys, see Wells, *West Side Story*, 141–88.

7. Frederick Wertham, *Seduction of the Innocent* (New York: Rinehart and Company, 1954).

8. James Burkhart Gilbert, *A Cycle of Outrage: America's Reaction to the Juvenile Delinquent in the 1950s* (Oxford: Oxford University Press, 1999), 64.

9. Arthur Laurents, *Original Story by Arthur Laurents: A Memoir of Broadway and Hollywood* (New York: Applause, 2000), 338.

10. Evan Hunter, *The Blackboard Jungle* (New York: Simon and Schuster, 1954).

11. Amanda Vaill, *Somewhere: The Life of Jerome Robbins* (New York: Broadway Books, 2006), 273.

12. That said, jazz music was part of the world of young professionals, not teenagers, being considered somewhat cerebral.

13. Stearns, *American Cool*, 195.

14. Stearns, *American Cool*, 257.

15. Gilbert, *A Cycle of Outrage*, 74.

16. Barry Seldes, *Leonard Bernstein: The Political Life of an American Musician* (Berkeley: University of California Press, 2009), 69–72.

17. Gilbert, *A Cycle of Outrage*, 63.

PART III

The Legacy

West Side Story and the Voice

SYLVIA STONER-HAWKINS

'I say it is not an opera', Mr. Bernstein offered. 'It's a work on its way toward being one. Some parts are operatic, but it isn't one.'[1]
'The American theatre took a venturesome forward step last evening. This is a bold new kind of musical theatre – a juke-box Manhattan opera.'[2]

Although many have speculated as to which genre *West Side Story* belongs – it is a musical that at times requires vocal skills often demanded of opera singers. Bernstein wrote for the voice with a keen understanding of how drama becomes heightened through music. Since *West Side Story* broke the mould of traditional musical comedy, the vocal demands are equally non-traditional. By examining the vocal writing, one can understand Bernstein's sense of character and how each musical number propels the story through song.

The main singing roles of Maria, Tony, Anita, and Riff require two classically trained 'legit' singers for Maria and Tony, and two Broadway belt/character voices for Anita and Riff. Bernstein divides the solo material so that the majority of singing falls to the star-crossed lovers, which leaves less singing for Riff and Anita, but more room for dance to be incorporated into their performances. Although Bernstein writes sensitively for each kind of singer, occasionally the vocal categories blur. At times, Anita is required to perform in a more classical style as in the 'Tonight' Quintet and 'I Have a Love'. Tony also has moments of standard Broadway belt mix in his solos 'Something's Coming' and in the 'Tonight' (Quintet). Bernstein's use of the voice paves the way for the modern musical, where composers write less for a particular kind of voice and expect the singer–actor to be able to sing in many different kinds of styles.

The Vocal Writing in *West Side Story*

In the opening scenes of the show, Bernstein sets up a strong vocal contrast between Riff and Tony. The 'Jet Song', led by Riff, begins seamlessly from underscored dialogue. This integration of speech into song helps Riff ease into song from his extended speech about Tony's loyalty. The song's opening lines are set in a typical mid-range that allows for the baritone (or bari-tenor) to easily start pitching speech instead of creating a full tone. Bernstein recognised the importance of the singer–actor being able to deliver text and have its meaning carry from the stage into the theatre. Although rhythmically challenging for a singer, the use of hemiola allows for Riff to separate his words, using strong rhythmic accents that create the impression of a rough, streetwise gang leader. When Riff's line eases into a tune ('You're never alone . . . ') in 6/8 time, the line suggests a jazzy swing with angular intervals. Moving through these vocal register shifts in a melody with such wide intervals can make the voice sound rough. This is because of the constant transitions between the low and high range of the voice. The actor may also choose to carry the chest register up past this transition to create a strong belt sound, as in the phrase 'You're well protected', which takes Riff to his highest solo note in the show, an F4.

With the change of scene, Tony sings in a completely different vocal style in 'Something's Coming'. In contrast to Riff's angular, loud, and rhythmic melody, Tony starts at a *pianissimo* volume in falsetto and then simply holds a note for several bars. As the song develops, Tony sings in eager rhythmic articulation, but the melodic line follows a smoother trajectory. This allows the voice to create a steady flow of tone without abrupt register shifts. Like his friend Riff, Tony has moments of sung speech with 'It may come cannonballing . . . ' or 'I got a feeling' on the second verse, as the line swells to a *fortissimo* E4 sustained over eight bars. However, despite his impetuous arc into sustained high notes, both Tony and Maria always quieten down from such *crescendi*, as can be heard later in their duets 'Tonight' and 'One Hand, One Heart'. This is true for Tony in his first number, as he continues to have moments of *sotto voce* that swell into broad phrases, which Bernstein indicates should be sung 'warmly, freely'. Despite the swell, the song concludes as it starts, again *pianissimo* and *sotto voce*, sounding unresolved, so as to leave the question 'Who knows?' lingering in the air, unanswered.

It is easy to compare the structure of 'Maria' to a *bel canto* operatic tenor aria. The expanded structure of Tony's solos 'Something's Coming' combined with 'Maria' reflects the traditional form of a flowing cavatina followed by a fiery cabaletta, separated by 'A Dance at the Gym'. Naturally, Bernstein understood such operatic forms and knew how to sustain a steady musical build up for maximum dramatic effect. Beginning with a gentle recitative style as Tony learns Maria's name, Bernstein bridges the transition into the aria-like section through a gentle melodic pull first with Tony singing 'Maria' on a perfect fourth, then the next phrase as a perfect fifth, and finally the glorious tritone, which seems both unexpected and bent towards tonal resolution. The challenge vocally, of course, is to maintain accurate pitch on the changing, wide intervals. As Tony continues into the *Moderato con anima* section the melody becomes stepwise and more lyrical. This scalar movement allows for the singer to create a smoother legato and richer tone, especially as Bernstein moves the melody through the singer's *passaggio* and into a higher tessitura.

The *passaggio* literally means 'passage' in Italian and the term applies to the transition from one register, or area of the voice, to another. Singers experience a specific kind of vocal production in one register and an altered or totally different production in another, dependent upon the degree of tension in the thyroarytenoid muscles and changes to the vocal fold length and vibration. Vocal pedagogue Cornelius Reid noted: 'The smooth and easy negotiation of the *passaggio* without the loss of range, resonance, or flexibility is the hallmark of technical mastery.'[3] Because of the stepwise writing in 'Maria', Tony transitions smoothly into a head dominant tone without too much exposure of a register shift. Shifting between registers in musical theatre requires the performer to decide how to shift in a way that supports the character. Tony often sounds more operatic at this point because that is what is needed for efficient vocal production; for most actors using a belt sound in this range could potentially damage the voice during long runs of the show. Delaying a transition from chest voice into a head dominant voice produces a belt or belt-mix that has an extremely different sound than transitioning earlier into a dominant head register, which produces a more classical tone.

Bernstein's overall trajectory for 'Maria' follows a similar pattern as Tony's first solo. As with 'Something's Coming', the first broad *crescendo* in 'Maria' ends abruptly with a *subito piano* indicated for the lyric 'say it soft and it's almost like praying'. Dramatically, it helps rein in the dynamics so that the second, broader *crescendo* can move to the climax of the song. Vocally, it is an opportunity for the singer to relax any tension and sing with less pressure by using his falsetto (if desired) before he returns to the next section of intense singing. Falsetto singing eases the stress at this point because only a portion of the vocal folds are in contact, as opposed to full voice when the folds are in full contact and vibrate their full vocal length. At the climactic moment, Bernstein's score indicates that he originally wrote a B♭4 to be sustained at a *forte* over three bars at the climax of the song. In the iconic Deutsche Grammophon recording of 'Maria' performed by José Carreras, he sustained the B♭4 effortlessly under the baton of Bernstein.

Likewise, musical theatre tenor Matt Cavenaugh sailed through this sustained B♭4 in the 2009 revival. However, most singers prefer to sing the *ossia* line that allows them to sing several shorter phrases and at lower pitches. This line proves a bit less strenuous and allows brief pauses of relaxation in a very high range. Following this second *crescendo*, Tony once again ends in *subito piano* and falsetto, creating an overall boy soprano effect, reminiscent of an innocent prayer.

Following 'Maria', Tony has a brief exchange of dialogue with Maria that sets up the 'Balcony Scene' duet. This is the third singing number in a row that involves Tony. Following his pseudo-cavatina/cabaletta aria, Tony now sings an extensive duet with Maria. It is important that the singer–actor paces himself through these three numbers, so that he has the stamina to maintain a consistent tone and perform the nuanced dynamics required in these three songs.

Tony has a brief vocal break at the start of the 'Balcony Scene', when Bernstein gives Maria an opportunity to start the duet with a solo section. Once again, Bernstein grows the solo vocal line out of spoken word and he suggests Maria begins 'freely' at a low dynamic level. A common speaking tone for most female voices begins around A3, and Bernstein sets her starting note only a half-step higher at B♭3. This allows for the drama to be more integrated from the spoken word into singing, and slowly allows the audience to alter how they listen to the words, which makes the text more understandable and the singing more believable. Her melodic line creates a beautiful arc into her *passaggio* and then gracefully descends. This rise and fall of the melody naturally encourages a dynamic swell in the middle of the phrase. These opening solo lines encourage use of the head voice and legato singing, and in this soprano range the voice sounds light, giving the impression of a soubrette or ingénue. The duet builds in anticipation as Tony interrupts Maria, followed by Maria interrupting, or overlapping, Tony's line prior to their first kiss.

With the start of the *molto allegro* section, Maria begins again with a solo. Her melodic line broadens into longer phrases that linger in her middle voice, eventually rising into the upper range of her *passaggio*. Sondheim's 'simple' lyrics help Maria sing fewer consonants and more vowels as she leaps from the vowel [i] of 'on-ly' on F4 into D5, F5, and E♭5 on the words 'you to-night'. This proves to be another 'operatic' moment in *West Side Story*, because the text cannot be Maria's first priority at this moment. She needs to focus on creating a consistently free tone as she moves into her upper register. It is harder to maintain clarity in the lyric because ' ... vowels must be modified for the resonator (vocal tract) to work efficiently'.[4] Also, using head register dominance for a vocal line that hangs in this tessitura allows for efficient breath flow, especially over sustained notes. The classically trained singer will most likely choose to modify the diphthong vowel in the word 'say' and 'today' so that the F5 and G♭5 can be sustained on a modified 'eh' without spreading the mouth, causing loss of air and tonal focus.

The duet continues in a restatement of Maria's 'Tonight' solo material, this time sung in unison octaves. Tony, most likely a tenor or bari-tenor, must face similar issues of shifting registers and potentially modifying vowels as he moves into the higher tessitura. Maintaining breath energy, a clear and precise tone, and singing with expression requires adequate vocal technique. Actors cast as Tony must understand how to shift vocal registers seamlessly in order to give consistent performances throughout the run. The conclusion of the duet offers one final challenge to the singers – they end in *pianissimo*, perhaps suggesting a blissful whisper that floats into the clouds as both soprano and tenor are required to sustain a *dolcissimo* A♭5. This kind of vocal float can be achieved more easily by the tenor if he flips into falsetto, but the soprano needs both relaxation and agility to support her intonation at such a low dynamic level in this range. Although Bernstein wrote for the singers to be in unison, it is common for Tony to conclude this duet a perfect fourth lower on E♭4. This is certainly an understandable adjustment in light of the vocal load for Tony thus far in the show.

The next two musical numbers, 'America' and 'Cool' (their order in the Broadway/stage musical adaptation), remind us that this show is not an opera but a musical. The style of singing is markedly different than that of Tony and Maria and there are definite elements of comedy interspersed. Bernstein attempts to create a Latin-sounding vocal number with 'America'. Sondheim noted that the original scene conceived by Arthur Laurents was to have been an argument between Anita and Bernardo, 'then Jerry Robbins said he didn't want boys in this dance ... "all girls"'.[5] Of course, in both movies this number returned to Laurents's original concept and included Bernardo and the other members of the Shark gang.

In the stage version, 'America' includes solos for Rosalia and Anita with the Shark girls as ensemble. The vocal style depends of course upon the casting, but in most recordings this number is sung with an affected Puerto Rican accent, which often results in a nasal tone and bright chest dominant sound. Most of the melodic material is in a possible belt range for both altos and sopranos. In this ensemble, Anita sings the lowest line and Rosalia tends to remain in a more mezzo-soprano range. Rosalia's solo is usually performed in a mix of head and chest register, with a sense of legato.

Bernstein suggests that she sings 'nostalgically' of Puerto Rico, while Anita repeats Rosalia's melody 'mockingly', and thereby creates a speech-like character sound that can be quite pointed and *marcato*. Anita opens into a full belt on her *subito forte* line, 'I like the island Manhattan . . . ' This strong tone creates an energetic transition into the 'Tempo di Huapango' vocal ensemble of Anita and the Shark girls (except Rosalia). This is clearly written in a way that allows the performers to both dance and sing. Vocal phrases are short and rhythmic, with little or no sustained singing, which allows for more manageable air flow while executing challenging choreography.

'Cool' provides a stark contrast to 'America' by situating the two gangs (as noted above, the Shark men appear in the film versions of 'America') in back-to-back group numbers. The Jets sing in more of a contemporary pop or musical theatre tone as opposed to the more classically trained sounds of Tony and Maria. With the intent to calm his gang, Riff begins 'almost whispered' as he speak-sings the opening lines of the number. The vocal style remains consistent for Riff to what he did in the 'Jets Song', but this time there is a definite swung, jazz style. Bernstein marks the tempo as 'Solid and boppy', which gives Riff the opportunity to use both smooth and rhythmic articulations of the text. On the fuller, longer notes, Riff can also embellish the tone with some vibrato as is consistent with the big band style popular songs of the 1930s and 40s. The vocals at the start of this number clearly lead into the extended dance section, followed by a reprise of the opening lines by the ensemble, and ending with Riff returning to his whispered, falsetto singing at the end.

After two traditional musical theatre songs, Bernstein returns to semi-operatic writing with 'One Hand, One Heart'. Sondheim explains that this was previously an instrumental tune that Bernstein wrote for *Candide*, but strictly in dotted half notes: 'I had to ask Lenny for more notes.'[6] Thankfully, Bernstein included a few more quarter notes to give Sondheim the opportunity to write more words, and the performers more melody to sing, which propels the text. Since this is the wedding scene at the dress shop, both Tony and Maria speak their vows. Tony's opening solo line responds to Maria's spoken text and continues the profession of vows in song in a *dolce piano* tone. The first phrase arcs to C♭4 on 'hands', to D♭4 on 'hearts', and to E♭4 on 'vows'. Because of the close stepwise progression and repeated pitches, the overall line of the melody is intuitively easier for a singer to sing legato. When the register changes are gradual, the tone remains consistent. Throughout this duet Maria must float the voice in the *passaggio* on G♭5 and Tony often moves to falsetto on

G♭4. Following the instrumental interlude, Bernstein modulates on the reprise from G♭ to A♭, so Maria floats a step higher, to A♭5. Tony's melodic writing moves down to a falsetto F4 and ends on a low A♭3. Intonation in sustained soft singing is always challenging, but the soft high notes again seem to lift these lovers into their dreams and out of reality.

The blaring horns of the next musical number awaken both the audience and the dreamers as the plot turns to the 'Tonight' (Quintet). If the director chooses to have both gangs sing in addition to Bernardo and Riff, this is the only number that involves almost the full company. Unlike other musicals which include some full company number in both acts, often bookended at the beginning and ends of acts, this number appears in the middle of the show at the height of tension. This 'Fast and rhythmic' agitated ensemble opens in a speech-like range with little pitch movement for the opening gang's phrases. Sung *marcato* (with a marked accent), it is easy to understand the text, whether sung by a solo voice or the entire gang. Also, it is interesting that the same melodic structure appears for both gangs. In some way, Bernstein helps to unify these two groups and suggest that such emotion reflects the overall human condition, regardless of race.

In contrast to the shouting quality of the gangs, Anita sings with a sultry articulation, but still maintains the same shifting rhythmic patterns as the gang ensemble. Although the meter shifts are written to follow a natural speech pattern of the text, Anita has to make those shifting rhythmic patterns sound relaxed and easy, while still singing accurately. Following Anita, Tony sings a reprise of 'Tonight' from the earlier 'Balcony Scene'. Much of the prior dynamic shaping returns to these long phrases, but his solo section ends on a broad *crescendo* on 'night'. Interrupting Tony's reverie, Riff reintroduces the gang counter-motive to 'Tonight'. Following Riff's solo, the two motives (gang *vs* lovers) build intricately into a quintet that is clearly the most contrapuntal and harmonic vocal section of the entire show. With the harmony shifting every two bars or fewer, the ensemble needs to be keenly aware of the chromaticism of each vocal line in order to shift in tune with each other. Bernstein's dynamic markings provide guidance to the storytelling, as if to shift the scene from one location to another while the group sings together. Therefore, the performers must be sensitive to their dynamics so that they know when the focus is on their story and when it is not. The climactic ending has a driving *crescendo* throughout the ensemble, with every voice ending at the top of its range, including Maria who sustains a C6 for the last four bars.

Following 'The Rumble', 'I Feel Pretty' provides a fresh start in Act II and breathes some momentary hope and light into the tragedy. This number features Maria and the three girls at the dress shop: Consuelo, Rosalia, and Francisca. Set in 3/8 time, the music feels like a fast waltz, and Bernstein indicates that Maria should begin singing 'with pulse'. Since dialogue precedes the singing, Bernstein starts Maria in her speaking range, and much of this melody lies in a more speak-singing range. Her friends respond to Maria's solo by teasing her, and often the tone is a bit nasalised and pointed. Future productions of *West Side Story* will need to carefully evaluate this number and other 'exotic' treatment of the Puerto Ricans, whether through exaggerated accents, or other stereotypes. Certainly, singers cast in these roles should accurately represent this ethnic group and perform with cultural authenticity. While singing in Puerto Rican dialects, there is a different vowel formation and resonant space than what is typical of *bel canto* vocal training. Since Bernstein did not consciously write for the Latinx voice, musical directors and vocal coaches must be aware of and sensitive to these differences.

The 'Ballet Sequence' involves two singing sections. The first is a brief duet between Tony and Maria, which begins the ballet. These few lines definitely seem to be lifted out of an opera. Both characters sing in a middle to high range in long phrases. Since Bernstein is knowingly guiding us into a dream sequence, this heightened delivery of text seems absolutely appropriate. 'Somewhere' also appears in the ballet and is performed by 'A Girl'. Whoever is cast to sing this solo needs to feel comfortable singing such an exposed line. Maintaining accurate intonation in these wide intervals is challenging at the least, especially with the orchestra responding in canon to the vocal line. Yet the vulnerability of this bare vocal line beautifully mirrors the plight of the young lovers. When the lush chords of the orchestra finally move homophonically with the voice, the result is transcendent on 'Someday, Somewhere' and 'Somehow, Someday, Somewhere!' The last two lines of the song conclude the ballet, this time shared by Tony and then Maria. Bernstein begins and ends the ballet with their voices, bringing them back to their tragic reality.

In the original stage production, 'Gee, Officer Krupke' follows the ballet. The song's vaudevillian slapstick continues an emotional roller coaster, careening the story from the ballet's tragedy into comedy. Conceived as a comedic social commentary that parodies the gang members' plight as juvenile delinquents, the vocal lines are basically sung speech, often in character voices. For example, Bernstein's score indicates that Baby John put his voice in falsetto when he pretends to be the social worker. Also, since this is an extremely physical number, the phrases need to be short enough to allow for adequate breath when needed.

Although 'Krupke' brings high energy into the show, the true '11 o'clock' number lies in 'A Boy Like That/I Have a Love' duet between Anita and Maria. This was the only number for which Sondheim wrote all of the lyrics first, then Bernstein set the text to music. For the most part, according to Sondheim, other musical numbers developed collaboratively between the two, with a constant interchange of textual ideas and melodies.[7] The stakes are high as the tempo starts *Allegro con fuoco*. Anita must find a steely quality in her belt voice to maintain volume and resonance in the low pitches at the start. The metric shifts between 4/4, 3/4, and 3/2 create a rhythmic ambiguity that heightens the tension and escalates the conflict. Also, each of Anita's phrases end with a driving *crescendo*. When singing the role of Anita, one needs to establish a pace of this intensity to avoid vocal tension but still invest emotionally, without compromising her stamina. Anita's solo culminates in a sustained Db5 on the words 'heart' and 'smart', which allows her to sing on an 'ah' vowel and gives her more flexibility in how to focus her tone. She could sing it in a mix, full-on belt, or more of a twang to achieve the necessary *crescendo*.

The dramatic contrast between the two women's voices further illustrates the conflict. Anita's belting can only be subdued by Maria's operatic high notes. Rhythmically, Anita continues with her earlier motives over which Maria sustains longer and higher notes. As the duet continues into Maria's solo, 'I Have a Love', the tessitura drops so that she can now sing more calmly. The ascending sevenths are challenging leaps for accurate intonation, but such an interval truly sounds like yearning in the voice. At the *con espansione* end of the solo, Maria's vocal writing turns more operatic with higher tessitura and longer sustained phrases. Her last note of a sustained G5 over four bars breaks Anita's anger, and the two reconcile by singing in thirds and unison. Such a consonant ending offers a final glimpse of comfort and hope, at least for the two characters.

The last moment of singing occurs in the 'Finale', as Maria cradles the dying Tony who sings, 'Hold my hand and we're halfway there ... ' Maria joins him with, 'Hold my hand and I'll take you there somehow ... ' Tony dies in song as Maria continues, 'Someday!' then 'falters and stops'. Indeed, singing takes over when spoken text can no longer express the heightened emotional state. It would seem awkward to break into an *a cappella* singing at another point in the story, but as a brief reprise of a hope that could not be realised in their world, this is the perfect end to a dreamer's life.

The Voices of *West Side Story*

Bernstein's vocal writing in *West Side Story* created a descriptive road map for character development and provided a crucial element to the storytelling. There are three specific performances that offer vastly different interpretations of this vocal map: the original Broadway cast recording, the 1984 recording conducted by Bernstein himself with opera singers, and the 2009 bilingual Broadway revival. Additionally, the 2021 movie built upon ideas from the 2009 revival and further developed vocal color and interpretation.

Both of the Broadway recordings were sung by performers who in some way are 'triple threats', capable of acting, singing, and dancing the role. Often in singing callbacks for the roles in *West Side Story*, the groups of performers could be divided between 'singers who act' or 'actors who sing'. The principal roles of Tony, Maria, Anita, and Riff perform a large amount of singing with varying styles. Only Tony and Maria are not dance-heavy roles and must perform the most operatic style of singing. The 1984 recording by Bernstein represents the only time that he personally conducted his score and was directly involved with the casting: 'When I knew we were going to have a recording, I decided to go for sound. For the first time in my life, we can have exactly the singers we want.'[8]

The original Broadway cast recording features a group of then 'unknown'[9] performers with Larry Kert as Tony, Carol Lawrence as Maria, Chita Rivera as Anita, and Michael Callan as Riff. After many weeks of auditioning, Larry Kert, a bari-tenor, was cast as Tony. Kert apparently never intentionally auditioned for the role since the character was described as a 'high tenor'. During the previews, producer Goddard Lieberson observed, 'I hope Kert gets his first two songs into shape . . .'[10] As of opening night, Walter Kerr of the *Herald Tribune* observed, 'When hero Larry Kert is stomping out the visionary insistence of "Something's Coming" both music and tumultuous story are given their due.'[11] Obviously, Kert grew stronger with more runs of the show. It was Lieberson who encouraged the artistic team to make a cast recording, but CBS President William Paley strongly reacted to the vocal lines, ' . . . there's nothing in it anybody could sing, too depressing, too many tritones, too many words in lyrics, too rangy – "Ma-ri-a" – nobody could sing notes like that, impossible.'[12] Perhaps that is what makes *West Side Story* remarkable; 'anybody' cannot sing it. It is a challenging work that requires sensitive casting and patient coaching.

These leading performers trained arduously to get the roles in their voices. Carol Lawrence spoke kindly of Bernstein's style as a vocal coach: 'None of us was an opera singer, and we knew it, yet we were singing opera. If Lenny saw that we were having difficulty with a passage in a song, he would say: "Tell me, how does that note feel in your mouth? If it doesn't feel comfortable, I'll change it."'[13] This approach gave the performers comfort and support in their roles, thus giving them the confidence to attain stellar performances. Chita Rivera remarked that Bernstein, '... taught me how to hit those notes.'[14] The role of Anita requires a strong belt, but also a flexible head–chest mix, specifically in the 'Tonight' (Quintet). Anita provides mezzo-soprano counterpoint to the soaring lines of Maria's high soprano, which naturally carries Anita's phrases into a higher range. In order to blend in this range with the operatic quality that Maria needs to produce for her notes, Anita cannot carry a belt into her E♭5 or F5 and has to allow for a more resonant space that is head voice dominant and perhaps vibrato in the tone in order to tune and blend with Maria. In the original Broadway cast recording, Chita Rivera sang most of this line down the octave and occasionally jumped to the written octave in a belt mix. In the 1961 movie adaptation, with most of the singing dubbed by 'ghost singers', the role of Anita in the 'Tonight' (Quintet) was dubbed by Marni Nixon, who also dubbed Maria, because the vocal line was too high for Betty Wand, who dubbed the rest of Anita.[15] The 1984 opera recording added the Shark Girls towards the end of the 'Tonight' (Quintet) to create a full company number, singing the lines as written. For the 2009 Broadway revival, Karen Olivo also sang Anita in the original range, with some edits at the very end of the ensemble.

For the 1984 recording conducted by Bernstein with opera stars José Carreras, Kiri Te Kanawa, and Tatiana Troyanos, among others, the range of the vocal lines did not pose an issue. The major challenge for the operatic voices was dramatic interpretation. The rich instruments of Dame Te Kanawa and Carreras bring unfitting maturity to the young lovers Maria and Tony. Whereas the sound itself proves thrilling, the story seems distant and often disconnected to the music. Bernstein's son, Alexander, and daughter, Jamie, convincingly portrayed Tony and Maria in the speaking scenes that precede the singing numbers. Yet the recording loses the sense of integration from their spoken word into the sung vocal lines of Carreras and Te Kanawa. Classical training rarely focuses on sung speech unless the role requires secco recitative. Even then, when opera singers are expected to declaim their text, they still must maintain spacious resonance for an easy transition into full singing. Also, the tone for classical voices most likely shifts into a dominant head voice earlier than musical theatre singers, who have a more dominant chest mix in the middle voice. This is most visible in Troyanos's interpretation of Anita. Her velvety mezzo-soprano switches into a headier mix at C4 and D4, whereas Chita Rivera sang in a belt-mix style on those notes.

Likewise, most of these opera singers were schooled in *bel canto* technique, which generally trains the voice using consonant passages often in scalar motion and in sequence of half or whole steps. Bernstein's writing for Tony and Maria often leans towards *bel canto* at its most operatic moments, such as in the beginning of the 'Balcony Scene'. But when these singers are faced with wide intervallic leaps the continuity of tone quality seems more of a priority than acting the text. Vowels become modified to enhance the tone but decrease the understanding of the words. The consistent use of vibrato also obscures the communication of the text and occasionally misplaces stress on unstressed syllables. Whether sung by singers who primarily perform opera or musical theatre, the songs have a transportive and staying power.

'The consummate craftsmanship of *West Side Story* with its matchless ability to weave a solemn narrative through music and dance, still dazzles after more than 50 years. Leonard Bernstein's majestic score, in particular, is undiminished . . . fueled by testosterone and rage, and some of the most achingly beautiful expressions of love ever sung', writes David Rooney of the 2009 Broadway revival.[16] Directed by the then 91-year-old Arthur Laurents, this revival took risks to reimagine the story. Laurents strove for a more realistic interpretation than he felt was possible in the 1950s. For some critics, Laurents's attempts at realism enhance the show, and for others it seemed more like a gimmick. One of the most dramatic changes to the show was provided by Lin-Manuel Miranda's translations of lines and lyrics into Spanish for some of the Puerto Rican characters. Ideally, a bilingual performance gives the Sharks more presence, dignity, and ' . . . adjust[s] balance with the Jets, who always tended to dominate the proceedings'.[17] It also creates more of a division between the two cultures, and the sound of the sung Spanish adds a very different dimension to the characters. Unfortunately, the use of Spanish did not go over well with the audience and the creative team restored much of the English later in the run.

Unlike in opera, there was no attempt to provide supertitles in this production, which fuelled some criticism because entire scenes would be performed in Spanish. For others, the use of Spanish added to the drama and overall experience. A powerful example of the use of both languages was heard in 'A Boy Like That/Un Hombre Así'. The musical argument begins in Spanish as Anita chides Maria. However, at the midpoint of the duet, just prior to the musical shift into 'I Have a Love', Maria departs from her native Spanish and speaks the lyric, 'You should know better!' in English. This shift to English in this moment demonstrates her love for Tony, even at the cost of losing her own brother. After that, the duet continues in English. In a way, it signals that Anita accepts this love, which is understood when she sings with Maria at the consonant, harmonic end of this duet.

Karen Olivo's performance of Anita drew critical acclaim, including the Tony Award for Best Performance by an Actress in a Featured Role in a Musical. She was the first Broadway Anita to receive such an award. Vocally, she maintained exceptional power and nuance throughout her musical numbers. Also impressive was the portrayal of Maria by Josefina Scaglione, who was hailed for her operatic training and ease in the upper register. Tony's portrayal by Matt Cavenaugh drew mixed reviews, noting the challenges of this role. Occasionally critics compared Cavenaugh to Kert's performance, noting the vocal demands and dramatic challenges of portraying a convincing Tony. Although their voices were completely different, Cavenaugh a tenor, and Kert more of a baritone with a high extension, it seems likely that the critics found comparable interpretation styles.

Although some confessed that they resented the missing Sondheim text, the sound of the Spanish brought a new authenticity to the world of *West Side Story*. This revival added the voice that was missing in the original production, that voice of the marginalised and stereotyped Puerto Ricans, which was previously ignored and unheard. Likewise, the gender lines blurred in this production. Bernstein originally indicated that the song 'Somewhere' should be performed by 'A Girl'. In the 2009 revival, the character of a young Jet named Kiddo, a young boy soprano (Nicholas Barasch) sings 'Somewhere'. Critic Adam Feldman notes the significance of this adaptation for the twenty-first-century Broadway audience: ' . . . the show had to adapt, and Laurents has labored – within the constraints of what remains a faithful account of a 1950s musical – to disguise its traces of old-fashioned corn and bring its themes into hardened focus'.[18]

And the adaptations continued with the 2021 movie version, directed by Steven Spielberg with new dialogue by playwright Tony Kushner. This film reframes the story through a sociological lens that prioritises racial equity. Similar to the 2009 revival, many scenes were completely in Spanish without translations to amplify the Puerto Rican voice in the story and acknowledge 'that America is not a monolingual country'.[19] An important addition to the vocal landscape was including 'La Borinqueña', the Puerto Rican anthem, after the first gang altercation. Vocal coach and consultant for the film, Jeanine Tesori, collaborated with Puerto Rican dialect coach Victor Cruz to coach the actors on the transition from speaking into singing. Rachel Zegler integrated speech into song with ease as a stunning Maria. Cast when she was only 16 years old, she was the first Colombian to win a Golden Globe award for Best Actress. Tesori's coaching manifests in these singers' honest performances, taking them 'inside out' in their lyrical interpretation. She explains: 'you're singing, and you're not singing, you're actually working something out inside that we happen to (the audiences will) eavesdrop on ... '[20] Additionally, the benefits of audio engineering made it possible to capture live vocals on set. Although the majority of the numbers were prerecorded, 'The balcony scene, the duet between Tony and Maria, was all done live. Rita Moreno singing "Somewhere", that was all live. Ariana DeBose and Rachel Zegler doing "A Boy Like That" and "I Have a Love" live, when you watch that passion and power, belting at each other, it's all real, all happening live on the set', explains vocal producer Matt Sullivan.[21] Occasionally, keys were lowered by a step ('Something's Coming', 'Maria', 'Balcony Scene', and 'I Feel Pretty') and songs were reassigned ('Cool', 'Somewhere'), but the integrity of the story remained. What was exemplary in this film was the seamless integration from spoken text into sung lyric, which resulted in a compelling reimagining of the 1957 musical.

When considering the vocal writing of *West Side Story* across more than sixty years of interpretation, the genius of the team of Bernstein, Robbins, Laurents, and Sondheim accounts for its longevity. The songs challenge the performers to throw themselves into the operatic passion, but also maintain a vocal technique that cultivates stamina and efficiency. Likewise, the genre of musical theatre continues to evolve and include extremely varied vocal styles. The combination of operatic and popular singing in one musical seems more common now than in 1957. Singers are expected to have the ability to 'cross over' from opera into musical theatre and vice versa. From the theatre to the opera house, to film, productions of *West Side Story* abound with vitality and relevance, and these voices will be heard for years to come.

Notes

1. John Rockwell, 'New Recording of *West Side Story*', *New York Times*, 7 September 1984, Section C, 3. Used by permission of The Leonard Bernstein Office, Inc.
2. John Chapman, *Daily News*, quoted in Steven Suskin, *Opening Night on Broadway: A Critical Quotebook of the Golden Era of the Musical Theatre* (New York: Schirmer Books, 1990), 695.
3. Cornelius Reid, *A Dictionary of Vocal Terminology* (New York: Joseph Patelson Music House, 1983), 265.
4. Berton Coffin, *Phonetic Readings of Songs and Arias* (Metuchen, NJ: Scarecrow Press, Inc., 1982), ix.
5. Stephen Sondheim, 'Song Specific Commentary by Stephen Sondheim', Extras: *West Side Story* (United Artists, 1961). Streaming on iTunes.
6. Sondheim, 'Song Specific Commentary by Stephen Sondheim'.
7. Sondheim, 'Song Specific Commentary by Stephen Sondheim'.
8. Humphrey Burton, 'A Session Report by Humphrey Burton First Featured in the April 1985 Edition', *Gramophone*, 26 August 2015, www.gramophone.co.uk/features/article/bernstein-s-west-side-story (accessed 11 July 2011).
9. Richard L. Coe, 'On the Aisle: *West Side* has that Beat', *Washington Post*, 20 August 1957, quoted in: Nigel Simeone, *Leonard Bernstein*: West Side Story (Farnham, Surrey: Ashgate Publishing Company, 2009), 116.
10. Goddard Lieberson, letter to L. Bernstein, 30 August [1957], in Leonard Bernstein Collection, Library of Congress, quoted in Simeone, *Leonard Bernstein*, 142.
11. Walter Kerr, '*West Side Story*', *Herald Tribune*, 27 September 1957, quoted in Simeone, *Leonard Bernstein*, 123.
12. Otis Guernsey, *Broadway Song & Story: Playwrights/Lyricists/Composers Discuss their Hits* (New York: Dodd, Mead, 1985), 46. Used by permission of The Leonard Bernstein Office, Inc.
13. Carol Lawrence, *Carol Lawrence: The Backstage Story* (New York: McGraw Hill, 1990), 46.
14. Chita Rivera, speaking on: 'A Place for Us: 50 Years of *West Side Story*', presented by Scott Simon, National Public Radio, 26 September 2007; quoted in Simeone, *Leonard Bernstein*, 50.
15. Michael Portantiere 'It All Began Tonight: Marni Nixon and Jimmy Bryant Reminisce about Recording Maria's and Tony's Songs', https://westsidestory.livejournal.com/125418.html (accessed 11 July 2021).
16. David Rooney, '"West Side" Revival Reaches New Heights', *Variety*, 23 March 2009, 20, 24.
17. Elisabeth Vincentelli, 'Shark Attack! *West Side Story* Feels Pretty Good', *New York Post*, 20 March 2009, 45.

18. Adam Feldman, '"West Side Story": A Broadway Classic Leaps to New Life', *Time Out New York*, 26 March–1 April 2009, 103.

19. John Schilling, 'Composer Jeanine Tesori Talks "West Side Story" Music', *The Brooklyn College Vanguard*, 9 December 2021, https://vanguard.blog .brooklyn.edu/2021/12/09/composer-jeanine-tesori-talks-west-side-story-music/ (accessed 7 July 2022).

20. Schilling, 'Composer Jeanine Tesori Talks "West Side Story" Music'.

21. Jon Burlingame, 'How *West Side Story*'s First-Class Music Team Preserved the Authenticity of Leonard Bernstein's Score', *Variety*, 10 December 2021, http:// variety.com/2021/artisans/news/west-side-story-john-williams-leonard-bernstein-1235131071 (accessed 19 April 2024).

14 | *West Side Story / Suite*

Jerome Robbins's Choreo-Directing on Broadway, Hollywood, and Ballet Stages

DUSTYN MARTINCICH

For Jerome Robbins, musical theatre dance provided spectacle, but its primary function was to communicate story, acting as a cohesive thread between visual, aural, and textual elements. Robbins turned dance into a common language in the world of the play, an extension of a character's vocabulary. For *West Side Story*, Jerome Robbins envisioned a prominent ensemble comprised of singing–acting dancers responsible for conveying essential narrative elements. By centering the action of the ensemble, movement and music lead lyrics, book, and design in translating given circumstances and character action. He enhanced aesthetic unity, thematic synthesis, and flow by developing a choreo-direction process which integrated American Stanislavski-based method acting principles with staging and dance composition. This ultimately contributed to the legacy left by *West Side Story* on film, Broadway, and in concert dance.

Setting the Stage for Choreo-Direction

Robbins's custom of working with storyboards guided his approach to *West Side Story* 'with the same time-free, space-free, image-evocative method of a ballet.'[1] Laurents's short libretto, heavy in stage direction and exposition, allowed movement to lead storytelling. Working with Laurents's descriptions of action ('a boy being tripped up, or being sandbagged with a flour sack or even being spit on'), character traits ('the boys . . . vital, restless, sardonic'), and dialogue (Anita: 'You saw how they dance: like they have to get rid of something, quick')[2] gave Robbins inspiration to thread both traditional dance and physical gesture through the narrative.

As a director, Robbins laced 'all of the visual elements of the production – the moving human body, sets, and lights' to create a cohesive aesthetic.[3] He relied on the expertise of long-time collaborators in concert dance and Broadway: lighting designer Jean Rosenthal, scenic artist Oliver Smith, and costume designer Irene Sharaff. These collaborators knew 'the

231

kind of fluid, almost cinematic dance action'[4] that created spatial clarity to support character-driven, movement-focused, non-verbal storytelling. Integrating design elements, Robbins used the raised levels and fences of the set for multi-level tableaus and jumps; allowed for lighting to enhance movement, mood, and fluidity between scene shifts; created patterns that featured the colours Sharaff assigned to each group (golds, greens, and brown for the Jets; purples, reds, and black for the Sharks); and devised character-driven gestures and choreography based on the cut of Sharaff's costumes. As Priscilla Peña Ovalle notes, Robbins set 'straight lines and short gestures for the Jet women,' who were mostly dressed in pencil skirts and 'supple, sweeping movements from Anita and the Shark women,'[5] who were dressed in ruffled, full skirts. Intentionally enhancing design's power of visual storytelling through his choreography and staging, non-textual elements provided clarity in defining relationships, character, and mood.

Arguably, it was Bernstein's music that most inspired Robbins's staging. Bernstein's complicated, layered rhythms spoke to Robbins's use of Stanislavskian beat changes as well as character action and emotion in his choreography. Throughout their careers, both artists sought projects that told 'American' stories to create an 'American' aesthetic in music and ballet. Bernstein and Robbins were both inspired by popular American rhythms – blues, jitterbug, mambo, and cha-cha – and accompanying dances. Robbins and his assistant Peter Gennaro, who primarily choreographed the Sharks, infused these African American and Latinx vernacular dances into movement vocabulary, including, as Julia Foulkes notes, 'pounding heels, swirling skirts, and matador-like side bends with arms curving high above the head to convey ethnic particularities.' She continues, the 'elements alluded in a diffuse, generalized way to Spanish-speaking cultures.'[6] Though Robbins and Gennaro employed mambo and other social dances as ways to establish character, time period, and relationship, the 'genericness of "Latin" culture embedded in its music and choreography'[7] was not specifically Puerto Rican in terms of cultural identity, but became defined as such when West Side Story went to film.

Robbins's choreography and direction of the ensembles 'forms the structure and language of the gangs ... these characters dance their moods, intentions, and tragic ends.'[8] Dance vocabulary works as emotionally motivated character movement, like the extended battement à la second with arms outstretched in an 'L' which is a move of longing or power. The iconic chassé could be translated as expansive, a confident, easy staking of land in the 'Prologue,' where in 'Cool' it is confined and low to the ground, like a coil compressed then released.

As choreo-director, Robbins could 'demand unity both in the larger production, and within the individual performers.'[9] Unlike shows that distinguish between the singing chorus and the dancers, Robbins's *West Side Story* employed performers who could act, sing, and dance. These triple-threat performers were 'quick-witted, reflexive, mercurial, versatile – not *danseurs nobles* or prima ballerinas but *dancers*, who could follow [Robbins's] sketched gestures (he rarely used ballet terminology) and read his intentions from his merest glance.'[10] Robbins prepared the dancing actors by offering 'contextual research' such as 'postings of newspaper articles about Puerto Rico, juvenile delinquents, and general struggles in the city.'[11] He also employed non-traditional rehearsal practices like working with the Sharks and Jets separately to build competition and tension.

In creating the ensemble, Robbins required actors to develop backstories that would 'convey the situation, mood, and meaning between people.'[12] He coached dancers to attack movement as their character would, asking them to give purpose to why they moved. The dancer invested, then, in distinct character choices, incorporating personal gestures and idiosyncrasies into their translation of the choreography. As Deborah Jowitt points out, Laurents's descriptions in the libretto gave insight into characters: 'A-Rab is "an explosive little ferret who enjoys everything and understands the seriousness of nothing," Action, "a catlike ball of fury."'[13] Nuanced variations of shared movement vocabulary included manipulating the tension, dynamics, and exerted energy. A-Rab's bursts of laughter made his choreographed movement seem more indirect and unpredictable. Action, on the other hand, bursts in a more direct, pouncing manner. As Keith Garebian writes, 'Exactness or precise replication of a line or step was not as significant as youthful springiness, grace of carriage, strength in stopping and starting.'[14] Unison choreography then symbolizes connectedness and power as a group, intentionally making it have greater impact.

With Robbins directing through dance, the Sharks and Jets ensembles become leads in the story. While Gennaro worked with the Sharks, Robbins focused on building the specificity of the Jets ensemble. The gangs' collective physical distinctions helped to define them. These communities act as 'both a destination for characters in a musical and an omnipresent environment for them.'[15] Robbins's choreo-direction establishes the love story of Tony and Maria in the context of their identities to the Jets and the Sharks, whose 'restlessness and hostility,' as Jowitt describes, 'emerge primarily through rhythmic motion' as they perform as gendered, 'American,' New York youth.[16] By blending acting methods with narrative-driven dance composition through the use of dance-led numbers (which are almost void of text), character-led numbers (which have lyrics and dance breaks), and fights, transitions, and tableaus, Robbins stylistically unified the production.

Dance-Led Numbers

West Side Story opens with a snap – a physical gesture, signaling that dance and music will lead the storytelling. As Mary Jo Lodge points out, 'shows that begin with a focus on dance ... struggle less with embracing their later dance moments.'[17] Numbers like the opening 'Prologue' and later 'The Dance at the Gym' and 'Somewhere' are staged in an open space, making dance central to storytelling, and feature signatures of Robbins's style: pedestrian gestures that serve as deliberate stage business and lay foundations for dance vocabulary, movement that visualizes Bernstein's complex rhythms, and clear stage patterns propelled by urgency and motivations stemming from characters' anger, fear, and an assertion of turf.

In the 'Prologue,' the Jets establish themselves as an 'ensemble comprised of idiosyncratic characters who maintain their individuation, even as – through shared movement, motive, and melody – they move as one.'[18] When the curtain rises, they are mid-scene, leaning on Smith's set. Their first snap is direct, impatient, attention-seeking, coded, and one of Robbins's signature pedestrian gesture-turned-dance moves. It synthesizes the music and offers immediate subtext, as Ying Zhu and Daniel Belgrad point to the 'muscular tension building beneath the surface, a tension that is revealed only when it is released as a sound ... an apt physical synecdoche of coolness.'[19] The snap leads to larger, gross motor movement akin to more familiar dance vocabulary where, as Jowitt describes 'bravado, stealth, fear, playfulness, and anger meet in combat, revealed in actions that shrug their way into dance and as quickly drop back into everyday behavior.'[20] The repeating sweeping arm gesture and head pan indicate an assertion of power and relaxation for the Jets. They strut through New York streets, growing in confidence as the music swells until the abrupt entrance of Bernardo. The cut-off in the music and forward momentum of the movement establishes his antagonistic relationship with the Jets. Repeated cut-offs and crescendos align with the rise in tension of the movement – jumps and turns get tighter, pivots get more syncopated. The Sharks also snap to keep cool, but their phrasework is smoother and more vertical.

In the beginning sections, Robbins interjects gestures of feigned civility (a bow) between punctuated pushes (and lines like 'Beat it') to highlight rising tension between the Sharks and Jets as they establish space as territory. This culminates when a Jet is tripped by a Shark. The Shark shrugs on beat in a mocking apology. The Jet extends a hand which shifts from a handshake to a shove. Finally, the Shark's 'spit gesture' sparks a music change that initiates a chase as both the Sharks and Jets begin to run. Robbins uses stark diagonals for entrances and exits as if groups are dodging through streets and alleyways, building on group patterns of 1-on-3 or 3-on-3 that occurred in the first part of the number. The Sharks and Jets move urgently, with punctuated exchanges that are executed with the ease of people who are familiar with the Upper West Side landscape, having fought there before. These opening sequences lay the groundwork for sonic and physical themes that are replayed through the show.

The 'Dance at the Gym' is another diegetic, dance-led number that opens mid-scene and further defines group identity and character relationships. In the open space of the community gymnasium, Robbins employs thematic movement vocabulary like the snap and the *battement à la second*, and redefines actions found in the 'Prologue' like meeting, waiting, and battle. Robbins's choreography for the Jets and Gennaro's for the Sharks emanate from specific vernacular dance styles; each team watch their 'rival(s) dance and respond accordingly with movements that escalate in complexity.'[21] With brass and percussion, the dynamic changes in music signal changes in the accompanying vernacular dances: blues, promenade, mambo, jive, and cha-cha.

Robbins's unison 'blues' choreography, with explosive, ungendered, and initially touchless movement, establishes the space as a place to practice rituals of courtship and freedom, following the libretto's description: 'Jitterbugging wildly with their bodies but their faces, although they are enjoying themselves, remain cool, almost detached … The dancing is a physical and emotional release for these kids.'[22] The couples then collapse into heteronormative pairings and move with their own character styles, circularly moving hips in a Mooche-like blues motion. Robbins stages Baby John and his partner in an awkwardly stiff variation, signaling his inexperience. This couple moved against the flow of the group, a trademark storytelling method he uses to 'shake up the ensemble patterns.'[23]

When community organizer Glad Hand initiates a 'get-together dance,' a way to urge participants to 'become a community *as a result* of the dancing, rather than through a shared social or cultural heritage,'[24] the groups divide into two circles, boys on the outside, girls on the inside. As the 'Promenade' plays, the characters collectively walk upright, without hips or punctuation, to 'Latin music as their parents might listen (or dance) to.'[25] When the music ends with Shark men facing Jet women, a silent beat of recognition of the outcome is broken when Bernardo gestures for Anita, cuing the mambo face-off.

The face-off features 'Cuban mambo-style hip swings and layered rhythms for the Puerto Rican Sharks' signature moves, and jitterbug athletic swings and turns for the Jets.'[26] Anita and Bernardo, representing the Sharks, set the tone with 'arms held aloft and framing the face, chest high, in a pose reminiscent of flamenco,' states Foulkes (see Figure 14.1). She continues: 'the Jets respond with clucking heads and broad, gymnastic lunges to bluesy jazz,'[27] replicating movement qualities seen in the 'Prologue,' 'Cool,' and other Jets numbers. The groups form two, independent dance circles with featured dancers: Anita's high kicks, layouts, and skirt movement versus Riff's athletic gymnastics. Again, patterns and costuming define affiliation. As the dance-off escalates, 'both gangs take on the characteristics of each others' signature moves ... with the Jets adopting "flamenco" arm positions and the Sharks taking on jitterbug.'[28] When Tony and Maria see each other, their look pauses the motion, shifting

Figure 14.1 Silvia Álvarez as Anita and Oriol Anglada as Bernardo in 'The Dance at the Gym' in SOM Produce's production, Madrid, 2018. (Photo by Javier Naval, in public domain.)

music and movement to 'a streamlined cha-cha, which becomes "almost a minuet" . . . a blending of cultures.'[29] Tony and Maria's duet is echoed by three additional couples performing a wordless flirtation through direct eye contact, circular *port de bras*, and delicate non-touches, all nods to romantic ballet *pas de deux*. The addition of finger snapping here is a flirtatious gesture. The light, uplifted qualities complement Bernstein's 'con grazia' note on the score and provide contrast to the explosive, quick mambo.

Robbins aligns Tony and Maria's cha-cha in the gym with the staging and vocabulary of his fantasy ballet, 'Somewhere,' which is charged with Maria and Tony's hopes for the utopic future. Staged after the Rumble and Bernardo's death, 'Somewhere' features a principal *pas de deux* and *corps de ballet* relationship staged in front of 'Smith's airy, white and blue backdrop of sky and sea, with Manhattan in the distant background.'[30] Furthest from stylistic realism, Maria, Tony, and the ensemble, dressed in 'soft pastel versions of what they have worn before,' perform mostly unison balletic choreography with a presentational focus and male/female lifts, 'movements which are not out of character but suddenly released from the tension of their realistic city problems.'[31] Working from simple, replicated duets that echo Maria and Tony, the vocabulary emphasizes harmony as the ensemble locks hands, gazing peacefully toward that hopeful future.

Character-Led Numbers

Robbins integrated method acting and choreographic approaches to convey given circumstances, and defined specific movement qualities using character objectives. As Ray Miller states, Robbins 'demanded not only high technical proficiency from the performers, but also a psychological understanding of character that would inform movement, voice, and musical choice.'[32] He also used spatial patterns to convey characters' hierarchy and power shifts within the gangs. For example, he often staged Bernardo and Riff at the center or front of their group and moved Tony to the periphery. Anita and Maria are similarly mirrored with the Shark women. Jet numbers like 'Cool' and 'Gee, Officer Krupke' exemplify this character-led choreography, where movement is part of a scene and the choreography sacrifices pure spectacle to continue the thread of a scene's intention.

For 'Cool,' the music and dance 'represent(s) a visceral kinetic struggle between chaos and order, repression and expression.'[33] Described in Bernstein's score as 'solid and boppy,' Robbins's movements exude

Robert Farris Thompson's tenets of Africanist aesthetics of get down, swing, a sense of anticipation, and ephebism, which he describes as 'youthfulness'; qualities of strength, flexibility, speed, and intensity in all parts of the body.[34] Finger snapping returns as a thematic gesture of cool and connection. Individual Jets burst from this state of cool with forceful reaches – they punch their fists in their palms, hit Bernstein's unexpected sonic accents, and regain composure again. The coiled energy of the strings, muted horns, and guttural vocal gestures are enacted through contractions, tight turns, and low *chassés*. Arms and legs release outward and are drawn back quickly. The movement's darting, flicking, and hitting qualities and constant syncopation and pauses in phrases, produces an unsteadiness, similar to the pulsing nature of Tony's more pedestrian footwork in his earlier number 'Something's Coming.'

Robbins's direction and choreography merges in eliciting actors to embody characters' objectives (to block, to push, to suppress) as well as individual traits. For example, A-Rab's sharp, sudden, reactionary movement quality throughout the scenes manifest in 'Cool' in his solo through repeated punches, gun-shaped hand gestures, and vocal 'Pow!' As Belgrad and Zhu point out, 'over the course of the dance, A-Rab's uncontrollable violent gesture will not be fully eliminated, but rather disciplined and integrated into the choreography,'[35] like in the crescendo of the dance break when the Jets finally find unison after individual bursts, or what Miller describes as an example of 'a highly stylized, deeply resonating expression of the emotion behind that gesture ... Robbins moves from a literal interpretation of gesture to a multi-layered movement phrase.'[36] The repetition of thematic gesture, therefore, acts as marker for a character's physical 'voice.'

The movement is a coded, physical language of youth, something not understood by adults, echoing Laurents's use of slang in the libretto. In 'Gee, Officer Krupke' exaggerated physical posturing seen in scenes with Krupke become the basis for the pantomime. The number is a satire following Riff through the life of a juvenile delinquent. Repeated gestures of violence like slapping and hitting with a newspaper emphasize the rhythmic staccato and frame of verse, chorus, break. Transitions between each mini-scene incorporate movement that mock adults who failed them – from an angular polka to a slap fight to drunken staggering. In one of *West Side Story*'s only comedic moments, Robbins ensures that physicality prioritizes the characters' truthfulness, emotionality, and relationships.

Fights, Transitions, Tableaus

Robbins created fights, tableaus, and transitions to serve the narrative and create flow between scenes. Mirroring the Montagues and Capulets in *Romeo and Juliet*, the rivalry between the Sharks and Jets always made physical altercation a possibility. The 'Prologue' introduced violent actions like spitting, slapping, tripping, and punching, and they evolved as extensions of the choreography throughout the production. In the 'Prologue,' 'the stakes of brawling are not lethal,' says Belgrad and Zhu, but are 'movements that clearly belong within a vocabulary of play.'[37] Accompanying leaps, turns, and reaches indicate lightness, and fighting in this instance releases tension. However, when there is a real threat of battle in the 'Rumble,' Robbins stages fights with more intensity, where the movement is 'exactingly performed to specific beats, even in the silent passages'[38] and playfulness is omitted. Robbins creates a 'back and forth between movement that is "realistic" in the sense that there is a push, or shove, or a strike with the knife toward the opponent, and a turn or somersault or jump that is more recognizable from dance.'[39] Though movement remains similar to earlier choreography, it is performed with more directness, sharpness, and with a quicker and more syncopated tempo.

This specificity and attention to tempo also kept the gestures connected to the dance movement in terms of quality and attack. When Robbins was directing the argument between Anita and Maria after Bernardo was killed, he choreographed the movement in terms of counts. As Carol Lawrence remembers: 'You had to slap her on this count, pick up the knife on that count.'[40] Additionally, Robbins staged the Jets' attempted rape of Anita with a choreographic approach: Anita *chaînés* through the line of Jets while staggering, being physically manipulated by each man before they throw her to the ground and physically place the unwilling Baby John on top of her. Unlike other fight sequences, the staging is unbalanced, and the patterns are asymmetrical – one Anita against all of the Jets.

Robbins engaged deliberate and simple storytelling through physical gesture in staging transitions. For instance, Maria's twirling in her dress that signals her excitement and delight, make a subtextual and aesthetically pleasing transition from the dress shop to the gym. This kind of character-driven action combines costume, set, lights, and movement to convey Maria's femininity and sensuality as the twirl lifts a certain veil to reveal her legs. The dizzying repetition of the action with the fabric is a metaphor for Maria's tumultuous feeling of anticipation. The gesture coupled with

Bernstein's transitional build culminating in a full brass blast reminds audiences that the story is also about lovers, not just violence between the two gangs.

Finally, Robbins employs tableaus to convey narrative, giving the audience time to register a stage picture that would communicate power, focus, relationship, and character intention. Examples of tableaus are found in moments of pause, one of Bernstein's signature cut-offs, in 'The Dance at the Gym,' and the 'Jets' Song,' and for many face-offs between the gangs. After Tony is killed, Robbins stages a tableau around Maria for her monologue and final music. The stillness maintains the electricity between characters, delivering the audience to the realization that the dream of 'Somewhere' had been erased. The stillness also guarantees that the audiences will not be released from this tension at the end of the show.

From Stage to Screen

Most audiences know *West Side Story* as a film from 1961, which differs from the stage production in several ways in terms of staging and content. In the film, the camera impacted how movement could convey realism and metaphor; the cinematography emphasized the percussive cut-offs and tension. For example, in the 'Prologue,' Jowitt quotes Robbins saying, 'when the walk began to build and hint at dance, "the camera WHIPS and we pick up the Jets in the new location."'[41] The camera also contributed to artful, emotionally resonant transitions, like the soft, dreamlike fade between the scene in the dress shop and the gym. Film could take choreography to larger spaces and real locations, which opened up possibilities for staging and patterns, as well as serve Robbins's desire to create an authentic reality. For instance, the low ceilings of the parking garage 'made us feel the weight of the world on our shoulders,' dancer Robert Banas remembers. He continues, 'We felt contained, cramped, restricted, and asphyxiated, which certainly mentally and physically enhance the choreography.'[42] Additionally, the camera enhanced urgency and confrontation, like in 'Cool' when the dancers move toward the camera in their crouched position, as if chasing the camera and then pouncing.

Scene order and casting shifted to accommodate for cinematic storytelling. For instance, the 'Prologue' doubled in length and 'Officer Krupke' and 'Cool' were switched. Staging 'Cool' after the 'Rumble' gives the song to Ice, the new leader of the Jets, and the actors shifted their objectives to coping with the shock of and response to Riff's death rather than preparing for battle. Another change included adding Shark men back to 'America.' For the stage, Robbins had 'insisted that the song be for the girls only, as it was the only chance for a full-out all-female dance number.'[43] Primarily choreographed by Gennaro, the piece is a character-led number about Puerto Rican immigrants living in America, a mirror in a way to 'Gee, Officer Krupke' for the Jets. However, as Brian Herrera notes, 'instead of culminating in a single exuberant dance, the screen version of the number punctuates each rhymed quatrain of "in America"'[44] giving the number a feeling like it is an extension from the mambo footwork in the dance-off from 'The Dance at the Gym.' Adding back the men gives more power to the Shark males, and offers another kind of 'battle,' though dance breaks are seemingly disconnected from the narrative and instead accentuate the virtuosity of the female dancers. The number is driving, insistent, and indulging in musical theatre dance trends that feature virtuosic technical skills with constant turns, changing of direction, leaps, kicks, and layouts keeping with the *tempo di seis* and *huapango* rhythms.

Finally, the dream ballet 'Somewhere' was omitted from the film 'because its otherworldliness could not fit the hyperrealism of the medium'[45] and because the leads were not dancers. Its omission, as Foulkes notes, 'portended the steps away from West Side Story's vision of hope,' now only centering the better future for Tony and Maria, not the rest of the community. The absence of the dream ballet also solidified a previous divide between lead vocalists and ensemble dancers, given that audiences never see Tony and Maria dance other than in the cha-cha.

With Robbins's reputation for being difficult and his inability to meet deadlines, he was released from the project, and director Robert Wise and choreographer Peter Gennaro took over piecing together Robbins's motifs and visual aesthetic. For Robbins, his work as choreo-director would remain in the bodies and experiences of the performers executing character-based choices through movement.

'West Side Story Suite'

West Side Story's next evolution came in the form of concert dance with the 'West Side Story Suite' first in *Jerome Robbins' Broadway* (1989), a dance-focused musical revue, then as a repertory piece for the New York City Ballet (NYCB) (1995). The 'Suite' distilled the production to its dance numbers: 'Prologue,' 'The Dance at the Gym,' 'Cool,' 'America' (restored to the Broadway version of just Shark women), 'The Rumble,' and

'Somewhere.' Robbins also added a new solo for Tony in 'Something's Coming.' Visually, the original costume design, minimalistic set, and mood-enhancing lighting were maintained, keeping the period-style as well as the aesthetic connection between theatrical storytelling elements. The cast included Sharks and Jets ensembles, Maria, and Tony. Officer Krupke, a stand-in for all adults, became embodied in the sound of a police whistle.

The 'Suite' premiered in *Jerome Robbins' Broadway* alongside other numbers from Robbins's Broadway repertoire from 1944 to 1964.[46] It was an athletic feat for dancers who moved from number to number with no scenes between. The 'Prologue' opened in the same vein as the musical with a snap and a group of men. Numbers typically ended in a presentational front-facing and a unison bow of the head, like a concert dance piece. The dynamic connectedness between the movement and music featured prominently, and the growing tension over the course of the 'Suite' toward the 'Rumble' was rarely broken by text. Tony and Maria were left to tell their story via dance. Robert LaFosse, who is the 'ideal Robbins dancer' according to *Time*'s Martha Duffy, was cast as Tony, singing and dancing in the new 'buoyant flying solo' 'Something's Coming.'[47] For this new piece of choreography, Tony's movement harkened to Robbins's former solos from his earlier days with Ballet Theatre. With footwork that hits the score's pulsing undercurrent, Tony's upper body suspends the shapes with ease, allowing his voice to hold notes at the ends of lines. Bernstein said the piece would 'give Tony balls – so that he doesn't emerge as just a euphoric dreamer,'[48] and Robbins's new choreography matches this characterization. Privileging acting above athletic jumps, Tony performs simple reaches and quick footwork; he executes pirouettes that sail, floating with anticipation, contrasting the tight turns in numbers like 'Cool.'

The 'Suite' features a more equal balance of dancing for men and women. By incorporating 'Somewhere' and reverting back to the original staging for 'America,' there is more opportunity for women, especially Shark women, to establish themselves as integral parts of the story. Adding more women gives Maria a female community to either fit into or reside outside of, and 'America' offers virtuosic female dancing. The movement vocabulary highlights the female legs, hips, backs, and pounding footwork; however, it continues to remain unspecific in terms of conveying movement specific to Puerto Rican culture of the 1950s. However, by the 1990s, with salsa and Newyorican culture engrained in musical theatre and popular dance, the general Latinx dance style is even more accepted as an identity marker as well as an American movement style. The driving rhythm is persistent and their movement, next to 'Cool,' is the longest consecutive all-out dancing in the show.

By the time the 'Suite' premiered, Robbins's choreography and style was recognized and studied by Broadway and ballet dancers, which was helpful in translating the choreography to new media. There were, however, significant differences between the 'Suite' performed in *Jerome Robbins' Broadway* and NYCB, most notably in terms of the dancers's approach to choreography and use of space. For the revue on Broadway, the Imperial Theatre's house seats 1,400 people, with less depth from the front of the stage to the back wall, which highlighted the compositional patterns made by the 38-person cast who dart in strong diagonals and quick pivots like they are in alleyways absorbed in the bustle of the city. The proximity of the stage to the audience made facial expressions and physical gestures easy to read by the audience. The main challenge facing the Broadway 'Suite' cast was not overdoing the performance and not giving into the larger, more trick-based exaggerations of the body and face. The dancers, well-trained as triple threats and jazz dancers, delivered more release and recovery than previous dancers, owing to the style of the popular studio technique of the 1980s and 1990s. *Battements* are higher, but still have control, isolations in contractions are more defined as shapes, and there is the sense that turns can go on forever if the music allowed. Vocal gestures, in lieu of most lyrics, weave into the language of the dance scene as much as any *battement*, pivot, or turn.

When the 'Suite' shifted to NYCB, there was doubt that ballet dancers could handle the demands of acting the choreography. It premiered in the New York State Theatre (now the David H. Koch Theatre), a deep, winged space where the stage is separated from the 2,500-seat audience by a visible orchestra. The expansive space highlights the form and shape of bodies as well as dynamic spatial patterns and use of compositional canons. The dancers worked expertly with Bernstein's complex musical structures, grand crescendos, and moments of ease and subtlety, like in 'Somewhere' and the cha-cha at the 'Dance at the Gym.' However, the ballet dancers' unfamiliarity with works that demanded they sing, speak, and dance led Robbins to bring in Broadway dancers (Robert LaFosse and Nancy Ticotin) to the NYCB performance to cover the roles of Tony and Anita. Like the film, translating *West Side Story* for the concert dance stage gave the piece longevity, a legacy captured and archived when it moved into the NYCB repertory, and was theirs alone from 1995 to 2007.

Revivals (1980, 2009) and Revisals for Stage (2019) and Film (2021)

Robbins directed and choreographed the *West Side Story* revival in 1980 with assistance from 1957 production veterans Tom Abbott and Lee Becker Theodore. The production remained true to the original and made some room for new dancers' interpretations. After Robbins's death, Arthur Laurents, in collaboration with Lin-Manuel Miranda, directed and revised a 2009 production. Revised to incorporate Spanish language for the Sharks, former Robbins dancer Joey McKneely was hired to reimagine the choreography with Robbins's foundation. McKneely, who worked on *Jerome Robbins' Broadway* and in staging and choreographing various tours of *West Side Story*, attempted to make the dance, as he put it, 'the emotional glue.'[49] However, to update and foreground the text meant that the role of dance necessarily had to adjust. It also had to transfer to contemporary times and bodies. Some adjustments were slight, where McKneely felt the work needed, as Lisa Jo Sagolla writes, 'alteration to retain the original choreography's emotional impact,' and other adjustments were music-bound. Sagolla continued, 'jumps in the "Cool" number . . . needed extra time to extend their air position to the extreme point of its line.'[50] The same adjustments needed to be made for the *battements*, which were higher than those in the 1950s. Other adjustments factored in contemporary situations, like intensifying the fight choreography around Anita's rape sequence.

In 2019, Ivo van Hove and Anne Teresa de Keersmaeker collaborated on a new *West Side Story* project. The piece is of a solidly European, postmodern aesthetic, full of multi-media elements and minimalist gestural abstraction. The goal of the production – deemed controversial for its dismantling of Robbins's work, convening an all-white creative team, and its casting choices – was to modernize the story and dig into the identity politics of the characters. The production cut 'I Feel Pretty' and 'Somewhere' as well as other dance segments of the score and dialogue. De Keersmaeker's movement vocabulary was in many ways opposing Robbins: 'If Robbins' dance floated up, De Keersmaeker's shifts down and side to side.'[51] However, in speaking with Sylviane Gold, de Keersmaeker said she was interested in 'the way the Robbins dances evolve out of casual, everyday moves . . . There's something about simplicity and readability in Jerome Robbins's movement that is extremely efficient.'[52] She, like Robbins, went to clubs to watch young people dance, so as to situate the movement in the contemporary period, giving authentic period style to the choreography. Inspired by music of the day's youth, she also looked at hip hop, break dance, martial arts, and contemporary vernacular dance forms, bringing former Miami City Ballet principal Patricia Delgado and Tony-winning choreographer Sergio Trujillo on as consultants. Like Robbins, she worked with dancers to establish the needs of the story and the truth of the characters.

In 2021, *West Side Story* returned to the screen with director Steven Spielberg at the helm and a heavy book revision by Tony Kushner. The Oscar-nominated film featured choreography by NYCB resident choreographer and artistic advisor Justin Peck. A descendant of Balanchine and Robbins's influences, Peck is known for collaborating with an eclectic array of musicians, reimagining classic stories, and building strong ensemble work. His collaborations have led him to his Tony-Award winning choreography for the Broadway revival of *Carousel* (2018), as well as dance for camera and feature film projects. He is intimately familiar with Robbins's work at NYCB, having performed in the 'West Side Story Suite.' For this film, he paid homage to Robbins while pursuing his own choreographic aesthetics that supported a contemporary approach to the story.

Similar to Robbins's approach, Peck used dance to convey character tensions, the power of group identity, and the reactions to the changing community landscape of the Upper West Side. Dance is employed to emphasize the complexity of emotions that cannot be expressed through lyric or book. He also brought in his wife Patricia Delgado and Craig Salstein, a former soloist at American Ballet Theater, to assist in choreographing the Shark sequences, as Robbins did with Peter Gennaro. Peck wove visible references to Robbins (and Gennaro) throughout in the film: *chassés* as Jets accumulate as an identified gang in the 'Prologue'; snapping used to direct attention and keep time; outstretched arms as groups rush into a rumble; and the 'Mambo!' face-off staging, use of blues and swing social dance motifs, rhythmic footwork for the Sharks choreography, and the box step with arms outstretched in a snap for the cha-cha-cha in the 'Dance at the Gym.'

Peck's choreography was clearly customized to suit the cinematography (instead of the cinematography being customized to suit the choreography). This can be seen in the 'Prologue' which focuses on setting up the world of the Upper West side where Peck's choreography is only occasionally given focus to highlight the individual groups' identities. The Jets stake their territory by hitting strong, clear shapes as they accumulate in number and are interrupted by their main obstacles (the Sharks or other Puerto Rican residents in the neighborhood, building demolition and construction sites, or interactions with cops). Dance evolves into realistic running or fighting, which is staged without syncing with the score's detailed rhythms.

The 'Dance at the Gym' sequence highlights the talents of the dancing cast, especially the women led by Tony-Award winner Ariana DeBose as Anita and Paloma Garcia-Lee as Graziella. Peck's choreography is driving and athletic, featuring quick footwork and a fusion of ballet, mambo, swing, and jazz-inspired partnering. His compositional patterns and Spielberg's camera angles emphasize Broadway designer Paul Tazewell's costumes which pay homage to the original designs of women's skirts and the vibrant colours that signal gang affiliation. Like the 'Prologue' the dance is interrupted by conflict and scene vignettes. Unlike in the original film, some characters who are important catalysts in the story get a feature. Anybodys is briefly featured dancing with the Jets, and is shown rejected when the movement transitions to heteronormative social partnering, emphasizing Anybodys's inability to 'fit' in this world. Similarly, Chino, an accountant/square who is Bernardo's chosen date for Maria, is given a solo moment to initiate a dance that, when Bernardo and Anita join, gets adopted by both Sharks and Jets.

'America' is staged as in the original film, with Shark men and women in playful battle. However, instead of framing the piece in one location, the piece roams through the neighborhood streets, stopping in the boxing gym and threading through resident protesters and market vendors with no clear destination. This number employs dance to provide spectacle, featuring DeBose and David Alvarez (Bernardo) in a visual back-and-forth argument that emulates the lyrics. Men and women dance with their gender separately at first, then eventually move to full-touch partnering, demonstrating their reconciliation. The number culminates with the Sharks dancing in the middle of an intersection, clogging traffic and being witnessed by white and Puerto Rican onlookers. There is a brief addition of children to the choreography. The new incorporation of the community members as witnesses who don't get to participate in the dancing (with the exception of a brief incorporation of children at the end) or even seem to support it indicates that the Sharks are outcasts like the Jets.

'Cool' is transformed again, now taking place between 'One Hand, One Heart' and 'Tonight' (Quintet) in the story. The number, no longer about the Jets working through a collective anguish, is a duet between Tony and Riff that demonstrates the divide between Tony and the Jets and a premonition of the coming violence. Symbolically shot on mid-demolition structures, the staging, which contradicts Tony telling Riff to keep cool, creates a keep-away fight for the possession of a gun. These actions antagonize Riff, and Peck's signature tight core turns accented by rhythmic footwork or quick and distal dabs and flails remain central as the duo leap over broken floorboards and swing on dislocated pipes. Tony and Riff are mostly at odds, circling, chasing, or pushing against one another, with occasionally unison phrases, until their 'dance' becomes actual fight choreography. A five-on-one keep-away adding other Jets to Riff's side culminates with the lyric 'Pow!', now identified with the literal gesture of a gun-shaped hand aimed at Tony.

In the original, the music and dance were carefully entwined; in this film, the choreography appears to ride alongside Bernstein's score as opposed to with it. 'I Feel Pretty' and 'Gee, Officer Krupke,' which would be opportunities for more dance, are staged to enhance set pieces or camera movement. The main shifts that privilege book over music or movement also shift the film's delivery: nonverbal storytelling is diminished to privilege more dialogue used to flesh out the backstory for the lead male characters (Tony is just out of prison, Bernardo is a boxer) and introduce the new character of Doc's widow, Valentina, played by Rita Moreno. Interrupting the 'Dance at the Gym' with audible lines when Sharks and Jets clash, when Glad Hand and Krupke interject, or when Tony enters relegates dance and music to the background. Giving Valentina 'Somewhere' to sing solo and stationary strips the movement from a song meant for a dream ballet.

Ultimately, dance serves the film's cinematography and direction. Because Peck's vocabulary (or the way it is shot) lacks release or fluidity, it misses some of the complexity and nuances of Bernstein's score that Robbins was so apt to synthesize. Instead, dance sequences for Sharks and Jets keep a consistent tempo and aesthetic no matter the musical structure or rhythm – tight, crisp, sharp. Contrasting fluidity is only reserved for Tony and Maria. As the film, like the 2019 musical, reimagines and attempts to update the story, it also ventures away from core elements of the project that made it so unique in its own time.

The Legacy

West Side Story's lasting impact on musical theatre dance and concert dance can be seen in dance-led, integrative productions; in choreography and movement direction that honors character and circumstance over spectacle; and in triple threat performers. As Lodge writes, 'the era of the triple threat performer not only led to changes in who danced, but in fact, since dance could be interspersed throughout the production, in how dance could be used.'[53] *West Side Story* was the first large-scale Broadway project for a choreo-director which empowered Robbins to thread all production elements seamlessly to serve the story and create movement vocabulary that fits the needs of the character and scene. Robbins activates the ensemble, not just as background or spectacle, but as a key force that drives narrative forward with clear characters and intention. Through its film, revivals, and tours, *West Side Story* was seen by audiences around the world, solidifying its iconic status, setting it up for numerous references, satires, and quotations in popular culture, from Gap commercials (2000) to *The Simpsons* (2011) to *Glee* (2011). With this wide audienceship came more glaring issues of generalizing Latinx culture in Robbins's and Gennaro's choreography and with Bernstein's music, which 'spurred long-standing cultural debates interrogating the musical's particular contributions to the limiting repertoire of Latina/o depictions in US popular performance.'[54] Though popular ethnic dance forms were part of musical theatre dance training and performance of the time, this translation of 'Americanness' often lacked the specificity necessary in understanding Puerto Rican identity for *West Side Story*.

West Side Story demonstrated that audiences are collaborators who are capable of engaging with a musical that does not shy away from rape, violence, and racism. Where dance had previously translated the inner psyche and subtext that text could not, Jerome Robbins used his talents as a choreographer as well as a director to stage scenes and dance that conveyed fear, angst, hate, and deep inner turmoil through realistic gesture. As the dance work was archived and copyrighted in film and ballet repertory, it accumulated staying power because, like the text and music, *West Side Story* is forever captured and referenced in our history of American art.

Notes

1. Deborah Jowitt, *Jerome Robbins: His Life, His Theater, His Dance* (New York: Simon & Schuster, 2004), 284.
2. Arthur Laurents, et al., *West Side Story: A Musical* (New York: Random House, 1958).

3. Ray Miller, 'Dance in the Broadway Musicals of Shakespeare: Balanchine, Holm, and Robbins' in *The Oxford Handbook of Shakespeare and Dance*, ed. Lynsey McCulloch and Brandon Shaw (Oxford: Oxford University Press, 2019), 13.

4. Amanda Vaill, *Somewhere: The Life of Jerome Robbins* (New York: Broadway Books, 2006), 277.

5. Priscilla Peña Ovalle, *Dance and the Hollywood Latina: Race, Sex, and Stardom* (New Brunswick, NJ: Rutgers University Press, 2011), 118.

6. Julia L. Foulkes, *A Place for Us*: West Side Story *and New York* (Chicago, IL: University of Chicago Press, 2016), 51.

7. Frances Negrón-Muntaner, 'Feeling Pretty: *West Side Story* and Puerto Rican Identity Discourses' in *Social Text;* 18, no. 2 (1 June 2000): 83–106, 95.

8. Foulkes, 77.

9. Mary Jo Lodge, 'Dance Breaks and Dream Ballets: Transitional Moments in Musical Theatre' in *Gestures of Music Theatre: The Performativity of Song and Dance*, ed. Dominic Symonds and Millie Taylor (New York: Oxford University Press, 2014), 82.

10. Vaill, 293–94.

11. Foulkes, 72.

12. Foulkes, 19.

13. Jowitt, 275.

14. Keith Garebian, *The Making of* West Side Story (Buffalo, NY: Mosaic Press, 2016), 13.

15. Bethany Hughes, 'Singing the Community: The Musical Theatre Chorus as Character' in *Gestures of Music Theatre: The Performativity of Song and Dance*, ed. Dominic Symonds and Millie Taylor (New York: Oxford University Press, 2014), 271.

16. Jowitt, 266.

17. Lodge, 79.

18. Brian Eugenio Herrera, *Latin Numbers: Playing Latino in Twentieth-Century U.S. Popular Performance* (Ann Arbor, MI: The University of Michigan Press, 2015), 106.

19. Ying Zhu and Daniel Belgrad, 'This Cockeyed City is THEIRS: Youth at Play in the Dance of *West Side Story*,' *Journal of American Studies* 51, no. 1 (2017): 87.

20. Jowitt, 279.

21. Lodge, 88.

22. Laurents, *West Side Story*, 32.

23. Misha Berson, *Something's Coming, Something Good*: West Side Story *and the American Imagination* (Milwaukee, WI: Applause Theatre & Cinema Books, 2011), 122.

24. Sherril Dodds, *Dancing on the Canon: Embodiments of Value in Popular Dance* (New York: Palgrave Macmillan, 2011), 49.

25. Elizabeth A. Wells, West Side Story: *Cultural Perspectives on an American Musical* (Lanham, MD: Scarecrow Press, 2010), 125.

26. Rachel Duerden and Bonnie Rowell, 'Hierarchical Reversals: The Interplay of Dance and Music in *West Side Story*' in *Bodies of Sound: Studies across Popular Music and Dance*, ed. Sherril Dodds and Susan C. Cook, 135–48 (Burlington, VT: Ashgate Pub., 2013), 136.

27. Foulkes, 54.

28. Duerden and Rowell, 143.

29. Foulkes, 54.

30. Berson, 12.

31. Foulkes, 59.

32. Miller, 17.

33. Berson, 124.

34. Robert Farris Thompson et al., *African Art in Motion: Icon and Act in the Collection of Katherine Coryton White* (Los Angeles: University of California Press, 1974), 7–9.

35. Daniel Belgrad and Ying Zhu, 'Dancing with Knives: American Cold War Ideology in the Dances of *West Side Story*', *Kyiv-Mohyla Humanities Journal* 3 (2016): 1–22, 13.

36. Miller, 14.

37. Belgrad and Zhu, 4.

38. Berson, 126.

39. Miller, 15.

40. Vaill, 283.

41. Jowitt, 286.

42. Foulkes, 139.

43. Stephen Sondheim, *Finishing the Hat: Collected Lyrics (1954–1981) with Attendant Comments, Principles, Heresies, Grudges, Whines, and Anecdotes* (New York: Knopf, 2010), 41.

44. Herrera, 119.

45. Foulkes, 187.

46. With permission of the Jerome Robbins Estate, I viewed the rehearsal of *Jerome Robbins' Broadway* filmed without costume or scenery on 14 November 1988.

47. Martha Duffy, 'West Side Glory,' *Time*, 29 May 1995.

48. Jowitt, 277.

49. Julie Bloom, 'Rekindling Robbins, a Step at a Time,' *New York Times*, 4 March 2009.

50. Lisa Jo Sagolla, 'A *West Side Story* that Resets the Choreographic Balance,' *American Theatre*, March 2020.

51. Ruthie Fierberg, 'What Does *West Side Story* Look Like with New Choreography?' *Playbill*, 9 December 2019. www.playbill.com/article/what-does-west-side-story-look-like-with-new-choreography (accessed 20 April 2024).

52. Sylviane Gold, 'What It Takes to Radically Reimagine *West Side Story*,' *Dance Magazine*, 19 February 2020. www.dancemagazine.com/broadways-new-west-side-story/ (accessed 20 April 2024).

53. Lodge, 83.

54. Herrera, 98–99.

Exoticism, Race, and the Broadway Musical
in the 'City of Waltzes'

Marcel Prawy's 1968 *West Side Story* Production
at the Vienna Volksoper

MARTIN NEDBAL

On 28 February 1968, a production of *West Side Story* opened at the Vienna
Volksoper, the second most important opera theatre in the Austrian capital
after the Vienna State Opera. One of the main reasons for the Volksoper's
decision to stage *West Side Story* was that Leonard Bernstein was working
in Vienna with increasing frequency. Bernstein made his debut at the
Vienna State Opera in 1966 with Verdi's *Falstaff*, and he returned in
1968 for a production of Richard Strauss's *Der Rosenkavalier*. Already in
1956, moreover, the Vienna Volksoper produced Bernstein's musical
Wonderful Town. The Volksoper's *West Side Story* was in fact promoted
as an early celebration of Bernstein's fiftieth birthday. The staging of
Bernstein's work contributed to the rise of the Austrian metropolis as
a European centre of American musical theatre. As this chapter shows,
the main link between Bernstein, Broadway, and Vienna was Marcel Prawy
(1911–2003), a well-known Austrian dramaturg, opera connoisseur, and
critic. Prawy was also one of the first European producers of American
musicals. In his 1996 memoir, Prawy claimed that in his pioneering
productions of American musicals on European stages, he aimed to enlarge
the operatic repertoire:

I assumed from this (and you must know that I am describing a world that was
quite different from the present one) that they [musicals] were an interesting
enrichment of the operatic repertoire. Musicals belong to the opera, with a style
that is appropriate for opera, sung with great voices, played by large orchestras, i.e.,
an inebriation with music. We viewed this artform (in contrast to unsuccessful
modern operas) as a success formula for modern opera ...[1]

This approach is also apparent in Prawy's adaptation of *West Side Story*,
which imputes Central European cultural viewpoints and preferences into
the American artform, particularly in its representation of ethnic conflicts.
Marcel Prawy was born in 1911 as Marcell Ritter Frydman von Prawy
into a prominent Viennese Jewish family. During his studies of law at the

University of Vienna, he also attended Egon Wellesz's musicological lectures and became an opera enthusiast. After finishing his law degree in 1936, Prawy became an assistant to the Italian pro-Fascist film director and screenwriter Carmine Gallone. During the work on Gallone's 1936 film *Opernring* (English title: *Thank You, Madame*) in Vienna, Prawy became acquainted with Polish opera singer and film star Jan Kiepura, and soon became the secretary to Kiepura and his wife, Hungarian actress and soprano Marta Eggerth. Thanks to Kiepura and Eggerth, Prawy was able to emigrate to the United States after the Anschluss of Austria in 1938. His employers soon became involved with Broadway, most prominently in the 1943 production of Lehár's *The Merry Widow* at the Majestic Theater, and Prawy got to meet leading personalities of the American musical theatre, such as Irving Berlin, Cole Porter, Richard Rodgers, and Jerome Kern. Prawy was fascinated by the differences between European opera and American musicals:

I discovered this completely new world, which was still in its infancy, and made an indescribable impression on me: the living authors, who could be reached on the telephone, who stopped for tea in the afternoon instead of being buried at Vienna's Central Cemetery. Also greatly impressive was the unsubsidised theatre, which does not receive a single penny from the state, where people either go bankrupt or become millionaires. Where something could run for months – which was quite long in that time – or several years, and everyone became rich, or, if the critiques were bad, the theatre would be closed by the next morning and people could no longer afford to buy breakfast.[2]

Prawy eventually obtained American citizenship and enlisted in the US army, but returned to Vienna after the end of World War II. Back in Austria, he made use of his knowledge of American musical theatre when he organized a series of theatrical evenings in Vienna's Kosmos-Kino (later also 'cosmos theatre'), where he introduced and explained excerpts from American musicals to Austrian audiences. In 1955, Prawy became the chief dramaturg at the Vienna Volksoper (under the director Ernst Marboe) and in that position, he introduced American shows to a musical public until then solely devoted to operas and operettas. Prawy himself claimed that his were the first productions of musicals on the European continent.[3] Yet, already in 1948, Czech actors Jiří Voskovec and Jan Werich, who, similar to Prawy, spent World War II in the USA, introduced Prague audiences to *Finian's Rainbow*, though with a radically revised plot.[4] Prawy's first American import was Cole Porter's *Kiss Me, Kate!*, which was enormously successful after its Volksoper premiere on

14 February 1956. The next American musicals at the Volksoper were Bernstein's *Wonderful Town* in 1956 and *Annie Get Your Gun!* in 1957, which nevertheless did not achieve the same success as *Kiss Me, Kate!* Due to the misfortunes of the two shows, the protests against introducing musicals in the 'city of operettas and waltzes,' and also the death of Prawy's supporter and the Volksoper director Marboe, the Volksoper returned to American works only in the mid 1960s. First, in 1965, Prawy produced *Porgy and Bess*, followed by *West Side Story* in 1968. Prawy's final two musical productions at the Volksoper were *Show Boat* in 1971 and *Carousel* in 1972. His musical-related activities ended in 1972, when he was hired by the Vienna State Opera to work on programming and public outreach and education.

Prawy became an admirer of Leonard Bernstein's music at a time when Bernstein was mostly unknown as a composer in Europe. Prawy and Bernstein first became acquainted when Prawy was preparing the 1956 production of *Wonderful Town*, which was the first Bernstein stage work to be performed in Europe. In 1957, Prawy attended the Broadway premiere of *West Side Story*. According to his biographer Otto Schwarz, Prawy wanted to bring *West Side Story* to Vienna soon after the American premiere but had lost his influence in Volksoper after the death of director Marboe in 1957.[5] Prawy continued to keep in touch with Bernstein, and in 1965, he approached Bernstein with the offer to conduct the Volksoper production of *Porgy and Bess*. At that time, however, Bernstein was already engaged to conduct Lucchino Visconti's production of Verdi's *Falstaff* at the Vienna State Opera. Prawy's interest in *West Side Story* was reignited in February 1964, when the Finnish troupe from the Tampere Theatre gave four guest performances of a 1963 Finnish adaptation of Bernstein's musical at the Theater an der Wien.[6] Prawy thought *West Side Story* was 'the masterwork of masterworks' ('Meisterwerk aller Meisterwerke') and eventually approached Bernstein about producing the work in Vienna.[7] Bernstein's only condition supposedly was that 'Tony and Maria . . .must sing like Rudolfo [sic] and Mimi in "La Bohème!"'[8] Prawy also claims that he decided to produce *West Side Story* at the Volksoper in 1968 to celebrate Bernstein's fiftieth birthday.[9] For that year, Bernstein was also engaged by the Vienna State Opera to conduct a new production of Strauss's *Der Rosenkavalier*, so he was to be in Austria and experience the performances of his own musical.

In preparing the Volksoper *West Side Story*, Prawy returned to his practice, applied already in *Kiss Me, Kate!*, *Wonderful Town*, and the Kosmos-Kino shows, of translating works of American musical theatre into German. Prawy must have started the *West Side Story* translation already in the summer of 1966, because he claims he was working on it during his summer stay on the Canary Islands.[10] Once finished, Prawy's German translation pleased Bernstein, who supposedly told Prawy that *West Side Story* was better in German than in English.[11] Prawy's claim contrasts with many contemporaneous critiques that suggested that the German version was not as harsh-sounding as the English version, which made the work seem more sentimental.[12] As with most foreign-language adaptations of stage works, Prawy's *West Side Story* differed in significant details from the original text by Arthur Laurents and Stephen Sondheim. In Prawy's own estimate, the adaptation's lyrics kept only about 40 percent of the original meaning because, according to Prawy, Americans think and speak too quickly and the American language is therefore untranslatable.[13] The differences between Prawy's German adaptation and the English original also suggest that Prawy was concerned about making the American work more understandable for Viennese audiences not only through his approach to language and the poetic properties of the lyrics, but also by subtle but significant changes in the work's meaning. Most prominently, Prawy aimed at increasing the Broadway work's exoticist elements.

As earlier critics and researchers have pointed out, both the original 1957 musical and the 1961 film combine negative stereotypes with sympathetic agency in how they depict *West Side Story*'s two ethnic groups, the American-born characters, represented by the Jets, Doc, and the policemen, and the Puerto Rican characters, represented by the Sharks and their girls. Ralph Locke explains, for example, that *West Side Story* has many hallmarks of earlier exoticist operas and operettas: the exotic group, the Puerto Ricans, are presented as the Other and are effeminized, the Polish-American Tony is portrayed as 'the courageous yet sensitive Self,' and, similar to many earlier Western or proto-Western opera heroes, is depicted as he 'intrudes, at some peril, into a forbidden, darker-skinned region, which is represented by the tender and beautiful Maria, the exotic Other, the Desired One.'[14] At the same time, Locke continues, few earlier exotic works 'focus as unremittingly on the search for a place of reconciliation as *West Side Story* does . . . the death of exoticism – the show finally suggests – may permit the birth of a multiracial, multiethnic, mutually tolerant society.'[15] In discussing the 'Dance at the Gym,' Locke also suggests that there is something specifically American about *West Side Story*'s mixture of exoticist and de-exoticizing elements: the fact that both ethnic groups participate and delight in the Mambo, a Latin dance, and the fact that through the enjoyment of the music the audience is 'drawn into caring' about the on-stage characters, parallel the processes in which white America often resents 'the intrusion of darker-skinned populations into its protected domains, but, on the cultural level, it absorbs elements of the Outsider, quickly domesticates and masters them.'[16] Bernstein's Puerto Ricans, in other words, are both a source of alienation and absorption; they are presented in a way that not only stresses ethnic differences but also makes the mainstream white audience sympathize with them.

A significant aspect of Prawy's attempt to translate the Broadway show for Central European audiences is that the Viennese adaptation to some extent abandons *West Side Story*'s original ambiguity of representing the Other. To clearly bring out the ethnic differences in his German-language adaptation, Prawy decided to cast the American-born characters with native German speakers and the Puerto Rican characters with non-German performers, hired outside of German-speaking lands after hundreds of auditions in New York and Madrid. To be sure, the original Broadway production of *West Side Story* also aimed at an ethnic authenticity by casting some of the Puerto Ricans with Latin-American actors – this was the case especially with Chita Rivera in the role of Anita, who had Puerto Rican ancestry. At the same time, other performers in the Puerto Rican roles on Broadway were of European descent – this was the case with the original Maria, Carol Lawrence. Prawy's approach to casting and how it was perceived in the contemporary press, however, leaned even more toward racial stereotyping. Most of the reviews of the 1968 production hail Prawy's distinction between the two ethnic groups as the most remarkable achievement, which makes it seem as if the general perception of the musical in 1968 centered on how it depicted ethnic difference, not common humanity. The ethnicity of the Volksoper cast and particularly of the Puerto Rican impersonators became a source of immense fascination for Austrian and German critics and called forth animalistic and sexual imagery. These critics, moreover, tended to further exoticize the American performers, sometimes referring to all of them as 'coloured' ('farbig').[17] Particularly fascinating and exotic to many critics was the Italian-American Carmine Terra in the role of Bernardo. The Viennese journal *Wochenpresse* described him as 'interestingly exotic' ('interessant-exotisch'), and the reviewer for the journal *Wiener Zeitung* referred to him as 'a nimble, ready-to-jump beast of prey' ('feinnerviges, sprungbereites Raubtier').[18] The critics found Arline Woods, the Volksoper Anita, similarly fascinating and exotic; *Der Merker* called her 'a sexually charged temperament bomb' ('sexladene Temperamentsbombe').[19] The critic for the Swiss journal *Tages-Anzeiger* likewise rates the racial aspect of the Volksoper production as significant when he writes that he was initially skeptical about the show, expecting a musical turned into an operetta ('ein Musical à la viennoise') and wondering whether the songs were already too well known and outdated, especially because of the popularity of the film and the recordings of the English version. But the German production was eventually a pleasant surprise for the critic, particularly because the racial difference was brought out so effectively through the actors' accents.[20]

Prawy's German translation contributes in several details to the sharper ethnic differentiation of the two groups portrayed in the musical. For the most part, Prawy's text is sensitive to both the poetic meanings and the rhymes and rhythms of Stephen Sondheim's original lyrics. This can be seen already in the very first stanza of the opening 'Jet Song':

Stephen Sondheim's lyrics	Marcel Prawy's translation	English translation of Prawy's translation
When you're a Jet,	Ein echter Jet	A true Jet
You're a Jet all the way	Ist es vom Kinderbett	Remains a Jet from his child's bed
From your first cigarette	Bis zum letzten Gebet,	To the last prayer,
To your last dyin' day.	Denn ein Jet bleibt ein Jet.	Since a Jet stays always a Jet.

To create a close rhythmic connection between the original text and the German translation, Prawy often departs from the original meaning. These phrases at times make the Jets more outspoken about their racist attitudes. In the opening of the first-act quintet 'Tonight' ('Heut Nacht'), for example, Prawy sharpens the phrases with which the Jets refer to the Sharks. Prawy changes the Jets' line 'The Puerto Ricans grumble "fair fight"' to 'Die Kokosfresser heulen: "Zweikampf"' ('The coconut eaters howl: "combat"') and the line 'We're gonna cut 'em down to size/Tonight' to 'Das Pack von Wilden wird heut klein – ganz klein' ('The pack of the wilds will be diminished today'). Another change that intensifies the Jets' racist views comes in Action's quatrain from 'Gee, Officer Krupke':

Stephen Sondheim's Lyrics	Marcel Prawy's translation	English translation of Prawy's translation
Dear kindly social worker,	Mein Fräulein Jugendpfleger!	Dear Miss social worker
They say go earn a buck.	Bei Arbeit wird mir schlecht.	I get sick at work.
Like be a soda jerker,	Zum Schuften nimmt man Neger,	For drudgery there are the Negroes
Which means like be a schmuck.	Dafür sind sie grad recht.	That is something for them.

The heightened racism of Prawy's portrayal of the Jets intensifies the differences between the white characters and the Puerto Ricans. It is easy to imagine that the sharpened representation of racial conflict in the Volksoper *West Side Story* may have resonated with the experiences of Prawy and other members of the Viennese Jewish community. In his memoir, for example, Prawy remembers with revulsion that the representation of the Black jazz band fiddler Jonny in the Vienna State Opera 1927 production of Ernst Krenek's *Jonny spielt auf* caused week-long demonstrations with placards that reviled Blacks and Jews.[21] Gertrud Marboe, the wife of Ernst Marboe, the Volksoper director who helped Prawy produce *Kiss Me, Kate* in 1956, wrote, furthermore, that some members of the Viennese musical establishment opposed the introduction of musicals at the Volksoper with 'a certain anti-Semitism' ('einem gewissen Antisemitismus').[22] By making the Jets more explicitly racist, Prawy may have been making the Puerto Ricans more sympathetic to those who had experienced racial oppression, possibly because he himself, as a Jew in Vienna, may have to some extent identified with the Puerto Ricans.

The emphasis on ethnic difference in the Viennese adaptation is quite audible in the cast recording of the 1968 production, released by the CBS prior to the Volksoper premiere.[23] In the original Broadway recording from 1957, the Puerto Rican characters clearly deliver their songs with a Hispanic accent, but overall it is not difficult to recognize that most of them are native English speakers. In the Austrian recording, by contrast, not only do the performers have a foreign accent but they also put on a much more pronounced Hispanic accent, although many of them were not native Spanish speakers. These differences become particularly obvious in the most famous Puerto Rican number of *West Side Story*, the song 'America.' In the Broadway recording, Chita Rivera as Anita attempts to make the song's second stanza sound Hispanic but her American accent shines through. The Viennese Anita, Arline Woods, by contrast, sings in a more pronounced mixture of foreign accents, so that her phrases are nearly incomprehensible. In comparison to the Broadway Rosalia and Anita, furthermore, the Viennese performers sing in voices that are breathier, filled with more pronounced changes in timbre and vibrato, fluctuating tempo, and improvised sound effects.

A similar transformation occurs with the Viennese Maria. For the Volksoper production, Prawy hired Julia Migenes, a native New Yorker of Greek and Irish-Puerto Rican descent. As the *New York Times* noted in a 1981 interview, despite her appearance, Migenes spoke with a pronounced New York accent.[24] In the Viennese recording, Migenes nevertheless puts on a faux-Hispanic accent that was much stronger than that of Carol Lawrence, the original Broadway Maria. This becomes quite obvious from the Broadway and Vienna recordings of 'I Feel Pretty.' Migenes's appearance and her vocal delivery of the role made a strong impression on the Viennese audiences and critics, most of whom perceived her as a Puerto Rican, not an American singer. Even after her Vienna debut in *West Side Story*, Migenes cultivated an exotic image for her European fans. In 1980, for example, she produced an LP entitled *Latin Lady*.[25] She also appeared in a number of exotic roles in Europe, including as Carmen in Francesco Rosi's 1984 film version of Bizet's opera, where she starred next to Plácido Domingo. In the years following her Viennese appearance in *West Side Story*, the Austrian press treated Migenes as a fascinating, exotic Other. In 1970, for example, the tabloid *Bunte Österreich Illustrierte* featured Migenes in a story titled 'Der Vorhang fällt, die Liebe bleibt' ('The Curtain Falls, the Love Remains'), which reports on her romantic relationship with Heinz Marecek, one of the Volksoper Jets.[26] The story concludes with an endearing, yet clearly exoticizing episode, in which Marecek nearly broke up with Migenes when he realized she had a quite significant weakness: she could not learn how to make Viennese Palatschinken, crêpe-like pancakes served with jam. To avoid destroying her relationship to the good-looking Austrian, the article adds, Migenes gave up pursuing Palatschinken recipes altogether. The myth of Migenes's exotic, Caribbean origin remained so strong in Austria that it is still presented as a fact in a 2012 PhD dissertation about Broadway musicals in Austria written at the University of Vienna, where Migenes is presented as born in Puerto Rico.[27]

Besides the vocal delivery, it is also once again Prawy's German translation that transforms Maria's image in the Volksoper production. Stephen Sondheim's original lyrics of 'I Feel Pretty' show Maria as joyfully playful yet also able to assess her emotions with a tongue-in-cheek attitude:

I feel pretty, oh so pretty
I feel pretty and witty and bright
And I pity any girl who isn't me tonight.

Prawy's translation is somewhat awkward and therefore presents a more simplistic and naïve image of Maria:

Marcel Prawy's translation	English translation of Prawy's translation
Weil ich nett bin, einfach nett bin,	Because I am nice, simply nice,
Und adrett bin, und süß und gescheit,	And cute, and sweet and smart,
Tun mir Mädchen, die nicht ich sind,	I pity the girls who are not me very
heute sehr, sehr leid.	much today.

Whereas Sondheim's Maria reflects on her emotions and to some extent makes fun of them as well, Prawy's Maria is simply describing her basic qualities. The Viennese Maria's ingenuousness is enhanced in the 1968 recording, where 'I Feel Pretty' proceeds in a slower tempo than in the original 1957 recording. As a result, the Viennese rendition of 'I Feel Pretty' becomes more sentimental and artless, similar to utterances from earlier Viennese operetta characters who were socially inferior, such as the introductory song 'Ich bin die Christel von der Post' ('I Am Christel, the Post Mistress') for the main non-noble heroine of Friedrich Zeller's 1857 classic *Der Vogelhändler* ('The Bird Seller'). Another famous operetta aria with which Viennese audience members may have associated the Austrian Maria's 'Weil ich nett bin' is Chinese Princess Mi's 'Im Salon zur blauen Pagode' ('In the Salon of the Blue Pagoda') from Lehár's 1929 *Das Land des Lächeln* ('The Land of Smiles'). At the same time, Mi's aria is in some ways more complex than Maria's because the easily exotic music (based on simple, repetitive, pentatonic tunes) clashes with her tongue-in-cheek lyrics that criticize the treatment of women in traditional Manchu society.

The exoticizing approach to Maria in the Volksoper *West Side Story*, was balanced by the Viennese approach to Tony. Whereas Maria became a more clearly exotic Other, Tony is easily identifiable as a Viennese hero. The particulars of the Viennese Tony are most closely related to the approach and skills of Tony's Volksoper impersonator, Adolf Dallapozza. Whereas Migenes got her first stage experiences on Broadway, Dallapozza was an Austrian-born operatic singer and a member of the Volksoper ensemble at the time of the *West Side Story* production. For the Volksoper audience, he was therefore a familiar figure, unlike Migenes, a newly arrived foreigner. In the 1968 recording, moreover, Dallapozza stands out because of the operatic quality of his voice and the Viennese accent with which he pronounces Prawy's German text. This is particularly obvious from a comparison of the 1957 and 1968 recordings of Tony's 'Something's Coming.' What in the 1957 recording sounds typically 'Broadway-like' transforms in the 1968 recording into an operetta cavatina, a style with which the Viennese audiences could easily identify. Bernstein himself picked up on Dallapozza's qualities of a good Austrian/European/ white boy when he cast him as the simple-minded and good-natured Jaquino in his production of Beethoven's *Fidelio*, created with the Vienna State Opera team at the Theater an der Wien to celebrate Beethoven's bicentennial in 1970.

The intensity of ethnic characterization in the Volksoper *West Side Story* seems to have influenced many Austrian critics, who viewed racial conflict as the defining issue of the work. For the critic of the Vienna journal *Neue Front*, Prawy's adaptation, although it was not in the original language, managed to present a genuine vision of how America, the American temperament and *joie de vivre*, are 'overshadowed by wildness, brutality, racial hatred, and unruly youth.'[28] The reviewer for the *Salzburger Volkblatt* was critical of the work's overall premise, because the story of Romeo and Juliet was overwhelmed, optically and acoustically, by racial questions and gang violence.[29] The reviewer also imagines many audience members objecting that what was depicted on the stage in the Volksoper *West Side Story* 'is not our world, not our idea of art' ('dies ist nicht unsere Welt, nicht unsere Vorstellung von Kunst'). The critic fears that the Austrian youth might try to imitate what they see on the stage. In other words, the *Salzburger Volksblatt* critique suggests that to some commentators the Volksoper production completely suppressed the humanistic elements of *West Side Story*; where Bernstein's work to some extent promotes multicultural understanding, some Volksoper audience members only saw racial violence and hate. The strong differentiation between the Jets and the Sharks in the Volksoper production might have also been the reason why Bernstein himself thought, as reported in several German reviews, that *West Side Story* was ideologically outdated by 1968. The *Zürcher Spiegel* critic, for example, explains why he perceived the Volksoper performance as too sentimental and at times dull:[30]

A possible reason might be that the interior political developments in America in the last three years have affirmed Bernstein's own worry that the fast transformation of racial problems in the US have already outpaced *West Side Story*, that the piece that was so intensely topical in 1957 no longer possesses any timeless value because the timeliness has vanished – nothing alters more rapidly than timely matters!

German critics were also quite opinionated about Bernstein's music and their criticism is also based on exoticist and racialized viewpoints. Bernstein's score became an object of exotic admiration mainly because it contains references both to North American and Latin American musical idioms. Most critics found particularly appealing those portions of Bernstein's score that were most unlike traditional European classical music, whereas they strongly objected to the lyrical, expressive, and most opera- and operetta-like selections. As the reviewer for the Graz journal *Südost-Tagepost* put it: the dance-like and rhythmic sections are very effective, but the lyrical ones are quite banal ('alles Tänzerisch-Rhythmische ist sehr wirksam, alles Lyrische eher banal').[31] The critic for the journal *Wiener Montag* was more explicit about the exoticist bent of his musical preferences when he wrote that lyrical numbers such as 'Maria' are inexcusable, but Bernstein's music is redeemed by his reliance on 'Mittel-, Latein- und Color-Amerika [middle, Latin, and coloured America].'[32] Numerous reviewers went as far as to reject the lyrical numbers of *West Side Story* as 'kitschy.' The critic for *Der Merker*, for example, claimed that some numbers, such as 'Maria,' are so kitschy as to exceed the bearable level of Viennese operettas.[33]

At the same time, the Volkoper *West Side Story* came to be viewed as reflecting specifically Viennese qualities, particularly by German critics outside of Austria. Especially interesting reactions come from reviewers in Switzerland, where the Volksoper toured with *West Side Story* in 1970. The *Zürcher Zeitung*, for example, pointed out that Dallapozza brought numerous 'Viennese moments' to the performance of Tony.[34] The *Zürcher Spiegel* was more critical, claiming that the Volksoper production included too many satirical slips into the manners of German-Austrian musical comedy, particularly in the 'cheap' 'Tonight' (Quintet) and in 'Gee, Officer Krupke.'[35] The critic also thought that Dallapozza's presentation in 'Maria' was unbearably 'schmaltzy.' Because they were viewed as a product of both Broadway and Austria, the Zurich performances of the Volkoper *West Side Story* added yet another layer of exoticism to the famous musical: it became a mixture of American musical theatre and Viennese operetta.

The Volksoper *West Side Story* shows that works of musical theatre do not necessarily reflect only the social, cultural, and political environment in which they were created, but that they continue to acquire new and significant meanings and associations through the processes of adaptation and cultural transfer. Marcel Prawy and his team not only created a landmark production that made *West Side Story* one of the most often performed works of American musical theatre in Europe but also left behind a fascinating record of how German-speaking Central Europeans of the mid twentieth century approached the complicated issues of racism and multi-culturalism.

Notes

1. Marcel Prawy, *Marcel Prawy erzählt aus seinem Leben* (Vienna: Kremayr und Scheriau, 1996), 108. 'Ich bin davon ausgegangen (Sie müssen wissen, dass ich eine andere Welt beschreibe als die heutige), dass das eine interessante

Bereicherung des Opernrepertoires ist. Das Musical gehört in die Oper, mit einem operneigenen Stil, mit grossen Stimmen gesungen, von grossem Orchester gespielt, also ein Rausch von Musik. Wir haben darin (zum Unterschied von erfolglosen modernen Opern) ein Erfolgsschema einer modernen Oper gesehen …'

2. Prawy, 102. 'Ich habe dort also diese vollkommen neue Welt, die in den Kinderschuhen steckte, kennengelernt, und sie hat unbeschreiblichen Eindruck auf mich gemacht: die lebenden Autoren, die man am Telefon anrufen konnte, die am Nachmittag zum Tee kamen und nicht auf dem Zentralfriedhof lagen. Ungeheuren Eindruck machte auch das nicht subventionierte Theater, wo der Staat keinen Heller gibt, wo die Leute entweder Pleite machen oder Millionäre werden. Wo etwas Monate – damals war das sehr lang – oder ein paar Jahre lief, und alle entweder reich wurden oder das Theater am nächsten Morgen schon gesperrt wurde und die Leute ihr Frühstück schon nicht mehr bezahlen konnten, wenn die Kritik schlecht war.'

3. Prawy, 107.

4. Conspicuously, Prawy admits in his memoirs that one of the works he considered as a potential first musical to be produced in Vienna was *Finian's Rainbow*, which suggests that he may have been aware of the earlier Prague production. Prawy, 124.

5. Otto Schwarz, *Marcel Prawy 'Ich habe die Ewigkeit noch erlebt': Ein grosses Leben neu erzählt* (Vienna: Almathea, 2006), 171.

6. Schwarz, 172. The performance of the Finnish *West Side Story* in Vienna is discussed in Aino Kukkonen, *Heikki Värtsi: laidasta laitaan* (Helsinki: Like, 2011), 55–56. See this volume's final chapter for more on this production of the show in Tampere, Finland, and in Vienna.

7. Prawy, 119.

8. Prawy, 119.

9. Prawy, 179.

10. Prawy, 71.

11. Prawy, 126.

12. This idea appears, for example, in Ruediger Engerth, 'Keine Lerche in Manhattan: Glanzvolle Erstaufführung der *West Side Story* von Leonard Bernstein in der Wiener Volksoper,' *Salzburger Nachrichten*, 1 March 1968, and Gerd Kriwanek, 'Musical erobert Wien: Grosser Erfolg für die *West Side Story* in der Volksoper,' *Volkszeitung Kalgenfurt*, 2 March 1968.

13. Prawy, 126.

14. Ralph Locke, *Musical Exoticism: Images and Reflections* (New York: Cambridge University Press, 2009), 268–73.

15. Locke, 274–75.

16. Locke, 270–71.

17. Otto F. Beer, 'Wird Wien eine Musical-Stadt? *West Side Story* folgt dem "Man von La Mancha,"' *Süddeutsche Zeitung*, 3 March 1968.

18. Manfred Vogel, 'Volksoper: West-Side-Fest; Bernsteins *West Side Story*,' *Wochenpresse*, 6 March 1968 and Heinrich Neumayer, 'Virtuoses Musical-Theater: Wiederaufnahme von Bernsteins *West Side Story* in der Volksoper,' *Wiener Zeitung*, 12 January 1969.

19. I.M.S., 'West Side Story,' *Der Merker: Mitteilungsblatt des Vereines Opernfreunde* 13, no. 3 (March 1969): 10.

20. Walter Boesch, 'Romeo und Julia in Manhattan: Viermaliges Gastspiel der Volksoper Wien mit *West Side Story* im Zürcher Opernhaus,' *Tages-Anzeiger*, 4 May 1970. 'Den besten Einfall aber hatte Prawy in Bezug auf die Besetzung: da die Handlung bekanntlich auf den – auch rassischen – Gegensätzen zwischen zwei Banden New-Yorker Halbstarker beruht, den weissen "Jets" und den puertorikanischen "Sharks" (Haie), die in diesem Musical nach Shakespeares "Romeo und Julia" stellvertretend für die Montagus und Capulets stehen, musste für eine nichtangelsächsische Version ein einigermassen glaubhafter Konstrast geschaffen werden; das Problem wurde durchaus einleuchtend dadurch gelöst, dass man die Puertorikaner und ihre Mädchen von Ausländern, zumeist Amerikanern, auch solchen dunkler Hautfarbe, spielen liess, die Eingeborenen Manhattans hingegen von deutschsprachigen Bühnenleuten . . . .'

21. Prawy, 48.

22. Prawy, 103.

23. On the recording, see Prawy, 121 and 184. Leonard Bernstein, *West Side Story*, Originalaufnahme der deutschsprachigen Bühnenfassung der Wiener Volksoper, nach einer Idee von Jerome Robbins, deutsches Buch und Gesangstexte Marcel Prawy, CBS S 70 040, 1968, LP.

24. John Rockwell, 'Julia Migenes-Johnson, from Ingenue to the Met,' *The New York Times*, 5 January 1981, p. 16.

25. Julia Migenes, *Latin Lady*, Ariola 31 879 0, 1980, LP.

26. *Bunte Österreich Illustrierte*, 31 March 1970.

27. Wilhelmine Brandtner, 'Dr. Marcel Prawy – Pionier und Wegbereiter des Musicals vom Broadway nach "Good Old Europe"' (Ph.D. diss., University of Vienna, 2012), 153.

28. '-ring [*sic*],' 'Volksoper Wien: Prominententreffen in *West Side Story*,' *Neue Front*, 9 March 1968. 'Die *West Side Story* bleibt trotz des deutschen Wortes die unverfälschte Vision Amerikas, seines Temperaments, seiner Lebensfreude, überschattet von Wildheit, Brutalität, Rassenhass und einer ungebärdigen Jugend.'

29. Walter Zeleny, '*West Side Story* in der Volksoper,' *Salzburger Volksblatt*, 4 March 1968.

30. 'Gastspiel im Opernhaus: *West Side Story*,' *Zürcher Spiegel*, 5 May 1970. 'Eine gewisse Rolle mag dabei spielen, dass eben doch Bernsteins Befürchtung, "bei der raschen Veränderung der Rassenprobleme in den USA wäre das Werk bereits überholt", durch die innenpolitischen Entwicklungen der letzten drei

Jahre bestätigt wurde, dass überhaupt das 1957 hochaktuelle Stück nicht mehr überzeitliche Gültigkeit hat, weil es auf Aktualität abgestimmt wurde – nichts altert schneller als die aktuellen Dinge!'

31. Heinrich Neumayr, 'Romeo und Julia in Manhattan: Leonard Bernsteins *West Side Story* in der Wiener Volksoper,' *Südost-Tagepost*, 1 March 1968.

32. Franz Hrastnik, 'Die "Kehr-Side" der *West Side Story*,' *Wiener Montag*, 4 March 1968.

33. 'I. M. S.,' '*West Side Story*,' *Der Merker* (March 1969): 9–10 (9).

34. 'Romeo und Julia in den Slums von New York: Gastspiel der Wiener Volksoper mit "West Side Story" im Opernhaus,' *Zürcher Zeitung*, 6 May 1970.

35. *Zürcher Spiegel*, 5 May 1970.

16 | *West Side Story* Abroad as an American Icon

EMILY ABRAMS ANSARI, ANNE SEARCY, PAUL R. LAIRD,
GONZALO FERNÁNDEZ MONTE, ELIZABETH A. WELLS, AND
AINO KUKKONEN

The USSR

EMILY ABRAMS ANSARI AND ANNE SEARCY

With its tense, explosive, and ultimately tragic portrayal of two societies irrationally set against each other, *West Side Story* was in many ways a quintessential Cold War narrative.[1] This was likely no accident, given the committed leftist, pacifist views of its creators.[2] It should come as no surprise, then, that its early history in the Soviet Union is intimately bound up with the complexities and contradictions of this ideological conflict and military stand-off.

Like many products of American culture at this time, the relationship of *West Side Story* to the Cold War is fraught with contradictions. On one level, the musical's plot offered a profound challenge to American exceptionalism – the longstanding American ideology that understands the United States as having special, even unique features, which was used to justify global dominance during the Cold War. *West Side Story* was a musical about a great American city, yet it made plain that life in such cities was far from perfect, and that different racial groups did not always live peacefully alongside one another. This critical stance presented a challenge to US government efforts to downplay the gravity of inter-ethnic conflict in the USA abroad, particularly the headline-grabbing protests of the civil rights movement. The Soviet government was quick to exploit any evidence that democratic capitalism might not, in fact, produce racial or economic equality of opportunity, as the United States claimed.

Yet while *West Side Story* challenged American nationalist attitudes in its plot, musically it provided a remarkable, almost utopian representation of the nation in sound. In this way, it can be understood to prop up nationalist agendas. Bernstein's score shows his longstanding commitment to musical Americanism – the quest for a uniquely American sound in music – fusing jazz, European high culture, and distinctly American folk music traditions to create American music for all Americans.[3] Ironically, the music's cultural nationalism was one of many aesthetic and musical features the show shared with the official Soviet artistic language, socialist realism. Among the other common characteristics were accessibility, appeal to an international literary canon, and the integration of music, dance, and drama.[4]

West Side Story's complicated relationship to its nation of origin profoundly shaped the story of its reception in the Soviet Union. Some Americans, including US diplomats working in the USSR, felt its distinctly American features and its popularity with audiences meant it could effectively serve the US government's Cold War cultural diplomacy efforts. They argued that a Soviet tour of the musical, funded by the State Department, might help convince the Soviet people of the sophistication and vigour of American culture. Its honest portrayal of US social problems was no issue, they argued, because this aspect made plain the freedom of expression that the US government permitted American artists.[5]

If *West Side Story* was to undertake a Soviet tour, as *Porgy and Bess* had so successfully done in 1955–56,[6] it would need financial, logistical, and political support from the State Department. Without such support no US arts organization could visit the USSR. Such tours became much more possible in 1958, when Premier Khrushchev and President Eisenhower signed an agreement that allowed for artists, academics, and businesspeople from each country to visit their colleagues in the other, thereby facilitating conversation between the superpowers. Beginning that year, Hal Prince in particular worked hard to make the case that a *West Side* production would be ideal for such an exchange, finding support from previous cultural diplomats and government officials, and even visiting the USSR to explore possibilities in July 1959.[7]

But any such tour needed the approval of State Department officials and their advisory panels of experts in the arts. Both the Drama Advisory Panel and the Music Advisory Panel refused to approve a *West Side* Soviet tour when one was proposed in February 1958, arguing its story would bolster Soviet propaganda efforts more than those of the United States. The Music Panel 'agreed that the show was wonderful', but felt that 'showing the gang warfare of New York will not help our cultural relations'.[8] For the Drama Panel, similarly, 'Gore, bloodshed and mayhem would add to the poor opinion of America that Europeans already have.'[9] A year later, the Drama Panel decided it was willing to support a tour, but State Department officials continued to block it, just as they did in 1963, when the producers of its European tour tried one more time.[10]

Soviet artists sent as cultural diplomats to the United States were, perhaps surprisingly, major players in this push for a Soviet tour. One of the first Soviet artists to see *West Side Story* was choreographer Igor Moiseyev, whose folk dance troupe undertook a cultural diplomacy tour to the United States in 1958. On his return, Moiseyev gave a speech at the Central House of Actors in Moscow in which he praised American theatre, particularly *West Side Story*. Moiseyev emphatically recommended the musical to his audience, calling it a 'choreodram', an alternative term in Russian for the *drambalet,* the socialist realist style of ballet. He went on to name Jerome Robbins the greatest choreographer of the time. Even though Moiseyev did draw attention to the American problems of racism and juvenile delinquency portrayed in the musical, the overwhelming impression of his speech was deep admiration for the performance and particularly for Robbins.[11] Unfortunately for Moiseyev, when the *New York Times* ran an article about the speech, Soviet Minister for Culture Nikolai Mikhailov reprimanded the choreographer for having made a 'gross political error'. Moiseyev pushed back via a letter to the Ministry of Culture, in which he cited American pianist Van Cliburn's recent victory in the Tchaikovsky Piano Competition as a basis for allowing, where appropriate, honest praise of American culture.[12] Other Soviet artists saw *West Side Story* on cultural diplomacy tours as well, including dancers from the Bolshoi Theatre in 1959. In interviews with the American press, the Soviet dancers commented approvingly on the 'tension of the acting and dancing'.[13] Georgi Orvid, the Bolshoi's director, remarked that the musical would be welcomed in the Soviet Union.[14]

Yet despite such encouragement, the State Department continued to deny a *West Side* tour of the Soviet Union. In this context, it was the 1961 film that was ultimately responsible for bringing *West Side* to Soviet audiences for the first time, rather than a live performance. The book of the show was translated into Russian and published in a Soviet theatre journal in the late 1950s. A performance with little singing and dancing that emphasized the inter-racial conflict was planned, but this does not seem to have taken place.[15] Meanwhile, Soviet cosmonaut Gherman Titov saw the film in Washington with forty other Soviets during an official exchange in 1962. That same year, the film was shown at the Moscow Film Festival, with audiences lining up for four hours to see it and responding enthusiastically.[16] Given the State Department's longstanding anxiety about how the work might be interpreted in the USSR, the US delegation to the festival felt it necessary to emphasise that the depiction of gang warfare in New York was not representative of all US society.[17] Over the next decade many US cultural diplomats on official exchange brought copies of the film to the Soviet Union to distribute as well, further increasing access to the show amongst Soviet musical theatre fans.[18]

The first live performances of *West Side Story* in the Soviet Union were locally organized productions. The first seems to have been in October 1962 at the National Academic Opera Company in Yerevan, Armenia, and another took place in December 1964, in Tallinn, Estonia.[19] Neither production provided royalties to the work's creators, despite the authors' concerted efforts to obtain payment once they learned of the performances.[20] (This was anyway an impossibility for productions staged by a non-US company in the Soviet Union, because the United States and the Soviet Union had no formal royalties agreement.) In 1965 the Moscow Operetta Theatre staged it and a tour of performances by the Leningrad Lenin Komsomol Theatre took place 1968–71.[21] These productions relied on rather literal translations of the book, meaning a lot of the slang and humour did not come across. Such companies staged *West Side* as a critique of US social culture. The Moscow production, for example, began with a spoken prologue: 'Comrades, we would like to tell you about good boys brought up in hatred and shackled by hatred.'[22] Early on, therefore, both the musical's criticism of American society and its creators' left-leaning politics were important reasons to produce *West Side Story* in the Soviet Union. As it became ever more present in Soviet theatres and on Soviet screens, however, emphasis on the political faded away in favour of admiration for the music and choreography and delight at the show's popularity with audiences.[23]

Indeed, *West Side Story* turned out to align surprisingly well with Soviet aesthetics. Soviet officials and critics appreciated that the musical was an adaptation of Shakespeare, whose plays were widely admired and performed throughout the USSR.[24] They likewise praised the fact that it was set in the current day and dealt with social issues. More than anything else, though, *West Side Story* overlapped with Soviet aesthetics in its blend of music, dance, and theatre. Soviet aesthetics often called for such a synthesis of artistic forms, an aesthetic value that coincided fairly neatly with the Golden Era ideal of integration in the American musical theatre.[25] Composer Arkady Ostrovsky remarked in an interview with journal *Sovetskaia muzyka* that the 'synthesis' of art in the film of *West Side Story* was unforgettable, a 'union of orchestra, song, ballet, dramatic action, the play of colours, style of cinematography'.[26] In 1966, the editorial board of *Teatr* called the genre of the musical 'very contemporary and very democratic' – strong words of praise in the jargon of Soviet aesthetics – and used *West Side Story* as their leading example.[27]

Once *West Side Story* took hold in the Soviet repertoire it never went away, and it remains a mainstay in Russia today. From the mid 1960s on, theatre and music critics regularly argued about how best to produce *West Side* and other American musicals. The question of whether or not to stage those musicals in the first place, however, was never raised.[28] From this period onward, critics regularly used *West Side Story* as a point of reference to judge other works, including Soviet productions of *Rite of Spring* and *Carmen.*[29] In 1976, *Sovetskaia muzyka* ran a glowing nine-page profile of Bernstein that praised *West Side Story* in the highest possible terms.[30] By the 1970s, *West Side* had so thoroughly worked its way into the repertoire that Soviet figure skaters and rhythmic gymnasts were regularly using its music at international events.[31] In the twenty-first century, *West Side Story* continues to enjoy a strong reputation in Russia as one of the central pillars of an international repertoire of musical theatre.[32]

Spain

PAUL R. LAIRD AND GONZALO FERNÁNDEZ MONTE

West Side Story first came to Spain as the 1961 film, which became extremely popular and made a sizable impression on Spanish culture. This however did not inspire the bringing of a stage version of the show to the country as the first live performance only took place in 1983. It is tempting to blame this gap on Francisco Franco's right-wing dictatorship, but Anglo-American musicals started to play in the country with some regularity in the 1960s and such progressive shows as *Hair* and *Jesus Christ Superstar* played in major Spanish cities in 1975, the year that Franco died.[33] No tours of *West Side Story* played in Spain before the 1980s, and it would have been difficult to assemble a Spanish cast in the 1960s or 1970s given the demands of finding a number of triple-threat actors who could also dance and sing well. Musical theatre was not yet that well established in Spain.

Traveling Spanish journalists saw the stage show in New York, London, and Paris in the years before the film appeared. Gustavo Puiche attended *West Side Story* in New York in 1957 and wrote about it in *La Hora*, calling it 'a new "thing," perfectly developed,' a winning mixture of drama, tragedy, opera, and ballet.[34] Another reporter, Guy Bueno, saw the London production in 1958 and praised it in *Falange.*[35] Spanish journalists also wrote about the 1961 European tour produced by Felix Marouani, which premiered at the Alhambra Theatre in Paris.[36] The film did not open in Spain for more than a year after the US premiere in October 1961 and eight months after it won ten Academy Awards. Interest was high when it debuted on 7 December 1962 at the Aribau Cinema in Barcelona, followed by a run at the Cine Paz in Madrid beginning on 1 March 1963. Few Spanish theaters had the necessary projecting equipment to show it, helping these engagements to extend as people from around Spain flocked to see the film when visiting these cities. Called *Amor sin barreras* ('Love without Borders'), the film played at Cine Paz until 1 April 1964 and at the Aribau for another six months. The film won Spanish cinematic prizes and the critics received it rapturously, one calling it ' . . . the most sensational, wonderful, and moving spectacle of our time.'[37]

Two international tours of *West Side Story* came to Spain in the 1980s. Austrian producer Till Polla collaborated with Francisco Bermúdez to offer an international tour at the Teatro Monumental in Madrid for ten days starting on 6 October 1983, the show's Spanish premiere.[38] The production, assembled in the USA, had already played in numerous countries. Dialogue and songs were in English. The instrumental accompaniment was an economic concession with six live musicians and the remainder of the orchestra recorded, an arrangement criticized in reviews. The show's press was mixed. Pilar Sierra of *El País* was somewhat impressed, stating that 'The lovers of musical comedy should not fail to go to this show, that, with a cheesiness that is all its own, retains the original freshness . . . '[39] Victor Manuel Burell panned the rendition in *Cinco Días*, describing most of it as 'deplorable.'[40] However, Fernando Bejarano of *Diario 16* noted that a full house ' . . . applauded with enthusiasm and shouted "*bravos*" . . . '[41]

The Broadway Musical Company of New York brought a touring production to Spain twice in 1988. Directed by Kathryn G. McCarthy and with choreography by Jane Setteducato, they billed it as the 'Original Broadway Production' based on staging and choreography of Jerome Robbins. They played at the Teatro Principal in Valencia from 18–21 February and then in August offered outdoor performances at festivals in Almería (in the Plaza Vieja), Santander (in the bullring), with another stop in San Javier (Murcia). This tour sometimes relied on local talent in the pit, including hiring the Orquesta Municipal de Valencia in February;[42] in Santander there were only eight musicians accompanying.[43] Reviews were mixed, with praise for the principals and ensemble but dissatisfaction with playing in the bullring and when comparing the production to the film's symphonic rendition of Bernstein's score.

The first professional production of *West Side Story* that originated in Spain was in 1996 and was directed by Barcelona-based Ricard Reguant, who had overseen adaptations of other American musicals.[44] He approached Music Theatre International for the rights, which included needing to hire one of the five choreographers whom Jerome Robbins had approved. Reguant chose Barry McNabb, who has Broadway credits as a dancer from the late 1980s and worked in Spain on several occasions.[45] Reguant collaborated with Focus, a company that had produced Anglo-American musicals adapted into Catalan. Albert Mas-Griera prepared the translation/adaptation in *castellano*, allowing performances elsewhere in Spain. They catered to the Spanish audience who knew the film by exchanging the placements of 'Cool' and 'Gee, Officer Krupke' and staging 'America' with the Shark men and women. At the time, it was the most expensive show ever produced in Spain with private money. The premiere was at Barcelona's Teatro Tivoli on 16 December 1996, where it played for five months, followed by a Spanish tour culminating in a run of more than three months at Madrid's Teatro Nuevo Apolo ending on 1 March 1998. Reguant and McNabb assembled a good cast that dealt with the show's varied challenges. The critical reception was generally positive. Eduardo Haro Tecglen, writing about the show in Madrid for *El País*, praised the young cast's dancing and liked some of the voices, but did not think that 'the production ... comes to the quality of the film that everybody has seen.'[46]

Theatrical director/choreographer Joey McKneely, who learned some of the *West Side Story* choreography from its creator as a dancer in *Jerome Robbins' Broadway*, and conductor Donald Chan, who has conducted the show more than 3,000 times around the world, teamed up for a production at the Teatro alla Scala (Milan) in 2000. It was the first musical ever to play there and did so again in 2003. Since then, McKneely and Chan have led a sporadic world tour that has played in many countries. During summer 2009, they were in Madrid from 25 June–5 July, Santander from 22–24 August, and Gijón 26–27 August.[47] Their cast included fine young talent, including Ali Ewoldt – one of two Marias on the tour – who also played the role in the American national tour based on the 2009 Broadway version directed by Arthur Laurents and choreographed by McKneely.[48] This international tour brought twenty-six pit musicians, mostly members of the Symphony Orchestra of Lithuania.[49] The production was in English with supertitles in the host language. It played outdoors in Madrid at the Casa de Campo, a large park, in a venue with 2,500 seats. Later that summer, the tour played as part of the Festival Internacional de Santander (also sponsor of the abovenamed 1983 tour's visit), but this time performances were indoors at the Sala Argenta del Palacio de

Festivales. When all tickets sold for three performances, they added a fourth. Two sold-out shows in Gijón were at the Teatro de la Laboral. Reviews demonstrate that it was a good production: a traditional realization of the show with a solid cast, but with costumes that more than one critic found too colourful and some inequality in the singing among principals. Julio Bravo of *ABC*, however, praised ' . . . this dazzling and emotional production, an example of quality and high artistry.'[50]

SOM Produce, a leading purveyor of musical theatre in Madrid, offered a fresh adaptation of *West Side Story* in 2018 in celebration of the 100th anniversary of Leonard Bernstein's birth. They advertised it as 'el clásico original de Broadway,' the first Spanish production based upon the 1957 stage version, eschewing changes introduced in the 1961 film. Noted Spanish director and writer David Serrano authored the adaptation/translation, working on Sondheim's lyrics with his brother Alejandro, a musician. Serrano's lofty goal was to produce a version sounding like it had originally been written in *castellano*.[51] In comparison to Mas-Griera's 1996 version, Serrano was less literal in approach and managed dialogue and lyrics that sounded somewhat more natural.[52] The director/choreographer was Argentinian Federico Barrios, who accepted SOM's lead and regarded Bernstein's music and Robbins's choreography as 'classic originals,' adding a few of his own subtle touches and encouraging constant interaction between characters.[53] Barrios chose his cast from about 3,000 aspirants, assembling a tight ensemble featuring several experienced actors from the Spanish musical theatre scene. The pit orchestra included eighteen musicians. The critical response was very positive, with high praise for producing a difficult show and for the realization of music and choreography. Critics were somewhat more ambivalent about the acting, but there were plaudits for Silvia Álvarez, playing Anita. Some thought that the set was too large for the stage, but numerous critics raved about the show and saw its realization as a victory for Madrid's theatrical community (see Figure 16.1). Nacho Fresno of *Shangay.com* stated: 'It is not an easy assignment to stage *West Side Story*. And if it can be done today with success in Madrid it is thanks to the very high level that we have in this country to present shows like this.'[54] Madrid is a much smaller center for the genre than New York or London, where it is hard to imagine a similar comment from a reviewer. The production opened at the Teatro Calderón on 3 October 2018 and ran until 2 June 2019, then embarking on a national tour that ended abruptly on 14 March 2020 because of the COVID-19 virus.

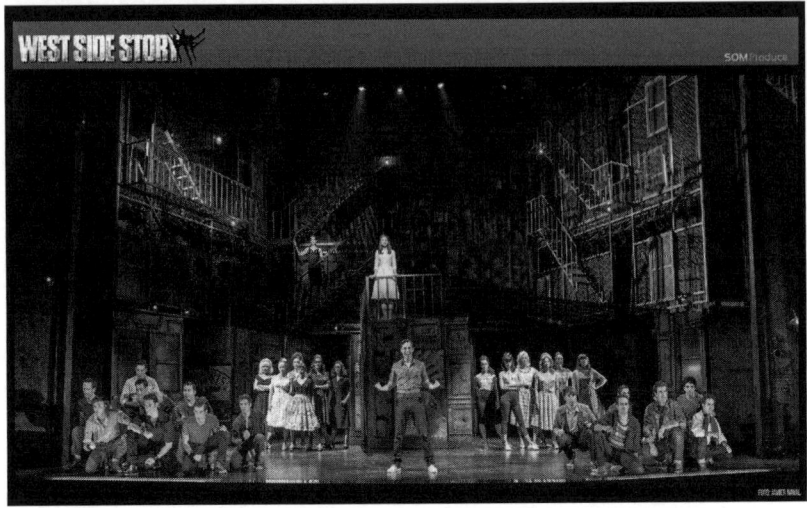

Figure 16.1 The 'Tonight' (Quintet) in SOM's production, Madrid, 2018. (Photo by Javier Naval, in public domain.)

London, 1958

ELIZABETH A. WELLS

When *West Side Story* opened in London's West End in 1958, no one could have predicted the enormity of the audience response. Although bootleg recordings of the work had been circulating for some time among the smart set ('Gee, Officer Krupke' was the favourite song), the more traditional musical *My Fair Lady* dominated the London stage at that juncture. Although *West Side Story* originally premiered in Manchester as a try-out city for London, it was not without a lot of preparation. This was not a straightforward transfer from one continent to another. Indeed, the British Actors' union had to hear from experts as to why the London production would not be cast, as was standard, by British actors. Testimony from American theatrical specialists argued that the style of dancing and acting, and the physical demands of the show, would be beyond the capabilities of most British performers at this time. The union acceded to the request and American dancers and singers (including Chita Rivera and Tony Mordente, from the original cast) flew to England to prepare the show. It is important to note that British musical theatre during the 1950s was still something of a lilac-scented affair: Noel Coward plays were popular, revue-like shows featuring famous London stage comedians and singers were everywhere, and the music hall style of production and consumption was the norm for London audiences. If they wanted to see balletic moves and more serious content, they would go to the ballet. Although a series of British musicals like *Fings Ain't Wot They Used to Be* and *The Crooked Mile* took on the lowlife or street people of London's Soho, they were still not as edgy or dark as *West Side Story*. Juvenile delinquents and their relationship to a curate were featured in the British musical *Johnny the Priest*, but the delinquents in that show were not particularly violent and mostly expressed their sense of disenchantment with dancing 'The Burp' and doing a little thievery. In some ways, although shows like this were dealing with some of the same issues raised by *West Side Story*, they weren't blockbusters. They paved the way for looking at the seamier side of life, but they often played in places like Stratford East, under the direction of iconoclasts like Joan Littlewood, not in mainstream London theatres. These 'Soho' musicals also coincided with the arrival of Brecht's plays in London, and both took some getting used to for audiences who were accustomed to much lighter fare. Although it is safe to say that London was gearing up for more serious content in their musical theatre, the average audience member would not have seen anything like *West Side Story* before.

After the generally good Manchester reviews, *West Side Story* opened at Her Majesty's Theatre in winter 1958. Hype that had preceded the premiere resulted in a star-studded audience: Noel Coward, Margot Fonteyn, and other luminaries of dance and stage attended. What they saw shook them to the core and resulted in a frisson of excitement over this supposedly new art form. 'Dansical' was the term newspapers used to describe this new kind of musical, recognizing the extent and seriousness of the dance numbers. 'Like a shark was let loose in an aquarium' wrote one critic of how opening night audiences responded to the work.[55] British culture was much more focused on ballet, and this art form was valued but also experienced by a wider swath of the population than in the United States. Certainly, nothing like this had ever been seen on a London stage, but it wasn't just the dance spectacle that resonated with audiences. Britain was having similar social problems, especially with juvenile delinquency, that America had suffered, and the work struck a chord with the British public. A famous judge, Justice Salmon, attended an early performance, and newspapers eagerly wanted to know what he thought of a work that was sympathetic to teenagers at the time he was sentencing the same kinds of characters to jail time for involvement in race riots.[56]

The work was not just popular, though. It caused musical theatre professionals and creators to rethink what it was they were doing to move their art form forward. One critic wrote that *West Side Story* made British musicals look like 'watery gruel' and called for a new kind of musical that would stare the American musical in the face.[57] The answer, for many, was not to replicate what the work did, but to create a sense of British identity in the wake of the 'American Invasion' that had taken over England particularly from *Oklahoma!* onwards. Although one would imagine that musical theatre changed drastically as a response to the success of the work, the most cogent response to it was *Oliver!* This musical (opening off the West End but soon transferring) premiered in 1960 and enjoyed great success. More importantly, it transferred to Broadway, so in essence reversed the direction in which musical theatre had been going for the last few decades. However, *Oliver!*, although about street urchins and containing some serious content, didn't really match the tragic content of *West Side Story*, and although it was British in its source material, was mostly written in the 'American' style that Britons had tried to depart from.

Ultimately, *West Side Story* ran longer in the West End than it had on Broadway, as unlikely as that may seem. When reviews of the electric audience response to the work reached *Variety*, the show, which had been running half-price tickets to encourage box office, suddenly started to sell out. It seemed that for Americans, an international imprimatur meant more to them than the New York critical response, which admittedly had been mixed. Harold Prince credits the newfound interest in the work to the London response, and so it was that the work was 'revived' the next year mostly with the original cast, after a short national tour. Although a film deal had already been struck with the original creators after a good showing at the Tony Awards, it is safe to say that the British response really cemented the popularity of the work with American audiences and it became part of the repertory and spawned other international productions.

Finland in the Early 1960s and a Visit to Vienna

AINO KUKKONEN AND PAUL R. LAIRD

After the introduction of *West Side Story* in London and that production's European tour, attempts began to mount the show in other countries. An effort by impresario Lars Schmidt to produce the musical in Copenhagen with a Nordic cast failed because they could not find enough qualified dancers.[58] An early such production took place in Finland. Rauli Lehtonen (1928–2014) was the young, energetic director of the Tampere Theatre (Tampereen Teatteri, founded 1904), located in that city in the southern part of the country. Tampere is the largest inland city in Scandinavia. Lehtonen was considering putting on a Viennese operetta, but his wife, having just seen the film of *West Side Story*, suggested that he produce the musical. Negotiations with Music Theatre International were difficult and Lehtonen sought assistance from the US Embassy in Helsinki. The licensing agency wanted to approve the translation and asked for at least fifty performances and an orchestra of twenty-two musicians. Finding dancers was again a major sticking point because jazz dance and related styles were new to Finland. Heikki Värtsi (1931–2013) was a young principal dancer in the Finnish National Ballet. His interest in jazz dance began in the early 1960s and he honed his skills by studying abroad and doing musical theatre and choreography for Finnish television. Värtsi's interest in the style led to him becoming one of its major exponents in Finland; in the 1960s he founded a school at the Helsinki City Theatre that eventually led to the establishment of the professional Helsinki Dance Company.[59] He became the show's choreographer and co-director along with Lehtonen, traveling to New York in 1963 to study jazz dance and the right dance style with an assistant of Jerome Robbins. Värtsi had seen the musical already in London and first thought it was impossible to perform it in Finland. However, he designed his own choreography suitable for the Tampere Theatre cast, and it became the cornerstone of the show's success. The production's contract specified that Robbins would come to Tampere to approve the choreography, but the American director/choreographer never arrived. Sauvo Puhtila (1928–2014), a noted Finnish composer, lyricist, and journalist, translated the book and lyrics of *West Side Story* for the production.

The Nordic premiere of the show took place at the Tampere Theatre on 13 November 1963.[60] The musical played often over the next few years, 146 times before a total audience of 70,000 by the time that the company mounted *West Side Story* at Vienna's Theater an der Wien in April 1965,[61] an event described below. As was the case elsewhere that the show played, it inherently carried a political message. The family of counselor George M. Ingram from the US Embassy was invited to the premiere. Later also the Finnish president Urho Kekkonen, who was skillfully balancing his nation's foreign policy during the Cold War, saw the performance. The musical engendered discussion in reviews of social problems in the United States. Tampere was a strong theatrical centre but also known as an industrial, workers' city, and Värtsi states in his memoirs that he faced some criticism for promoting a distinctly American musical. *West Side Story* became somewhat of a sensation in Finland, with productions following at the Turku City Theatre (directed by Gordon Marsh) in 1964 and the Finnish

National Ballet at the Finnish National Opera in Helsinki in fall 1965 with Heikki Värtsi serving as choreographer and playing the role of Bernardo.[62] In Helsinki the production was a success, but it raised questions of high and low culture that are embedded in the musical itself; some commentators questioned whether it was suitable for the National Opera.[63] Other productions later in the decade took place in the city theatres of Kuopio and Kotka. From the late 1950s onward other American musicals, such as *Annie Get Your Gun*, *My Fair Lady*, and especially *Fiddler on the Roof*, also became popular in Finland, replacing the operetta repertory in theatres.

It is extraordinary to consider the notion that the first time that *West Side Story* played in Vienna it was a Finnish production.[64] Alois Brunnthaler, editor-in-chief of the *Arbeiter-Zeitung*, was an advocate for Finland in Vienna and served as impresario for the Tampere Theatre company's visit. Help with expenses came from the cities of Vienna and Tampere and the Finnish Cultural Ministry, and the ensemble had free use of the Theater an der Wien. The company of twenty actors, twenty-two dancers, twenty-six musicians, and twenty-two technical and other staff members enjoyed receptions held by Mayor Franz Jonas of Vienna and the Finnish Embassy. The sold-out show played four times over three days, the premiere attended by numerous dignitaries and greeted at its conclusion with eighteen minutes of applause. The orchestra, led by Finnish conductor Juhani Raiskinen, who later became the director of the Finnish National Opera, included fourteen Viennese violinists to augment the sound of the strings. In Vienna, Raiskinen's 'non-academic' and care-free touch was admired. The cast performed mostly in Finnish, but did learn some lines and lyrics in German, including the song 'Maria.' Although the Theater an der Wien had recently been renovated, the Finns found themselves disappointed with the lighting equipment. Some of the show's lead actors recorded their songs from the show for radio broadcast. The brief run coincided with an exhibition of Finnish design at the Volkshallen. Critics were mostly positive about the production, enjoying the young, lively cast; the reviewer for the *Neues Österreich* even suggested that this cast might succeed on Broadway. The writer for the *Kurier* noted that *West Side Story* is a demanding show that one would think would only be attempted by Europe's largest theaters, but then one has the surprise of this company from Tampere coming in with a spirited cast, good conductor, and rich choreography. The *Expressen* criticized what seemed to be the production's amateurish look, but also praised the lively performance with a fast tempo. What seemed like a courageous attempt for Rauli Lehtonen and his collaborators found success in both Tampere and Vienna.

Notes

1. Early reviews noted this, too. See Julia L. Foulkes, *A Place for Us*: West Side Story *and New York* (Chicago, IL: University of Chicago Press, 2016), 95–96.

2. Elizabeth A. Wells, West Side Story: *Cultural Perspectives on an American Musical* (Lanham, MD: Scarecrow Press, 2011), 14, 203–04. Emily Abrams Ansari, *The Sound of a Superpower: Musical Americanism and the Cold War* (Oxford: Oxford University Press, 2018), 184–87. Bernstein had long collaborated with leftists who sought, as Carol Oja writes, 'art that would help make a better world'. Carol J. Oja, *Bernstein Meets Broadway: Collaborative Art in a Time of War* (New York: Oxford University Press, 2014), 295. A counter-perspective is offered by Daniel Belgrade and Ying Zhu, who argue that the dances of *West Side Story* 'reproduce the cultural logic legitimating Cold War militarism'. Daniel Belgrad and Ying Zhu, 'Dancing with Knives: American Cold War Ideology and the Dances of *West Side Story*', *Kyiv-Mohyla Humanities Journal* 3 (2016): 1–22.

3. Ansari, *The Sound of a Superpower*, 162–99.

4. 'Davaĭte sporit' dal'she', *Teatr* (June 1966): 44–45.

5. See for example Max Frankel, 'Drama Mailbag: American in Moscow Explains Why *West Side Story* Should Go There', *New York Times*, 13 September 1959: X5.

6. Michael Sy Uy, 'Performing Catfish Row in the Soviet Union: The Everyman Opera Company and *Porgy and Bess*, 1955–56', *Journal of the Society of American Music* 11, no. 4 (November 2017): 470–501.

7. Foulkes, *A Place for Us*, 100–02. Wells, *West Side Story*, 226.

8. Music Advisory Panel Meeting Minutes, 19 February 1958, Bureau for Educational and Cultural Affairs Historical Collection (MC468), Special Collections, University of Arkansas (hereafter CU collection), Box 100, Folder 2. This attitude was likely also informed by the panel's general antipathy toward Bernstein's music, which they felt was too commercial to need government support. Music Advisory Panel Meeting Minutes, 19 March 1958, CU Collection, Box 100, Folder 2.

9. Drama Advisory Panel Meeting Minutes, 21 February 1958, CU Collection, Box 102, Folder 6, quoted in Foulkes, *A Place for Us*, 103–04.

10. Foulkes, *A Place for Us*, 103, 181.

11. 'Doklada I. A. Moiseeva "Kul'turnaia zhizn" Ameriki', 11 December 1958, Russian State Archive of Contemporary History (RGANI) fond 5 opis 36 delo 57 listi 223–30.

12. Letter to Minister of Culture from Igor Moiseyev, 19 February 1959, RGANI fond 5 opis 36. delo 57 listi 195–97. Diana Adams Schmidt, 'Moiseyev Glows in Report on U.S.', *New York Times*, 19 January 1959. All translations from Russian by Anne Searcy, except where otherwise noted.

13. Foulkes, *A Place for Us*, 100. Edith Evans Asbury, '*West Side Story* Host to Frolicsome Bolshoi Dancers', *New York Times*, 30 April 1959.

14. Richard L. Coe, 'Bolshoi Notes U.S. Reaction', *Washington Post Times Herald*, 15 May 1959.

15. Louise Calta, 'Producers Pleased at Plans in Soviet to Stage US Show', *New York Times*, 4 September 1959: 11, and 'Russians to Stage *West Side Story*', *New York Times*, 4 December 1959: 37, both quoted in Wells, *West Side Story*, 226. Scholars have not found evidence that this planned performance actually took place. Foulkes, *A Place for Us*, 103. Neither *Sovetskaia muzyka* nor *Teatr* mentions a 1959 performance.

16. Foulkes, *A Place for Us*, 182.

17. Foulkes, *A Place for Us*, 182.

18. One example of such a cultural diplomat was Robert Wise, who participated in an official film exchange in 1971. Sergei Zhuk, *Soviet Americana: The Cultural History of Russian and Ukrainian Americanists* (London: I. B. Tauris, 2018), 138.

19. Foulkes, *A Place for Us*, 182. See also '*West Side Story* is Staged in Soviet', *New York Times*, 31 December 1964: 11.

20. Foulkes, *A Place for Us*, 183.

21. Foulkes, *A Place for Us*, 183.

22. Foulkes, *A Place for Us*, 183. Translation from Foulkes.

23. S Finklstaïn, 'Kompozitory SSHA Segodnia', *Sovetskaia muzyka* (October 1959): 179. An article about musicals from 1975 mentions the 'mechanical soul of a capitalist city', but that is an aside in an essay mostly on aesthetics and even that overt a reference is unusual for later Soviet coverage of the musical. Nina Velekhova 'Porazmyslim!', *Teatr* (September 1975): 51. 'Nelegkii uspekh', *Teatr* (August 1965): 118.

24. Natalia Khomenko, 'Feeling the Love in Soviet Russia: The Slippery Lessons of *Romeo and Juliet*', in *Shakespearean International Yearbook 18*, ed. N. Khomenko, et al. (New York: Routledge, 2020), 85–101.

25. 'M. Tariverdiev: Ya za sintegicheskii teatr!' *Teatr* (January 1966): 75–76. Zhukov, 'Zametki ob operette', *Teatr* (June 1966): 51.

26. Interview with A. I. Ostrovsky, *Sovetskaia muzyka* (December 1967): 77.

27. 'Davaïte sporit' dal'she', *Teatr* (June 1966): 44–45.

28. V. Kurochkin, 'Nastupat' shirokim frontom', *Sovetskaia muzyka* (October 1964): 30. Kaarel Ird, 'Opera i zritel', *Teatr* (September 1971): 51–54. B. Pokrosvskii, 'Opera i rezhisser', *Sovetskaia muzyka* (April 1970): 117–88. Iu. Frid, 'Ostorozhno: muzyka!', *Sovetskaia muzyka* (February 1973): 55.

29. V. Gaevsky, 'Vesna sviashchennaia', *Teatr* (October 1965): 37. 'Preobrazhennaia "Karmen"', *Sovetskaia muzyka* (June 1966): 132.

30. G. Shneerson, 'Leonard Bernstein', *Sovetskaia muzyka* (October 1976): 113–21.

31. M. Eratova, 'Volshebnye mgnoveniia', *Izvestiia*, 6 December 1976. 'Turniry, kubki, chempionaty', *Izvestiia*, 12 November 1977.

32. Aleksei Filipiov, 'Vykhodnye s Teatrom Pushkina', *Izvestiia*, 11 October 2002. Iuriĭ Gladil'shikov, 'Massandry, polnye pechali', *Izvestiia*, 23 April 2003.

33. For information on musical theatre in Spain, see: Mia Patterson, *75 años de historia del musical en España (1930–2005)* (Madrid: Ediciones y Publicaciones Autor, 2005); and Íñigo Santamaría and Xavier Martínez, *Desde* Al Sur del Pacífico *hasta* Más allá de la Luna: *casi 6 décadas de teatro musical en España*, 3 vols. (N.p.: Gráficas EUJOA S.A., 2016). For more on *West Side Story* in Spain, see: Paul R. Laird and Gonzalo Fernández Monte, West Side Story *in Spain: The Transcultural Adaptation of an Iconic American Show*, Elements in Musical Theatre (Cambridge: Cambridge University Press, 2022).

34. Gustavo Puiche, 'El último estreno de la temporada en Broadway: *West Side Story*, versión neoyorquina de *Romeo y Julieta*,' *La Hora*, 28 November 1957: 15–16. All translations from Spanish are by Paul R. Laird and Gonzalo Fernández Monte.

35. Guy Bueno, '*West Side Story*, comedia musical norteamericana, triunfa en Londres,' *Falange*, 20 December 1958: 5.

36. Federico García-Requena, 'Romeo y Julieta (versión 1961),' *Blanco y Negro*, 22 April 1961: 40–44.

37. 'Desde hace casi cinco meses, un éxito sensacional,' *El Mundo Deportivo*, 14 April 1963: 10.

38. Maruja Torres, '*West Side Story* se presenta en Madrid con la coreografía de Jerome Robbins,' *El País*, 5 October 1983, https://elpais.com/diario/1983/10/06/cultura/434242812_850215.html (accessed 27 September 2020).

39. Pilar Sierra, 'Un clásico musical todavía vivo,' *El País*, 9 October 1983: 53.

40. Victor Manuel Burell, 'MUSICA MODERNA: Estreno de *West Side Story*,' *Cinco Días*, 8 October 1983: 23.

41. Fernando Bejarano, '*West Side Story*, canto a la nostalgia,' *Diario 16*, 9 October 1983: 40.

42. Adolf Beltrán, 'Una compañía de Broadway representa en Valencia *West Side Story*,' *El País*, 29 February 1988: 31.

43. 'La ópera *West Side Story* triunfó ante la juventud cántabra,' *Diario 16*, 20 August 1988, supl. *Verano y Humo*: 4.

44. For more information on this production, see: Santamaría and Martínez, *Desde* Al Sur del Pacífico, vol. 3, 1296–97.

45. https://barrymcnabb.com/bioresume/ (accessed 2 January 2021).

46. Quoted in Santamaría and Martínez, *Desde* Al Sur del Pacífico, vol. 3, 1297.

47. For more information on this production, see: Santamaría and Martínez, *Desde* Al Sur del Pacífico, vol. 3, 1298–99.

48. Santamaría and Martínez, *Desde* Al Sur del Pacífico, vol. 3, 1299.

49. Julio Bravo, 'Broadway se instala en la Casa de Campo,' *ABC*, 24 June 2009: 63.

50. Julio Bravo, 'El genuino sabor americano' *ABC*, 29 June 2009.

51. Personal interview with David Serrano by Paul R. Laird and Gonzalo Fernández Monte, Madrid, Spain, 6 January 2019.

52. This is a general conclusion from our comparison of these two adaptations of *West Side Story* into Spanish; for details, see Laird and Fernández Monte, West Side Story *in Spain*, 48–67.

53. Personal interview with Federico Barrios by Paul R. Laird and Gonzalo Fernández Monte, Madrid, Spain, 4 January 2019.

54. Nacho Fresno, 'Crítica: *West Side Story*, cuando lo "vintage" es historia del género musical (y de la danza y la música),' *Shangay.com*, 21 October 2018.

55. Anthony Cardew, 'London Cheers New Star Rita as *West Side Story* Wows 'Em', *London Daily Herald*, 13 December 1958.

56. Harold Conway, 'This Knocks *My Fair Lady* for Six', *London Daily Sketch*, 13 December 1958.

57. 'The Theatre: A Musical That Makes the Others Look Pale', *London Sunday Express*, 12 January 1959.

58. Most of the information in this paragraph was kindly supplied in an English summary by Aino Kukkonen, author of the following chapter in Finnish: 'Jazzia ja Jameksia – tanssi musikaalissa *West Side Story*,' in *Suomen teatteri ja draama*, ed. Katri Tanskanen and Mikko-Olavi Seppälä (Helsinki: Like, 2010), 279–90. Thanks to Martin Nedbal, for the initial contact with researcher Kukkonen.

59. Aino Kukkonen : *Stretch – Tanssiryhmä teatterissa* (Helsinki: Like 2003, with English summary); Lena Hammergren, 'Dancing African-American Jazz in the Nordic Region,' in *Nordic Dance Spaces: Practicing and Imagining a Region*, ed. Karen Vedel and Petri Hoppu (London and New York: Routledge, 2014), 101–28, see 111.

60. Teatterimuseo/Teatermuseet/Theatre Museum (accessed 24 May 2021).

61. Panu Rajala, *Tunteen tulet, taiteen tasot. Tampereen Teatteri 1904–2004* (Hämeenlinna: Karisto, 2004), 479–85.

62. *Dance Info Finland*, https://tanka.danceinfo.fi/tanka-en-US/Performance/3641 (accessed 24 May 2021).

63. Aino Kukkonen, *Heikki Värtsi – Laidasta laitaan* (Helsinki: Like, 2011), 160–61.

64. Most of the information in this paragraph, including references to the three reviews of the production, comes from Kukkonen's summary of information available on the Tampere Theatre company's visit to Vienna, available from these three books: Kukkonen, *Heikki Värtsi: Laidasta laitaan*, 155–56; Rauli Lehtonen, *Tuntematon teatterinjohtaja* (Hämeenlinna: Karisto, 1997), 277–81; and Rajala, *Tunteen tulet, taiteen tasot*, 479–85. See also Chapter 15 in this volume, by Martin Nedbal, concerning the show's reception in Vienna in the 1960s.

Select Bibliography

Acevedo-Muñoz, Ernesto. West Side Story *as Cinema: The Making and Impact of an American Masterpiece.* Lawrence: University Press of Kansas, 2013.

Ansari, Emily Abrams. *The Sound of a Superpower: Musical Americanism and the Cold War.* Oxford: Oxford University Press, 2018.

Armstrong, Linda. '*West Side Story* is the Worst!' *The New York Amsterdam News,* June 24, 2009.

Baber, Katherine. *Leonard Bernstein and the Language of Jazz.* Urbana, IL: University of Illinois Press, 2019.

"'Manhattan Women': Jazz, Blues, and Gender in *On the Town* and *Wonderful Town.*' *American Music* 31, no. 1 (Spring 2013): 73–105.

Banfield, Stephen. *Sondheim's Broadway Musicals.* Ann Arbor: University of Michigan Press, 1993.

Barranger, Milly S. *A Gambler's Instinct: The Story of Broadway Producer Cheryl Crawford.* Carbondale, IL: Southern Illinois University Press, 2010.

Belgrad, Daniel, and Ying Zhu. 'Dancing with Knives: American Cold War Ideology and the Dances of *West Side Story.*' *Kyiv-Mohyla Humanities Journal* 3 (2016): 1–22.

Bernstein, Leonard, *The Leonard Bernstein Letters,* edited by Nigel Simeone. New Haven, CT: Yale University Press, 2013–2017.

West Side Story. Originalaufnahme der deutschsprachigen Bühnenfassung der Wiener Volksoper. Nach einer Idee von Jerome Robbins. Deutsches Buch und Gesangstexte Marcel Prawy. CBS S 70 040, 1968, LP.

Berson, Misha. *Something's Coming, Something Good:* West Side Story *and the American Imagination.* Milwaukee, WI: Applause Theatre & Cinema Books, 2011.

Bloom, Julie. 'Rekindling Robbins, a Step at a Time.' *New York Times,* March 4, 2009. www.nytimes.com/2009/03/08/arts/dance/08bloo.html#:~:text=Rekinding%20 Jerome%20Robbins%20for%20New,Story'%20%2D%20The%20New%20York %20Times.

Brandtner, Wilhelmine. 'Dr. Marcel Prawy – Pionier und Wegbereiter des Musicals vom Broadway nach "Good Old Europe."' Ph.D. diss., University of Vienna, 2012.

Brantley, Ben. 'Our Gangs: Keep Cooly Cool Boy, Real Cool.' *New York Times,* March 20, 2009.

Bryer, Jackson R., and Richard A. Davison. *The Art of the American Musical: Conversations with the Creators.* New Brunswick, NJ: Rutgers University Press, 2005.

Burton, Humphrey. 'A Session Report by Humphrey Burton first featured in the April 1985 edition.' *Gramophone*, August 26, 2015. www.gramophone.co.uk/features/article/bernstein-s-west-side-story.

Carter, Marva Griffin. *Swing Along: The Musical Life of Will Marion Cook*. Oxford: Oxford University Press, 2008.

Cho, Sumi, Kimberlé Williams Crenshaw, and Leslie McCall. 'Toward a Field of Intersectionality Studies: Theory, Applications, and Praxis.' *Signs* 38, no. 4 (Summer 2013): 785–810.

Clum, John M. *The Works of Arthur Laurents: Politics, Love, and Betrayal*. Amherst, NY: Cambria Press, 2014.

Coffin, Berton. *Phonetic Readings of Songs and Arias*. Lanham, MD: Scarecrow Press, Inc., 1982.

Conlon, John J. 'Jerome Robbins.' *Magill's Literary Annual 2005*, June 2005, 1–3.

Conrad, Christine. *Jerome Robbins: That Broadway Man, That Ballet Man*. 1st ed., London: Booth-Clibborn Editions, 2000.

Crawford, Cheryl. *One Naked Individual: My Fifty Years in the Theatre*. Indianapolis: Bobbs-Merrill, 1977.

'Who Would Want to See a Play about an Unhappy Salesman?' *New York Times*, March 20, 1977. www.nytimes.com/1977/03/20/archives/who-would-want-to-see-a-play-about-an-unhappy-salesman-a-producers.html.

Crenshaw, Kimberlé Williams, Luke Charles Harris, Daniel Martinez HoSang, and George Lipsitz, eds. *Seeing Race Again: Countering Colorblindness across the Disciplines*. Berkeley: University of California Press, 2019.

Crist, Elizabeth B. 'Mutual Responses in the Midst of an Era: Aaron Copland's *The Tender Land*, and Leonard Bernstein's *Candide*.' *The Journal of Musicology* 23, no. 4 (2006): 485–527.

Davids, Julia, and Stephen La Tour. *Vocal Technique: A Guide for Conductors, Teachers, and Singers*. Long Grove, IL: Waveland Press, Inc., 2012.

Dodds, Sherril. *Dancing on the Canon: Embodiments of Value in Popular Dance*. New York: Palgrave Macmillan, 2011.

Dolan, Jill, and Stacy Wolf. 'Jewish American Performance: An Introduction.' *TDR: The Drama Review* 55, no. 3 (2011): 18–20. www.muse.jhu.edu/article/448646.0900300302543&site=eds-live.

Duerden, Rachel, and Bonnie Rowell. 'Hierarchical Reversals: The Interplay of Dance and Music in *West Side Story*.' In *Bodies of Sound: Studies across Popular Music and Dance*, edited by Sherril Dodds and Susan C. Cook, 135–148. Burlington, VT: Ashgate Pub., 2013.

Duffy, Martha. "West Side Glory." *Time*, May 29, 1995.

Dziemianowicz, Joe. '"West Side" Revival is Halfway There.' *Daily News*, March 20, 2009.

Eisler, Garrett. 'Kidding on the Level: The Reactionary Project of I'd Rather Be Right.' *Studies in Musical Theatre* 1, no. 1 (2006): 7–24.

Engel, Lehman, and Howard Kissel. *Words with Music: Creating the Broadway Musical Libretto*. New York: Applause Theatre and Cinema Books, 2006.

Everett, William A. 'Oscar Hammerstein II and the Performativity of Race and Intersectional Oppression in American Musicals from Show Boat (1927) to Carousel (1945).' *Arti musices* 50, nos. 1–2 (2019): 355–375.

Feingold, Michael. 'Revival of the Fittest.' *Village Voice*, May 6, 2003.

Fierberg, Ruthie. 'What Does *West Side Story* Look Like with New Choreography?' *Playbill*, December 9, 2019. www.playbill.com/article/what-does-west-side-story-look-like-with-new-choreography.

Foulkes, Julia L. *A Place for Us:* West Side Story *and New York*. Chicago: University of Chicago Press, 2016.

Garebian, Keith. *The Making of* West Side Story. Buffalo, NY: Mosaic Press, 2016.

Gennaro, Liza. 'Evolution of Dance in the Golden Age of the American "Book Musical."' In *The Oxford Handbook of the American Musical*, edited by Raymond Knapp, Mitchell Morris, and Stacy Wolf, 52–61. Oxford: Oxford University Press, 2011.

George-Graves, Nadine, et al. 'Dance in Musical Theater.' In *The Oxford Handbook of Dance and Theater*, edited by Nadine George-Graves, Chapter 9. Oxford: Oxford University Press, 2015.

Gilbert, James Burkhart. *A Cycle of Outrage: America's Reaction to the Juvenile Delinquent in the 1950s*. Oxford: Oxford University Press, 1999.

Gold, Sylviane. 'What It Takes to Radically Reimagine *West Side Story. Dance Magazine*, February 19, 2020. www.dancemagazine.com/broadways-new-west-side-story-2645184837.html.

Grossman, Barbara Wallace. 'Musical Theatre Directors.' In *The Oxford Handbook of the American Musical*, edited by Raymond Knapp, Mitchell Morris, and Stacy Wolf, 281–293. Oxford: Oxford University Press, 2011.

Guernsey Jr., Otis L. 'Landmark Symposium: *West Side Story.*' *The Dramatists Guild Quarterly* 22, no. 3 (Autumn 1985): 11–25.

Hall, Karen. *So You Want to Sing Music Theater: A Guide for Professionals*. Lanham, MD: Rowman & Littlefield, 2014.

Harburg, E. Y., and Fred Saidy. *Finian's Rainbow*. New York: Random House, 1947.

Harrah, Scott. 'Score, Dances Are Best Reasons to See "Story."' *The Village Voice*, April 22, 2009.

Harris, Paul. 'A Bilingual Dazzler.' *Variety*, January 12, 2009.

Heath, Karen Patricia. 'Roger L. Stevens: The Great Facilitator.' In *The Palgrave Handbook of Musical Theatre Producers*, edited by Laura MacDonald and William A. Everett, 207–215. New York: Palgrave Macmillan, 2017.

Herrera, Brian Eugenio. *Latin Numbers: Playing Latino in Twentieth-Century U.S. Popular Performance*. Ann Arbor, MI: The University of Michigan Press, 2015.

Hinton, Stephen. *Weill's Musical Theater: Stages of Reform*. Berkeley and Los Angeles: University of California Press, 2012.

Horowitz, Mark Eden. 'Early Signs of Talent: Wisconsin Archives Reveal Sondheim's Youthful Evolution.' *The Sondheim Review* 21, no. 2 (Spring 2015): 32–33.

Hughes, Bethany, 'Singing the Community: The Musical Theatre Chorus as Character.' In *Gestures of Music Theatre: The Performativity of Song and Dance*, edited by Dominic Symonds and Millie Taylor, 263–275. New York: Oxford University Press, 2014.

Hunter, Evan. *The Blackboard Jungle*. New York: Simon and Schuster, 1954.

Ignatiev, Noel. *How the Irish Became White*. London: Routledge, 1995.

Ilson, Carol. *Harold Prince: From* Pajama Game *to* Phantom of the Opera. Ann Arbor, MI: UMI Research Press, 1989.

Jowitt, Deborah, and Jerome Robbins. *Jerome Robbins: His Life, His Theater, His Dance*. New York: Simon & Schuster, 2005.

Keathley, Elizabeth L. 'Postwar Modernity and the Wife's Subjectivity: Bernstein's *Trouble in Tahiti*.' *American Music* 23, no. 2 (Summer 2005): 220–256.

Kendi, Ibram X. *Stamped from the Beginning: The Definitive History of Racist Ideas in America*. New York: Bold Type, 2016.

Kennerly, David. 'Best Side Story.' *Gay City News*, April 2, 2009.

Khomenko, Natalia. 'Feeling the Love in Soviet Russia: The Slippery Lessons of Romeo and Juliet.' In *Shakespearean International Yearbook* 18, edited by Tom Bishop, Alexa Alice Joubin, and Natalia Khomenko. New York: Routledge, 2020.

Kisselgoff, Anna. 'Dance View; City Ballet, at the Boiling Point.' *The New York Times*, July 2, 1995.

'Jerome Robbins, 79 is Dead: A Giant of Ballet and Broadway.' *The New York Times*, July 30, 1998.

Kukkonen, Aino. *Heikki Värtsi: laidasta laitaan*. Helsinki: Like, 2011.

'Jazzia ja Jameksia – tanssi musikaalissa *West Side Story*.' In *Suomen teatteri ja draama*, edited by Katri Tanskanen and Mikko-Olavi Seppälä, 279–290. Helsinki: Like, 2010.

Lahr, John. 'Turf Wars: *West Side Story* and God of Carnage on Broadway.' *The New Yorker*, March 30, 2009.

Laird, Paul R. West Side Story, Gypsy, *and the Art of Broadway Orchestration*. Routledge Research in Music Series. London and New York: Routledge, 2022.

Laird, Paul R., and Gonzalo Fernández Monte. West Side Story *in Spain: The Transcultural Adaptation of an Iconic America Show*. Cambridge Elements in Musical Theatre. Cambridge: Cambridge University Press, 2022.

Laurents, Arthur. *The Bird Cage*. New York: Dramatists Play Service, 1950.

A Clearing in the Woods. New York: Random House, 1957.

Mainly on Directing: Gypsy, West Side Story, *and Other Musicals.* New York: Knopf, 2009.

Original Story by Arthur Laurents: A Memoir of Broadway and Hollywood. New York: Knopf, 2000.

The Rest of the Story. New York: Applause Theatre and Cinema Books, 2010.

Selected Plays of Arthur Laurents. With an Introduction by Gabriel Miller. New York: Back Stage Books, 2005.

The Time of the Cuckoo. New York: Random House, 1953.

Laurents, Arthur, Stephen Sondheim, and Leonard Bernstein. *West Side Story.* New York: Random House, 1958.

Lawrence, Greg. *Dance with Demons: The Life of Jerome Robbins.* New York: Putnam and Sons, 2001.

Leonard Bernstein: Reaching for the Note. DVD. Directed by Susan Lacy. New York, NY: American Masters–Thirteen/WNYT, 1998.

Lesser, Wendy. *Jerome Robbins: A Life in Dance.* New Haven, CT: Yale University Press, 2018.

Locke, Ralph. *Musical Exoticism: Images and Reflections.* New York: Cambridge University Press, 2009.

Lodge, Mary Jo. 'Dance Breaks and Dream Ballets: Transitional Moments in Musical Theatre.' In *Gestures of Music Theatre: The Performativity of Song and Dance*, edited by Dominic Symonds and Millie Taylor, 75–90. New York: Oxford University Press, 2014.

Long, Robert Emmet. *Broadway, the Golden Years: Jerome Robbins and the Great Choreographer–Directors, 1940 to the Present.* New York: Continuum, 2001.

LoVetri, Jeannette. *The LoVetri Institute for Somatic Voicework.* Baldwin Wallace University, Ohio, 2019.

Manago, Jim. *Love Is the Reason for It All: The Shirley Booth Story.* Albany, GA: Bear Manor Media, 2008.

Marshall, Lea. 'Is It Time to Retire *Fancy Free?' Dance Magazine*, April 19, 2019. www.dancemagazine.com/fancy-free-ballet-2634991525.html.

Martins, Peter. 'Jerome Robbins at New York City Ballet.' YouTube, accessed August 24, 2020. www.youtube.com/watch?v=Rigl9ejpuV4.

May, Elaine Tyler. *Homeward Bound: American Families in the Cold War Era.* New York: Basic Books, 2008; 1988.

Miller, Ray, 'Dance in the Broadway Musicals of Shakespeare: Balanchine, Holm, and Robbins.' In *The Oxford Handbook of Shakespeare and Dance*, edited by Lynsey McCulloch and Brandon Shaw. Oxford: Oxford University Press, 2019. https://doi.org/10.1093/oxfordhb/9780190498788.013.13.

Nash, Jennifer C. 'Re-thinking Intersectionality.' *Feminist Review* 89, no. 1 (2008): 1–15.

Negrón-Muntaner, Frances. 'Feeling Pretty.' *Social Text* 18, no. 2 (2000): 83–106. https://doi.org/10.1215/01642472-18-2_63-83. Accessed January 2020.

Nixon, Marni, and Jimmy Bryant. 'It all Began Tonight: Marni Nixon and Jimmy Bryant Reminisce about Recording Maria's and Tony's Songs.' Interview by Michael Portantiere, *West Side Story*, January 10, 2012. https://westsidestory .livejournal.com/125418.html.

Oja, Carol J. *Bernstein Meets Broadway: Collaborative Art in a Time of War*. Oxford: Oxford University Press, 2014.

'*West Side Story* and *The Music Man*: Whiteness, Immigration, and Race in the U.S. During the Late 1950s.' *Studies in Musical Theatre* 3, no. 1 (2009): 13–30.

Ovalle, Peña Priscilla. *Dance and the Hollywood Latina: Race, Sex, and Stardom*. New Brunswick, NJ.: Rutgers University Press, 2011.

Pollack, Howard. *George Gershwin: His Life and Work*. Berkeley: University of California Press, 2006.

Marc Blitzstein: His Life, His Work, His World. Oxford: Oxford University Press, 2012.

Prawy, Marcel. *Marcel Prawy erzählt aus seinem Leben*. Vienna: Kremayr und Scheriau, 1996.

Preston, Katherine K., ed. 'Irish American Theater: *The Mulligan Guard Ball* (1879) and *Reilly and the 400* (1891).' In *Nineteenth-Century American Musical Theatre*, edited by Deane Root, volume 10. New York: Garland, 1994.

Prince, Harold. *Contradictions: Notes on Twenty-Six Years in the Theatre*. New York: Dodd, Mead & Company, 1974.

Ramsey, Burt. *The Male Dancer: Bodies, Spectacle, Sexualities*. New York: Routledge, 1995.

Rockwell, J. 'New Recording of *West Side Story*.' *New York Times*, September 7, 1984.

Roediger, David R. *Working toward Whiteness: How America's Immigrants Became White – The Strange Journey from Ellis Island to the Suburbs*. New York: Basic Books, 2018.

Rooney, David. '"West Side" Revival Reaches New Heights.' *Variety*, March 23, 2009.

Sagolla, Lisa Jo. 'A *West Side Story* That Resets the Choreographic Balance.' *American Theatre*, March 2020. www.americantheatre.org/2020/01/30/ a-west-side-story-that-resets-the-choreographic-balance/.

Schlundt, Christena L., et al. *Dance in the Musical Theater: Jerome Robbins and His Peers 1934–1965 – A Guide*. New York: Garland Pub., 1989.

Scholick, Jennie. 'Poetry and Politics in Jerome Robbins's Age of Anxiety.' *Dance Chronicle* 41, no. 1 (2018): 78–98. doi:10.1080/01472526.2018.1414547.

Schorske, Carina del Valle. 'Let *West Side Story* and Its Stereotypes Die.' *New York Times*, February 24, 2020.

Schwartz, Michael. 2017. 'The Nice One: The Productions of Robert Griffith.' In *The Palgrave Handbook of Musical Theatre Producers*, edited by

Laura MacDonald and William A. Everett, 191–197. New York: Palgrave Macmillan. https://doi.org/10.1057/978-1-137-43308-4_19.

Schwarz, Otto. *Marcel Prawy "Ich habe die Ewigkeit noch erlebt": Ein grosses Leben neu erzählt.* Vienna: Almathea, 2006.

Sebesta, Judith. 'Angry Dance: Postmodern Innovation, Masculinities, and Gender Subversion.' In *Gestures of Music Theatre: The Performativity of Song and Dance*, edited by Dominic Symond and Millie Taylor, 146–160. New York: Oxford University Press, 2014.

Secrest, Meryle. *Leonard Bernstein: A Life.* New York: Random House, 1994.

Seldes, Barry. 'Bernstein and McCarthyism.' In *Leonard Bernstein and Washington DC: Works, Politics, Performances*, edited by Daniel Abraham, Alicia Kopfstein-Penk, and Andrew H. Weaver, 67–85. New York: University of Rochester Press, 2020.

Leonard Bernstein: The Political Life of an American Musician. Berkeley: University of California Press, 2009.

Sheward, David. '*West Side Story.*' *Backstage*, March 26, 2009.

Simeone, Nigel, ed., Leonard Bernstein, *The Leonard Bernstein Letters.* New Haven, CT: Yale University Press, 2013–2017.

Simeone, Nigel. *Leonard Bernstein: West Side Story.* Farnham, Surrey: Ashgate, 2009; new edition Abingdon and New York: Routledge, 2016.

Sondheim, Stephen. *Finishing the Hat: Collected Lyrics, 1954–1981, with Attendant Comments, Principles, Heresies, Grudges, Whines and Anecdotes.* London: Virgin Books, 2010.

Look, I Made a Hat: Collected Lyrics (1981–2011) with Attendant Comments, Amplifications, Dogmas, Harangues, Digressions, Anecdotes and Miscellany. New York: Alfred A. Knopf, 2011.

'Song Specific Commentary by Stephen Sondheim.' Extras: *West Side Story.* iTunes, 1961.

Starr, Larry. *George Gershwin: Yale Broadway Masters.* New Haven and London: Yale University Press, 2011.

Stearns, Peter N. *American Cool: Constructing a 20th Century Emotional Style.* New York: New York University Press, 1994.

Strizek, Andrei. 'Celebrating 60 Years of *West Side Story* – and the Musical Genius of Leonard Bernstein.' AU News, Europe News, Show/Author Spotlight, September 26, 2017.

Suskin, Steven. *Opening Night on Broadway: A Critical Quotebook of the Golden Era of the Musical Theatre.* New York: Schirmer Books. 1990.

Swayne, Steve. 'Hearing Sondheim's Voices' [by Steven Robert Swayne]. Ph.D. diss., University of California, Berkeley, 1999.

'Hindemith's Unexpected Grandson.' *Hindemith-Jahrbuch* 32 (2003): 215–234.

How Sondheim Found His Sound. Ann Arbor: University of Michigan Press, 2005/2007.

'Music for the Theatre, the Young Copland, and the Younger Sondheim.' *American Music* 20, no. 1 (Spring 2002): 80–101.

'Sondheim's Piano Sonata.' *Journal of the Royal Musical Association* 127 (2002): 258–304.

'Williams College before, during, and after Sondheim.' In *Sondheim in Our Time and His*, edited by W. Antony Sheppard. New York: Oxford University Press, 2022.

Teachout, Terry. 'Tough Guys Don't Dance.' *The Wall Street Journal*, March 20, 2009.

'What Jerome Robbins Knew that Leonard Bernstein Didn't: Important-itis and its Dangers." *Commentary Magazine*, November 2019. www.commentarymagazine.com/articles/terry-teachout/what-jerome-robbins-knew-that-leonard-bernstein-didnt/.

Thompson, Robert Farris, et al. *African Art in Motion: Icon and Act in the Collection of Katherine Coryton White*. Los Angeles: University of California Press, 1974.

Tobias, Tobi. 'The Show Goes On.' *New York Magazine*, June 12, 1995.

Vaill, Amanda. *Jerome Robbins, by Himself*. New York: Alfred A. Knopf, 2019.

Somewhere: The Life of Jerome Robbins. New York: Broadway Books, 2006.

Vincentelli, Elisabeth. 'Shark Attack! *West Side Story* Feels Pretty … Good.' *New York Post*, March 20, 2009.

Walsh, Michael. 'Gentrified Bernstein's Musical Gets An All-star Operatic Cast.' *Time*, April 1, 1985.

Warman, Jonathan. 'Wherefore Art Thou Tony?' *New York Blade*, April 3, 2009.

Wells, Elizabeth A. West Side Story: *Cultural Perspectives on an American Musical*. Lanham, MD: Scarecrow Press, 2011.

Winer, Linda. 'Tragic Story Sings in Any Language.' *Newsday*, March 20, 2009.

Wolf, Stacy. *Changed for Good: A Feminist History of the Broadway Musical*. New York: Oxford University Press, 2011.

A Problem Like Maria: Gender and Sexuality in the American Musical. Ann Arbor: University of Michigan Press, 2002.

Wood, Elizabeth. 'Sapphonics.' In *Queering the Pitch: The New Gay and Lesbian Musicology*, 2nd ed. New York: Routledge, 2006; 1994.

Wright, Trudi. '*Pins and Needles* (1937): Everything in Moderation.' *Studies in Musical Theatre* 7, no. 1 (2013): 61-73.

Zacharek, Stephanie. 'Come Again? Revivals of *West Side Story* and *Blithe Spirit* Work, More or Less – More Thanks to Two Performances.' *New York Magazine*, March 30, 2009.

Zadan, Craig. *Sondheim & Co.*, 2nd ed. New York: Harper & Row, 1989.

Zhu, Ying, and Daniel Belgrad. 'This Cockeyed City is THEIRS: Youth at Play in the Dance of *West Side Story*.' *Journal of American Studies* 51, no. 1 (2017): 67–91.

Zhuk, Sergei. *Soviet Americana: The Cultural History of Russian and Ukrainian Americanists*. London: I. B. Tauris, 2018.

Zinn, Joshua. 'Leonard Bernstein's Modern Day Romeo and Juliet: A Conversation with conductor Timothy Meyers about Houston Grand Opera's current production of West Side Story.' *Houston Public Media.org*, April 27, 2018.

Index of Songs

General Index

Made in the USA
Monee, IL
07 July 2026

56550161R00179